TIME ALLOWED FOR READING.

This book should be returned on or before the date last stamped below. If kept beyond that date a fine of one penny per week or part of a week will be incurred.

Ancient Cities

General Editor : B. C. A. WINDLE, F.R.S., F.S.A.

EDINBURGH

A HISTORICAL AND TOPOGRAPHICAL
ACCOUNT OF THE CITY

The Castle
from the
Grassmarket

EDINBURGH
A HISTORICAL AND TOPOGRAPHICAL ACCOUNT OF THE CITY

WRITTEN BY
M. G. WILLIAMSON, M.A.
ILLUSTRATED BY
HERBERT RAILTON

A MEDIÆVAL CITY

LONDON
METHUEN AND CO.

First Published in 1906

TO

MY MOTHER

WHO FIRST TAUGHT ME TO LOVE THE PAST

AND

WITHOUT WHOSE ADVICE AND ENCOURAGEMENT

THIS BOOK

COULD NOT HAVE BEEN WRITTEN

CONTENTS

LIST OF ILLUSTRATIONS

FULL PAGE

xi

SMALLER ILLUSTRATIONS

xii

ADDITIONAL ILLUSTRATIONS

PREFACE

THE aim of the author in writing this book has been, as far as possible, to connect the history of Edinburgh with the description of the chief objects of interest, and thus to make the history a living reality to the reader. Accordingly the first three chapters have been devoted to an outline of the history of the city, while in the later chapters parts of the history have been given in greater detail, and have been linked with the objects round which that history centres. In addition to the historical and descriptive part of the book, chapters dealing with Literary Men and Social Life and Customs have been added, which, it is hoped, may in some measure enable the twentieth-century visitor to realise the strange admixture of charm and squalor in the Edinburgh of long ago. An Itinerary has been added to enable strangers to use the time at their disposal to the best advantage. An index will also be found at the end of the book.

It is impossible to mention all the books which have been consulted, but reference must be made to a few which have been specially helpful. Among these are Daniel Wilson's *Memorials of Edinburgh in the Olden Time*, Grant's *Old and New Edinburgh*, Abercromby's *Martial Achievements of the Scottish Nation*, Lindsay of Pitscottie's *Chronicles*, Dr. Robert Chambers's *Traditions of Edinburgh* and *Minor Antiquities of Edinburgh*, Dr. William Chambers's *Historical Sketch of St. Giles' Cathedral*, Lockhart of Carnwath's *Memoirs*, *The Lives of the Lindsays*, Cockburn's *Life of Jeffrey* and *Memorials of his own Time*, the *Letters of Mrs. Patrick Cockburn*, Miss Dunlop's *Anent Wester Portsburgh*, the *Autobiography of Dr. Carlyle of Inveresk*, Lockhart's *Life of Scott*, Henry Grey Graham's *Social Life in the Eighteenth Century*, Mr. John Geddie's *Romantic Edinburgh*, and Stevenson's *Picturesque Edinburgh*.

M. G. W.

CHAPTER I

EARLY HISTORY

LIKE most towns whose history stretches far back into the past the origin of Edinburgh is a matter of considerable doubt. In bygone days town records were not kept with the scrupulous accuracy of the present day, and even if they had been, it would have availed little, for the national records were twice destroyed by ruthless English invaders—by Edward I. and by Cromwell.

But while facts are hard to obtain, legend obligingly gives us full details, and if they are less veracious than circumstantial, we must not be too critical. Stow's *Summarie of Englyshe Chronicles* fixes the date of the foundation of the Castle as 989 B.C.—nearly three hundred years before Rome was founded! He thus describes the state of things then existing: 'Ebranke, the son of Mempricius, was made ruler of Britayne; he had, as testifieth Policronica, Ganfrida, and other twenty-one wyves, of whom he receyved twenty sons and thirty daughters, which he sent into Italye, there to be maryed to the blood of the Troyans. In Albanye (now called Scotlande) he edified the castell of Alclude, which is Dumbritayn;[1] he made the castell of Maydens, now called Edenbrough; he made also the castell of Banburgh in the twenty-third yere of his reign. He buylded York citie, wherein he made a temple to Diana

[1] Dumbarton.

A   I

and set there an "Arch-flame," and there was buried;
when he had reigned forty-nine yeares.' It is sufficient
to remark in passing that in the Middle Ages all self-
respecting nations thought it necessary to claim kindred
with Troy. In the twelfth century Geoffrey of Monmouth compiled (*he* said translated) a Latin history of
Britain, claiming as ancestor of the Britons, Brutus,
great-grandson of Æneas. This legend is better known
in its English version, 'The Brut of Layamon.' But
such procedure was universal in those days—quite re-
gardless of probability or even of possibility. Very
mediæval too is the curious confusion which makes this
British king who—if he had any religion at all—was
probably a Druid, worship Diana, and found a temple in
her honour.

Probably the only part of this legend which has any
foundation in fact is the statement, implied rather than
expressed, that the Castle of Edinburgh was first
founded, and that the town gradually grew up around
it. That is what we should expect, not only because
this was the most general origin of towns in early days,
but still more because of the natural position of Edinburgh.

The rock rises abruptly from a flat plain which extends
to the south-east in almost unbroken level stretches.
With foes swarming on every side, what more obvious
than that this splendid natural fortress, further fortified
by the Nor' Loch, should be utilised and improved.
This conjecture is confirmed by history of a somewhat
more reliable nature than Stow's *Summarie*. We read of
the Castle being occupied as early as the fifth century by
the Picts, from whom it was taken in 452 A.D. Picts
and Angles struggled to retain it, and with varying
success the struggle went on until the reign of
Malcolm II.

The most probable account of the origin of the name
Edinburgh is that which derives it from the Northum-

2

brian King Eadwine (Eadwinesburg). This monarch ruled with so strong a hand that it was said, ' A woman with her babe might walk scathless from sea to sea in Eadwine's day.' Eadwine fought with Britons on the west, Mercians on the south, and Picts on the north— all with considerable success—and though Eadwine's strong and merciful rule is forgotten by all except the student of history, the city which he named still survives and flourishes.

After this the history of Edinburgh is almost a blank until the reign of Malcolm Canmore, familiar to readers of *Macbeth* as the son of Duncan. This king had married the Saxon Princess, Margaret, whose goodness was so undeniable that she was canonised, and is even now spoken of by the good Protestants of Edinburgh as ' St. Margaret.' In 1093 Malcolm and his eldest son Edward were killed while besieging Alnwick Castle. Donald Bane, Malcolm's brother, thereupon put himself at the head of those who were dissatisfied with Margaret's anglicising tendencies, and laid siege to Edinburgh Castle. Margaret, overwhelmed with grief, died immediately after her husband, and there was some difficulty in removing her body. But Donald, while guarding the regular accesses, overlooked a small postern-gate. Accordingly the body of the Queen was secretly carried through the gate down the cliff, along the road to Queensferry, and across to Dunfermline, where—in the Abbey Church—her grave may still be seen. Prince Edgar, the heir, escaped by the same method, and cast himself on the protection of his uncle, Edgar Atheling, who was then living in England. Tradition assigns this very postern-gate as the scene of the famous interview between Dundee and the Duke of Gordon.

Alexander I. seems to have lived a good deal in Edinburgh, but we hear little about the town till the important reign of David I. Modern criticism declares that Holyrood owes its name to the portion of the True Cross

bequeathed by St. Margaret to her children, and, like the
Scone Stone of Destiny, appropriated by Edward I. It
is now at Durham. But while this explanation seems
reasonable we should be sorry indeed to lose the story of
the White Hart. The story goes that on 'Rood Day'
(Good Friday) David decided to go out hunting in spite
of the horrified remonstrance of a canon called Alkwine.
Possibly he had not yet earned his title of St. David—in
any case he seems to have had his due share of royal
obstinacy. The country round Edinburgh was one vast,
almost impenetrable forest through which ranged 'hartis,
hyndis, toddis,[1] and sic like manner of beastis.' The King
and his train,—possibly out of bravado—made such a
hullabaloo that all the animals were roused out of their
dens. By some mischance, the King was separated from
his attendants, was thrown from his horse, and was on the
point of being gored to death by a hart with 'auful and
braid tyndis' when a cross was miraculously placed in his
hands, at sight of which the hart speedily fled. David
could hardly do less than found an Abbey on the spot
where he had been so miraculously delivered from the
consequences of his own wrong-headed folly, and in
honour of its origin the Abbey was named 'Holy Rood.'
Whether we accept this story or the one quoted above,
the fact remains that the Black Rood was a treasured
possession until it was annexed by Edward I.

David's generosity to the Church did not end there.
He made over to the Canons of Holyrood the Church of
St. Cuthbert, which he endowed with valuable revenues,
and the chapels of Corstorphine and Liberton. He also
presented the canons with the dues of the Port of Perth,
and built a mill for their own use, which gives its name
to the district of Canonmills. But perhaps the most
important of his benefactions was the right granted to
the canons to erect a burgh between the Abbey and the
Castle ; this burgh received the name of the 'Canon's

[1] Foxes.

4

gait,' and we know it as the long straggling street called
'Canongate.'

In addition David founded the Abbeys of Melrose,
Dryburgh, Newbattle, Cambuskenneth, Kelso, and Jedburgh, besides many other churches,—so one hardly
wonders that King James vi., his less wealthy, and certainly less generous, descendant, should have petulantly
remarked that St. David was 'a sair sanct to the crown.'
David was a brave soldier and a sagacious ruler as
well as a generous patron of religion. In his reign
Edinburgh became more a royal residence than it
had previously been. He died at Hexham in 1153—
his attendants found him kneeling and discovered he was
dead.

David was succeeded by his grandson Malcolm iv.,
sometimes called Malcolm the Maiden. This name was
given him, partly because of his extreme youth (for he
succeeded at the age of twelve), and partly because of
his mildness of disposition, which his indignant subjects
thought made him too much of a tool to the English
King, Henry ii. In this reign Fergus, Lord of Galloway,
died in Edinburgh, having become an Augustinian monk
in disgust after three decisive defeats. Malcolm, like his
grandfather, lived a great deal more in Edinburgh than
earlier sovereigns had done, and this example was followed
by his brother and successor William i., better known as
William the Lion.

If Malcolm was too yielding to the English King,
William rushed to the opposite extreme and was absurdly
warlike. The struggle does not concern us here; it is
sufficient to note that one condition of the disastrous
Treaty of Falaise was that Edinburgh Castle should be
ceded to England. This is the first time—leaving out
of account mythical Trojans and unauthenticated legendary history about Picts and Saxons—that we find
Edinburgh Castle a cause of dispute between England
and Scotland, but it is the first of a long series of

5

struggles for this strong point of vantage. However,
what was lost in the fortune of war was restored in the
course of true love—or at least successful matrimony.
Twelve years after the Treaty of Falaise a marriage was
arranged between William and Ermengarde de Beaumont,
cousin of King Henry, and Edinburgh Castle was restored
to Scotland as part of her dowry.

With the exception of his war with England, William's
reign was in the main prosperous, and that of his son
Alexander II. was even more so. He also is closely connected with Edinburgh in more ways than one. He
seems to have emulated rather the munificence of his
great-grandfather than the warlike achievements of his
father, for we find him founding churches and abbeys,
though without David's reckless generosity. Indeed, the
resources of the Crown did not permit this; but what
he could do Alexander did. The mendicant orders
benefited chiefly by his generosity. The most interesting, historically, of his foundations were the Blackfriars
Monastery and the Collegiate Church of St. Mary's-in-
the-Field. The Blackfriars Monastery has long since
disappeared, but its name still survives in a rather dirty
street connecting the High Street with the Cowgate. St.
Mary's-in-the-Field is now no more; its site is occupied
by the Old University buildings. Before it disappeared
it was to gain notoriety under its other name of the
'Kirk-o'-Field.' Alexander was an assiduous patron of
religion in other ways than founding monasteries. Accordingly we find him receiving a Papal Legate (Cardinal
l'Aleran). Edinburgh became still more important when
the Legate convened a Provincial Synod. Alexander had
held Parliaments in Edinburgh, so Church and State
alike combined to raise the prestige of the city.

In spite of this, however, Alexander's daughter-in-law,
the English Princess Margaret, wife of Alexander III., had
opinions about the city which can hardly be described
as complimentary. 'A sad and solitary place, without

verdure, and, by reason of its vicinity to the sea, un-
wholesome.' One wonders if the English princess was
afflicted by the east wind and the 'easterly haar,' which
residents in Edinburgh know only too well. In this reign
the old claim of homage was revived by Henry III., but
Alexander was equally determined to keep peace with
England and to avoid in any way compromising the
national independence, and contrived with great tact to
avoid the vexed question. As was only to be expected,
when the sovereign was a boy, with no one nearly related
to him, his various collateral relatives disputed considerably about the succession. Alexander II. had nominated
Bruce as his successor, in default of a son, and now the
great rivals the Bruces and the Comyns each tried to
establish their supremacy in the kingdom. To complicate
matters still further we find Alan Durward, Earl of March,
intriguing to have his wife recognised as Alexander's
heir, and even applying to the Pope to help him. It was
this nobleman who 'liberated' Alexander and Margaret
from Edinburgh Castle, where they were kept prisoners
by the Comyns. The Comyns, however, with the help of
the Queen-Mother and her second husband, seized the
King again at Kinross. Alexander seems to have displayed considerable tact in these difficult situations. He
could fight well when there was any necessity for so
doing, as is shown by the result of the famous battle of
Largs, 1263. In the disastrous wars which followed
people looked back to the reign of Alexander III. as to a
sort of 'golden age.' The old rhyme 'Quhen Alysandyr
our King wes dede' voices the popular sentiment.
During this prosperous reign the importance of Edinburgh steadily increased. In spite of the low opinion
entertained of Edinburgh Castle by the Queen, Alexander and Margaret seem to have lived there fairly
constantly. In Edinburgh also all judicial business was
transacted, and there too state records and the regalia
were preserved. All Alexander's children predeceased

him, and on his death the crown passed to his granddaughter Margaret, known as the 'Maid of Norway.' It
was decided to bring her to Scotland, but she became
very ill and died at Orkney before reaching our
country.

This led to the long and disastrous wars with England.
In considering this part of the history of Scotland it
must not be forgotten that Edinburgh, though it had
been frequently used as a royal residence, was far from
being what we should now call the capital of the country.
If any place deserved that name it was Scone, where the
Scottish monarchs were crowned on the Stone of Destiny.
As far as residence was concerned they lived as much in
Edinburgh, perhaps, as anywhere else, but Edinburgh
was not then a Scottish town. In Anglo-Saxon days
'Scotland' originally meant Ireland, but the term gradually was extended so as to include those western parts
of what we now call Scotland which were inhabited by
the Scots—Argyle, etc. After the union of the Picts
and the Scots under Kenneth M'Alpine the term was
applied to the northern part of the country ; but Strath-
clyde, Galloway, and Lothian were not included. The
Firth of Forth was known as the 'Scots' Water' in
much the same way as we speak now of the 'English
Channel.' In royal proclamations the King's subjects
were referred to as Francs (Normans), Scots, Galwegians,
and Angles (i.e. inhabitants of Lothian). Galloway was
held by the kings of Scotland by inheritance through
the mother of Duncan. Lothian was held as an English
earldom. So far as can be discovered from the mass of
conflicting testimony, Malcolm II. got Lothian after the
battle of Carham in 1018, the object being to buy him
off and prevent his ravaging the English border further.
Cnut, who succeeded about this time, seems to have
insisted on some sort of homage, but all is rather vague.
What we do know is that Lothian was peopled by Anglo-
Saxons who had fled north after 1066, and so racially

8

was distinct from the other parts of Scotland, which were mainly Celtic (except in those parts where the Danes had settled). The King's tenure of Lothian was in some way different from his possession of the Celtic parts of his kingdom. So we do not find Edinburgh attacked by the English because it was the capital of Scotland, but because the Castle dominated the surrounding country and made a splendid base of operations. Much light might have been thrown on these and similar disputed points if we had had contemporary documents. It is interesting to find Edward ordering John de Lithegreynes, William of Lincoln, and Thomas of Fisherburn to search out all such documents as bore on the succession to the Scottish crown. This search was to be made in Edinburgh Castle. Edinburgh was honoured by attention from Edward which it could well have dispensed with. Holinshed gives a graphic account of the siege and surrender of Edinburgh, town and Castle, in 1291 : ' He planted his siege about the Castell, and raised engines which cast stones against and over the walls, sore beating and bruising the buildings within ; so that it surrendered by force of siege to the King of England's use on the 15 daie after he had first laid his siege about it.' Edward visited Edinburgh again in the following year when he was adjudicating the respective claims of Bruce, Baliol, Hastings, the Count of Holland, and the other competitors for the crown. We hear no more of Edinburgh till 1296. Events had followed each other in rapid succession. First the claim of the French King to Edward's homage, next the conclusion of the first Franco-Scottish alliance, and last, Baliol's rash act in renouncing all fealty to the English King. Edward in great wrath marched north, took Berwick and Dunbar, marched to Edinburgh and took up his quarters at Holyrood. Patriotic Scottish chronicles accuse Edward of having annexed the Scottish regalia—which he would no doubt have gladly done but for the fact that, so far as we know,

9

such a thing did not then exist. There was only the
crown, which Edward afterwards took from Baliol and
presented as a votive offering at the shrine of St. Thomas
à Becket. Edward was so little ashamed of the property
he annexed that he had an inventory made of it, and
those who wish may still see the list—which consists
chiefly of plate and jewellery. It is possible some of
these articles bore the royal arms of Scotland—which
might explain the complaints about the regalia. It is
interesting to read of some of the items: 'unus ciphus
de ovo griffini fractus in toto argento munitus,' and 'una
nux cum pede argentia deaurata fracta.' We find a
reference to these in the *Scotichronicon*:

> ' Hic rex sic totam Scotiam fecit sibi notam
> Qui sine mensura tulit inde iocalia plura.'

But Edward appropriated Scottish property which was
more valuable by far than mere 'iocalia.' When he was
at Perth he annexed the Stone of Destiny on which—at
Scone—Scottish monarchs were crowned. And from
Holyrood he took the 'Black Rood' from which the
Abbey derived its name. Not content with appropriat-
ing the Rood, Edward further infuriated the Scots by
using it to administer oaths of allegiance to himself.
This made the crime of a broken oath all the greater,
since the oath had been sworn on the Black Rood. It
was while he was in Edinburgh at this time that he compelled the chief men of the kingdom to acknowledge him
as Lord Paramount, receiving their submission in the
church in the Castle. Tradespeople as well as nobles
were compelled to acknowledge Edward, for we find the
townspeople, led by William de Dederyk, Alderman of
Edinburgh, swearing fealty to him. For some time we
hear little of Edinburgh. The next notice is merely a passing reference. In 1304 Edward summoned a Parliament
to Perth, and we find Edinburgh, Haddington, and Linlithgow—the three Lothians—sending only one sheriff

to represent them. The chief scenes of the war which was being fought out between England and Scotland were laid elsewhere—chiefly in the neighbourhood of Stirling, where the three great battles of Stirling Bridge, Falkirk, and Bannockburn were fought. But if the actual struggle was fought out elsewhere, the taking of Edinburgh Castle by Randolph is one of the most picturesque episodes in the war. The Governor of the Castle was Piers Leland, a Gascon, but the garrison, suspecting him of a desire to treat with the Scots, imprisoned him. Randolph was determined to win this important stronghold, but did not quite see how to do it, when William Frank came to the rescue. Frank had been one of the Scottish garrison before the Castle had been taken by the English. His lady-love lived in the Grassmarket—a more pleasing abode then than now—and as he was unable to see her during the day, he used to clamber down the Castle Rock at night. Practice having made him perfect in this achievement, he offered to guide Randolph and a picked body of men by the path he knew so well. It was a distinctly risky experiment, but Randolph thought it well worth trying. An unpleasant incident occurred as they were quietly climbing up the rock. An English soldier dislodged a large stone, which he rolled down almost on the top of them, shouting, 'Aha! I see you well.' They feared all was discovered, but had sufficient presence of mind to crouch down, making no sound, and to their great relief discovered the English soldier had been trying to alarm his comrades as a diversion. They got up without further misadventure, and climbed over the wall successfully by means of scaling-ladders. Frank went first to show the way, then Sir Andrew Gray, and Randolph himself was the third. Once within the walls, the taking of the Castle was a comparatively simple matter, as the English were all asleep and unarmed, with the exception of the sentries, who were unable to make any effective resistance. This was in 1312. The

imprisoned governor, Leland, gave some colour to the
suspicions of his garrison by entering the Scottish
service. Barbour tells us that Bruce created him Viscount of Edinburgh, but seems to have distrusted him as
a renegade, and eventually he declared that Leland had
an English heart, and resorted to the drastic measure of
ordering him to be 'hangit and drawen.'

We find Bruce holding a Parliament at Holyrood in
1327, and his last Parliament was held in Edinburgh in
1328. But even then Edinburgh was far from being
considered a town of much importance except from a
military point of view, and its extreme accessibility from
England made the castle not altogether as desirable for
a royal residence as the great strength of its position
might lead one to infer.

It was in Edinburgh that Edward Baliol held his
Parliament of the 'Disinherited Barons' in 1333. The
Scots retained no record of this Parliament, but this is
compensated for by the immensely long account found
in the English records. The Church had loyally supported Bruce in his struggle with England, but we find
seven prelates, and among them the Bishop of Dunkeld
and the Abbot of Inchaffray, attending this Parliament
and acknowledging Edward Baliol as King of Scotland
and Edward III. of England as Lord Paramount. Four
representative barons are next mentioned, viz. Patrick
Dunbar, Earl of March, the Earl of Athole, Lord Bell-
mont (or Beaumont), who, like the Earl of Athole, was
connected with the Comyns, and Richard Talbot, who
called himself Earl of Mar—probably he had been
created earl, by Edward Baliol. After these great barons
there were others : 'et aliis quamplurimis baronibus mag-
natibus proceribus et hominibus tam clericis quam laicis
dicti regni Scotiæ.' The business seems to have been
carried through under the direction of Anglo-Norman
lawyers. Apart altogether from the favourable nature
of the terms—to England—there is the indirect evidence

of the involved and highly technical language. It is hard at first to be absolutely clear as to the meaning of all this, but it resolves itself in the end into two main conditions, viz. that Edward Baliol (and other Scottish kings after him) should hold the Scottish crown merely as a vassal of the King of England and should acknowledge the suzerainty of England; and secondly, that Baliol should give some tangible expression of his gratitude to Edward for helping him to gain the Scottish crown, and that this should take the form of a rent charge of two thousand 'libratæ' with so much Scottish land as security. The town and district of Berwick-on-Tweed were then handed over to Edward. So much was sanctioned by Parliament, and Edward Baliol on his own responsibility proceeded to complete the two thousand 'libratæ' by adding the town, castle, and county of Roxburgh, Jedburgh, Peebles, Dumfries, and the Lothians. If England held sovereignty over the south of Scotland and suzerainty over the rest, it seemed as if Scotland would become a vassal state.

But the Scots could not give up their independence without a struggle. In 1337 a force, headed by Guy, Count of Namur, landed at Berwick and marched on Edinburgh to the help of the English. The Castle at that time was quite incapable of adequate defence, so the Earl of Moray led the Scottish troops out to the Boroughmuir to await the arrival of the English. A knight who followed the Count of Namur challenged any Scot to fight with him. The challenge was accepted by a man called Richard Shaw, and both the combatants fought with such determination that each killed his opponent. When the armour of the dead combatants was removed it was discovered—to the considerable amazement of every one—that this adventurous stranger was a woman. What were her motives in following the English to battle, and especially in challenging a Scottish adversary, remained always a mystery. The battle

seemed to be won by the English when the unexpected
arrival of William de Douglas changed the result and
the English fled to Edinburgh itself. They retreated
in fair order through St. Mary's Wynd, but their retreat
was cut off by another party of Scots led by David
de Anand. After fighting gallantly they surrendered,
and were allowed to go free provided they promised
never again to bear arms against King David. In the
following year Edward rebuilt and fortified Edinburgh
Castle. But if the English held the principal strong-
holds the Scots were tolerably successful in their own
methods of warfare, which are described so graphically
by Froissart. The exploits of Alexander Ramsay are
specially interesting. He raised the siege of Dunbar
and then concealed himself and his followers in a cave
near Hawthornden, and made raids on the English whenever he got a suitable opportunity. Yet in spite of the
courage and determination of the Scots it seemed as
if the work of Bruce was to be undone. Knowing as
we do the military skill of Edward III. and the Black
Prince, we can see that the danger was even greater than
it appeared at the time. One thing saved Scotland—
the outbreak of war between England and France in
1338. After that fortress after fortress surrendered to
the Scots. Edinburgh was won by an ingenious stratagem. A Scottish captain, Walter Curry, appeared
at the Castle and told the governor he had brought a
cargo of wine from an English vessel. He skilfully
upset the wine casks, and some Scots under the command
of William de Douglas, who had been concealed near
at hand, rushed out of hiding and made themselves
masters of the Castle. This was the last important
stronghold held by the English, and when the Scots
took possession of it in the name of King David, the
invaders were forced to retreat.

Soon after David himself and Queen Johanna landed
in Scotland. One would have supposed that David had

had enough of adventures, and would have been glad to have some quiet time to get the country settled after its varied vicissitudes. But David had lived so long in France that he became imbued with the rashness which was the curse of France in those days and which caused most of her defeats. Accordingly in 1346 he led a Scottish army across the border, hoping to win a victory in the absence of Edward. But no proper precautions had been taken, and the result was a crushing defeat at Nevill's Cross. David himself was taken prisoner along with 'four earls, two lords, the Archbishop of St. Andrews, one other bishop, one knight, and many others.' The number of those killed was also very great. But in some ways the sorest loss was the 'Black Rood' which Edward I. took possession of, but which had been eventually restored to Scotland as stipulated by treaty. This loss to Scotland was a great gain to Durham Abbey, where the relic was kept. David was kept in captivity for a considerable time, during which time Edward anxiously but unsuccessfully tried to win recognition as King of Scotland. In 1357 a Parliament was held in Edinburgh to arrange about his ransom. David's brother-in-law, Robert the Steward of Scotland, presided over this Parliament, which included delegates from seventeen burghs. It is interesting to note that this is the first time Edinburgh is given the place of honour. This is characteristic, because Edinburgh was emphatically the capital of the Stewarts, more especially of the later Stewarts. Up to this time it was regarded chiefly as a border town, a place where Parliaments were sometimes—but by no means invariably—held, and where the King sometimes lived. Abercromby does not give a specially flattering account of it: 'Edinburgh was then but a small burgh, or rather, as Walsingham calls it, a village, the houses of which, because they were so often exposed to incursions from England, being thatched for the most part with

straw and turf; and when burnt or demolished, were
with no great difficulty repaired. The strength of the
Castle, the convenience of the Abbey, the fruitfulness of
the adjacent country and its no great distance from
the borders, made after Kings chuse to reside for the
most part, to hold their Parliaments and keep their
courts of justice, in this place.' It is curious to read
that when they were threatened by an English army
the method of defence adopted by Edinburgh citizens
was to hide any wealth they had, drive off their cattle,
and take with them the thatched roofs of their houses.
Naturally any damage done was speedily repaired! The
history of the Stewarts is also the history of the evolution of this little border village which was to attain
widespread celebrity as the capital of Scotland.

CHAPTER II

EDINBURGH UNDER THE STEWARTS—ROBERT II. TO JAMES VI.

Holyrood Palace

DAVID II. died in 1369 and was succeeded by his nephew, Robert the High Steward of Scotland. Marjorie Bruce had married Walter Fitzalan, in whose family the office of High Steward had become quasi-hereditary, and Robert was thus the obvious heir of his childless uncle, David II. Robert pursued the policy of Bruce, which was to become traditional in the house of Stewart—enmity with 'our auld enemies of England,' alliance with 'our auncient allies of France.' He sent Sir Archibald Douglas and Walter Wardlaw to Paris in 1371 to arrange a treaty of alliance. The treaty set forth among other terms that neither Scotland nor France was to make peace or war with England without the consent of the other. The Scots received a body of thirty French knights with great hospitality. But even Scottish hospitality could not stand the two thousand French soldiers who came over shortly afterwards and who expected the Scots to provide those luxuries which they were accustomed to in France. Worst of all, they

B

dared to criticise Edinburgh itself—now more and more recognised as the capital—and to declare that it was neither so large nor so fine as the second-rate French towns. These French knights, moreover, were addicted to plundering the Scottish peasants, and were in every way unsatisfactory allies, so they were speedily got rid of. Froissart voices the feeling of the French in the unflattering picture he gives of Edinburgh at this time : 'Edinburgh, though the Kynge kepte there his chefe resydence, and that is Parys in Scotland ; yet it is not like Tourney or Vallenciennes, for in all the town is not four hundred houses ; therefore it behoved these lordes and knyghts to be lodged about in the villages.' The accommodation of 'the villages' seems to have been limited, for we find the knights scattered as far apart as Kelso and Fife. But the Scots had sufficient good sense to profit by the criticisms of these candid friends, for we find Scottish architecture of this and succeeding ages closely modelled upon French styles—to the great improvement of Edinburgh and other towns. Even now some of the old houses show traces of French influence, though unfortunately many of them have been pulled down to make room for modern 'improvements.' In spite of injured national pride the Franco-Scottish alliance continued. In 1383 Robert held his court in Edinburgh, and received an ambassador from Charles VI. for the purpose of concluding a treaty offensive and defensive against England. The Duke of Lancaster— better known as John of Gaunt—marched north at the head of an immense army. He had been hospitably entertained in Edinburgh, and gratitude prevented his destroying the city. But it did not interfere with the raid of the Scots into England, so the Duke returned and revenged himself on the town he had previously spared, and Edinburgh was *again* reduced to ashes. Fortunately the architecture was of a style which was easily replaced, otherwise these incessant English incursions and con-

18

flagrations would have been expensive as well as annoying. But while the houses were easily rebuilt, one thing was destroyed which has not been and could not be adequately replaced—the original church of St. Giles. This was built in early Norman style and must have been extremely beautiful. A doorway which survived the conflagration was pulled down about 1760. An impression of an engraving of it may still be seen in the Signet Library, and one cannot but wonder why work of such rare beauty, which escaped the English, the Reformers, and the Covenanters alike, should have been sacrificed to the execrable taste of an age which seemed bent on destroying all that was old and beautiful and replacing it by all that was new and hideous. War with England continued all through the reign of Robert II. It was in this reign that the famous battle of Otterburn was fought. Though better known than other similar conflicts, it was only one of those skirmishes which, caused though they were by family rather than by national hatred, still served to keep up a spirit of opposition between the two countries. In 1389, however, a truce was made between England and France which included Scotland and lasted for ten years. Robert himself had always deprecated the ceaseless wars with England, and rejoiced greatly over the truce, but did not live long to enjoy it, for he died in the following year (1390).

He was succeeded by his eldest son John, who was, however, crowned as Robert III., because the Scots had such a hatred for the Christian name borne by Baliol. In spite of the truce Robert III. entertained French ambassadors in Edinburgh in 1390, and renewed the alliance which his father had entered into. After the expiry of the truce Henry IV. marched north in 1400 with a large army, disregarded the Duke of Rothesay's chivalrous offer, and sat down before Edinburgh Castle, hoping to carry through a successful siege. He was vanquished, however, not by the Scottish arms, but by the Scottish

climate. The east wind and easterly haar seem to have
been as trying then as now ; Henry complained bitterly
of the cold and rain and lack of food, and eventually
crossed the border, leaving things pretty much as he had
found them. To his honour be it said, Henry did not
indulge in pillage, and he made a special point of protect-
ing churches and religious houses. Two canons of Holyrood begged him to spare the Abbey and Monastery, to
which Henry replied : ' Never while I live shall I cause
distress to any religious house whatever, and God forbid
that the monastery and Holyrood, the asylum of my
father when an exile, should suffer aught from his son.
I am myself a Cumin, and by this side half a Scot ; and I
came here with my army, not to ravage the land, but to
answer the defiance of certain amongst you who have
branded me as a traitor, to see whether they dare to make
good the opprobrious epithets with which I am loaded in
their letters to the French King, which were intercepted
by my people and are now in my possession. I sought him
in his own land, anxious to give him an opportunity of
establishing his innocence or proving my guilt ; but he
has not dared to meet me.' This must refer to Albany,
who had avoided a battle, while the Duke of Rothesay
was anxious for a chivalrous display of strength, and when
Henry would not grant that, bravely stood the siege in
the Castle. Probably Henry was more anxious to revive
the claim to Scottish homage than to redeem his
character, and it may be that the rumour that Richard II.
was alive and in Scotland had something to do with
his action ; but whatever were his motives it was undoubtedly a gain that this English invader did not, like
most of his countrymen, burn and pillage all he could lay
hands on. The murder of the Duke of Rothesay at
Falkland was followed by the disastrous defeats of Nesbit
Moor and Homildon Hill, and these again by the seizure
of the young Earl of Carrick, the King's only surviving
son, on his way to France. Robert died in 1406 after

seeing his armies defeated, one son murdered, the other a prisoner, and all power in the hands of that most unscrupulous brother, Robert, Duke of Albany.

Edinburgh during the regency of Albany underwent some vicissitudes. It seems, however, to have been fairly prosperous, for we find it contributing 50,000 merks, as its share of the ransom of James I. in 1424.

With the accession of James I. a new era began for Edinburgh. We have said that Edinburgh is the capital of the Stewarts; it rose with them, and when they deserted it, it sank—not into insignificance (its memories averted that fate), but into a mere shadow of its former self. And if Edinburgh is the capital of the Stewarts it is pre-eminently the capital of the Jameses. Rightly or wrongly, the Scottish people take comparatively little interest in Robert II. and Robert III. There is a halo of misfortune around the Duke of Rothesay, but even he seems shadowy, and the majority of people feel that they know far less about the Edinburgh of Robert II. and Robert III. than they do of the days of Robert I. It is true that James I. himself did not live a great deal in Edinburgh. His plans for the subjugation of the Highlands, especially of that very troublesome vassal, Alexander, Lord of the Isles, necessitated a good deal of the business of government being transacted at Perth, as it was nearer the Highland line than Edinburgh was. And Perth will be for ever associated with the death of the poet king and with Catherine Douglas's heroic, though unavailing, attempt to save him. But James and his queen, Jane Beaufort, 'the fairest and the freshest yonge flour,' as he called her, lived a good deal in Edinburgh, which they visited first of all, even before the King's coronation at Scone. James was a very different ruler from his well-meaning but somewhat feeble father. Lesley, Bishop of Ross, gives a graphic account of his strong and merciful rule. In Father James Dalrymple's translation of this history we read: 'Efter the corona-

21

tioune of King James the first, and frome Scone he was
now cum till Edinburghe; a diligent and sharpe compte
he requyres of al quha war gouernouris in his absence;
and how mony he fand were uniust in thair office, he
seueirlie punissed.' He goes on to explain about the
aforesaid punishments, showing that James meant to
be feared as well as loved. But James was not content
with merely punishing the offenders. He at once began
the constructive work of building up a strong and just
government. We find him holding many parliaments,
and it was in this reign that others besides the nobility
were first represented. It is true that the object of this
innovation was to relieve the lesser barons from what
they found an intolerable burden, but its importance
can hardly be overestimated. Several Acts of Parliament throw curious sidelights on the manners of the
time. A rather amusing provision was passed in the
Parliament of 1425, 'Anent hostillaris in villagis and
burowyis.' It seems that innkeepers complained that
their profits were small owing to the reprehensible habit
of travellers staying with any friends they might happen
to have in the place—a habit not unknown in our own
day. Accordingly, to pacify them, travellers were ordered
to put up in 'the hostillaries; bot gif it be the persones
that leadis monie with them in companie, that sall
have friedome to harberie with their friends; swa that
their horse and their meinze be harberied and ludged
in the commoun hostillaries.' The greatest nobles of
all usually—like royalty—lodged in monasteries. Some
of the sumptuary laws enacted by Parliament are also
curious. The common people seem to have been anxious
to imitate their betters in the matter of dress, and the
upper class emphatically objected to this. Accordingly
none but knights and lords possessed of at least 200
merks a year were allowed to wear silk or fur, 'and
none uther wear borderie, pearle, nor bulyeone, bot
array them in honest arraiments as beltes, broches, and

22

chienzies.'[1]   But the Act of Parliament which tells most
of the Edinburgh of that day is that which enacts that
various precautions shall be taken to avert the danger
of fire.   Town officials are ordered to have in readiness
' siven or aught twenty fute ledders as well as three or
foure sayes to the common use, and sex or maa cleikes
of iron, to draw down timber and ruiffes that are fired ';
and as a preventive measure it is enacted, ' that na fire
be fetched fra ane house, til ane uther within the town,
bot within covered weshel or lanterne under paine of ane
unlaw.'   All this gives us interesting information about
the style of architecture.   Obviously houses were built
of wood and covered with thatch, and equally obviously
they cannot have been more than two stories high, if
' timber and ruiffes ' could be drawn down with ' cleikes.'
The lofty houses of old Edinburgh were not yet.   As
a natural consequence of this wise and strong government
the country became prosperous, and commerce increased
considerably.   We find Scotland trading with Lombard
merchants, and it is interesting to find one of their vessels
described by the chroniclers as ' navis immanissima ' (an
enormous vessel) wrecked in the Firth of Forth and
driven ashore at Granton.

Edinburgh is important politically as well as socially
in this reign.   It was at Holyrood that the Earl of Ross
made his dramatic appearance in 1430.   Besides being
Earl of Ross he was also Lord of the Isles, and held
almost undisputed sway in the West Highlands.   Abercromby in the *Martial Achievements* remarks : ' His
power was immense, indeed, too much so for a subject,
and too potent subjects are seldom good ones.'   His
pretensions were as great as his power, but his rebellion
was quite unsuccessful.   Accordingly his only hope was
to trust to the King's clemency, so he appeared one day
at Holyrood while Mass was being said.   His whole
appearance was most wretched, he was only half clothed

Edin-
burgh
under the
Stewarts :
Robert II.
to
James VI.

[1] Chains.

23

and his manner showed the utmost distress. Falling
on his knees he presented the hilt of his sword to the
King, to intimate that he cast himself entirely on his
mercy. James yielded to his wife's entreaties and spared
the suppliant's life, but 'to prevent future temptations'
imprisoned him in Tantallon. His mother, the Countess
of Ross, described by Abercromby as 'a haughty resent-
ing woman who set him on to the perpetration of his
enormities,' was also prevented from doing further harm
by being shut up in the island of St. Colme. However,
she was soon released, and even the archculprit himself was not long detained. Not only was he set free to
celebrate the happy event of the Queen's giving birth to
twin sons, but he was actually asked to stand sponsor,
though some writers deny this. Certainly one of the
royal twins, who did not live long, bore the name of
Alexander, the other was James, afterwards James II.
Though the final tragedy of the reign took place at
Perth, Edinburgh was closely connected with it, inasmuch
as James was there just before going to Perth; and it
was at Edinburgh that he got several warnings, to which
he paid just as much attention as his great-grandson
James IV. did to the various portents which happened
before Flodden. The result of this was, in the words
of the old song, that

> 'A woman was Scotland's mail,
> A wean wore Scotland's crown,'

a state of things too sadly common in the history of
Scotland and of the Stewarts.

Throughout the reign of James the influence of the
Queen had always been on the side of mercy. But she
roused herself from her grief and pursued the murderers
with a vindictiveness which hitherto had been quite
foreign to her nature. Sir Robert Graham himself was
executed at Stirling, and his execution was accompanied

24

with such torture that he is reported to have said:
'I doubt me full sore that an ye continue thus your
torments upon my wretched person, that for the pain
ye will constrain me to deny my Creator, and if so,
do I appeal you before God the high and chief Judge
of all mankind after their deserts at the universal
doom, that ye been the very cause of the loss of
my soul.' Edinburgh was, however, the scene of most
of the executions, notably that of the Earl of Athole,
an old man, who was tortured for three days and
then beheaded. Æneas Sylvius, the Papal Nuncio,
who was present at the execution, remarked 'that
he was at a loss to determine whether the crime
committed by the regicides or the punishment inflicted upon them by the justice of the nation was
greatest.'

Edin-
burgh
under the
Stewarts:
Robert II.
to
James VI.

James II. was the first Scottish King to be crowned in
Edinburgh, or rather at Holyrood, Scone being too un-
pleasantly near Perth to be safe. The first Parliament
of James II. was held in 1437. The Queen was
appointed guardian of the princesses and of the King
until he came of age, and Archibald, Earl of Douglas
and Duke of Touraine, was appointed Lieutenant-General
of the Kingdom—he, however, died in about a year, so
had little influence on the state of affairs. In spite of
the Queen-Mother being guardian of the young King,
Crichton, the governor of Edinburgh Castle, kept him
so strictly confined that his mother hardly ever saw him.
Queen Jane was a Plantagenet, which is to say she was
a woman of determination. She laid her plans with
great skill, pretended to be on the best of terms with
Crichton, visited the young King at the Castle, and then
said she was going on a pilgrimage to the shrine of Our
Lady at Whitekirk. But what she did not tell Crichton
was that among her luggage was a box containing the
young King himself. To preserve the unfortunate child
from suffocation the Queen had had holes bored in

the lid of the box. Whitekirk is near Brechin, so the
traveller from Edinburgh would naturally proceed to
Leith, sail east down the Firth, and then north to
Brechin. But Whitekirk bears no memories of the
pilgrimage of Queen Jane. She went to Leith, as was
to be expected, but she sailed *west* to Stirling to join
Sir Alexander Livingstone, and she took with her her
precious luggage.

If this episode has in it something of comedy, the next
scene connected with Edinburgh Castle was tragic
enough. Livingstone and Crichton buried their feud
in face of the great danger to be feared from the Earl
of Douglas. It is true he was a mere boy at the time,
but his power was so great as to constitute a serious
menace to the Crown. Accordingly he was invited to
Edinburgh, and so unsuspicious was he that he brought
his brother along with him. The King was charmed to
have youthful companions and greeted them warmly.
The banquet was proceeding most successfully when,
according to one version, the fatal bull's head made its
appearance; according to the other, Crichton and Livingstone accused the Earl and his brother of being
traitors to the King. Realising too late their danger,
the young brothers tried to defend themselves, and the
King clung to Crichton and begged their lives—a curious
experience for a king. But Crichton sternly told him
not to ask mercy for traitors who had plotted against
him. There must have been some form of trial, but the
result was inevitable and they were beheaded; in the
words of the old writer they 'shook their heads from
them.' One chronicler says the place of execution was
'in the back court of the Castle that lyeth to the west,'
while another fixes it in the great hall of the Castle. In
1753 some workmen found the golden handles and
plates of what is supposed to have been the Earl of
Douglas's coffin. Even in the disturbed state of the
country this crime, with its cruelty and treachery,

26

made a deep impression, as is shown by the popular rhyme :

> ' Edinburgh Castle, towne, and tower,
>   God grant thou sinke for sinne ;
> An' that even for the black dinner
>   Earle Douglas gat therein.'

The Douglases afterwards gained possession of the King and used his power for their own ends, but Crichton contrived to make quite satisfactory terms for himself. It is a relief to turn from these records of murder and civil war to other matters.

The war with England had the indirect effect of causing walls to be built round Edinburgh. The city of that day seems to have stretched from the West Bow to the Netherbow, and from the Nor' Loch to what is now the part between the High Street and the Cowgate. This was now enclosed by walls in 1450—for the better security of the city against the English, the burgher guard being a sufficient additional protection. Needless to say the citizens rose greatly in importance after this. Patrick Cockburn of Newbigging, Provost of Edinburgh, was appointed Governor of the Castle, and was one of the commissioners who settled the truce with England after the battle of Sark in 1450. We see the growing importance of the burgher class in the repeated sumptuary laws. For instance, in 1457 citizens are ordered, 'that they make their wives and daughters gangand correspondant with their estate ; that is to say, on their heads short curches, with little hudes ; and as to their gownes, that na women weare mertrickes nor letteis nor tailes unfitt in length, nor furred under, bot on the Haliedaie. And in like manner, the barrounes and other puir gentlemen's wives. That na laborers nor husbandmen weare on the wark day bot grey and quhite ; And on the Halie-daie, bot lichtblew, greene, redde, and their wives richt-swa ; and curchies of their awin making, not exceeding the price of xi pennyes the elne.'

27

The first result of the truce with England was the marriage of the King to Mary of Gueldres. This had been previously arranged, but she could not sail until she was sure she would not be captured by a hostile English fleet. Mary was attended by a brilliant train, and her appearance was the signal for gaiety and rejoicing of every kind. Masks, revelry, and tournaments followed each other, the Scottish and Burgundian knights striving with each other in amicable rivalry. These gay scenes took place at Stirling, but the marriage itself was celebrated at Holyrood.

Even the wedding festivities were not sufficient to ensure peace, for the Earl of Douglas rebelled almost immediately. A Parliament held in Edinburgh shortly after this passed various enactments against this unruly subject. His subsequent assassination by the King, the relations with England and the death of James himself while besieging Roxburgh Castle in 1460, belong to general Scottish history rather than to the history of Edinburgh. It was about this time that Henry VI. of England with his wife and son fled to Scotland for protection from the victorious Yorkists. The Scots took up the Lancastrian cause, but their help was rather a questionable advantage to Henry, for the inhabitants of the northern counties of England so dreaded a Scottish invasion that they were inclined to look with suspicion on a king who had Scottish allies. But what was an undoubted boon to Henry was the shelter granted him in Edinburgh. He and Margaret and Prince Edward were accommodated in the monastery of the Greyfriars in the Grassmarket, and so grateful was Henry that he granted the citizens of Edinburgh a charter enabling them to trade with England on most favourable terms. This is interesting as showing Henry's good intentions and in casting a light on the trading arrangements of that day, but as Henry never recovered his throne it had no practical outcome. Shortly after this

28

the Queen-Mother, Mary of Gueldres, died and was buried in the church she had recently founded and endowed—the Collegiate Church of the Holy Trinity, now known as 'Trinity College.'

In 1471 James III. married the Danish Princess Margaret. They were a youthful pair, for he was only nineteen and she was twelve. She was beautiful and became very popular. Moreover she brought as her dowry the islands of Orkney and Shetland, which the Scots had long coveted, and which had been sometimes held by Scotland and sometimes by Denmark. The festivities which accompanied her wedding were splendid, and all seemed to promise well. But James had more than his own share of troubles. John of the Isles had for some time been at feud with the Earl of Huntly and the other loyal lords in the north, and what was worse, was in alliance with Edward IV. of England. He was accordingly in 1475 cited to appear before Parliament, and as he did not do so he was attacked by Argyle, Athole, Crawford, and Huntly, and was compelled to beg for mercy. He retained most of his estates, but was deprived of the Earldom of Ross (which was now added to the Crown lands), and from this time he sat in Parliament as Lord of the Isles. But James had even more formidable foes—those of his own household. His brothers, Alexander, Duke of Albany, and John, Earl of Mar, were accused of plotting against him, and were accordingly imprisoned, Mar in Craigmillar and Albany in Edinburgh Castle. Mar took ill and was removed to Canongate, where he died. This was most unfortunate for James, who was straightway accused of having poisoned him—though there was no evidence pointing that way. Albany's escape from Edinburgh Castle is one of the many romantic stories connected with it. The French King sent a vessel which contained some Gascony wine. Albany asked for some casks, which were accordingly sent, but in place of wine one of them contained a letter

29

telling him the danger he was in and a coil of rope to help
him to escape. Albany invited the captain of the guard
to come to supper to taste the wine, and when the soldiers
were intoxicated, he and his servant fell on them and
despatched them. The servant then slipped down the
rope to test it, but it was much too short, and he fell a
considerable distance and broke his thigh bone. Albany
accordingly lengthened the rope by adding sheets from
his bed, and so gained the ground in safety. He carried
his servant to a place of safety and then made for Leith,
where he got on board the French boat and sailed for
France.

It was about this time that some unfortunate women
were tried and burnt in Edinburgh as witches. They
are said to have confessed that the late Earl of Mar
had bribed them to plot against the King by means
of waxen images and incantations. James's rebellious
barons were a greater source of danger to him than
these unfortunate old women. Soon after the conspiracy
against Cochrane, the King's favourite, we find in 1481
a curious situation—James, a state prisoner in Edinburgh
Castle, conspiring with the Earl of Douglas, also a
prisoner, but a prisoner because of his rebellion against
the King. At last James in his despair appealed to his
rebellious brother Albany, and through him to Edward
IV. of England. Accordingly the Duke of Gloucester
marched north with a large army, encamped on the
Boroughmuir, and was joined by Albany. These
noblemen persuaded the barons to set the King free.
James on his release made haste to leave the Castle, and
as Lindsay tells us, 'lap on a hackney to ride down
to the Abbay, but he would not ride forward till the
Duik of Albanie his brother lap on behind him; and
so they went down the geat to the Abbay of Hallyruid-
house, quhair they remained ane long tyme in great
mirrines.' The loyalty of the burghers at this time
formed a pleasing contrast to the rebellion of the nobles;

they never deserted the King in his worst days and— strongest proof of devotion—were always willing to supply him with money. In recognition of their various services James granted them the ' Golden Charter,' by which provosts and bailies were made sheriffs within the bounds of their territories. It was at this time, too, that the King formally sanctioned the use of the 'Blue Blanket' as the ensign of the city guard. Tradition declares that the order of the Blue Blanket was instituted in the eleventh century by Pope Urban II.—but it does not need this further halo of antiquity to enhance its importance. James also made over to the town of Edinburgh all the customs of the harbour of Leith and jurisdiction over the coast roads. It is therefore easy to understand why James was so popular in Edinburgh; and if anything were wanting to complete the popularity, it was added by the devotion to religion which he exhibited by riding in procession from Holyrood on Wednesdays and Fridays to the various churches in the town. Unfortunately for James, he did not evoke the same admiration among his nobles and the rest of his subjects; hence the battle of Sauchieburn in 1488.

James IV. was crowned in Edinburgh that same year. His reign had a most unpromising beginning, but, though to his latest day he never ceased to regret the part he took in the rebellion against his father, Scotland's prosperity never was greater than under this monarch. The cloud which rested on the King did not trouble the nation. The chivalrous inclinations of James led to his subjects cultivating tournaments, weapon-shows, and other trials of arms. These usually took place near the King's stables under the Castle Rock; the name still surviving in King's Stables Road. James encouraged these displays by all means in his power, especially by offering special prizes to be striven for, such as a gold-headed spear. Scotland became justly celebrated, and

as Lindsay tells us, ' the fame of his justing and turney
spread throw all Europe, quhilk caused many errand
knyghtis cum out of uther pairtes to Scotland to
seik justing, because they hard of the kinglie fame
of the Prince of Scotland. Bot few or none of them
passed away unmarked and oftymes overthrowne.'
James also took care to give his subjects plenty of
practice in real war as well as in these chivalrous
encounters.

But he was far from being merely a fighter. We
find him arranging a curious experiment—more in the
line of James VI., one would think. He directed that,
in order to discover what was the original language,
two children should be sent to Inchkeith and brought
up by a dumb woman. The conclusion come to was
that ' they spak gude Ebrew'—poor children! James
would not have been a Stewart if he had not loved and
encouraged literature. We have nothing of his composition except his reply to Dunbar's petition, but we
have abundant evidence of his literary taste in the men
he gathered round him. Gavin Douglas and Kennedy,
and, greatest of all, Dunbar, were each singled out for
special favour. In their compositions old Edinburgh
stands out clearly before us with its narrow streets
blocked with ' booths,' the houses with their forestairs,
and the curious medley of nobles, fishwives, beggars, and
minstrels, all jostling each other in inextricable confusion. The greatest occasion of national rejoicing was
of course the King's marriage to Margaret Tudor. The
account given in the *Thrissil and the Rois* is too well
known to need more than a passing reference; by all
accounts Edinburgh must have been a gay city on that
auspicious occasion. The houses were decorated with
tapestry in the most lavish manner, the fountains ran
wine, the windows were thronged with gaily dressed
lords and ladies. In honour of the Queen various plays
were performed, and—strange combination—sacred relics

were produced for her benefit, such as the arm of
St. Giles. Allegorical and historical scenes were also
enacted, such as the Archangel Gabriel saluting the
Virgin Mary, Prudence triumphing over Sardanapalus,
Justice treading Nero under foot, etc., all with a truly
mediæval disregard of the appropriateness of time and
place. The royal pair were received at Holyrood by
the Archbishop of St. Andrews and a train of ecclesiastics.
The dresses were as gorgeous as the festivities : ' every
man apointed himself richly for the marriage, the ladies
nobly aparelled, some in gowns of cloth of gold, others
of crimson, velvet and black ; others of satin, tynsell,
and damask, and of chamlet of many colours ; hoods,
chains and collars upon their necks. . . . The Kyng
sat in a chayre of cramsyn velvet, the pannells of that
sam gylte, under his cloth of astat of blew velvet fygured
of gold,' while the Queen was ' crowned with a varey
ryche crowne of gold, garnished with pierry and perles.'
The Archbishop of Glasgow performed the ceremony.
The marriage brought nothing but harm to James himself, as there were constant disputes between England
and Scotland about Margaret's dowry ; but as an incident in the history of the Stewarts its importance can
hardly be over-rated. And if it affected the Stewarts
themselves it affected their capital no less, though less
directly. For the Stewarts owed to this marriage the
fact that they became kings of England and Ireland
as well as of Scotland, and it was owing to this that
Edinburgh in later generations sank from her proud
position of capital of a great independent country to
being little better than a provincial town.

The incident of Perkin Warbeck does not concern us
here, as it was mainly at Stirling that James entertained
him so hospitably. But this was the beginning of the
strained relations with England which eventually led
to the battle of Flodden. James had been warned by
his wife and by his nobles that it was sheer folly to

Edin-
burgh
under the
Stewarts:
Robert II.
to
James VI.

c

risk the welfare of the kingdom by a chivalrous desire to accept the challenge of the French Queen to ride for her sake three feet on English ground. Whether the warnings which followed were a mere trick of the Queen, or whether they were really supernatural, every one must decide for himself. The only warning which happened in Edinburgh is graphically described by Lindsay: 'There was a cry heard at the market cross of Edinburgh, about midnight, proclaiming, as it had been, a summons which was called by the proclaimer thereof the summons of Plotcok (Pluto) desiring all earls, lords, barons, gentlemen, and sundry burgesses within the town to compear before his master within forty days; and so many as were called were designed by their own names. But whether this summons was proclaimed by vain persons, night-walkers for their pastime, or if it was a spirit I cannot tell. But an indweller in the town, called Mr. Richard Lawson, being evil-disposed, ganging in his gallery-stair fornent the Cross, hearing this voice, thought marvel what it should be; so he cried for his servant to bring him his purse, and took a crown and cast it over the stair, saying, "I for my part appeal from your summons and judgment and take me to the mercy of God." Verily he, who caused me to chronicle this, was a sufficient landed gentleman, who was in the town in the meantime, and was then twenty years of age; and he swore after the field there was not a man that was called at that time that escaped, except that one man that appealed from their judgment.' Readers of *Marmion* will recognise the incident, though in the poem de Wilton takes the place of 'Mr. Richard Lawsoun.' In spite of the warnings alike of earth and Heaven James gathered his army on the Boroughmuir. The Bore Stone where the royal standard was raised, may still be seen built into the wall enclosing Morningside Parish Church. The most melancholy thing about the defeat of Flodden was that it was so unnecessary.

The old song 'The Flowers of the Forest' voices the general sentiment when it says:

> 'Dool for the order sent our lads to the border,
> The English for aince by guile won the day.'

Other writers, however, blame Scottish recklessness rather than English 'guile.' Sir David Lindsay in his *Testament and Complaynt of the Kingis Papyngo* ascribes all manner of virtues to James:

> 'Ane greater nobyll rang nocht in to the eird . . .
> For he was myrrour of humylitie
> Lode stern and lampe of liberalytie.'

He then goes on to speak of 'that most dolent day'—Flodden, and concludes his remarks by saying it was

> 'Nocht be the vertew of Inglis ordinance
> Bot be his awin wylfull mysgovernance.'

The Scots, however, forgave James's wilfulness in consideration of the gallant fight he made. In spite of the terrible slaughter there was much to strengthen the national pride in that battle, where

> 'Groom fought like noble, squire like knight,
> As fearlessly and well.'

And the Scots would not have been human if they had failed to contrast Flodden with Bannockburn: James IV. fighting to the death, with Edward II. fleeing for his life.

The news of Flodden did not immediately reach Edinburgh, but rumours of the disaster were heard long before they were authenticated. The city was in a wretched plight. Not only were the provost and all the chief men of the city among the slain, but the great border lords had also fallen. Therefore there was, on the one hand, nothing to prevent a victorious English army marching straight to Edinburgh, and on the other

35

there were no adequate means of defence. But while
one would have expected, under these circumstances,
that the town would be given up to panic, we find the
magistrates acting with the greatest presence of mind.
They ordered the women not to waste time crying and
clamouring on the public streets, and told them they
would do better to betake themselves to the churches
and offer prayers for the nation in its perilous condition.
This proclamation begins with warning the people not to
believe the worst until belief is forced on them : 'For sa
meikle as thair is ane greit rumber now laitlie rysin
within this toun, tueching our Soverane Lord and his
army, of the quhilk we understand thair is cumin na
veritie as yet quhairfore we charge straigtlie, and com-
mandis that all maner of personis, nyhbours within the
samen, have reddy their fensible geir and wapponis for
weir, and compeir therewith to the said president's at jow-
ing of the commoun bell, for the keeping and defens of the
toune against thame that wald invade the samyn, and also
chairgis yt all wemen . . . yat yai . . . be not seen upon ye
gait clamorand and cryand under ye pane of banesing
of yr personis but favoris. And yat the uther wemen
of gude pass to ye Kirk and pray quhen tyme requiris
for our Souerane lord and his army and nythouris
being thair at, and hold yame at yair previe labouris off
the gait within yair houses as efferis.' Never had the
condition of affairs seemed more desperate, never did the
courage of the citizens rise higher. 'It is the language of
Rome when Hannibal was at the gates' is the testimony
of Scott, and Aytoun in *Edinburgh after Flodden* gives a
vivid picture alike of the distress of the citizens and of
the steadfast courage which animated them. Men and
money were soon forthcoming, a town guard was
appointed, and £500 Scots levied for artillery and forti-
fications. The town had long since grown beyond the
wall of James II., so a new wall was built enclosing the
suburb of Cowgate. Parts of the 'Flodden wall,' as it is

36

still called, may be seen in the Vennel, a street opening off the Grassmarket. Even now we can see by the inferior workmanship how hastily it was built. This incident had a considerable effect on Edinburgh architecture. Previously the tendency had been to live in low two-storied houses and to extend the town towards the country. But for two hundred and fifty years hardly a house was built outside the Flodden

The Flodden Well

wall, and when more accommodation was necessary the city grew in height, not in extent. A truce with England was speedily arranged. Shortly afterwards the Pope sent his legate to convey two gifts to James—a consecrated cap and a sword: the latter may still be seen, as it forms part of the Regalia at the Castle.

All through the wretched time of the minority of James V. Edinburgh had its full share of the disturbances which distracted the country. The various nobles who were at feud with each other fought even in the streets of the town. The encounter between Arran and Angus (whom Margaret had married), which is known as 'Cleanse the Causey,' is the best known of these meetings, but it is far from being unique. Readers of *The Abbot* will remember how Roland Graeme some years later came to the help of Lord Seyton when he was in difficulty, and

37

the graphic account of the fray given by Scott may be taken as typical of such occurrences. It was impossible for Margaret to hold the Regency, as that would have given too much power to the already powerful Douglases. Accordingly John, Duke of Albany—son of the energetic brother of James III.—was asked to come to the rescue. He arrived in Edinburgh in 1515, and at once did his best to check the prevalent disorders. We read with considerable relief that ' evill doaris wes punnesit; amang the quhilkis ane Petir Moffet, ane gret rever theif was heidit, and for exampill of utheris, his head wes put on the West Port of Edinburgh.'

Edinburgh is now the undisputed centre of government. We find the nobles meeting the Governor in the Abbey of Holyrood, we find criminals and recalcitrant lords tried in Edinburgh, and in cases of condemnation we find the heads of the aforesaid nobles fixed on the Tolbooth or West Port of Edinburgh. We find the provost rising in importance too: his salary was increased, so was the number of his attendants.

All this time Edinburgh Castle was the residence of the young King. Gavin Dunbar, the future Archbishop of Glasgow, superintended his education, while Sir David Lindsay was his favourite companion. After he had lost the royal favour by his uncompromising attacks on the clergy, Sir David conjured James to remember those happy old times :

> ' How as ane chapman beris his pack
> I bure thy Grace upon my back
> And sumtymes stridlingis on my nek,
> Dansand with mony bend and bek ;
> The first sillabis that thow did mute
> Was *pa, da, lyn,* upon the lute ;
> Than playit I twentie springis perqueir
> Quilk was greit plesour for to heir
> Fra play thou leit we never rest,' etc.

The unfortunate King was considerably neglected by the

great lords who tried to gain possession of his person. We hear melancholy tales of the royal apartments falling into disrepair and being put right only through the generosity of his tutor. The King's wardrobe seems to have been quite as dilapidated as his dwelling, for on one occasion at least he was reduced to begging a new doublet and a pair of stockings from his half-sister the Countess of Morton.

At last, in 1524, King James was solemnly ' erected ' King, and was after this supposed to rule without the help of a regent, though at this time he was only twelve years old. Margaret, who was now acting in the interests of England, was anxious to neutralise the power of Beaton, Archbishop of St. Andrews, who was the real head of the French party. Wolsey tried to get possession of his person, but found that in subtlety Beaton was quite equal to himself. However, Margaret continued to persuade the Archbishop to come to Edinburgh, and, having got him there, she imprisoned him in the Castle. Margaret had, however, considerable difficulty with her husband, the Earl of Angus, or, as she most appropriately called him, ' My Lord of *Anguish*.' He and Lennox marched into Edinburgh early one morning, and were only persuaded to withdraw by the unanswerable logic of the Castle guns. The popular feeling ran very high against England, in fact the English envoy wrote to Wolsey that the women in the streets cursed him, and even accused him of being the cause of the bad harvests ! But popular sentiment had little effect on the nobles, and in 1525 we find a three years' truce with England concluded, and later on in 1528 a five years' peace.

It was not till 1528 that James escaped from the Douglases, although Lennox and some of the other nobles had gallantly tried to rescue him. From this time on he ruled as well as reigned, and showed all the vigour of the Stewarts in dealing with unruly subjects. He dealt with them firstly by force of arms,—as in the

39

case of that noted Border freebooter Johnnie Armstrong of Gilnockie; but the year 1532 is memorable, not only for Edinburgh, but for the whole of Scotland, as the date when the College of Justice was founded. Scotland is justly proud of her system of law and of her law-courts; it is strange to look back to those turbulent days when the Court of Session, as we know it, first came into being. 'The Session' had been founded by James I. and improved by James II., while the 'Daily Council' was instituted by James IV. The College of Justice was to a certain extent modelled on the 'Daily Council,' but it also bore a close resemblance to the Parlement de Paris, the supreme legal body in France.

In 1536 James went to France to seek a wife in the person of Marie de Vendôme. But the lady was so plain-looking that James flatly refused to have her, and married instead Magdalene, daughter of François I. The King and Queen landed at Leith on Whitsun Eve. The Queen on landing fell on her knees and kissed the soil of Scotland, and then proceeded to Holyrood. Her entry into Edinburgh itself was most brilliant, for the people had made all imaginable preparations in her honour, and her own train was dazzling. It contained among others a little boy of thirteen, who was then of small account, but who was afterwards to become famous as the poet Ronsard. But neither the warm reception of her subjects nor her distinguished followers availed to protect the Queen from the biting winds of her new country, and within six weeks of her landing at Leith she died. She was buried at Holyrood near the grave of James II. We learn from Buchanan that this was the first occasion on which mourning was worn in Scotland. Pitscottie tells how the wedding festivities were succeeded by 'deregies and soull masses verrie lamentable to behold.' The lamentations were indeed universal, and Sir David Lindsay only expressed the general sentiments in his *Deploration of the Death of Quene Magdalene*. By no one, however, was she regretted so much as by the King.

It seems to have been in every sense of the word a love match, though it happened to harmonise with James's political aims.

But however much he mourned for Magdalene, duty to his subjects demanded that he should seek a second wife. He did not again visit France, but he sent David Beaton —nephew of James Beaton—to negotiate the matter. When he had wooed and won Magdalene another lady seems to have made a considerable impression on James, the young Duchesse de Longueville, daughter of the Duc de Guise. Her husband had since died, and James seems to have thought they might console each other. Henry VIII. wanted her as one of his numerous wives, but she prudently declined the honour. Accordingly Beaton brought her over in triumph to Scotland. While these negotiations were going on James was involved in unpleasant business not exactly suited to wedding festivities, viz. the trial and condemnation of the Master of Forbes and of Lady Glamis, sister of Angus. Lady Glamis must have been considered a dangerous woman, for she had been tried three times before,—the first time on the—to us—extraordinary charge of 'intoxicating' her husband. This was a good deal more serious than it sounds, as it meant *poisoning*. She was acquitted then and on two subsequent occasions. She was now, however, tried for attempting to poison the King, and was burned to death on the Castle Hill. Her noble birth and great personal beauty won for her general sympathy, which was changed to admiration by the courage with which she met her fate.

The people turned with relief from these gruesome events to preparations for welcoming the new Queen. We read of her being greeted with 'gold and spyces, wynes and curious playes.' A strange combination, but testifying the good will of the town, which was further shown by their undertaking the repair of Holyrood park walls and by contributing generously to the King's financial necessities. Although Mary of Guise was closely

41

connected with Edinburgh in her widowhood, she does not seem to have lived there much during the four years she was Queen-Consort. In the *Diurnal of Occurrents* we find this entry towards the end of the reign: ' Upon the last day of Februar thair was ane certaine of persones accusit for heresie in Abbay Kirk of Halyrudhous; and thair was condempnit twa blackfrieris, ane chanone of Sanct Androis, the vicar of Dollour, and ane lawit man that duelt in Stirling were brynt the same day on the Castell Hill of Edinburgh.' This entry has a sinister significance. If a desire for absolutism was one great cause of the downfall of the Stewarts, a passionate abhorrence of ' heresy' was another, and was no less fatal.

In December 1542 James v. died at Falkland—died, it is said, of a broken heart. His last words are almost too well known to need repetition: when he heard of the birth of a daughter he exclaimed, ' It (the crown) came with a lass (Marjorie Bruce) and it will gang with a lass.' Looking back on the struggles of his own minority James was justified in his melancholy prediction. That the crown did not go ' with a lass' is due mainly to the character of the Queen-Mother, Mary of Guise.

As was usual when the sovereign was a child, Scotland was torn by faction, and, as in the previous reign, it was no longer merely the rivalry of Boyd and Livingstone, Douglas and Gordon, it was the opposition of the French party and the English, and was further complicated by the religious question. Henry VIII. had already made his drastic changes in Church government, and had vainly endeavoured to persuade his nephew to follow his example. This James, alike from principle and policy, had refused to do. He had alienated the great nobles, the border freebooters and the Highland chiefs, and had to rely on the loyalty of the Church and of the common people, by whom he was much beloved as the Guidman of Ballengeich. Moreover, he seems to have been sincerely attached to the Church, while we know that Mary of

42

Guise would exert all her influence in that direction. There was, however, a large party among the nobles—headed by Angus—favourable to England and incidentally favourable to Church Reform; and the common people, while opposed to England, were by no means attached to the Church. The worldliness and—in many cases—the wickedness of the clergy had brought about this condition of affairs, which we see clearly portrayed in the satires of Sir David Lindsay.

Overtures of peace from England were accepted at a Parliament held in Edinburgh. Beaton, who opposed this, was imprisoned at Dalkeith. Soon after, however, the Papal Nuncio arrived, and did his utmost to break off these friendly relations. He was entertained with such splendour that he ever afterwards lauded Scottish hospitality. Some of the said hospitality seems to us rather absurd. For instance, Bishop Leslie tells us, 'The Earle of Murray makand him the banquet in his house, although he had great store of all kinds of silver wark, yet nottheless for the greater magnificence, he set forth ane cupboard furnished with all kinds of glasses of the finest chrystal that could be made; and to make the said patriarch understand that there was great abundance thereof in Scotland, he caused one of his servants, as it had been by sloth and negligence, pull down the cupboard cloth so that all the whole christellings suddenly were cast down to the earth and broken; wherewith the patriarch was very sorry, but the Earl suddenly caused bring another cupboard better furnished with finer chrystal nor that was; which the patriarch praised as well for the magnificence of the Earl as for the fineness of the chrystal, affirming that he never did see better in Venice where he himself was born.' The legate soon after left the country, having transferred his legatine powers to Cardinal Beaton.

Having regained his liberty and his power Beaton was able to break off the peaceful relations with England.

43

In 1544 Hertford appeared with a fleet in the Firth of
Forth. He speedily took Leith, overcame the very in-
adequate resistance which was offered him, and marched
on Edinburgh. He informed the citizens that he would
utterly destroy the city unless the young Queen was
immediately delivered up to Henry to be educated in
England and in course of time married to the Prince of
Wales (afterwards Edward vi.). The Provost, Sir Adam
Otterburn, thereupon remarked, 'That it were better
the city should stand on its defence.' Hertford tried
unsuccessfully to take the Castle, and in his wrath at
failure proceeded to revenge himself on the city. So
thorough was the devastation that it has been said that
nothing of the Edinburgh of that day remains but
the north-west wing of Holyrood and parts of the
Castle itself—which Hertford was unable to take. He
burned also Roslin and Craigmillar, and then marched to
Dunbar, destroying every abbey, town, and village between Dunbar and Edinburgh,—Musselburgh, Prestonpans, Port Seton, Haddington, and Dunbar itself being
a few of the places entirely burned by the English.
After the death of Henry these pleasant methods of
bringing about the marriage of Mary and Edward were
still continued by Hertford. The national and religious
sentiment of the people could not endure this alliance,
and they disliked above all the methods by which the
English sought to bring it about. The army which
marched to meet Hertford contained a large number of
priests and monks, who followed a banner representing
a woman kneeling before a crucifix. This banner bore
the motto ' Afflictæ ecclesiæ ne obliviscaris.' The battle
of Pinkie was fought on Saturday, 10th September
1547, a day long remembered as 'Black Saturday.'
Hertford thereupon marched to Leith and attacked
Edinburgh. It was said that in Edinburgh alone the
battle of Pinkie had left three hundred and sixty
widows, but the universal mourning only roused the

spirit of the citizens to greater efforts against England, and Hertford had to retire. He revenged himself, however, by removing the leaden roof of Holyrood, pillaging Leith, and burning what towns and villages he had previously omitted. Little wonder that the Earl of Huntly remarked, that while he had no 'objection to the match, he liked not the manner of wooing.'

Help from France soon arrived, and with it a proposal from the French King, Henri II., that the alliance between France and Scotland should be cemented by marriage between the young Queen and the Dauphin François. Henri also added that in the meantime he would gladly shelter Mary and superintend her education. This proposal must have been peculiarly gratifying to the Scots, and the courtesy with which it was expressed must have been a pleasing contrast to the rough and ready English methods. Mary of Guise showed her wisdom and her real love for her daughter by accepting the offer, but it must have been a sore trial to her to part from this dearly loved child. The French rendered great help in driving out the English, and also in helping to fortify Leith to enable it to resist future attacks. There were, however, some difficulties in having these French allies. Leslie gives a graphic account of a free fight which took place in the High Street, during which the Provost was killed. This matter was settled with some difficulty.

However, in 1550, peace was made with England. When the Queen-Mother returned from France in 1551 she held Parliaments in Edinburgh which transacted some important business. The property destroyed by the English was first dealt with. Some sumptuary laws were also passed which dealt not only—as formerly—with clothes, but also with the quantity and quality of food considered suitable for the rank of each individual. We read far less about clothes now than formerly; perhaps the satires of Sir David Lindsay had succeeded

45

where Acts of Parliament failed. But far the most interesting of these enactments is that which deals with printing books without licence. It enacts 'That na prenter presume to prent ony buikes, ballates, sanges, blasphemationes, rime, and tragedies, outher in Latine or English toung' without a proper licence. The penalty for infringing this act was confiscation of goods and banishment for life. In 1554 Mary at last persuaded Arran to hand over the Regency to her. It was undoubtedly time for some strong hand to seize the reins of government, the brawling in the streets (even of the capital) and the general disorders were frightful. The Laird of Buccleuch was killed in the streets of Edinburgh by the Kerrs, and the Scotts did not long remain indebted to their rivals. Lord Semple defied law and decency still further by stabbing Lord Crichton of Sanquhar in the house of the Governor of Edinburgh, —and owing to powerful friends was not molested in any way.

The new Regent at once introduced reforms, but, while the Parliament supported her in restoring order, they passed various acts relating to things religious in defiance of her wishes. The best known of these is the Act 'Anent Robert Hude and the Abbot of Unreason,' in which 'it is statute and ordained that in all times cumming, no manner of person be chosen Robert Hude, nor Little John, Abbot of Unreason, Queens of May, nor otherwise nouther in Burgh nor to Landwart, in onie time to cum,' under very severe penalties. 'And gif onie women or others about summer trees singand, makis perturbation to the Queenis lieges in the passage throw Burrowes and uthers Landward Towns, the woman perturbatoures for skafrie of money or utherwise, sall be taken, handled, and put upon the Cuck-stules of everie Burgh or Toune.' What delightful people our Scottish Reformers must have been when they considered it a crime to sing under summer trees! It is almost certain that these foolish restrictions of the amusements of the common people had a good deal to do with the general discontent. It was just at this time Knox returned to Scotland, and was cited to appear in Edinburgh in May 1556, but the case was dropped. He thereupon wrote to the Queen-Regent asking for reformation in the Church, but she handed his letter to the Archbishop of Glasgow, only remarking, ' Please you, my lord, to look at a pasquill.'

An agreeable change from these religious wranglings was afforded by the visit of the Danish ambassador. We read of the magnificent entertainment prepared for him in Edinburgh, and are somewhat amused to learn that it cost the truly extravagant sum of twenty-five pounds seventeen shillings and one penny—Scots (a little over £2 sterling). Is it wonderful that the poverty of the Scots was proverbial?

But this was merely an interlude—the religious strife waxed hotter than ever. The mob broke into St. Giles and destroyed the images of St. Francis and the Virgin Mary, and in 1558 they threw the famous image of St. Giles into the Nor' Loch, where it was customary to duck witches. Another image of St. Giles was borrowed from the Greyfriars, but it shared the fate of its predecessor. Knox gives a graphic account of these drastic measures: ' Down go the crosses, off go the surplices, round caps and cornets with the crowns. The Greyfriars gaped, the Black friars blew, the Priests panted and fled, and happy was he that got first to the house, for such a sudden fray came never among the generation of antichrist within this realm before.' It was in this year that Knox published his book against ' the Monstrous Regiment of Women,' otherwise Mary of England and the Regent,—but this vehement attack on ' Women's Rights ' brought him later small favour with Elizabeth.

The two years that followed are a melancholy record of brawling and pillage on the one side, and retaliatory

measures on the other. All these troubles seem to
have weighed heavily on the Queen-Regent. She died
in Edinburgh Castle on 10th June 1560. She tried
in vain to reconcile the opposing parties, to make things
easier for her daughter. On her deathbed she sent for
some of the more prominent 'Lords of the Congregation,'
the Duke of Chatelherault (Earl of Arran), the Earls
of Argyle, Marischal, and Glencairn, and her stepson
Lord James Stewart (afterwards Earl of Moray). Ig-
noring all she had suffered at their hands, the Regent
begged them to forgive her if she had ever in any
way offended them. The lords professed to be deeply
touched, but instead of leaving her to die in peace they
requested her to receive a Protestant minister, who
discoursed to her on the errors of Rome and dwelt on
the idolatry of the Mass. Instead of showing anger
at the insult offered to her religion Mary replied that
she looked for salvation only through the death of her
Saviour. Not content with this, the Protestant lords
refused to allow her funeral to be conducted according
to Catholic rites. Her body was therefore preserved
in a leaden coffin and taken to Rheims, where her sister
was abbess.

The violence of all classes of the community was far
from abating. Soon after the death of the Regent some
apprentices were severely punished for playing 'Robin
Hood.' The wrath of the mob was great, and serious
riots took place. Meanwhile Parliament passed more
stringent regulations. It was to this country that Queen
Mary came from sunny, light-hearted France, landing at
Leith on 19th August 1561. Not only was the country
divided on the religious question, but the great lords
were at variance with each other, and the whole country
was torn by religious and political feud. Worst of all,
there was no one whom this unhappy girl of nineteen
could thoroughly trust. In too many cases those who
professed to be most anxious to serve her had purely

selfish aims in view; but she, naturally, believed in the disinterestedness of her brother, whom she created Earl of Mar and then Earl of Moray—and who could blame her? Over and above the ties of kindred he owed everything he had to her: she showered titles and distinctions upon him and forgave his rebellions, times without number, only to be again deceived. But in the welcome bestowed on her there was no trace of future shadows, unless it were the ill-omened mist which shrouded everything when she arrived, a mist so thick that, as Knox tells us, 'in the memory of man at that day of the year was never seen a more dolorous face of the heaven.' This is rather different from the poetical account of her arrival which Hogg gives in the *Queen's Wake*. But the enthusiastic welcome she received seemed to leave nothing to be desired. Bonfires blazed in all directions, and loyal subjects serenaded her all night through at Holyrood. Needless to say the noise was execrable, and even had it been the sweetest melody imaginable, she would doubtless have preferred to rest after her long journey; but she took the welcome as it was meant, and expressed her pleasure that her subjects should be so eager to greet her. She was magnificently received when she made her public entry into the city. She was welcomed by a curious medley, including black slaves in gorgeous raiment and stately citizens suitably attired in black velvet with crimson satin doublets. The beautiful boy who presented her with the keys of the city presented her also with a Bible and Psalter, probably to her astonishment, as this was an innovation. Her surprise must have been intensified when a miracle play was performed representing the fate of Korah, Dathan, and Abiram as a warning to idolaters. In spite of these 'rifts within the lute' the day passed off most successfully. All the citizens were ordered to array themselves in satin, silk, or taffeta in honour of the Queen, and all deference was paid to

D

her and to the distinguished strangers who had come
with her from France—Brantôme and Châtelard, who,
along with the Queen, were entertained by a public
banquet. The streets were decorated in the most costly
manner imaginable to be in keeping with the dresses
worn, and the Queen seems to have disregarded all
minor drawbacks.

Mary Stewart was all her life an extremely tolerant
woman, willing to allow others to believe as they thought
best. But even toleration has its limits, and what Mary
could not tolerate was the intolerance then prevalent
in Scotland. It was manifestly unreasonable that the
Queen should be prevented from attending Mass, while
her subjects were free to attend Protestant churches.
Yet, when Mass was celebrated in the chapel at Holyrood
the Sunday after Mary's arrival, the mob were with
difficulty restrained from bursting in and interrupting
the service, and Knox from his pulpit fulminated against
'idolatry' in high places, telling his congregation that
he feared one Mass more than ten thousand armies
pledged to suppress religion. Mary might have attempted to coerce Knox; instead she trusted to that
charm of manner which had never before failed, and
tried to win him over by kindness. But Knox was
as impervious to her smiles as to her frowns, and expressed himself with even greater frankness than he had
previously done. 'Think ye,' said the Queen, 'that
subjects having power may resist their Princes?' To
which Knox returned the uncompromising reply, 'If
their Princes exceed their bounds.' We may regret
that the great reformer did not show greater courtesy
to one who was not only his sovereign but a young,
beautiful, and unprotected woman, but chivalry does
not seem to have been his strong point. This famous
interview is another of the memories which haunt the
old palace of Holyrood.

The Protestant lords were at this time anxious for

compromise, but compromise was hardly understood in the sixteenth century, and the lower classes accused them of treachery to the cause of religion. On 21st September 1561 the new statutes of Edinburgh were promulgated. These statutes ordered all malefactors to be turned out of the towns, and under 'malefactors' they classed all Roman Catholics. Mary, with the entire approval of the Protestant lords, imprisoned the magistrates and ordered others to be elected. Many other difficulties arose : the right of the Queen to attend Mass, the question of the Book of Discipline, and the settlement of the Church property. That Knox was no respecter of persons was shown by the fact that he severely criticised the festivities at the wedding of his friend and patron the Earl of Mar—better known by his later title Earl of Moray. He married Lady Agnes Keith, and the wedding was celebrated in St. Giles'. They were admonished to 'behave themselves moderately in all things,' but the preachers did not consider the gaieties which followed conformed to that recommendation. Knox blamed the Queen more than the actual culprits for the magnificence of these proceedings, but his strictures made a considerable breach between him and the Protestant lords. Maitland, among others, objected greatly to the tone of his prayers for the Queen, especially to his use of the phrase 'Illuminat hir hairt gif Thy gud plesour be,' and to the doubts cast on the possibility of her salvation.

In the midst of these disputes we find arrangements for the erection of a new tolbooth, the Kirk-o'-Field, granted as a site for a new school (afterwards the University), and Greyfriars monastery handed over to the town as a public graveyard. But these peaceful transactions were broken in upon by the violence of d'Elbœuf, Lord John of Coldingham, and Bothwell breaking into the house of a respectable citizen, and also by Arran's ridiculous plot to carry off the Queen.

51

But more serious trouble was imminent. Mary's
'fatal gift of beauty' had already involved her in great
trouble, viz. the unfortunate episode of Châtelard. She
may be said to owe all her subsequent troubles to her
unfortunate marriage with Darnley. After considering
the Archduke Charles of Austria and Don Carlos of
Spain, she was not likely to listen to Elizabeth's suggestion that she should marry Leicester unless Elizabeth
named Mary as her successor, which Elizabeth flatly
refused to do. It was about this time that Lennox and
Darnley returned to Scotland. Queen Mary's usual bad
fortune appeared here, for she fell madly in love with
Darnley. As a matter of fact their marriage at the
moment was the best possible policy, and if it had been
policy only it might have turned out well enough. But
Darnley had none of the qualities which could retain
love, and Mary and he became mutually jealous. As
the grandson of Margaret Tudor by her second husband
the Earl of Angus, Darnley's claim to the English
throne was second only to that of Mary herself, while
Lennox, his father, disputed with Chatelherault the
claim to the Scottish succession. Mary and Darnley
were 'proclaimed' in the Canongate Church, and on
29th July 1565 they were married by the Dean of
Restalrig in the Chapel Royal at Holyrood. Needless
to say, this marriage was a great trial both to the
Protestants lords and to Knox, who, Melville tells us,
'was like to ding the pulpit in blads and flee out of it.'
He paid another visit to Holyrood and asked the Queen
and the ladies-in-waiting if they thought they could
take their garnishings to Heaven. But there was
abundant cause for Knox's misgivings in the 'Round-
about' or 'Chaseabout Raid' which followed, and which
coincided with the beginning of the Counter-Reformation
on the Continent.

The one thing which prevented Mary's continued
triumph was the character of Darnley himself. He was

52

Doorway   Holyrood Chapel

both weak and wicked, and Mary found it impossible
to consult him on questions of policy. Her chief adviser
at this time was Rizzio, who was equally hated by
Darnley and by the Protestant lords: by Darnley
because he enjoyed Mary's confidence, by the Protestant
lords because he had brought about the marriage between
Mary and Darnley, and was supposed to be responsible
for Mary's policy. The main details of the murder of
Rizzio are well known. The Queen was at supper with
the Countess of Argyle, Lord Robert Stewart, Rizzio,
Beaton of Creich, and Arthur Erskine, when Darnley
suddenly appeared. His rooms at Holyrood were
immediately below those of the Queen and communicated
with them by means of a secret stair. There was nothing
remarkable in Darnley's coming in this way, but almost
immediately Lord Ruthven followed. He had risen
from a sick-bed, and his appearance was so ghastly that
Mary sprang to her feet, but Darnley put his arm
round her and prevented her taking any action.
Ruthven was followed by the other conspirators. Rizzio
tried to shelter himself behind Mary, but George
Douglas struck at him over the Queen's shoulder, while
Ker of Fawdonside held a pistol to her heart and
threatened to shoot her on the spot if she gave the
alarm. Morton and the other confederates then dragged
Rizzio into the outer room and there completed their
work.

For many a day his blood left a stain on the
floor supposed to be ineffaceable, and in later days
credulous tourists from many lands have gazed admir-
ingly at the red paint which was constantly renewed
for their benefit! Now, however, a brass plate marks
the place where Rizzio died. He was buried in the
passage leading from the quadrangle to the chapel, and
there the flat stone which marks his grave may still
be seen.

Darnley's conduct had been abominable, but either

from policy or because she realised he was the tool of others, Mary at once tried to detach him from his confederates, and succeeded so well that she persuaded him to escape with her to Dunbar. Darnley's conduct, however, did not improve, so Mary returned to Edinburgh. Holyrood had associations too tragic and too recent for her to care to return there, so she went to the house of a private citizen in the High Street, then to the house in Castlehill where her mother had lived, and finally, for greater security, she removed to the Castle.

There on 19th June a son was born to her—afterwards James VI. of Scotland, James I. of England. The room where James was born is still shown to visitors, and though now unfurnished is probably otherwise pretty much as it was then. It is a small room of peculiar shape commanding an extensive view and looking sheer down on the Grassmarket. The legend that James was let down from this window in a basket is quite unauthenticated, but it is one which the attendant seldom fails to produce for the benefit of tourists. The greatest joy prevailed in Scotland and corresponding gloom at the court of England. When she heard the news Elizabeth exclaimed, 'The Queen has a fair son and I am but a barren stock.'

Mary soon after pardoned about seventy people, including Morton, who had plotted the death of Rizzio. Darnley's position at this time was most unpleasant. He was estranged from Mary, and the return of the exiled nobles was an awkward circumstance, as they were in no mood to forgive him for having played them false. He left the Queen and went to Glasgow, where he took smallpox. His illness seems to have revived all Mary's affection, for she went to him and nursed him back to health, risking not only her life—she was a Stewart and knew no fear—but her beauty, which would have been a serious loss to her. When Darnley was

convalescent she persuaded him to return to Edinburgh
with her, and he was lodged in the house near the
Collegiate Church of St. Mary's-in-the-Fields (the Kirk-
o'-Field).   Mary spent a great part of each day with
him, and on 9th February 1567 she was with him in the
evening, but left to be present at a masque at Holyrood.
Bothwell's servants met her on her way back, ' gangand
before them with licht torches as they came up the
Black Frier Wynd.'   At two o'clock next morning the
Kirk-o'-Field was blown up with gunpowder, and the
dead body of Darnley was found in the garden.   No
one doubted for a moment that Bothwell was responsible,
but when he was brought to trial in the Tolbooth two
months later he was acquitted.   There were too many
others directly implicated in the murder—like Morton
and Maitland—for a thorough investigation to be considered safe.   Moray had taken good care to be away
from Edinburgh at the time.   The leading nobles also
signed a ' bond ' declaring that Bothwell was a suitable
husband for the Queen, though he had a wife living at
the time, whom he speedily divorced.

His abduction of the Queen followed a fortnight after
his acquittal.   When Bothwell brought Mary back
to Edinburgh she turned her horse's head towards
Holyrood, but Bothwell seized her bridle and compelled
her to ride to the Castle instead, a typical incident
surely.   They were married in the Chapel at Holyrood
on 15th May by Adam Bothwell, Bishop of Orkney.
Mary's next appearance in Edinburgh was a month
later, after the battle of Carberry Hill, when she was
imprisoned in the house of the Provost, Sir Simon
Preston, near the Tron Church.   Here she was insulted
by being confronted with a banner representing the
murder of Darnley and bearing the inscription, ' Judge
and revenge my cause, O Lord.'   This was too much for
the Queen, who exclaimed, ' Good people, either satisfy
your cruelty and hatred by taking away my miserable

life, or release me from the hands of such inhuman tyrants.' Thereupon some of the loyal citizens displayed the Blue Blanket and rushed to the rescue, but she was immediately removed to Holyrood. On 16th June 1667 Mary was removed from Holyrood to Lochleven, so she passes out of the history of Edinburgh. Yet her memory survives still, more strongly than ever, and when we walk along the cloisters of Holyrood or stand on the Castle battlements or wander through the aisles of St. Giles', it is the lovely and hapless Mary Stewart who fills our thoughts.

CHAPTER III

FROM this time on the character of Edinburgh changed considerably. During the twenty-five years that James reigned in Scotland, Stirling, not Edinburgh, was his chief place of abode, and after the removal of the King and Court to England, Edinburgh retained only a shadow of its former greatness—which was still farther attenuated by the Union of the Parliaments in 1707.

The first use the new government made of its power was to bring to trial certain attendants of the Queen on the charge of the murder of Darnley. Sebastian escaped, but Blackadder and the others were 'put in irins and tormentis for furthering of the tryall of the veritie,' and in spite of their—presumably well-founded—assertions of innocence they were executed on 24th June 1567. We find other incidents occurring in Edinburgh at this time: the magistrates' assertion of their superiority over Leith, the proclamation of Moray as Regent at the Cross of Edinburgh, and the siege of Edinburgh Castle, which was held for Queen Mary by Kirkaldy of Grange. The country was at this time torn by civil war, families were divided, and even children in their games declared themselves 'Kingsmen' or 'Queensmen.' Moray, however, contrived to reduce the country to something like order, but he was assassinated in 1570 by Hamilton of Bothwellhaugh. Knox preached his funeral sermon in St. Giles', the text being, 'Blessed are the dead which die in the Lord,' and he preached so eloquently that we are told ' he made three thousand persons to shed tears for the loss of such a good and godly governor.' He was buried in the south transept of St. Giles', which in his honour still bears the name of the ' Moray Aisle.' Knox died two years later and was buried in the churchyard of St. Giles. It is almost superfluous to refer to Morton's well-known eulogium, ' Here lies one who never feared the face of man.'

Moray had been succeeded by Lennox, and he in his turn by Mar. Morton now succeeded to that difficult office. Kirkaldy of Grange still held the Castle. There were minor inconveniences connected with this fact, besides the obvious awkwardness of having a hostile force in the midst of the capital. The Regalia was kept in the Castle for safety, so that when the crown jewels were wanted for state functions they ' might not be had,' and their place was taken by gilt imitations. The Castle was gallantly defended, but lack of provisions compelled surrender in 1573. No quarter for the leaders was to be expected from Morton, and Grange and his brother were accordingly ' hailit in cairtis bakwart ' to the Cross and there executed.

In 1579 James made his first public appearance in Edinburgh. He was received in the usual way with every magnificence and with allegorical representations. People representing ' Dame Music,' Peace, Plenty, Justice, Religion, etc., received him, and, the story of the judgment of Solomon was represented, and, in compliment to the ' British Solomon,' he was addressed in Latin, Greek, Scots, and Hebrew. The fall of Morton took place about this time. He had ruled with a high hand and had overcome his own enemies and the enemies of his house—the Hamiltons. But in 1580 he was accused and tried on the charge of Darnley's murder. It is undoubtedly true that Morton was mixed up in the affair, but his guilt

59

had been known for thirteen years. He was executed by
the 'Maiden,' a kind of primitive guillotine which he
himself is said to have invented. This, however, has
been denied, and some say it was used as early as 1560.
It may still be seen in the Antiquarian Museum. 1587
was an important year, as it was the date of Queen
Mary's execution. Many of the Scots agreed with the Earl
of Bothwell (Francis Stewart), who said a suit of mail was
the best mourning for the Queen, but James declined
to risk war. In 1587 also occurred James's would-be
dramatic feast, when he ordered all present to forgo
their feuds and pledge brotherly affection to each
other. The lords all took the hands of their enemies and
pledged each other at the Market Cross, but we do
not read that they laid aside their feuds afterwards.

In 1590 James married Anne of Denmark, and his
adventures when he went for her were most romantic—a
strange contrast to the rest of his career.

In the recent wars the Edinburgh Town Council had
gained a good deal of independence. They had successfully established their claim to superiority over Leith,
they had defied kings and regents. But James tranquilly
issued his orders for the reception of himself and his
Queen, and these orders were obeyed down to the smallest
detail, in spite of the trouble and expense involved therein.
The streets of Edinburgh, of Leith, and of the Canongate
were to be lined with armed men to keep off the rush.
The King and his bride, Anne of Denmark, landed at
Leith and then proceeded to Holyrood, where the Queen
was crowned a few days later, and not only crowned but
anointed with ' a bonye quantitie of oyll.' Another
accompaniment of the coronation was 'Mr. Andro
Meluene, principall of the College of Theolloges, making
ane oratione in twa hunder Lateine verse.' They were
received in Edinburgh with the usual magnificence
accorded to royal brides, and the usual incongruous
mixture of allegory and religion. The Queen received

the keys of the city from an angel, and they were met at
the Butter Trone by the Nine Muses, who ' greted them
with *psalms*.' They then proceeded to St. Giles' and
listened to a sermon. The Danish nobles who accompanied the Queen were, a few days later, entertained by
the magistrates to a banquet in the house of Thomas
Aitchisoun. This house may still be seen in the Cowgate. The accounts for the banquet may still be seen
and are very amusing reading. Evidently—as James
was at pains to inform his subjects—' A King with a new
married wife did not come hame every day.'

Shortly afterwards Edinburgh was perturbed by the
excesses of the Earl of Bothwell. He was the King's
near kinsman, as his grandfather was a son of James v.,
and his mother was the sister of the Earl of Bothwell so
notorious in the previous reign,—hence his title. It was
probably partly owing to his relationship with the King
that so many of his mad actions were condoned, but probably also his very daring was its own defence. In 1591
a friend of his was in danger on account of the witness of
a prisoner in the Tolbooth. Bothwell, without hesita-
tion, broke into the Tolbooth and carried off his man,
whom he lodged in Crichton Castle. Shortly afterwards he was tried before the Privy Council—*not* for this
escapade, but on the singular charge of having by witchcraft made the weather bad to keep the King in Norway.
His denial of this charge had no effect, and he was
imprisoned in Edinburgh Castle, but seems to have had
no difficulty in escaping. He was pursued to the borders,
but contrived to elude pursuit, only to return to Edinburgh—three days after his outlawry had been proclaimed
at the Town Cross—and dare the Chancellor or any one
else to touch him. But his crowning achievement was to
appear in Holyrood and defy the King himself. Eight
of his followers were taken and hanged, but Bothwell
himself escaped. Readers of *Old Mortality* are well
acquainted with his equally reckless and much more dis-

reputable grandson, who was killed at Drumclog in a
hand - to - hand fight with that doughty Covenanter,
Balfour of Burleigh. Truly there was no lack of incident
in old Edinburgh. 1595 was noted for the famous
barring-out on the part of High School boys.

In 1596 James's famous quarrel with the ministers
took place. Andrew Melville had roused James's royal
ire by describing him to his face as ' God's sillie vassal,'
but it was David Black who was the occasion—though
probably not the cause—of the upturn. Black declared
that for what he said in his sermons he was subject to the
jurisdiction of spiritual courts only. Thereupon James
ordered the Privy Council to take measures against the
ministers. The result was a riot, for which it was not
hard to persuade James that the ministers were responsible. James in great indignation left Edinburgh,
ordered the Parliament and College of Justice to be
removed, and even threatened to utterly destroy the town
and erect a monument on the ruins, ' as an infamous
memorial of their detestable rebellion.' The magistrates humbled themselves in the most abject manner, but
James for a long time refused to have anything to do
with them. At last, however, they proceeded to Holyrood, and humbly kneeling before their indignant
monarch, accepted his terms. These included giving up
to the King certain houses which had been built in St.
Giles' Churchyard. On this site Parliament House was
afterwards built. In addition James secured what might
be called an indemnity of twenty thousand merks, so he
emerged from the affair with considerable profit. In
1599 James and the ministers had another difference of
opinion. Some English actors came to Edinburgh—some
people think Shakespeare was in the company. In any
case they were warmly welcomed by James, who provided
them with a house and went to see them act, greatly to
the indignation of the ministers, especially as these
southern strangers gave performances on Sunday. James,

however, gave them to understand he would have no
interference. Although James scolded burghers and
ministers alike, he was on intimate terms with many of
the citizens, notably with George Heriot the goldsmith,
whose booth beside St. Giles' was often honoured with
royal visits. *The Fortunes of Nigel* gives a vivid picture
of the familiar terms existing between James and 'Jingling
Geordie' even in the English court, where much greater
state was preserved.

In 1603 the expected happened and Queen Elizabeth
died, naming as her successor James vi. of Scotland.
There were other claimants to the English throne—
notably Arabella Stewart and the descendants of Mary
Tudor—but there was no one whose claim was as strong
as that of James. The Scots must have expected this
for some time. It was better for James himself, better
for England, better for Scotland, that the two countries
should be united under one sovereign, but it was most
detrimental to the prosperity of Edinburgh. James
went to St. Giles' before leaving for England and listened
to a sermon which alluded in suitable terms to his approaching departure. At the end of the sermon James
himself delivered a farewell address to his subjects:
'Think not of me as of a king going from one part to
another; but as a king lawfully called, going from one
part of the isle to the other, that so your comfort may be
greater. And where I thought to have employed you
with some armour, now I employ only your hearts to the
good prospecting of me in my success and journey.' On
5th April 1603 James left Scotland, promising that he
would revisit it every three years, and as a pledge of
good faith left his children behind under the guardianship
of the Earl of Mar and some of the other leading nobles.

He reigned over England and Scotland for twenty-two
years, but in that time only once did he revisit his ancient
kingdom. Though his squabbles with the English
Parliament took up most of his time, James by no means

forgot his native country; perhaps he never cared so much for it—in a sentimental way—as when he was away from it. We find him solicitous about the means at the command of the magistrates for keeping up civic state, to aid which laudable object he granted them duties on wine. He was also grieved that the grandeur of London civic dignitaries should be so much greater than that of Edinburgh magistrates. Accordingly he sent to Edinburgh two gowns worn by London aldermen and requested the Edinburgh bailies to have their gowns made on that pattern. James also took a benevolent interest in things ecclesiastical. His great desire was to make the union between the two countries as complete as possible. He could make no progress in his aim of one Parliament, but he did his best to form the Church of Scotland on the model of the Church of England. This was the real object of his visit to Edinburgh in 1617. The Chapel at Holyrood was remodelled by Inigo Jones, and the service met with the approval of Laud, who was present—which speaks for itself. James also induced the estates to pass certain acts tending in the same direction. But with all his obstinacy James was too 'canny' to push matters to an extremity, so the 'deluge' did not come till after his day. Little of importance happened in Edinburgh during the remaining years of the reign if we except the visit of Ben Jonson to Hawthornden, which took place in 1619.

James died in 1625 and was succeeded by Charles I. Year after year he held out delusive hopes of a visit to his Scottish subjects, year after year something prevented him. At last in 1633 the long-promised visit took place. The people were delighted to have opportunity for display, and his welcome in Edinburgh was almost unparalleled, although Edinburgh was by no means remiss in its entertainment of its sovereigns. Drummond of Hawthornden was appointed to welcome the King, which he did in the most extravagantly complimentary manner.

All sorts of extraordinary people welcomed Charles, the nymph Edina, the nymph Caledonia, Mercury, Apollo, Endymion and the Moon being among the number, while his ancestor Fergus I. met him at the Tolbooth, and 'in a grave speech gave many paternal and wholesome advices to his royal successor.' The same old chronicler tells us that Mount Parnassus was represented 'with a great variety of vegetables, rocks, and other decorations peculiar to mountains,' and inhabited by gods and goddesses. This extravagant entertainment cost over £40,000. Charles I. had been crowned King of England, but his coronation as King of Scotland had not yet taken place. Accordingly he was crowned at Holyrood on 18th June with great magnificence. After he went south, however, Charles counteracted the favourable impression he had made, and drove his loyal subjects to rebellion by his want of tact. Like his father, he was anxious that the Church of Scotland should approximate more closely to the Church of England, but while James was content to 'ca' canny,' Charles introduced reforms with startling rapidity. As this annoyed the common people, Charles, if he had been wise, would have made a point of conciliating the nobles, instead of which he ordered them to restore Church lands to the Church. This was more than they could endure, so nobles and common people alike were opposed to the King's policy. On Sunday 23rd July the new service-book was read in St. Giles's for the first and last time, instead of Knox's prayer-book which the people knew. Row describes the book as a ' Popish—English—Scottish—Mass Service Book,' thereby giving the different reasons, religious and national, for the general opposition to it. The irate Jenny Geddes and her famed stool are too well known to need more than a passing reference, also her forcible, if somewhat inelegant, method of expression. Thereupon a violent riot ensued, and the Bishop was with difficulty rescued by the servants of Lord Wemyss. Dean Hannay, the special object of her indignation, also made good his escape. A somewhat similar scene took place in Greyfriars. Further comment is needless when we remember that for many years the memorable day was known as 'Stoney Sunday.' Jenny Geddes lived for some time after her sudden leap into notoriety. We hear of her after the Restoration keeping a cabbage-stall near the Tron; but she does not seem to have lived to see the policy carried out which she opposed in so vigorous and unusual a manner. Her stool may still be seen in the Antiquarian Museum.

Shortly after, the people petitioned the Privy Council in a 'Supplication,' to which Charles replied by a Proclamation stating that the service-book would be maintained. When the Privy Council were ready to make the Proclamation at the Cross of Edinburgh they found that their opponents had erected a scaffolding and were prepared to give as much trouble as possible. Gordon tells that Montrose, who was one of the malcontents, was resting on the scaffold when the Earl of Rothes said to him, 'James, you will not be at rest till you be lifted up there above the rest in three fathom of rope.' How true this prophecy was to prove neither of them could then know, still less that Montrose would die for the cause he was then opposing. The next development was the 'National Covenant,' which Johnston of Warriston (who drew it up) with great skill based on the 'Negative Confession.' This was drawn up in 1581 at a time when the Catholic League in France, the Inquisition in Spain, the intrigues of Queen Mary in England, and the power of the Roman Catholics in the north of Scotland seemed to menace the very existence of Protestantism. This document was signed by the nobles in Greyfriars Church, and by the common people outside in the Churchyard. It is said some of the people were so eager to show their earnestness that they *literally* signed it with their blood in place of ink. The document was four feet long, but there was not nearly sufficient room for all who wished to sign, so

Greyfriars Churchyard

when both sides were covered people signed their initials round the margin. Later the Covenant was again signed in a house which may still be seen in 'Covenant Close.'

In this desperate state of affairs Charles tried the expedient of a visit to Edinburgh, but it had little or no effect. One day, when he was playing the royal and ancient game of golf on Leith Links, he got a letter telling the appalling news of the Irish insurrection. As soon as he could, he dissolved the Scottish Parliament and hurried south, never to revisit his Scottish capital again. Throughout the course of the civil war we hear little of Edinburgh. The estates passed some drastic measures denouncing Episcopacy, condemning the bishops, and ordering every one under pain of excommunication to subscribe the Covenant. But the actual battles were fought elsewhere. The Castle indeed held out for King Charles, but had neither food nor ammunition, so speedily surrendered to Leslie. With the defeat of Montrose at Philiphaugh in 1645 the struggle entered on a new phase. All the prisoners without exception—men and women—were massacred in cold blood. This and the succeeding executions gave such joy to the extreme party that the Rev. David Dickson—an ex-moderator—only expressed the general sentiments of his party when he used the words 'the work gangs bonnily on.'

67

In 1648 Cromwell paid his first visit to Edinburgh. He stayed at Moray House and interviewed Argyle, Lothian, and some of the other Covenanting lords. Guthrie tells us that he discussed the impending execution of Charles with them, but this is unauthenticated.

In 1649 the execution of Charles came on his Scottish subjects like a thunderbolt. Rebellious they had undoubtedly been, they had striven to restrain the royal power, but regicide was another matter. They immediately proclaimed the Prince of Wales at the Cross as Charles II., but soon more cautious counsels prevailed, and they only offered him their support on condition he would sign the Covenant. Charles would rather have their support on these terms than not at all, but naturally enough he was unwilling to sign the Covenant unless as a last resource.

Accordingly Montrose made an unsuccessful attempt to win Scotland for the King. He was defeated in Ross-shire, and betrayed by Macleod of Assynt—who had once been his follower—for four hundred bolls of meal. The circumstances in which Montrose was brought to Edinburgh are well known. In Balfour's *Notes of Parliament* we read : ' Friday 17th May—Act ordaining James Graham to be brought from the Watergate on a cart bareheaded, the hangman in his livery, covered, riding on the horse that draws the cart—the prisoner to be bound to the cart with a rope—to the Tolbooth of Edinburgh, and from thence to be brought to the Parliament House, and there, in the place of delinquents, on his knees, to receive his sentence, viz.—to be hanged on a gibbet at the Cross of Edinburgh, with his book and declaration tied on a rope about his neck, and there to hang for the space of three hours until he be dead, and thereafter to be cut down by the hangman, his head, hands, and legs to be cut off and distributed as follows ;—viz. his head to be affixed on an iron pin, and set on the pinnacle of the west gavel of the new prison of Edinburgh ; one hand to be set on the port of Perth, the other on the port of Stirling; one leg and foot on the port of Aberdeen, the other on the port of Glasgow. If at his death penitent, and relaxed from excommunication, then the trunk of his body to be interred by pioneers in the Greyfriars; otherwise to be interred in the Boroughmuir by the hangman's men under the gallows.' This sentence was literally carried out. The author of the *Wigton Papers* tells us 'the reason of his being tied to the cart was in hope that the people would have stoned him, and that he might not be able by his hands to save his face.' But the majesty of his demeanour was such that even the women whose husbands and sons had fallen fighting against Montrose could only weep and pray for him, entirely forgetting their original purpose of stoning him. This awe which the common people felt did not apparently extend to the Countess of Haddington—Argyle's niece—or to Argyle himself. Together with Lord and Lady Lorn, and Johnston of Warriston, they were sitting in the balcony of Moray House, interested spectators of this pageant. The cart was stopped for a moment that Argyle might see his great enemy, but when Montrose calmly turned and looked at him Argyle was unable to meet his eye, whereupon an Englishman who was present exclaimed that it was no wonder, because for seven years Argyle had never dared to look Montrose in the face. All through the trial which followed Montrose showed himself worthy of the eulogium pronounced upon him by Cardinal de Retz: 'Montrose, a Scottish nobleman, head of the house of Graham, the only man in the world that has ever realised to me the ideas of certain heroes—whom we now discover nowhere but in the lives of Plutarch—has sustained in his own country the cause of the King his master with a greatness of soul that has not found its equal in our age.' When his sentence was read he only remarked 'that he was much indebted to the Parliament

Moray House in the Canongate

for the great honour they had decreed him, and that he was prouder to have his head placed upon the top of the prison than if they had decreed a golden statue to be erected to him in the market place, or that his picture should be hung in the King's bed chamber.' He thanked them for their care to preserve the remembrance of his loyalty by transmitting such monuments to the different parts of the kingdom ; and only wished that he had flesh enough to have sent a piece to every city in Christendom as a token of his unshaken love and fidelity to his King and country. He was visited in prison by Johnston of Warriston, who was much horrified to find Montrose engaged in arranging his hair, which he wore in long curls according to the cavalier fashion. Warriston told him he thought such an occupation most unbecoming when he ought to be thinking of serious matters, where-upon Montrose tranquilly replied, 'I will arrange my head as I please to-day, while it is still my own ; to-morrow it will be yours, and you may deal with it as you list.' That Montrose did not neglect serious thought at such a solemn time is amply proved—if proof be needed—by the well-known lines which he wrote on the windows of his prison with the point of a diamond :

> ' Let them bestow on every airth a limb,
> Then open all my veins, that I may swim
> To Thee, my Maker, in that crimson lake ;
> Then place my parboil'd head upon a stake ;
> Scatter my ashes, strew them in the air.
> Lord ! since Thou knowest where all these atoms are,
> I'm hopeful Thou 'lt recover once my dust,
> And confident Thou 'lt raise me with the just.'

Montrose was executed in May 1650, and met death with the same calm courage with which he had regarded the prospect. The sentence was carried out in every detail, but after the Restoration his ' dust ' was ' recovered ' and now rests in St. Giles', where there is a beautiful monument erected to him a few years ago by the clan Graham.

The Water Gate

The executions went on
with great vigour, so that
as Nicoll tells us, 'thair
wes daylie hanging, skurg-
ing, nailling of luggis,[1]
and binding of pepill to
the Trone, and booring
of tongues.'

In these cheerful cir-
cumstances the King's ap-
pearance must have been a
welcome change. Charles
showed he was the grand-
son of Henry IV. by con-
sidering that 'Scotland
was worth a Covenant.'
Accordingly he agreed to
the terms of the Cove-
nanters and came to Scotland in the summer of 1650.
Like Montrose, Charles entered Edinburgh by the Water
Gate, but was received with every appearance of loyalty.
After being greeted at the Castle by a royal salute, Charles
proceeded to Parliament House, where the magistrates had
prepared a banquet. One wonders if Charles thought of
his faithful follower who, three months before, had been
condemned to death in that very hall for overmuch
fidelity to his King,—but gratitude was not a prominent
feature of Charles's character. In spite of the welcome
afforded him, Charles did not care to stay in Edinburgh
itself, preferring 'ane ludging belonging to the Lord
Balmerinoch,' in the Kirkgate, Leith. Meanwhile Cromwell marched north, spreading terror far and near.
The memory of his Irish campaign, and especially of the
siege of Drogheda, was too vivid not to nerve the country
to opposition, and to this political opposition there were
added religious motives. The Scottish Presbyterians

[1] Ears.

were almost as far removed from the English sectaries on
the one hand as they were from Rome on the other, and
they regarded Cromwell and his Independents with the
utmost horror.

After the battle of Dunbar, Cromwell again visited
Edinburgh.   Words fail to express the feelings with
which the citizens regarded him.   True, the sternest
order prevailed.   Cromwell severely punished any soldiers
who plundered the citizens, or in any way misconducted
themselves.   But what the Covenanters could not endure
was the desecration of the churches.   The ministers
were driven away and their places filled either by
Independent preachers or—more frequently—by the
soldiers themselves.   We read of Cromwell holding forth
in St. Giles' Churchyard ; it is a matter for thankfulness
that he did not aspire to the church itself, or at least
that if he did, no record thereof remains.   This performance naturally scandalised the citizens of Edinburgh,
who—Pinkerton tells us—were aghast ' that men war not
aschamed to tak upon thame the functions of the
ministrie without a lauchfull calling.'   Part of Holyrood
was accidentally burnt at this time, and the soldiers
quartered there were removed to some of the churches,
so that—as Nicoll tells—' the College Kirk, the Grey-
freir Kirk, and that Kirk callit the Lady Yesteris Kirk,
the High Schule and a great pairt of the College of
Edinburgh wer wasted, their pulpites, daskis, loftis,[1]
saittes, and all their decormentis, wer all dung doun to
the ground by these Inglische sodgeris, and brint to
asses.'   Cromwell soon reduced the Castle.   This siege
is chiefly memorable because of the number of old buildings destroyed in the course of it, among others the
Weigh-house.   Cromwell did not stand alone in his
eloquence.   Shortly after this Lambert asked for ' the
East Kirk of Edinburgh, being the special Kirk, and
best in the town for his exercise at sermon.'   It was

[1] Galleries.

73

impossible to refuse this request, which was virtually a command, so 'weill giftit' soldiers occupied the pulpit. Another trial was the number of English immigrants into Leith—which made Edinburgh tremble for its hard-won superiority. In spite of all these troubles—or perhaps because of them (to conciliate the chief cause) —the Edinburgh Town Council decided to place a statue of Cromwell in Parliament Square. No sooner, however, had the block of stone arrived at Leith than the news of Cromwell's death arrived also. This block of stone, after some curious vicissitudes, was finally broken up, while the magistrates diplomatically changed their intention, and the equestrian statue of Charles II. was erected, which may still be seen in Parliament Square.

On the 11th May 1660 the town clerk went to Breda to carry the greetings of the Edinburgh magistrates to the King, and as a substantial expression of loyalty 'a poor myte of £1000 which the King did graciously accept as though it had been a greater business.' Amid the rejoicings of the citizens Charles II. was pro-claimed in the ancient Stewart capital. The first Parliament revived the ancient custom of riding in procession from Holyrood to the Tolbooth. One of the first acts of the Parliament was to collect and decently inter Montrose's remains. The coffin was taken to Holyrood and remained there till the following May, when it was taken to St. Giles and there buried in the south-east aisle. The condemnation and execution of Argyle soon followed. He had undoubtedly been rebellious against King Charles, but others had also. It is not easy to know why he was excepted from the indemnity. His cowardice in the Civil War had been lamentable, indeed he fled before the very name of Montrose. But when the end came he conducted him-self with a calmness and courage which amazed all who saw him, so great was the contrast with his former behaviour. Argyle, the Rev. James Guthrie, Captain

74

William Govan, and Johnston of Warriston form the
list of those who suffered in Scotland for past rebellion.
Warriston had fled to France, but was seized and tried.
At the time of Montrose's trial it was Warriston who
heaped insults on the prisoner, but when his turn to
suffer came he made a lamentable exhibition.

The next few years are a melancholy record of torture
and executions on the one hand, and of open and secret
rebellion on the other. It was in the lower hall of the
Parliament House that the examination of suspects took
place. In 1679 was fought the battle of Bothwell
Bridge. In one way the Council showed greater leniency
than formerly, for there were fewer executions. But the
great difficulty was how to dispose of the prisoners, as
there was not sufficient room in the Tolbooth. Accordingly they were imprisoned in the only available place,
viz. Greyfriars Churchyard. Among the various executions of the day we must note that of Major Weir in
1678, who was accused of being not a Covenanter but
a wizard. Readers of *Redgauntlet* know the name as
that borne by Sir Robert Redgauntlet's 'Jackanape.'
Major Weir himself was burned and his sister Grizel
was hanged, after having confessed many strange things,
among others that she and her brother were transported
about in a fiery chariot which was invisible to every
one else.

It is a relief to turn from these gruesome tales to the
visit of the Duke of York. He was sent to Scotland
that he might be out of the way of the troubles of the
Popish Plot and the Exclusion Bill. James's deliberate
policy was to ingratiate himself with the Scots so that
he might be able to trust Scotland in case of difficulties
in England. His ablest ally was his wife, Mary Beatrix.
She was both beautiful and charming, and her winning
manners only expressed her real goodness. She seems
to have overcome the opposition of the Scottish ladies
by a method not unknown in our own day—by inviting

75

them to tea. Tea was then an unknown luxury in
Scotland, and that, coupled with the Duchess's kindness
and charm of manner, seems to have had a considerable
effect. We read also of plays and masked balls which
enlivened the old palace, and in which 'the Lady Anne'
took a prominent part. Tennis and golf were also
favourite occupations. James, like his father, was very
fond of golf, and often played on Leith Links.

There were, however, troubles of various sorts, in spite
of the gaiety of the Court. There was the riot about
burning the Pope in effigy on Christmas Day. The
students were chiefly concerned in this riot, and were
therefore ordered to remove fifteen miles out of the city—
even in those days it seems 'students were students.'
Then there was continual trouble, not so much with the
moderate Covenanters, most of whom had accepted the
Indulgence and were now living as peaceable subjects,
but the more fanatical members of the party, now known
as Cameronians, would accept no compromise. In 1680,
by the 'Sanquhar Declaration,' they threw off their
allegiance to 'Charles Stewart' because of 'his perjury
and breach of Covenant to God and His Kirk.' Cargill
went a step further, and at a conventicle held at Torwood
he excommunicated the King, the Duke of York, Monmouth, Lauderdale, Rothes, Dalziel, and the Lord
Advocate. The Royalists might wax merry over this
performance, but it was a real source of danger to the
government, and no mercy was shown to Cargill when
he was taken prisoner. Argyle was imprisoned in the
Castle at this time, but contrived to escape in the disguise of a page through the cleverness of his stepdaughter, Lady Sophia Lindsay. As they were going
out, a sentinel seized Argyle's arm, and the supposed
page in a panic dropped the lady's train. She, however,
with extraordinary presence of mind turned and struck
his face with it—thereby smearing him with snow and
mud, which made an effective disguise—as she exclaimed,

'Thou careless loon.' This escape, however, only deferred his fate for four years.

In 1682 the Duke of York returned to England, and it is related as an ominous circumstance that 'Mons Meg' burst as it fired a salute in his honour. Three years later Charles II. died, and the Duke of York succeeded to the throne as James II. of England and VII. of Scotland. Shortly after James's accession Argyle invaded the country on behalf of Monmouth, but was unsuccessful, was soon taken prisoner and brought to Edinburgh. Argyle had—as Lord Lorn—watched Montrose being brought into Edinburgh, but Fountain-hall tells us 'our great men, not knowing their own destinies, thought it no fit copy to imitate, so that . . . he was met at the Watergate by Captain Graham's Company and the hangman, who tied his hands behind his back; and so the hangman going before him, he came up on his feet to the Castle, but it was casten to be so late that he was little seen.' Argyle met his fate with great calmness, saying he felt sure some one else would deliver Scotland. One of James's most typical actions was to order the chapel at Holyrood to be fitted up for the use of the Knights of the Thistle. The chapel at Holyrood had been used as their parish church by the inhabitants of the Canongate, but they were recommended to go to Lady Yester's Church. The present Canongate Church was built shortly after-wards.

James made a fatal mistake in trying to win over Scotland to Roman Catholicism. This policy could have but one result, and the Presbyterians, 'Moderates' and Cameronians alike, rose as one man to welcome the government of William of Orange. The Edinburgh mob fell on Holyrood Chapel, working irrevocable harm. Riots were inevitable, both sides fiercely maintaining their principles by force of arms. The Convention met in Edinburgh under the guidance of the Duke of

Hamilton. Many of the Royalist nobles declined to attend, as it was not summoned by King James. But Claverhouse—now Viscount Dundee—attended and did his best to win the Convention back to loyalty to King James. The Convention went further than the corresponding body in England, which declared that James had 'deserted' his kingdom, while the Scots said he had 'forfeited' it.

Finding he could make no impression on the Convention, and being moreover in hourly danger of assassination, Dundee left Edinburgh. The Duke of Gordon was at this time holding the Castle for King James, and Dundee interviewed him and begged him to hold out for six weeks. Dundee himself would raise the Highlands and bring him help at the end of that time. On being asked by the Duke where he meant to go, Dundee replied, 'Wherever the shade of Montrose may direct me.' Dundee did raise the Highlands and conquered the royal troops, but only to be killed at Killiecrankie in the moment of victory. Edinburgh Castle surrendered on 13th June 1689.

The enthusiasm with which William had first been received passed off. Even those who had no love for the Highlanders could not but feel distrust of the man who sanctioned the Glencoe massacre. But what touched the mass of the people far more was William's deliberate treachery in the Darien scheme. This nearly ruined the country, and the state of feeling engendered thereby was so bitter that William himself saw there were only two alternatives, either complete separation between England and Scotland or a far closer union than that which already existed. The mob of Edinburgh at this time behaved with great violence. Twice they broke into the Tolbooth and freed the prisoners, and they showed their indignation at the reprieve of some English sailors by attacking the Chancellor's carriage, breaking the windows, and dragging that dignitary himself out

78

on to the street. He was rescued with difficulty, and the mob was only pacified by the execution of the sailors. As regarded the question of a union with England there were three parties: (1) the government party, who were in favour of it; (2) the patriotic party, led by Lord Belhaven and Fletcher of Saltoun, who thought the union would not be for the prosperity of Scotland, but who, if they could have been convinced of this, would have supported it; and (3) the Jacobites and the Cameronians, who would not have it at any price. Of these Lockhart of Carnwath was the most zealous, and it must be confessed the most unscrupulous. Nevertheless his *Memoirs* are most amusing, and shed many interesting sidelights on the period. All through the War of the Spanish Succession the Scots kept up a lively trade with France, although England had concluded the Methuen Treaty with Portugal. The Scots would have been glad to have a commercial union with England, but England insisted on a legislative union or none at all. The special danger from the English point of view was, that at the Queen's death the Jacobites might persuade the Scots to return to their ancient allegiance. The Act of Security on the one hand and the Alien Act on the other produced relations which were distinctly strained, but the tact of Lord Somers overcame all difficulties, and the two countries became one as far as legislature, government, and trade were concerned. It is said that the Commissioners met in a summer-house in the grounds of Moray House, meaning to sign the treaty there, but the violence of the mob compelled them to withdraw to a house in the High Street near the Tron. The Scots kept their system of law and their Church—'The Church of Scotland as by law established' being Presbyterian. Not only so, but they insisted that the sovereign on his accession should take an oath to maintain the Church before he transacted other business, and this holds good even at the present day. After the

Union the process which was begun in 1603 was completed, and Edinburgh speedily declined in importance, though not in prosperity. We find that the Jacobite Rising of the '15 hardly came near Edinburgh at all.

The next important event is the Porteous Riot in 1736. Readers of *The Heart of Midlothian* are well versed in the story of Captain Porteous, but it may not be amiss to indicate the main incidents. Two smugglers, Wilson and Robertson, were tried and condemned. They made an ineffectual attempt to escape, but Robertson eventually succeeded in doing so. The Sunday before the day of their execution the two prisoners were taken to service at St. Giles', and Wilson contrived to engage the guards and let Robertson escape. The people admired this generous conduct, and made a disturbance at the execution of Wilson, whereupon Captain Porteous ordered the soldiers to fire on the mob. Several people were killed and wounded, and Porteous was accordingly tried for murder and condemned to death. George II. was abroad at the time, but his wife Caroline of Anspach was Regent in his absence, and she reprieved Porteous. The people of Edinburgh were furious, and they accordingly broke into the Tolbooth and seized Porteous. The most extraordinary feature of the whole proceeding was the calmness and deliberation with which the rioters acted. There was no apparent excitement, all was done quietly and gravely. There was no rope to be had, so they took one which was lying in a shop—leaving a guinea in its place. They intended to hang Porteous on a gallows, but came to the conclusion it would take too long, so they used a dyer's pole instead. After the execution the mob dispersed as suddenly as it had assembled. The best legal skill in Scotland was helpless in finding a clue to the instigators of the riot. Duncan Forbes—who was more prominent ten years later—was one of those who made unavailing attempts to track the culprits. Queen Caro-

line's rage was great. The Lord Provost was imprisoned,
and a bill was introduced into Parliament forbidding
him to hold any public office. This bill also threatened
to destroy the Nether Bow Port. The Duke of Argyle
and other Scottish nobles contrived to get these and
other penalties commuted for a fine. After this the
history of Edinburgh is uneventful for nine years.

But in 1745 its ancient splendours were revived.
Prince Charlie landed at Moidart. The Provost, Archibald
Stewart, was a Jacobite, though he did not dare to
proclaim the fact. However he did his best to dissuade
the citizens from fortifying the town, thereby rendering
valuable service to the Prince. The Jacobites realised
the necessity of keeping the Whigs in ignorance of their
real strength. They accordingly sent James Mohr
Macgregor (Rob Roy's son) to Edinburgh with instructions to minimise the strength of the Highlanders as
much as possible. He also circulated royal proclamations
and helped the Jacobite cause considerably. The Castle
was under the command of General Preston, who was,
however, superseded by General Guest, as it was thought
that Preston, being a Scot, might make terms with the
Jacobites. As a matter of fact, when Guest wished to
surrender, Preston insisted on holding out. When the
news came that the Prince was at Kirkliston it was
decided to send two dragoon regiments and the City
Guard to meet him. Dr. Carlyle of Inveresk gives a
most ludicrous account of how ex-Provost Drummond
rode at the head of the City Guard down the West
Bow, but when he reached the foot he found most of
his troop had mysteriously disappeared. The dragoons
behaved no better, in fact they strewed the roads with
pistols, carbines, and skull caps as they fled to Dunbar.
The city was still debating the question of surrender
when Lochiel's men solved the difficulty. The Nether Bow
Port was closely guarded, but it was opened to let out
a coach going to its stables in the Canongate, and in

that one moment the Highlanders sprang inside the
gate. So quietly was the surrender of the city accom-
plished that it has been said the citizens on waking
next morning 'found the government of the city
transferred from the magistrates in the name of King
George to the Highlanders in the name of King James.'
King James VIII. and III. was proclaimed at the Market
Cross and the Prince took the title of Prince-Regent.
He took up his quarters at Holyrood, whilst his army
encamped near Duddingston. An extraordinary out-
burst of loyalty for the exiled Stewarts ensued. Since
1682 no member of the royal family had set foot in
Edinburgh. The faults of the Stewarts were forgotten,
the people remembered only that they were 'kindly
Scots,' not foreigners like the Hanoverian line. Prince
Charlie himself won all hearts by his handsome face,
his charm of manner, and his perfect tact. Old family
heirlooms were sold to provide money for the campaign,
and fair ladies persuaded their husbands, brothers, and
lovers to fight for the Prince. Holyrood once more
was the scene of gaiety and joy. While the Queen
Mary rooms will be for ever associated with their
unhappy occupant, the Picture Gallery always brings
thoughts of her equally unfortunate descendant, especially of the ball given the night before Prestonpans.
A spectator may almost imagine that he sees Flora and
Fergus MacIvor, Rose Bradwardine and Waverley, but
the central figure dominating all is that of this gallant
and unfortunate Prince. After Prestonpans the Prince
returned to Holyrood. The Camerons paraded the
streets to the tune of 'The King shall enjoy his own
again,' and the greatest enthusiasm prevailed. As the
Highlanders were entering the city a gun went off
accidentally and struck Miss Nairn, a Jacobite lady.
'Thank God,' she exclaimed, 'that this accident has
happened to me. . . . Had it befallen a Whig they would
have said it was done on purpose.' Readers of *Waverley*

recognise Flora MacIvor in this enthusiastic Jacobite.
Most of the ministers fled from the city after Prestonpans, but it was at this time that the Rev. Neil M'Vicar,
minister of St. Cuthbert's, distinguished himself by
praying for 'King George,' and added, 'As for this
young man who has come among us seeking an earthly
crown, we beseech Thee that he may obtain what is far
better, a heavenly one.' The Prince must have possessed
the saving grace of humour, for when this was reported
he was greatly delighted.

On one occasion the Prince was almost taken prisoner
by the English soldiers in the Castle. He was at that
time at the house of Provost Stewart at the West Bow
and only escaped by a trap door. As he failed to take
the Castle he decided to march into England. The
results of that march and the retreat from Derby belong
to general history, and do not concern us here. When
the Highlanders came north, Hawley set up gallows in
the Grassmarket, declaring he would hang his prisoners
thereon. His only prisoner, Major Donald Macdonald
of Teindreich, was lodged in the Castle and finally sent
to Carlisle, where he suffered along with the other
Jacobites. Scott is said to have modelled Fergus Mac-
Ivor to a considerable extent on this gallant soldier,
who 'died with his last breath imploring a blessing on
Prince Charles.' It was his daughter who declined to
dance with the Duke of Cumberland when, struck by
her great beauty, he asked her at a ball at Bath. 'No,
sir,' replied this intrepid young person, 'I will never
dance with the murderer of my father.' A strange
experience for a royal duke, but perhaps not unsalutary
for his Grace of Cumberland !

Ere long Edinburgh had a visit from Cumberland
himself on his way north to Culloden. He insisted on
having the rooms which the Prince had had, and to show
his dislike of the ancient Scottish monarchs, from whom,
by the way, he derived any right he had to be there, he

83

encouraged his soldiers to cut up and deface a great
many of the portraits in the Gallery. Edinburgh was
again honoured by a visit from Cumberland—after
Culloden. His barbarity after the battle fortunately
does not come within our province. It was during this
visit that the standards taken at Culloden were burned
at the Cross by chimney-sweeps, while the Prince's own
standard was burned by the common hangman. Not
even the warmest admirers of the Georges could call the
Duke of Cumberland a generous foe. It was at this
time that severe penalties were exacted from all 'Papists,
Episcopals, Jacobites and disaffected persons.' In the
last-mentioned category nearly all Scotsmen might have
been included. The Lord Advocate, Duncan Forbes of
Culloden, had, more than any one man, contributed to
the triumph of the government, yet his remonstrances
were absolutely disregarded.

It is pleasant to turn from this account of cruelty and
ill-feeling to the next royal visit to Edinburgh, that of
Cumberland's great-nephew George IV. He came to
Edinburgh in 1822 and won all hearts by wearing the
Highland dress. The most enthusiastic Jacobites could
not refuse homage to the man who had erected a
monument in St. Peter's to the exiled Stewarts, especially
as the ancient line had now died out. It was on this
occasion that Scott vowed he would keep for ever the
glass out of which His Majesty had drunk, but unfortunately sat down on it in the course of a few minutes.

In 1830 Holyrood was granted as a residence to the
exiled King of France, Charles X. Old people speak of
the King himself, and still more of his daughter-in-law
the Duchesse d'Angoulême, the daughter of Louis XVI.
and Marie Antoinette. One old lady tells of how, when
she was a child, the Duchess presented her with a box of
French bonbons. When she was asked, 'What was the
Duchess like?' she replied, 'She had the saddest face I
ever saw.'

84

Edinburgh, alas, is no longer a royal residence, though
royal visits have been frequent. The curious mingling
of old and new constitutes the great charm of 'the grey
metropolis,' and this mingling is seen in the contrast
between Edinburgh as it usually is and Edinburgh as it
is for ten days in the year. We may say that it is like
an enchanted princess who is asleep, but, once a year,
awakes to some of her former glory. Every May the
Lord High Commissioner comes to represent the King at
the meetings of the General Assembly of the Church of
Scotland. Holyrood is no longer left to sightseers, the
great galleries are lighted up, beautiful dresses, Highland costumes, and officers' uniforms mingle together,
music and dancing bring back the glories of former days.
Every day a crowd assembles to cheer the King's representative and to watch the procession, made gay with
uniforms and curious costumes, and preceded by outriders.
But the magic awakening passes all too soon, and the city
relapses once more into her sober, respectable self until the
next May.

CHAPTER IV

THE CASTLE

IN considering the different objects of interest in Edinburgh the most important is the Castle. Considering the size and importance of Edinburgh there is singularly little to see, but there is a great deal to think about. Take away the history of Edinburgh and who would care to visit it? With this eventful history the Castle is more closely connected than any other historical monument. True, Holyrood has close associations with Mary Stewart and Prince Charlie, but there is no part of the history of Edinburgh, from St.

Castle Esplanade

86

Margaret onwards, that cannot trace some connection with the Castle.

Leaving the Castlehill we find ourselves on the Castle Esplanade, where soldiers may often be seen drilling. The moat is now drained, but what is left of it along with the drawbridge makes it possible—with the aid of a little imagination—to realise what it must have looked like in the olden days. As soon as he enters the portcullis the visitor to the Castle is usually beset with guides offering to conduct him round the various places of interest. For those who like a ' personally conducted ' visit it may be as well to state that there is an official tariff which can be seen at the gate.

After having left the portcullis behind, the visitor, still ascending, gains the Argyle Battery, where, if the day be clear, he is sorely tempted to remain and feast his eyes on the view. Wisdom, however, suggests that the King's Bastion is a better view-point, and that it is well not to linger too long on the lower level. Those who are ' fat or scant o' breath ' will do well to go up by the gradual incline, but those who are younger or stronger will find the steps leading to the Argyle Tower the better way. Half-way up the steps we come to the Argyle Tower itself. It was here than many prisoners were kept, Carstares among others. But the most important prisoners were those who gave their name to the Tower, the Marquis of Argyle—better known to some as ' Gillespie Grumach,' executed in 1661—and his son the Earl of Argyle, executed in 1685. There is little to see beyond the bare walls and the small window, but the security of the prison makes us wonder at the adroitness of Lady Sophia Lindsay in contriving the escape of her stepfather. A table with photographs and tartan boxes with views of Edinburgh forms a curious contrast to the memories of the Tower. Mounting the flight of stairs again we soon reach the King's Bastion, and look down from our superior height on the Argyle Battery. And

The Castle and National Gallery

not only on it, for *if* the day is clear a magnificent panorama is spread out before our eyes. Immediately below lie Princes Street Gardens, a curious oasis in the busy life of the town, though their peacefulness is rudely broken by the shriek of a North British engine as it rushes through. On rather a higher level Princes Street itself is seen,—higher than the gardens, but far below the Castle. The people and vehicles alike look like toys, and even the great hotels are not unlike doll's houses. A little to the right the Scott monument and the Calton Hill rise up, while the School of Art and the National Gallery at the foot of the Mound add to the incongruous contrast—incongruous from an architectural point of view—but are infinitely picturesque. From Princes Street the new town stretches northward to the Firth of Forth. From where the Firth meets the sea on the east to the narrow part above Queensferry on the

west a plain of waters meets the eye, having the Bass
Rock as a landmark to the east and the Forth Bridge to
the west. The latter can only be seen in part, but is
quite distinct. Beyond the Firth the Fife Lomonds
may almost always be seen, unless indeed Edinburgh is
at the moment indulging in an 'easterly haar,' by no
means an uncommon occurrence. The Ochils, too, are
often visible, especially if there is a touch of frost or a
little snow lying on the distant hills. But a very clear
day is required to see Ben Ledi, though it is quite possible to do so. It has often been stated that Lochnagar
can also be seen. It may be so. It would be interesting
to have so close a connection between Byron's 'dark
Lochnagar' and Scott's 'own romantic town'—another
link between these two great Scotsmen—for in Scotland
Byron, the son of Catherine Gordon of Gight, is always
considered a fellow-countryman.

Leaving the view, let us now turn our attention to 'the
great iron murderer Muckle Meg,' as this famous cannon
was emphatically described in 1650 when delivered up to
Monk. It is stated on the cannon itself that it was
forged at Mons in Flanders, but it has been more
recently proved that it was handed over to James II. in
1455 by the M'Lellans, when he was preparing to attack
the Douglases at Threave Castle. It was Mons Meg
which carried away the hand of Margaret de Douglas,
better known as the Fair Maid of Galloway. It was said
this was the judgment of heaven on the hand which had
been given in marriage to two brothers. The title (Mons
Meg) is explained in this way. The King rewarded the
smith, Brawny Kim, by bestowing on him the lands of
Mollance, and as his wife's name was Meg the cannon was
called in her honour 'Mollance Meg,' which afterwards
got contracted into 'Mons.' So good an authority as
Scott considered this origin of Mons Meg proved beyond
dispute. The mishap of 1682 has already been related
in an earlier chapter. After this 'Meg' remained very

quiet, but in 1745 was carried to the Tower along with
other trophies of the Jacobite rising. Owing to the
representations of Scott she was again restored to Edinburgh in 1829, when she was received with all possible
honour and was taken in a stately procession from Leith,
and attended by a military guard of honour. There she
still stands, an interesting relic of the past, though not
likely to be of practical use in time of danger. Fortunately defence of this kind is not likely to be needed.
'The gun,' however, fills a most important place in
Edinburgh life,—not Mons Meg, but a somewhat more
modern gun. At one o'clock precisely (Greenwich
time) the gun goes, and 'gun time' is the Edinburgh
expression for absolute accuracy of clocks and watches.

Just behind Mons Meg is St. Margaret's Chapel,
perched up on the rock. The chapel is named after the
the saintly wife of Malcolm Canmore, who was so closely
connected with Edinburgh Castle. Confused legends
speak of nuns in the Castle, but the legend may have been
invented to explain the old name of Castrum Puellarum
or the Castle of Maydens. Certainly, when she lived in
the Castle, Margaret insisted on having proper religious
ordinances, and there is no reason to doubt the tradition
which speaks of this chapel as her place of worship. The
chapel itself is very small, the nave measures only sixteen
feet six inches by ten feet six inches, while the chancel
is small even in proportion to the nave. The style of
architecture is Norman, severely plain without any of
the later florid ornamentations. The round chancel arch
is decorated only with plain moulding, while the chancel
is also quite plain, possibly because it is so small that
anything in addition to the altar would be superfluous.
The stained glass in the chapel is quite modern. The
south window in the chancel represents St. Margaret,
while those in the nave represent Malcolm Canmore and
David I., Margaret's husband and son. The west
window has the cross and monogram I.H.S. and bears

the following inscription: ' Hæc aedicula olim Beatæ
Margaretæ Reginæ Scotiæ quæ obiit M. XCIII. ingratæ
patriæ negligentia lapsa, Victoriæ Reginæ prognatæ
auspiciis restituta A.D. M.DCCCLIII.' The style of architecture is very like that of the earlier parts of Holyrood.
In and near Edinburgh there are quite a number of
churches and chapels which are either entirely or partly
Norman in style, viz. the earliest parts of St. Giles',
Duddingston, Ratho, Kirkliston, and Dalmeny. Another
relic of St. Margaret in the Castle is the Western Sally-
Port, by which after her death her body was conveyed
out of the Castle on its way to Queensferry and Dunfermline. Shortly after Margaret's death a church was
built and dedicated to her. No trace of it remains, its
site being now occupied by barracks. Leaving the
chapel we follow the road, which takes us to the quadrangle, on the north side of which this church was built.
Maitland tells us that it was a very large church, and
from its size he concludes that it was meant to supply
services not only for the garrison but for the inhabitants
of the parish of St. Giles, but this is by no means certain.
When David I. granted his charter to Holyrood he referred to this church, ' the Church of Edinburgh.' We
find it referred to again by Alexander III., while Robert II.
and Robert III. make due provision for St. Margaret's
Chapel at the expense of the customs. Unfortunately
no trace of this interesting old church remains, and it is
impossible even to be sure what it looked like. The
style of architecture would almost certainly be Norman,
and later on we hear of it being roofed with stone flags
and having had carved pinnacles. Beyond that we are
left pretty much to conjecture.

The western side of the quadrangle is all painfully
modern, but on the south and east sides we once more
find ourselves in the midst of ' days long since gone by.'
There is, it must be confessed, little trace in the Queen
Mary rooms of their former splendour. We read of

tapestries and brocades and cloth of gold wrought
with scriptural and legendary story—we read of them,
but do we see them? In the anteroom no furniture
at all except a plain wooden table in the middle of
the floor, and the walls formerly adorned with rich
hangings and tapestries have now no other adornment than the plain wooden panelling and one or two
pictures of Queen Mary herself, notably that of her
leaving Scotland. But over the doorway and all across
the ceiling we see H. & M., the initials of Mary and of
Darnley. The inner room was Queen Mary's bedroom,
where James VI. was born on 19th June 1566. The
room hardly accords with our ideas of royal state, its
length being only eight feet. It is a curious irregular
shape—more interesting than commodious—one would
suppose. It was here that Mary interviewed Darnley
and told him exactly what she thought of his conduct,
and illustrated her remarks by pointing to the unhappy
infant—then only a few hours old—which had made its
appearance in such troublous times. Mary must have
stood many times at the window (from which her infant
son was *not* let down in a basket) and gazed out on the
surrounding country. The view is not so extensive as
that on the north side of the Castle, but it has its own
special charm. Sheer down the rock may be seen the
open space of the Grassmarket with its wealth of historical association which, however, was still to come,
while above it may be seen Heriot's Hospital, which
commemorates 'Jingling Geordie,' so noted in the reign
of James VI. To the south-east lies Craigmillar, also
associated with Queen Mary, and Arthur's Seat guarding the city; while the view on the west is bounded by
Merchiston, where the inventor of logarithms was perhaps even then working out some of his mathematical
problems. There is little more to be seen in this room
than in the other, the old panelling is still there and
some remnants of old furniture. There is, however, the

92

inevitable table with photographs, etc. In 1830 excavation was going on when a curious discovery was made in the palace walls, viz. the body of a child wrapped in cloth of gold embroidered with the letter 'J.' What secret tragedy this conceals will never be known. Below the royal apartments and the banqueting-hall are the vaults where prisoners were confined. Some of the Jacobite prisoners in 1745 were shut up there, and all were not so fortunate as Lady Ogilvy, who escaped disguised as a washerwoman. The vaults, however, are chiefly important as being the place where the French prisoners were detained. We fear their stay in Edinburgh cannot have been altogether enjoyable, for we read of over forty being confined in one vault, a wooden framework being erected on which to hang the hammocks which rendered this economy of space possible. Doubtless, however, these French officers were not without some *divertissement* to lighten their imprisonment. Stevenson in *St. Ives* gives an interesting account of this episode centreing round his hero, the Vicomte Anne de St. Ives, who was one of the prisoners. Another of Stevenson's characters (not a 'hero' this time) was James Mohr, the father of Catriona. Readers of *Rob Roy* remember him as a promising young fellow, and are grieved to find how much he has deteriorated in his old age.

Another interesting feature of the quadrangle is the Crown Room, where the Regalia of Scotland are kept. The treasures in this room consist of the 'Honours of Scotland' (viz. the Crown, the Sceptre, and the Sword of State), the mace of office of the Lord High Treasurer of Scotland, and the golden collar of the Garter, an onyx stone with the order of St. Andrew on one side and the Thistle on the other, and the ruby ring worn by the Kings of Scotland. Let us first trace the history of the 'honours.' The crown is said to date from the days of Bruce, and may be the identical golden circlet which he wore over his helmet at Bannockburn by which Sir

Henry Bohun recognised him at the preliminary duel.
The crown, however, was not 'closed' till the reign of
James v. The tiara worn underneath was originally
purple velvet. The various vicissitudes which the crown
passed through had, however, a somewhat deleterious
effect on its appearance, and the velvet was renewed in
1685, the colour being changed to crimson. We read of
two ancient swords of state, one presented to James iv.
in 1507 by Pope Julius ii., and one presented to James v.
in 1536 by the Pope of that day to enable him to
fight against his 'heretic' uncle Henry viii. It is
doubtful which is the sword now in the Castle, but it
is probably the one of earlier date. The sceptre was
made in the reign of James v. and bears traces of French
workmanship. Charles i. was anxious to have the
regalia sent to London for his coronation, but the
Scots declined to part with their treasures. During
his visit to Scotland in 1633 Charles was crowned at
Holyrood, King of Scotland, England, France, and
Ireland. The regalia appeared again at the coronation
of Charles ii. at Scone in 1651, but it was shortly afterwards that the most adventurous part of its history took
place. When Cromwell marched north, one great object
of the Scots was to conceal the honours of Scotland.
Cromwell had destroyed the English regalia, and would
have doubtless destroyed the Scottish regalia also if he
had had the opportunity. The order of Parliament on
6th June 1651 runs: 'Instrumentis taken be the Erle
Mareschal upon the production of the honouris with his
dessyre represented to the Parliament that the same
might be put in some pairt of securitie; his Majesty and
Parliament ordanes the said Erle Mareschal to cause
transport the saidis honouris to the hous of Dunnottar,
thair to be keepit by him till further ordouris.' Dunnottar was held by Ogilvy of Barras, who was made
Lieutenant-Governor of the Castle by the Earl Marischal. Ogilvy was given soldiers and artillery, including

our old friend Mons Meg. In spite, however, of a
defence it was obvious the Castle could not ho
much longer. In this emergency the Countess-Dow
Marischal and Mrs. Ogilvy evolved a scheme wh
was successfully carried out. Mrs. Granger, wife of t
minister of Kinneff, got permission from the Englis
general to visit Mrs. Ogilvy. She brought out with her
the crown, while her maid carried the sword and sceptre,
concealed in ' hards,' *i.e.* bundles of lint ready for
spinning. So unsuspicious was the English general that
he helped Mrs. Granger to mount, little thinking that
she actually held the precious crown at that moment.
Ogilvy himself was told nothing, so that he might be able
to say truthfully he was ignorant of the matter. The
honours were then buried in Kinneff Church, as is
described by Mr. Granger in the account he gave to the
Countess-Dowager Marischal : 'I, Mr. James Granger,
minister of Kinneff, grant me to have in my custody the
Honours of the Kingdom, viz. the Crown, Sceptre, and
sword. For the Crown and Sceptre I raised the pavement stone just below the pulpit, in the night tyme, and
digged under it ane hole, and put them in there, and
filled up the hole, and layed down the stone just as it
was before, and removed the mould that remained, that
none would have decerned the stone to have been raised
at all; the Sword again at the west end of the church,
amongst some common seits that stand there, I digged
down in the ground betwixt the two foremost of these
seits, and layed it down within the case of it, and
covered it up, as that removing the superfluous mould
it could not be discerned by any body ; and if it shall
please God to call me by death before they be called for,
your Ladyship will find them in that place.' Dunnottar
surrendered three months afterwards, and great was the
rage of the English soldiers when they discovered that
the regalia had been removed. Suspicion might in
time have fallen on the Grangers, but the Dowager-

Countess Marischal adroitly turned the suspicion on her youngest son, the Honourable John Keith, who was abroad at the time. Keith told the same story, although it was at the risk of his life. At the Restoration those who had preserved the honours of Scotland were duly rewarded. Ogilvy was made a baronet, and his lands of Barras were in future to be held by blench tenure instead of ward-holding, 'in that he was instrumental in the preservations of His Highnesses's Crown, Sceptre and Sword, the ancient Honours of the Kingdom of Scotland.' John Keith, whose 'splendid lie' had probably saved the honours, was created Earl of Kintore and Knight-Marischal of Scotland. The Grangers had been severely interrogated and even tortured to make them reveal the hiding-place of the regalia, and their fidelity did not go unrewarded either. 'For as much as the Estates of Parliament doe understand that Christian Fletcher, spouse to Mr. James Granger, minister of Kinneff, wes most active in conveying the royal honours, his Majestie's Crown, Sword and Sceptre out of the Castle of Dunnottar, immediately before it was rendered to the English usurpers, and that be the care of the same wes hid and preserved; Therefore the King's Majestie, with advice of his estates in Parliament, doe appoint two thousand merks Scots to be forthwith paid unto her be his Majestie's thresaurer, out of the readiest of his Majestie's rents, as a testimony of their sense of her service.' After this, until the Union of 1707, the regalia, although appearing on public occasions, cannot be said to have played an important part in history. But at the time of the Union passions ran high, and it was emphatically stated by those opposed to the scheme that the honours of Scotland were to be taken to London as a visible proof that Scotland was no longer an independent country. It is doubtful whether this report was the cause or the effect of some of the bitterest opposition to the Treaty of Union. It was referred to by

Lord Belhaven in his historic speech: 'Hannibal is
come within our gates: Hannibal is come the length of
this table; he is at the foot of this throne; he will
seize upon these Regalia, he will take them as his *spolia
opima*, and whip us out of this house, never to return
again.' All this is to us the most ridiculous and ineffec-
tive bombast, matched only by the conclusion of the
passage, where Lord Belhaven added, 'Good God, what is
this?—an entire surrender! My lord, I find my heart
so full of grief and indignation that I must beg pardon
not to finish the last part of my discourse, that I may
drop a tear as the prelude of so sad a story.' But though
we may feel more moved to mirth than to tears, this
suggestion had a tremendous effect at the time. The
opponents of the Union, in the hope of wrecking the
project, proposed that it should be enacted in the Treaty
of Union that 'the Crown, Sceptre, and Sword of State,
Records of Parliament, etc., continue to be kept as they
are in that part of the United Kingdom now called Scotland, and that they shall remain so in all time coming,
notwithstanding of this Union.' This now forms part of
the Treaty of Union. Although the honours were not
removed to London—in fact this had never even been
contemplated—popular excitement ran so high that they
were deposited in the Crown Room in a large chest, supposed to be the 'blak kist' where James III. kept his
rather numerous jewels. There they remained till 1817.
The Crown Room itself was undisturbed till 1794, when it
was opened up during a search for some missing Parlia-
mentary records. At last in 1817 the Prince-Regent
issued a commission to certain public officers in Scotland
to search the Crown Room to see if the regalia were still
in existence. It is interesting to know that Sir Walter
Scott was one of those who were present when the chest
was opened and the regalia displayed to view. Along
with the crown, the sceptre, and the sword of state
was found also the silver rod or mace with a globe of

G

crystal beryl, which is the mace of office of the Lord High
Treasurer of Scotland. Beryl stones were considered by
the Druids to have special significance, and are spoken of
by Highlanders as 'Clach-bhuai,' or stone of power.
The following is the description of the regalia which
were buried with it in the 'kist' in 1707 : 'The crown
is of pure gold, enriched with many precious stones,
diamonds, pearls, and curious enamellings. It is composed of a fillet which goes round the head, adorned
with twenty-two large precious stones. Above the great
circle there is a small one formed with twenty points,
adorned with the like number of diamonds and sap-
phires alternately, and the points tipped with great
pearls ; the upper circle is elevated with ten crosses
floree, each adorned in the centre with a great diamond
betwixt four great pearls placed in the cross, one and one,
and these crosses floree are interchanged with the high
fleurs de lys, all alternately with the ten great pearls
below which top the points of the second small circle.
From the upper circle proceed four arches, adorned with
enamelled figures, which meet and close at the top surmounted by a *mond* of gold, enamelled blue, semee,
powdered with stars, crossed and enamelled with a large
cross patée, adorned in the extremities with great pearls,
and cantoned with other four in the angles. The tiar or
bonnet was of purple velvet, but in 1685 it got a cap of
crimson velvet, adorned with four plates of gold, on each
of them a great pearl, and the bonnet is trimmed up with
ermine. Upon the lowest circle there are eight small
holes, two and two on the four quarters of the crown,
which were for lacing or tying thereto diamonds or
precious stones. The crown is nine inches in diameter,
twenty-seven inches about, and in height from the under
circle to the top of the cross patée six and a half inches.
  'The sceptre; its stem or stalk, which is of silver
double over-gilt, is two feet long of a hexagon form,
with three buttons or knobs ; betwixt the first button

and the second is the handle of hexagon form, furling in the middle and plain. Betwixt the second button and the third are three sides engraven. From the third button to the capital the three sides under the statues are plain, and on the other three are antique engravings. Upon the top of the stalk is an antique capital of leaves embossed, the abacus whereof arises round the prolonged stem, surrounded with three little statues; between every two statues arises a rullion in the form of a dolphin; above the rullions and statues stands another hexagon button, with oak-leaves under every corner, and down it a crystal globe. The whole sceptre is in length thirty-four inches.

'The sword is in length five feet; the handle and pommel are of silver over-gilt, in length fifteen inches. The pommel is round and somewhat flat on the two sides. The traverse or cross of the sword, which is of silver over-gilt, is in length seventeen and a half inches; its form is like two dolphins with their heads joining and their tails ending in acorns; the shell in hanging down towards the point of the sword, formed like an escalop flourished, or rather like a green oak-leaf. On the blade of the sword are indented with gold these letters—Julius II. P. The scabbard is of crimson velvet, covered with silver wrought in philagram work into branches of the oak-tree leaves and acorns.' There is little to be added to this description except that the stone in the sceptre described as a crystal is really a beryl, and the statues mentioned in the description represent St. Andrew (the patron saint of Scotland), the Virgin Mary, and St. James. Underneath are the letters J. R. v., but the workmanship of the settings of the beryl belong to a more remote period than the reign of James v. The keys of St. Peter are worked into the filigree work of the sword—which is quite natural, considering that the donor of the sword was Pope Julius II. The sword-belt was not among the other treasures, as it remained with

the family of Ogilvy of Barras—as a memento of the
siege of Dunnottar, but was placed with the crown, sword,
etc., in 1893 by the Rev. Samuel Ogilvy Baker, a descendant of Ogilvy of Barras.

Along with the honours of Scotland there are in the
Crown Room the other jewels already referred to, whose
history is almost as eventful. As has been already stated,
these consist of the George, which is set with diamonds,
and the Golden Collar of the Garter, which accompanies
the George—this was given to James VI. by Elizabeth
when he was created a Knight of the Garter. There is
also a ruby ring set round with diamonds which was
worn by the kings of Scotland, and is interesting as having been worn by Charles I. at his coronation. The most
unique ornament, however, is that onyx which bears on
one side an image of St. Andrew surrounded by diamonds
and on the other the Thistle. A concealed spring hides a
beautiful miniature of Anne of Denmark, wife of James VI.
and I. These jewels were the personal property of the
King rather than national possessions like the regalia.
When James fled to France in 1688 he took them with
him. On his death they passed to his son, whom the
Jacobites called James VIII. and III. He in turn left
them to his elder son Prince Charles Edward, and on his
death in 1788 they passed to James's younger son Henry,
better known as Cardinal of York. Cardinal York was
the last of the direct line of Stewarts. He might have
bequeathed his belongings to the house of Savoy, the
descendants of the unfortunate Henrietta Maria, Duchess
of Orleans, the youngest daughter of Charles I. If primo-
geniture was the test they were undoubtedly the lawful
heirs to the throne of Britain, though their religion
excluded them from it. But Henry was wise enough
to recognise the inevitable. He knew that the house
of Guelph had come to stay, and came to the sensible
conclusion that it was better for such valuable jewels to
be in the possession of the sovereign *de facto*, even if he

did not think him the sovereign *de jure*. So the jewels
were bequeathed in 1807 by 'Henry by the Grace of
God to George by the will of man King of Great Britain
France and Ireland.' 'George by the will of man' was
of course George III., and we hear nothing of the jewels
for the next twenty-three years. But on the accession of
William IV. in 1830 they were handed over to Sir Adam
Ferguson, Knight, Deputy-Keeper of the Regalia of Scotland, with instructions to place them in the Crown Room,
where they may still be seen. Accordingly, when the
visitor has mounted the spiral staircase, he finds himself
in an octagon room strongly vaulted. There are only
four things to be seen in the room : the fireplace, the
' black kist,' the jewels themselves, and the table of photographs. The regalia and jewels lie on a table of pure
white marble. They are meant to be 'seen but not
touched,' and are protected from too curious a public by
a glass cover and also by a strong iron grating. Though
they are not to be touched they may be seen to great
advantage. In addition to the photographs, etc., which are
displayed on the table, there is a history of the regalia
by Sir Walter Scott which may be bought for sixpence.

The only other object of interest inside the Castle is the
great hall known as the Banqueting Hall or the Parliament
Hall. It occupies the south side of the quadrangle. It
was originally used for meetings of Parliament and for
ceremonial meetings of King and Nobles. In the reign
of James III. the nobility were thrown into a state of
frenzy by the rumour which was circulated that the King
had invited them to meet him in the Parliament Hall
that he might have a convenient opportunity of assassin-
ating them all. No such gruesome association, however,
hangs round the hall ; it tells of government and war,
and still more of recreation and feasting. Later on it
was converted into a garrison hospital, its beauties hidden
by whitewash. But in our own day it has been completely restored, and is now one of the most interesting

sights of the Castle. It is eighty feet long, thirty feet broad, and forty feet high. Its magnificent open roof gives an impression of even greater height than it really possesses. The walls are adorned with shields and coats of arms, armour of bygone days is to be found, while old banners are also displayed. The stained-glass windows are filled with the devices of most of the noble Scottish families.

This completes our survey of the Castle itself. The Wellhouse Tower, dating from 1450, is interesting historically. In ancient days the Castlehill had some sinister associations. Criminals were frequently executed there, and it was on the Castlehill that Lady Glamis was burnt alive within sight of her husband, who was at that time a prisoner in the Castle. Heretics and witches alike suffered here, although we also hear of witches being 'ducked' in the Nor' Loch. But in the *Diurnal of Occurrents* we find some curious entries: '9th March 1659 thair wes fyve wemen, witches brint on the Castell Hill for witchcraft, all of them confessand thair covenanting with Satan, sum of thaim renunceand thair baptisme, all of thame oft times dancing with the Devill.' In the eighteenth century the Castlehill seems to have had more cheerful associations. We read of it as a public promenade specially frequented by lovers. The road most favoured by them led from what is now the esplanade past the Wellhouse Tower and along the side of the Castlehill to St. Cuthbert's Church. There are many references to this promenade in the ballads of the time. The esplanade is now used for drilling soldiers, the Nor' Loch is drained, witches are no longer tortured and executed on the Castlehill; instead, children play in the Princes Street Gardens without let or hindrance, while, where the Nor' Loch itself flowed, the North British trains rush along, suggesting the utility of the present age as contrasted with the picturesque but somewhat uncertain 'good old days.'

CHAPTER V

HOLYROOD AND CANONGATE

The Girth Cross

WITH the exception of the Castle there is no building in Edinburgh so closely bound up with its history as the Palace and Abbey of Holyrood. Since its foundation by David I. it has always been closely connected, not so much with the history of Edinburgh itself, as with the history of the Scottish kings. Surely, if ghosts haunt any place in Edinburgh or its neighbourhood, they should be found here, and if they did appear they would make a strange medley: David I. himself, the royal Jameses, Mary Stewart, Rizzio, Châtelard, Darnley, Ruthven, Bothwell, Charles I., his son James when Duke of York, ' bonnie Prince Charlie,' George IV., and the French refugees of 1830. A goodly if somewhat incongruous company; but the chief interest of Holyrood will always be its association with Queen Mary and with Prince Charles Edward.

We have said that Holyrood was more closely connected with the personal history of the Scottish kings than with the history of Edinburgh as such. Not only so, it formed no part of old Edinburgh, and was con-

nected solely with the neighbouring burgh of Canongate.
As the burgh of Edinburgh clustered round the Castle
for protection, so did the burgh of Canongate gather
round the Abbey. The sacred character of the building caused it to be spared by some, at least, of the
English invaders, and the burgh doubtless shared this
immunity in times of war, while, in more peaceful times,
it grew rich and prosperous under the shadow of the
Abbey. As is usual in the case of very near neighbours,
the magistrates of Edinburgh and of Canongate were
not always on the best of terms, and when Holyrood
was no longer peopled by monks, the magistrates of
Canongate claimed that they had succeeded to the
rights and privileges of these earlier owners. Traces of
this claim may be seen in the title-deeds of houses and
property held in the burgh, which run in this manner :
'To be holden of the Magistrates of the Canongate as
come in place of the Monastery of Holy Cross.'

Another trace of the original character of Holyrood
was seen in its being used as a Sanctuary,—for crime of
all kinds until the Reformation, and afterwards for
debt only. This privilege was connected both with its
sacred character as a religious house and also with its
being a royal residence. Those who sought refuge in
the Sanctuary could go out without fear of capture
between midnight on Saturday and midnight on Sunday.
Many romances deal with this curious state of things,
but the true stories which are told are stranger than any
fiction : stories of men captured by such obvious artifices
as putting back the hands of the clock, and stories of
men escaping either by superior skill or more often by
superior speed. It is told of one man that he reached
the Sanctuary boundary just at midnight, and threw
himself across it, his feet still remaining outside. He
was, however, judged to have fairly won his freedom for
that time at least. Needless to say, this right of Sanctuary led to people of the most dubious character being

congregated together. Moreover, the available space was distinctly limited, so the ' Abbey Lairds,' as they were called, must often have been rather badly crowded. They were not left entirely to their own devices, though they were free from imprisonment. Their movements were supervised by the Bailie of the Abbey, or the Sanctuary Bailie, as he was sometimes called. It is interesting to note that Jeffrey's father once held the office. The boundary of the Sanctuary crossed the foot of the Canongate and ran up the Watergate and the Horse Wynd, taking in, not only the Palace, but the King's Park also. The Sanctuary rights only came to an end in 1880, when imprisonment for debt came to an end also, and the Sanctuary rights were therefore superfluous.

Outside the Palace may be seen a curious old building known as Queen Mary's Bath. Unauthenticated legend declares she was accustomed to bathe there in *milk*, but the spring of clear water bubbling up suggests a more probable liquid for her ablutions. Some years ago, when alterations were being made on the roof, a beautiful dagger was found, which is supposed to have belonged to one of Rizzio's murderers. This seems probable, as they would naturally leave the Palace that way. The dagger was described as being ' as though it had the King's arms on it done in gold.' It was lent as an ornament during the visit of George IV. and by most regrettable carelessness was lost. The only other noticeable feature before we come to Holyrood itself is the mansion-house of Croft-an-Righ (the King's croft), better known to readers of Scott as ' Croftangry.'

The Palace of Holyroodhouse, to give it its full and honourable designation, is not so much changed as one would expect. True, it is deserted by kings and their representatives for fifty weeks out of fifty-two, but then the interest lies in the historical, not in the modern apartments. True, the once fashionable suburb of Canongate is now degraded to a slum, and breweries surround the

Queen Mary's Bath

ancient Palace of the Scottish kings. But perhaps the
inhabitants of the slum are no more disreputable than
the 'Abbey Lairds,'—in any case, two sides of Holyrood
are left to the free air of Heaven, and the King's Park,
Arthur's Seat, and Salisbury Crags have changed little—
we may suppose—in the last eight hundred years. It
may be well to point out, for the benefit of those who
probably know but have never thought of the meaning
of the word, that Holyrood is etymologically the same as
Santa Croce.

As we enter the Palace we pass a fountain which the
late Prince-Consort ordered to be made on the model
of an old fountain at Linlithgow. We then reach the
great gateway which bears the royal arms. After
passing through the gateway we find ourselves in the

courtyard of Holyrood. The Palace is built round this quadrangle, while the cloistered walk under the pillars is a reminiscence of the purpose of the original building. On the south and east are the more modern parts of the building, which date only from the time of Charles II. It is in these rooms that the Lord High Commissioner and his suite live during the sittings of the Assembly, and it is there that he gives dinners and receptions. These rooms are gained by a door on the right hand of the entrance, but are not open to the public. To reach the historical rooms the visitor turns to the left, and if he is in doubt how to proceed, he will find full directions prominently displayed on the walls.

Immediately facing the visitor as he reaches the top of the stairs is the door which leads to the Picture Gallery. It was here that Prince Charlie gave the famous ball the night before the battle of Prestonpans. As we look at the embrasures of the windows we find ourselves wondering into which recess did the Prince draw Waverley for their private conversation, so real does it all seem to us, as we actually stand on the spot. We fear that even the most zealous supporter of antiquity could not maintain the genuineness of the portraits of the Scottish kings. On the face of it, how could the Flemish artist de Witt, working in A.D. 1685, have an accurate knowledge of the features and general appearance of Fergus I. who—the picture says—lived in 330 A.D. ? Even the early Jameses are, we fear, the result of imagination rather than knowledge. The earlier portraits were all destroyed by Cromwell's soldiers. There was, therefore, nothing to go upon in the portraits of early kings. The portrait of Queen Mary, however, in all probability is very like that unhappy princess. It certainly bears a great resemblance to several authentic portraits which we have of her, especially to that which may be seen at Azay-le-Rideau in Touraine. Scott in *The Abbot* truly says : 'It is in vain to say that the

portraits which exist of this remarkable woman are not
like each other; for amidst their discrepancy each
possesses general features which the eye at once acknow-
ledges as peculiar to the vision which our imagination
has raised while we read her history for the first time,
and which has been impressed upon it by the numerous
prints and pictures which we have seen. Indeed, we
cannot look on the worst of them, however deficient
in point of execution, without saying that it is meant
for Queen Mary.' We are far from suggesting that this
portrait is one of 'the worst of them,' but we do say
that it could represent no one but Queen Mary herself.
The portrait of Charles I. resembles the picture by
Vandyke which we all know so well, while de Witt was
a contemporary of Charles II. and James VII., and therefore drew them from personal knowledge. It has been
suggested that the portraits of the earlier Jameses were
copied from old pictures in the possession of Scottish
noblemen. Leaving the portraits of mythical Ferguses
and Kenneths, as well as of Wallace and Bruce and
the later kings of Scotland, we find at the end of the
gallery some curious old pictures, not hanging on the
walls like the others, but standing on the floor and protected by glass from the gaze of the too curious. These
strange old pictures, which date from the fifteenth
century, are said to have been originally placed in Trinity
College Church, which was founded by Mary of Gueldres.
In 1857 they were brought from Hampton Court, where
they had been placed. They represent James III. and
his son, Prince James, afterwards James IV., while on the
other side is an extraordinary representation of the
Holy Trinity. The other picture shows on one side
Margaret of Denmark, wife of James III., and on the
reverse Sir Edward Boncle, Provost of Trinity College
Church. The stiffness of the old figures is quaint in
the extreme, and the expression on the face of each of
the royal personages is simply ludicrous. We feel that

James iv. could not have looked like that. From the end window of the gallery close to these pictures we look out over the ruined chapel to the King's Park and Arthur's Seat. No amount of historical statements that Holyrood lay outside the walls, and apart from the life of Edinburgh, could bring the fact home to us so convincingly as this view over the open country. Close to the window is the door which leads to the passage communicating with the more modern parts of the Palace. At ordinary times it is shut and locked, but during the receptions of the Lord High Commissioner this door, and the corresponding one at the other end of the gallery, are thrown open, and smartly dressed modern people stream through the passage in search of—refreshment ! For—with bated breath be it spoken—it is in the Picture Gallery itself that refreshments are served. At such times the Queen Mary rooms are kept locked, but the Picture Gallery forms a link between old and new.

Leaving the Picture Gallery we find ourselves once more in the passage, whence on turning to the left we enter the first of Lord Darnley's rooms, viz. the Audience Chamber. This, like most of the rooms in Holyrood, is adorned with wonderful tapestry. One wonders when the ladies of ancient days found time to produce such elaborate work. Surely they must have been as diligent as the ideal Roman matron who sat at home and span. This room has also some interesting historical portraits of the Admirable Crichton, Charles ii. in armour, James vi. and his wife Anne of Denmark, the King of Bohemia and his hapless wife Elizabeth Stewart, whose beauty was such that the name by which she was best known was the 'Queen of Hearts.' But beauty was powerless to preserve her from misfortune, as it had been in the case of her grandmother Mary Stewart. There is also a portrait of her brother Henry, Prince of Wales, who died young, and a charming picture of the children of Charles i. copied from the well-known

picture by Vandyke. There is also a curious old clock
and a wonderful inlaid cabinet, which is equally interesting for the beauty of its workmanship and for its
ingenious secret drawer. A door on the left leads to
another room which, though classed among Darnley's
apartments, was never occupied by him, as it was not
built till the time of Charles II. There are several
portraits here : Charles II., James VI., James VII., Henry VI.,
and several of various members of the house of Hamilton.
Returning to the audience chamber we now proceed
to Lord Darnley's bedroom. The tapestry here is of
the same character as that in the audience chamber.
It is beautifully worked, but the design is not specially
interesting. This room, however, contains some very
interesting portraits, viz. Cardinal Beaton, the Countess
of Lennox (Darnley's mother), John Knox, Queen Mary,
Darnley and his brother, Sir William Hamilton, William
III. and his wife (another Queen Mary), the first Duke
of Hamilton, the Countess of Cassilis and St. Francis
of Assisi, a most extraordinary mixture, but none the
less interesting on that account. In this room may
also be seen a screen which was the property of Charles I.
The door on the left leads to the tiny turret room
which was Darnley's dressing-room. It contains only
four pictures, viz. Lady Mary Fielding, first Duchess
of Hamilton ; Lady Ann Cochran, Duchess of Hamilton ;
St. Margaret ; and St. Mark's, Venice. This cramped
little room is scarcely our idea of royal spaciousness,
but it is no smaller than the corresponding room which
belonged to Queen Mary, and it cannot even be said
that it is small in proportion to the bedroom and
audience chamber. On the left-hand side of the bedroom is a door leading to another turret room. The
tapestry here represents Meleager and Atalanta, and
has an appropriate background of woodland scenery.
But by far the most interesting feature of this room is
that it contains the foot of 'Queen Mary's private stair.'

This was reached by raising the tapestry, but could be kept concealed at will. Only a few steps at the foot are visible, while progress is barred by a strong iron gateway stretching across the stair. We remember in our childish days longing to explore the stair, but such curiosity met with no encouragement from the stern officials of the Palace. But even those who have passed the age of childhood feel that the story of Rizzio would be more vividly realised if they could creep up the secret stair, following the footsteps of Darnley and his fellow-assassins. As that is impossible we retrace our steps through the bedroom and

Scene of Rizzio's Murder

audience chamber, and mount the other staircase which, if we were not devoured with regrets for the secret stair, would have a great charm of its own. The steps are so curiously old-fashioned, even in their shallowness, and so worn with the tramp of many feet, that it is not difficult to conjure up romances about those who trod them in bygone days. At the top of the stair we see rooms which are also carefully barred off; but they are purely modern, and not even curiosity for this forbidden fruit can divert our thoughts from the Queen Mary rooms, in which the real interest of Holyrood centres.

Secret Stairway Holyrood Palace

In the passage at the entrance of the Queen Mary rooms may be seen the brass plate marking the spot where Rizzio died. No longer does the attendant

tell awestruck tourists that the blood of Rizzio can never
be washed out, and illustrate his remarks by pointing
to a red stain more suggestive of paint than of human
blood; but the simple brass plate is no less impressive
than the former legend,—on the contrary the impression
is deepened by the straightforward recital of facts,
leaving nothing which even the most flippant can turn
into ridicule. The first of the Queen Mary rooms is
the audience chamber, exactly above the corresponding
room in Darnley's suite of apartments. The tapestry
here is so frayed and the colours are so worn that it
is hard to decipher the original design, in spite of
the best endeavours of the skilled embroiderers who
at intervals repair the worn and faded tapestry in a
way that to those less skilful with the needle seems
little short of miraculous. The portraits, however, are
of considerable interest. Among them we see the
Regent Moray, the Duke and Duchess of Lauderdale,
and the beautiful Hortense Mancini (niece of Cardinal
Mazarin), whose history was no whit less romantic than
that of her better known sister Maria, who was so
nearly Queen of France. There are some other pictures,
including one of the Battle of the Boyne, but with that
exception they are of no historical interest. The curious
old fireplace with its wide hearth cannot be passed
unnoticed, and there are some embroidered chairs
dating from the days of Charles I. The bed has considerable memories of royal occupants of different sorts
and conditions. It was used by Charles I. when he
visited Scotland in 1633; his great-grandson, Prince
Charlie, slept in it during his stay at Holyrood in 1745,
and the Duke of Cumberland, with his usual lack of
magnanimity, insisted that it should be made ready
for him when he visited Edinburgh the following year
after Culloden. But perhaps the memories which most
haunt this room are the interviews between Queen Mary
and Knox which were held here. Even more interesting

than the audience chamber is Queen Mary's bedroom.
The panelled ceiling and the faded tapestry on the
walls—representing the story of Phaethon—are poor relics
of the luxury which her enemies accused Mary of indulging in. She must have felt this gloomy old palace
with its cramped accommodation a change indeed, after
the gaiety and brightness of sunny France. It is only
after visiting the magnificent salons of Fontainebleau
in the midst of its forest surroundings, and the picturesque châteaux of Touraine, that one can realise
something of what this change must have meant to
her. Her bed may still be seen, but it is frayed and
tattered to such an extent that one can hardly help
wondering how much longer it will hold together.
Under the tapestry may be seen the small door which
conceals the top of the secret staircase. There are only
four portraits in this room, but they are all of considerable interest, viz. Henry viii., his mother Elizabeth of
York, Queen Elizabeth, and Queen Mary. The little
dressing-room opening on the left is no larger than
that of Darnley exactly below. A door on the right,
close to the private stair, leads to Queen Mary's supping-
room. This of course was not the room where Queen
Mary held state banquets—its size prevented that—
but was her little private room where she received
only her intimate friends, her boudoir we might call
it. Standing here, it is easy to realise all the revolting
details of Rizzio's murder: Ruthven, Darnley, Ker of
Faudonside, Queen Mary, and the wretched Italian
himself, all seem to live before us. It must have been in
this room also—or else in the little dressing-room in the
other turret—that Mary tried to call for help during
her imprisonment, but her designs were stopped by
Ruthven's chivalrous threat to 'cut her into collops'
if she raised the people! The visitor doubtless feels
inclined to linger, but there is still much to be seen,
so we retrace our steps through the bedroom and

audience chamber, and down the worn stairs. After,
perhaps, a last glance at Darnley's rooms and the
Picture Gallery, we proceed downstairs and once more
gain the cloisters. As we walk along the north side
we actually pass over the grave of Rizzio. Another
version of the story says he was buried in the royal
vault of the chapel, but afterwards his remains were
interred in the nearest part of the chapel to the Palace;
while yet another tale declares that he lies buried in
the Canongate Churchyard. However that may be,
the name of Rizzio will always be associated with Holyrood, and there is a fitness in the tale which says he
is buried there.

Passing along the cloisters we reach a door which
leads us to the Chapel Royal. All that now remains
is the nave of the original building, and even that is in
a ruinous condition. Even in 1758 its condition was
such as to cause considerable alarm, and steps were
taken to preserve it, but the clumsy efforts of the builder
suggest zeal not according to knowledge. Incredible
as it sounds, he actually covered the roof with flagstones
which weighed down the frail old walls, and the whole
building collapsed ten years later. This attempted restoration really inflicted greater damage than any English
invasion, or even the heavy hand of time. The style
of architecture is partly Norman and partly Gothic.
Probably the earliest parts were Norman; but the whole
suggests transition. In some places one is led to suppose that the Gothic work has been placed on the top
of the Norman. Moreover, we find rounded windows,
chevron moulding, and the flat pilaster on the outside
walls, especially on the south wall, which are pure
Norman, as well as the pointed doorways and arches
and some more elaborate moulding which are Gothic
or Early English. A good general view of the chapel
is gained by first going out by the west door and
surveying the outside. The west door is very beautiful,

with a great deal of elaborate work representing birds and flowers, etc. It greatly resembles the west door of Poitiers Cathedral, and in recent years has been copied with considerable success by the architect who designed St. Mary's Cathedral. The large windows have a curious design of *fleur de lys*. The doorway and the pointed windows above show small sign of the ruin which prevails. It is in this doorway that Charles I. placed a slab bearing the inscription :

> ' He shall Build ane House
> For My name and I will
> Stablish the Throne
> of his Kingdom
> For ever.
>
> ———
>
> Basilicam hanc semi
> Rutam Carolus Rex
> Optimus instauravit
> Anno Dom
> CIƆ IƆ CXXXIII.'

The visitor of the philosophical turn of mind will doubtless meditate with interest on the inscription and the future events of the King's life. Re-entering the chapel we are anew impressed with the beauty of the ruin, and distressed that it should have been so neglected. The south aisle is almost intact, but on the north side only two sadly mutilated pillars remain. As the choir and transepts have vanished and only the nave remains, it is obvious that the east window is of comparatively modern date, having been built after the removal of the choir and transepts. The whole east wall shows traces of being built out of the remains of other parts. Some say it dates from the fifteenth century in the days of Abbot Crawford, others assign the credit (?) to Adam Bothwell, Bishop of Orkney and Lord Holyroodhouse, somewhere about 1570. We can only say that nothing is known to the credit of the Bishop of Orkney, and if he did not neglect repairing the chapel it is just what he would have

done. What would otherwise be a merely technical
question for antiquarians to settle derives a new interest
when we remember that Queen Mary's marriage both
with Darnley and with Bothwell took place in this
chapel, and we would fain know what the chapel looked
like at these eventful weddings. The east window is of
considerable size, being 34 feet 2 inches high by 20 feet
broad. The upper part of it is filled with diamond-shaped
stonework—what is technically called quatrefoil tracery
—while the lower part is divided by mullions into five
divisions,—we had almost said five panes, but glass there
is none. A transom crosses the mullions about half-way up.

Apart from the actual memories of the chapel, its great
interest for ordinary people who are not students of
architecture lies in its tombs. By far the most striking
of these is the monument to Lord Belhaven in the north-
west tower erected by his nephews Sir Archibald and Sir
Robert Douglas. There is a long Latin inscription in his
honour. This monument is life size and represents Lord
Belhaven in his insignia of office, robes, coronet, etc.
Some of the other tombs are those of Lord and Lady
Reay, Robert Cheyne, xii Prior of the Monastery of Holyrood, Margaret Erskin, Lady Alerdes, 'ane honest man
Robert Votherspone, Burgis and Deacon of ye Hammermen in ye Canogait, R.V.1520'; 'ye noble and poton
Lord James Douglas, Lord of Cairlell and Torthorall,
who married Daime Elizabeth Cairlell, air and heretrix
yarof, wha was slaine in Edinburghe ye xiii day of July
in ye zeier of God 1608.' The aforesaid 'Lord James
Douglas' was a nephew of Morton, and was assassinated by
a nephew of Arran. One of the most interesting monuments is that in honour of George Wishart, Bishop of
St. Andrews, better known as Montrose's chaplain, who
wrote a Latin history of the doings of 'the great
Marquis.' The grave of the fourteenth Earl of Sutherland is also prominent, and is interesting chiefly because
it displays not only his own arms but also those of some

116

of the many noble families with which he was connected,
e.g. Gordon, Lennox, Elphinstone, Perth, and Eglintoune.
These names also appear on the pillars. The inscription
gives him a fairly long pedigree, as it traces his descent
from ' Allan, Thane of Sutherland whom Macbeth in the
rage of his usurping tyranny, about the year of Christ
1057, made away with for endeavouring to restore the
kingdom to Malcolm III. lawful heir to the Crown.'
William, seventeenth Earl of Sutherland, and ' his amiable
Countess Mary, daughter of William Maxwell of Preston,
Kirkcudbright,' are also commemorated. There is an
interesting inscription to ' ane noble lady D. Isobel Ker,
Viscountess of Drumlanreg.' Her sister Margaret married
Lord Yester and founded Lady Yester's Church. The
inscription to the Countess of Eglinton is rather curious :
' D.I.H. Here lyes ane Nobil and maist vertuous Ladie
Deame Jeane Hamilton Countas of Eglingtoun, Dochter
to James Duke of Schattillarot (Châtelherault), sometyme
Governor of this Realme. She deceast in December MDXCVI.'
A contrast to this ' maist vertuous ladie ' is to be found
in Adam Bothwell, Bishop of Orkney and Shetland and
Commendator of Holyrood. It was he who celebrated
the marriage between Mary and Bothwell (to whom he
was not, of course, related—Bothwell's family name
being Hepburn). But when misfortunes came he was
quite willing to desert Mary and crown James, and he
moreover agreed ' to make a sermoun in the kirk of
Halierudehous, and in the end to confesse the offence in
mareing the Queine with the Erle of Bothwell.' This
far from admirable individual has, however, an extremely
laudatory Latin epitaph and some verses. Near the grave
of this belauded bishop may be seen the vault of the
Roxburgh family, which contains, among other famous
members of the family, the remains of the Countess of
Roxburgh who was governess to the children of James I.
But none of these graves—interesting as many of them
are—appeal to us like the royal vault, which may be seen

at the south-east of the chapel. This was restored in our own day by order of Queen Victoria. In 1688 the mob broke into Holyrood, plundering and burning, and even went so far as to break into the royal vault. David II., James II., James V., his first wife Queen Magdalene, and Darnley were among those who were buried there. Mary of Gueldres was buried in Trinity College Church, which she founded, but in 1848, in the course of some alterations, her remains were removed to Holyrood and deposited in the royal vault.

The Palace Gardens have a charm of their own, though not perhaps remarkable in any way. The sun-dial, which is attributed to Queen Mary, probably derived its name from Henrietta Maria, as it dates from her day rather than that of her husband's grandmother. The chief association that the gardens have for Edinburgh people is that they are the scene of the garden-parties which the Lord High Commissioner occasionally gives—wind and May weather permitting.

Closely connected with Holyrood was the burgh of Canongate. Strangers are usually under the delusion that the long winding street known as Canongate is merely a continuation of the High Street. This is not so. The burgh of Canongate grew up round the Abbey, from which also it derived its name. Even so late as 1513, when the Cowgate was enclosed within the city walls, no attempt was made to include the Canongate, whether because, even at that late date, the memory of its separate origin survived or, what is just as probable, that the sanctity of the monks was considered a better protection than city walls. If this were the case their reliance was misplaced, for Hertford's army in 1544 burned and pillaged to such an extent that no trace of the burgh of early days now survives. 1565 is the earliest date on any Canongate house, and there is no reason to suppose that any of the undated houses are older. The burgh of Canongate in olden days was

Tolbooth Wynd

indeed of considerable importance. It had its own
'Tolbooth,' where criminals were imprisoned, and it is
rather startling to find references to 'Parliament House.'
It is supposed, however, that this is meant to refer to
'William Oikis hous in the Canongat,' where the estates
met in 1571 when the vigour of the 'Queensmen' made
Edinburgh hardly safe, and when the Queen's Parliament
met in the Edinburgh Tolbooth.

The entrance to the Canongate was the Watergate,

Nisbet of Dirleton's House

through which many illustrious prisoners passed on their
way to Edinburgh, among them George, Marquis of
Huntly, and also Montrose and Argyle. It was through
this gate that Hertford led his army in 1544; here too
the Abbot of Kilwinning was killed on 'Black Saturday,'
1571; and here in 1601 the Earl of Bothwell's attempt to

seize the King proved a failure. Another entry at the Watergate, though less surely authenticated, is not without its own interest. In the city records for 1661 we read of Barbara Mylne, a witch, who was seen to 'come in at the Water Gate in likeness of a catt, and did change her garment under her awin staire, and went into her house.' It was close to the Watergate that 'Lucky Wood's' hostelry flourished in the time of Allan Ramsay.

Near the foot of the Canongate may be seen White Horse Close. It retains many of the features of bygone days, when, instead of being among the worst slums of Edinburgh, the closes off the Canongate were inhabited by the Scottish nobility. White Horse Close has, moreover, interesting associations. Probably, in spite of tradition, it has no connection with Queen Mary's White Horse, for the earliest date on any house is 1623, although one of the gables bears the date 1573. But it was here that the Royalist nobles were intercepted on their way to join the King at Berwick, Montrose being the only one who managed to carry out his purpose. This is known as the 'Stoppit Stravaig.' Many of the Highlanders lodged here in 1745, and it was to the hospitable house of Widow Flockhart that Fergus MacIvor conducted Waverley after his interview with the Prince.

Near White Horse Close may still be seen Whitefoord House, built on the site of 'my Lord Seaton's house in the Canongate,' which is noted historically for the visit of the French ambassador Manzeville in 1582, but has a far greater interest for all lovers of romance as the scene of Roland Graeme's exciting chase after Catherine Seyton. There is, however, now no trace of the 'projecting shield of arms supported by two huge foxes of stone' nor of the 'paved court decorated with large formal vases of stone, in which yews, cypresses, and other evergreens vegetated in sombre sullenness.' But Whitefoord House is not without an interest of its own, irrespective of site, as it

121

White Horse Close

was for some time the home of Lord Bannatyne, a fine specimen of a Scottish gentleman of the old school, and interesting, moreover, as the nephew of Lady Clanranald, who was imprisoned for helping Prince Charlie to escape.

Golfers' Land, on the south side of the Canongate, is connected with a tale setting forth the golfing prowess of John Paterson in the days when the Duke of York held court at Holyrood. Unfortunately the evidence is not considered absolutely unquestionable, for the story possesses considerable interest. Queensberry House has more general interest. It was built in 1681 by Lord Halton, but soon afterwards was acquired by the first Duke of Queensberry. He was a famous man in his day, celebrated for many things and for nothing more than for his inconsistency. He supported Charles II. and James VII., and earned the hatred of the Covenanters by his cruelty, but he was equally ready to serve the Prince of Orange when it was his interest so to do. He was miserly in the extreme, yet he built Drumlanrig, bought Queensberry House, and collected a fine library. He was almost illiterate, yet his letters—written by a secretary to his dictation—are well and tersely expressed. His son was High Commissioner of the Parliament which passed the Treaty of Union, and in consequence was heartily detested by the mob. They even went so far as to declare that the awful tragedy connected with his idiot son was a judgment on his unpatriotic conduct. His son and successor, the third Duke, was born there in 1688, and here the third Duchess, Prior's 'Kitty ever fair,' kept court attended by her protégé the poet Gay. Gay and Allan Ramsay struck up a friendship, and Gay used to visit Ramsay's shop at the Cross. Like most 'southerners' Gay had considerable difficulty in under-standing the phraseology of *The Gentle Shepherd*, but Ramsay explained the meaning of obscure words and phrases and the allusions to Scottish customs, which explanation Gay promised to pass on to Pope, who was

123

JENNY HA'S CHANGE HOUSE

another of Ramsay's admirers. 'Jenny Ha's Change House,' which was opposite Queensberry House, was also haunted by Gay when he was in Edinburgh. Queensberry House passed from the Douglases in 1801 when 'Old Q' sold it to the government. It was used first as barracks, then as a hospital, and is now a House of Refuge for the Destitute and Home for Inebriate Women. Near Queensberry House is Bakehouse Close, which contains Acheson House and the town house of the Marquis of Huntly, the front of which faces the street. Acheson House belonged to the Achesons of Gosford and bears their arms. One tale declares that Lady Jane Grey once visited this mansion, but its date (1633) settles that story.

The house of the Marquis of Huntly has many associations. It has curious timber-fronted gables adorned with Latin mottoes, *e.g.* 'Constanti pectori res mortalium umbra' and 'ut tu linguae tuae sic ego mear; aurium dominus sum.' This ancient building is now a public-house. 1510 is the year assigned for this house, but its name came from George, Marquis of Huntly, who killed 'the bonny Earl o' Moray.' His son, who was executed at the Cross in 1649, also lived here. In spite of his own loyalty—which indeed cost him his life—the daughter of this Marquis married Lord Drummond, son of the Earl of Perth, who, Spalding tells us, 'was ane preceise puritane and therefore weill lyked in Edinburgh.' In spite of the Puritanic tendencies of the bridegroom the wedding was the occasion of great festivities, which were celebrated in this old mansion.

124

Bakehouse Close

Hunrly House

The old burgh of Canongate had its own Tolbooth,
built 1591 (which may be known by its large clock), its
own parish church and its own churchyard. The old
church of Canongate was within the walls of Holyrood,
but when the Chapel Royal was appropriated for Roman
Catholic worship, the present Canongate Church was
built. Many interesting entries may be seen in the old
parish register. On 21st July 1565 'Harry Duk of
Albayne' and 'Marie be ye grace of God, Queene of
Scottis' were proclaimed. More tragic are the entries
'Monr Signior Dauid wes slane in Halyruidhous ye

126

Canongate Tolbooth

Canongate Cross

ix daye o' Merche
1565' and 'Ye
King's Grace blaun
up wi pudr in ye
Kirk-o'-Field, ye x
o' Februar 1566.'
In those days, of
course, the year
began with 25th
March, hence the
apparent confu-
sion of dates.

The Canongate
arms may be seen
represented pro-
minently on the
church as well as
on the Tolbooth
and Burgh Cross.
Even more interesting than these antiquities is the
long list of celebrities buried in the churchyard, which
may be seen at the gate. Among these may be mentioned Adam Smith, Dugald Stewart, David Allan
the artist, Bishop Keith, Dr. Adam Ferguson, historian
of the Roman Empire, etc. Alexander Runciman is here
also. His picture of the Prodigal Son is now remembered
only because the poet Fergusson sat as a model, and by a
curious coincidence he too is interred here. The tomb-
stone on his grave was erected by Fergusson's greater
successor, Burns, and the lines on it are by Burns.

Not far from the churchyard, on the other side of the
Canongate, is Moray House. It was built by the
Dowager-Countess of Home in the early years of the
reign of Charles I. She was a daughter of Lord Dudley,
and the Home and Dudley arms are still visible. It
passed in 1645 to her elder daughter, Margaret, Countess
of Moray. Cromwell stayed there when he came to

Here lies
ROBERT FERGUSSON POET
BORN SEP^t 1751
DIED OC^t 1774

No Sculptur'd Marble here nor
pompous lay
No storied Urn nor animated
Bust
This simple Stone directs Pale
Scotia's way
To pour her Sorrows o'er her
Poet's Dust

Fergusson's Tomb
Canongate Churchyard

Scotland in 1648, and he was visited by many of the Covenanting leaders, though he probably did not discuss the King's impending execution with them, in spite of Guthrie's statement to that effect.

In 1650 Lady Mary Stewart, eldest daughter of the Earl of Moray, was married to Lord Lorn, son of Argyle. The wedding festivities were in progress when Montrose was brought into Edinburgh as a prisoner. It was from the very balcony, which may still be seen, that Argyle watched his great rival, and turned away unable to meet his gaze. It is a curious illustration of the uncertainty of political power in those days that three of the wedding party who enjoyed this triumph over Montrose in the course of a few years suffered the same death at the same place, *i.e.* Argyle himself, Johnston of Warriston, and the bridegroom Lord Lorn, afterwards Earl of Argyle. After Dunbar Cromwell again visited Edinburgh and stayed at Moray House, where he once more received his Scottish allies—who were not, however, as numerous as formerly. We hear nothing more of Moray House until the Union of the Parliaments. Considerable interest attaches to it as the residence of Lord Chancellor Seafield. It must at that time have been frequented by many famous men, and the old thorn-tree in the garden could doubtless tell many strange tales if it could only speak. The signatories of the Union met in the quaint old summer-house, but were compelled by the violence of the mob to seek refuge in a cellar belonging to one of the High Street houses. Moray House is now the Normal Training College of the United Free Church. St. John Street opens off the Canongate just beside Moray House, and is no less interesting than that famous mansion, though its associations are literary rather than historical. It was here that Mrs. Telfer, sister of Tobias Smollett, lived, and it was here doubtless that her brother got his knowledge of the Edinburgh of that day which he depicts so vividly in *Humphrey Clinker*. Dr. John Gregory, Lord Monboddo, and his beautiful daughter Bess Burnett, were also among the residents. More famous still was James Ballantyne, who entertained his friends—Scott himself among them—when he brought out a new Waverley novel. The Canongate Kilwinning Lodge of Freemasons, of which Burns was a member and also poet-laureate, may still be seen, and is probably not so much changed as many of the other places of interest. Another famous man, Murray of Broughton, was also a member of that Lodge, but the stern justice of the eighteenth century had no mercy for the traitor, and his name was removed from the roll of members.

On the other side of the Canongate was St. John's Cross, where King James was received by the Canongate authorities when he returned ' like a saumon ' to Edinburgh. There also Charles I. knighted the Provost when he entered the city in 1633.

Jack's Land, which is nearly opposite St. John Street,

has some interesting associations. It was at one time the residence of the lovely Susannah, Countess of Eglin- ton. The way in which the Earl of Eglinton conducted his 'coortin' sheds a curious sidelight on the manners of those days. Her father was Sir Archibald Kennedy of Culzean, a stout old cavalier who had followed Claver- house. No sooner did he bring his beautiful daughter to Edinburgh than he was besieged by suitors for her hand. One of these was Sir John Clerk, and Sir Archibald con- sidered his suit so far as to consult Lord Eglinton, who made the—to modern notions—astounding reply, 'Bide a wee, Sir Archie, the Coontess is gey sickly.' The 'sickly' Countess departed this life most opportunely, and the Earl espoused Susannah, who was his third wife, though he himself was at this time just about forty. One of Susannah's stepdaughters, Lady Effie, was the wife of that zealous Jacobite, Lockhart of Carnwath,— 'Union' Lockhart he was called sometimes, from the prominent part he played in obstructing the Treaty of Union. Lady Effie was as ardent a Jacobite as her husband, and her adroitness saved him from many awk- ward situations. She frequently disguised herself as a man and haunted the coffee-houses in the hope of getting information, and on one occasion, when it suited her plans better, she disguised her sons as women. The Countess of Eglinton does not seem to have imitated the unconventionality of her stepdaughter, but she also was a strong Jacobite. She received Prince Charlie at her house in 1745, and in recognition of her hospitality he bestowed on her his full-dress plaid. Jack's Land had another famous resident—albeit a very different person from the Countess of Eglinton. From 1753 to 1762 David Hume lived here, and it was here that a con- siderable part of his history was written. In Big Jack's Land lived Dalzell of Binns, who combined in an extra- ordinary degree the most chivalrous loyalty to his King with the most relentless cruelty to the Covenanters. It

Playhouse Close

is not generally known that his devotion to religion led him to build a private chapel. Fortunately for himself he died before the Romanising tendencies of James VII. became apparent.

Playhouse Close is interesting as being the site of the first regular theatre in Edinburgh. Dramatic representations ceased at the time of the Reformation, but were revived under the Duke of York in the form of masques, etc. The Revolution, however, put a stop to this, and it was not until 1714 that we hear of a representation of *Macbeth* at the Tennis Court. This was the occasion of a riot, as some of the audience were anxious for the song 'May the King enjoy his ain again,' while others as strenuously opposed it. An Italian dancer, Signora Violante, gave her performances at Carrubber's Close, and shortly afterwards a regular theatre was opened in Playhouse Close. The drama of *Douglas* was one of the pieces produced here.

New Street, opposite Playhouse Close, has reminiscences of Lord Kaimes and Lord Hailes, and of the Earl of Angus, whose town house was here. But Morocco Land has a story connected with it which seems more in keeping with Grimm's *Fairy Tales* than with sober history. In the early part of the reign of Charles I. a number of riotous young men broke into the Provost's house, and assaulted that dignitary. The ringleader, Andrew Gray, son of the Master of Gray, was taken, imprisoned in the Tolbooth, and condemned to death. He escaped, however, the night before the day fixed for his execution, and was heard of no more. In 1645 Edinburgh was visited with pestilence, and was also in great fear of the armies of Montrose. Another terror was now added, for a curious ship appeared at Leith, obviously with hostile intentions. The alarm of the citizens did not decrease when they discovered that the vessel was an Algerian pirate ship. Some of the crew landed, and seem to have met with no opposition when they passed through the

133

Reid's Close

Watergate and marched up the Canongate to the Netherbow Port. There they were interviewed by the Edinburgh
magistrates, who offered to ransom the city, but seemed
to make little impression on these pirate rovers. The
Provost, Sir John Smith, persuaded his brother-in-law,
Sir William Gray, to try his persuasive power, and this
time the Moorish leader seemed more inclined to listen.
He agreed to accept a large ransom, provided the Provost
would give up his son to him. But the Provost had
only one daughter, who was at that time seriously ill from
plague. There was great anxiety on her account, as her
cousin, Egidia Gray, had just died. On hearing this the
Moorish leader demanded that she should be given up to
him, promising that, if he did not succeed in curing her,
he would leave the city without ransom. The Provost
could hardly bring himself to surrender his only child,
but as there was no other way out of the difficulty he
was persuaded to do so. The joy of the Provost may be
imagined when his daughter was restored to him safe and
well. The Moorish leader proved to be Andrew Gray,
who had been taken prisoner and kept as a slave by
the Moors, but was fortunate enough to gain the favour
of the Emperor of Morocco, who set him at liberty.
Determined to wreak his vengeance on the children of
the Provost of Edinburgh he returned, only to find in the
object of his hatred a near kinswoman, whom he first
cured and—for the tale would be incomplete without
this—finally married. Gray had made a rash vow never
to enter Edinburgh except sword in hand, so having
made his peace with the magistrates, he kept this vow by
living outside the Netherbow Port in the house which is
still known as Morocco Land. Whether the tale is true
or not we leave our readers to determine. Certainly a
Moor's head still adorns Morocco Land, but whether it is
the result or the cause of the story we do not pretend
to say. Passing by Cranston Street—the old Leith
Wynd—which was one entrance to Edinburgh, we come

Brown's Close

to St. Mary Street and Jeffrey Street. A little east of St. Mary Street was the White Horse Inn, where the waiter horrified Dr. Johnson by using his fingers instead of sugar-tongs. St. Mary Street and Jeffrey Street are separated from the Canongate by no visible wall of separation, for the old Netherbow Port is now swept away, yet they are outside the bounds of the old burgh of Canongate, and will be dealt with in a later chapter.

Stooping Stone

St Giles' Cathedral

CHAPTER VI

ST. GILES'

OF all churches in Edinburgh the best known, alike to inhabitants and visitors, is the Cathedral Church of St. Giles. Not only is it important on account of its site, its antiquity, and its architecture, but it is bound up inextricably with the history of the town. In pre-Reformation times St. Giles' made no claim to cathedral rank, that dignity came later, and was of short duration. But even without that it has many claims on our interest.

St. Giles is not a specially well-known saint, nor is he connected in any way with local Scottish tradition. Giles is the French form of the Latin Egidius, and it may be noted in passing, that while Giles was a common name for men, the feminine form, Egidia, was often bestowed on Scottish ladies of rank. Princess Egidia, daughter of Robert II. who married William de Douglas, is perhaps the best-known example of the name, but many others are to be found. St. Giles, who was a native of Athens, wandered west, and finally took up his abode at Nîmes, in the south of France. Being a hermit, he lived quite alone, until chance brought him an unexpected companion. A hind, pursued by the dogs of Flavius Wamba, King of the Goths, took refuge with the hermit and remained with him as his constant companion. In pictures St. Giles is always represented with the hind beside him, but there is no foundation in fact for the

139

picture of Lucas van Leyden, which represents St. Giles
sheltering his companion with a hand pierced by an
arrow intended for the hind. It is interesting to note
that a hind figures in the arms of the city of Edinburgh.
This hind must not be confused with the hind which
attacked David I., and which is to be found in the arms
of the burgh of Canongate. St. Giles died in 451 A.D.,
and churches, chapels, and hospitals were immediately
dedicated to him. It is said that in England a hundred
and forty-six churches were founded in his honour. Of
religious buildings dedicated to him one of the best
known is the St. Giles hospital for lepers, founded in
London by Matilda, wife of Henry I., in 1117. Possibly
the association with Edinburgh had something to do
with the name. As regards the Edinburgh church, it
seems probable that some Benedictine follower of St.
Giles brought the name from the south of France to
Edinburgh.

It is not certain if the earliest church on this site was
originally dedicated to St. Giles, though there is no
proof to the contrary. It is known that there was a
church in Edinburgh in 854, as Simeon Dunelmensis refers
to it. It was, however, at that time under the jurisdiction of Lindisfarne, but in 1020 the province of Lothian
was ceded by Eadulf to Malcolm II. It is possible, however, that, although Edinburgh was in things civil under
the rule of the Scottish kings, St. Giles' in things ecclesiastical was under the jurisdiction of Lindisfarne. This,
we know, was the case with the Priory of Coldingham.
The title of the chief dignitary connected with the
church—Perpetual Vicar of the Church of St. Giles—
together with the absence of cathedral rank, gives considerable force to the arguments in favour of this supposition. In the reign of Alexander II., Baldredus,
Deacon of Lothian, and John, Perpetual Vicar of the
Church of St. Giles, appear as witnesses to papal bulls
and to charters of the church of Megginche.

The original building was replaced in 1120 by a church of early Norman architecture. The prosperity of St. Giles' was greatly helped by the kings of Scotland selecting Edinburgh Castle as a residence. David I., as was to be expected, dealt generously with the church. In his day St. Giles' was a small parish church. Wilson in his *Memorials of Edinburgh* speaks of a print representing ' a beautiful Norman doorway which formed the entrance to the nave of St. Giles church on the north side and was only demolished about the year 1760. It stood immediately below the third window from the west within the line of the external wall. A plain round archway that had given access to it was obliterated in the alterations of 1829. This fragment sufficiently enables us to picture the little parish church of St. Giles in the reign of David I. Built in the massive style of the early Norman period, it would consist simply of a nave and chancel united by a rich Norman chancel-arch; altogether occupying only a portion of the central aisle of the present nave. Small circular headed windows, decorated with zig-zag mouldings, would admit the light to the sombre interior; while its west front was in all probability surmounted by a simple belfry, from whence the bell would daily summon the natives of the hamlet to matins and vespers, and with slow measured sounds, toll their knell as they were laid in the neighbouring church-yard. This ancient church was never entirely demolished. . . . The Norman architecture disappeared piece-meal, as chapels and aisles were added to the original fabric by the piety of private donors, or by the zeal of its own clergy to adapt it to the wants of the rising town. In all the changes that it underwent for about seven centuries, the original north door, with its beautifully recessed Norman arches and grotesque decorations, always commanded the veneration of the innovators, and remained as a precious relic of the past, until the tasteless improvers of the eighteenth century demolished it

without a cause, and probably for no better reason than
to evade the cost of repair.' An impression of this doorway may still be seen in the Signet Library.

Though the original fabric was Norman, the prevailing
style of architecture is pure Gothic. This points to the
fact that it was probably in the reign of David II. that
the church was altered and enlarged, as pure Gothic is
not found later than the fourteenth century. It is in
this reign that we find the first reference to chantries in
St. Giles'. We also find endowments given to the church
at this time. The Vicar of St. Giles' held the 'Sant
Geilies Grange,' a farm about a mile south of the church.
This farm gives its name to the present church and district of Grange, though there is now no connection with
St. Giles'.

St. Giles', being the metropolitan church of Edinburgh,
had its share in the various vicissitudes which befell the
city. In 1385 it was burned and almost completely
destroyed by an English army under Richard II. Little
of the church remained except the choir, the nave, the
base of the spire, and the beautiful north doorway which
has been already referred to. In addition to rebuilding
the town the citizens determined to rebuild the church.
Accordingly in 1387—in the reign of Robert II.—it was
agreed to build five chapels in St. Giles'. The chapels
were to be of stone, they were to have pillars and vaulted
roofs and to be lighted with windows. In its best days
St. Giles' had forty altars and was served by seventy
priests. Little more was done architecturally until 1460,
when the choir was enlarged and the pillars altered. An
Act of Council, slightly modernised, gives this account of
the origin of the Preston Aisle : ' Be it kenned to all men
by these present letters, we, the provost, bailies, counselle
and communitie of the burgh of Edynburgh to be bound
and obliged to William Prestoune of Gourton and to the
friends and sirname of them, that for so much that William
Prestoun the father, whom God assoile, made diligent

labour by a high and mighty prince (the king of France, Charles VII.) and many other lords of France, for getting the arm-bone of St. Gile, the which bone he freely left to oure mothir Kirk of St. Gile of Edynburgh withouten any condicion. We, considering the great labour and costs that he made for getting thereof, promise that within six or seven years in all the possible and goodly haste we may, that we shall build an aisle furth from our Ladye Aisle, where the said William lies, the said aisle to be begun within a year, in which aisle there shall be brass for his lair in bost (*i.e.* embossed) work, and above the brass a writ specifying the bringing of the Rylik by himself into Scotland, with his arms, and his arms to be put in hewn work, in three other parts of the aisle, with book and chalice and all other furniture belonging thereto. Also that we shall assign the chaplains of whilome Sir William of Prestoune, to sing at the altar from that time forth. . . . Item that as often as the said Rylik is borne in the year, that the sirname and nearest of blood of the said William shall bear the said Rylik, before all others, etc. In witness of which things we have set to our common seal at Edinburgh the 11th day of the month of January in the year of our Lord 1454.'

The other arm-bone is at Bruges in the Church of St. Giles. Preston's arms are on a pillar on the south side of the choir, and consist of the heads of three unicorns.

It was soon after this—in 1466—that St. Giles' was transformed from an ordinary parish church into a collegiate charge with 'a chapter to consist of a Provost, Curate, sixteen Prebendaries, a Minister of the Choir, four choristers, a Sacristan and a Beadle.' These were in addition to the chaplains who served the various altars.

It was at this time that the Pope granted a bull making St. Giles' independent even of the authority of the Bishop

of St. Andrews, and under no jurisdiction but that of the
Pope himself.

When St. Giles' became a collegiate charge the Perpetual Vicar William Forbes was created the first
Provost. He, however, is not so well known as his
successor, the famous Gavin Douglas, the poet who
wrote two allegorical poems, 'King Hart' and the
'Palace of Honour,' but is remembered chiefly as the
translator of the *Aeneid*. This was the first time Virgil
had been translated into Scots, and it is wonderfully well
done considering the inaccurate knowledge of that day,
while the Prologues (which are original) abound in extra-
ordinarily vivid descriptive touches. Equally interesting
at this time, though not equally well known, is Walter
Chepman 'the Scottish Caxton,' who, along with Andrew
Myllar, introduced printing into Scotland in 1507,—
needless to say under the patronage of James iv., whose
interest in literature and letters seems to have been
unbounded. Chepman was connected with St. Giles'
in many ways, notably in founding the aisle which
bears his name. It is south of the Preston Aisle and
east of the south transept. Chepman was buried here
in 1532.

Of the riots which accompanied the Reformation and
the hard treatment meted out to the image of St. Giles
we have already spoken (in chap. ii.). The church was
cleared of 'images,'—and of almost everything else, too.
But melancholy as was its aspect it was never deserted
as long as Knox preached. The choir was set apart for
worshippers, the other parts of the church being used as
a place of resort where citizens could meet their friends
and discuss the political situation. But even this—
doubtless interesting—conversation was not proof against
the extraordinary interest Knox always excited. There
were no seats in the church, those who cared brought
their own stools, but the majority of people preferred to
stand. So great was his popularity that Knox often

preached to an audience of three thousand. The great reformer might be stern to weakness in others, he did not, however, spare himself. Twice on Sundays, and three times on week days, did this indefatigable man preach in St. Giles'. History does not record when he found time to prepare so many sermons, and one cannot but suspect that he occasionally favoured his audience with 'cauld kail het again.'

It was not till just before the death of Knox that the church began to be divided. The first division was the Tolbooth, which was in the south-west part of the church. In early days Parliaments used to meet in St. Giles' and civil dues were sometimes paid there—hence the name Tolbooth or Town House.

The Reformation, while it swept away much that was inseparably connected with St. Giles' in the days of 'the old religion,' did not touch the secular purposes for which the church was used and which seem to us now such desecration of the sacred building. Business was transacted in the south aisle, and idlers lounged in and out to gossip with their friends and see what was going on. An analogy to the English proverb 'to dine with Duke Humphrey' sprang up in connection with Regent Moray. Sempill, writing about those idlers who used the south aisle for secular purposes, makes one of them say:

'I dined with saints and gentlemen,
  Ev'n sweet Saint Giles and the Earl of Murray';

meaning that he had had no dinner, and wandered about in St. Giles' for lack of more congenial occupation. Bills were often made payable 'at the Earl of Moray's tomb' as a convenient meeting-place.

Charles I., in his endeavour to establish Episcopacy in Scotland, determined that St. Giles' should be a worthy cathedral for the newly created Bishop of Edinburgh. Accordingly he gave orders that the partitions should be

K

removed ' according to the first Intentioun of the Erectors
and Founders thairof; which was to be keiped conforme
to the Largeness and Conspecuitie of the Foundatioun and
Fabrick; and not to be indirectlie parcelled and disjoinit
by wallis and Partitiounis as now it is withouten anie
warrant from anie of oure Royal Predecessoures. Oure
Pleasure is that with all diligence you caus raze to the
Ground the East wall of the said Churche; and sick-lyke,
that you caus raze to the Ground the Wester-wall therein,
betwixt this and Lambas inseuing at or before which
Tyme we require you to caus finish the new Tolbuith,
to the effect it may be for the Use of oure Churche and
uther Judicatories and Commissiounes, as the Tyme and
Occasioun shall require.' These orders were given in
1633, and in 1636 the Town Council requested James
Hannay, Dean of St. Giles', to go to Durham and study
the architecture of the Cathedral and especially of its
choir, so that he might be able to direct the restoration
of St. Giles' on somewhat similar lines. But Jenny
Geddes and her stool sternly protested against the new
order of things, and in 1639 Episcopacy was abolished
and St. Giles' once more became a parish church. Episcopacy was restored at the Restoration, but was again
abolished after the Revolution of 1688, and St. Giles' is
now that curious anomaly, a Cathedral without a Bishop.
Beauty or ugliness of architecture hardly seem grounds
for a struggle of national importance, but though not
the cause they seem to have become the badges of the
opposing parties. Charles I. wanted St. Giles' restored
to something of its original beauty; therefore in 1639
the popular party who were then in power ordered
the partition walls to be rebuilt and its condition of
artificial ugliness resumed. Not only so, but fresh partition walls were built. By a curious parallel church
extension in the eighteenth century was carried on
somewhat on the lines of town extension in the middle
ages. The town did not dare to spread itself out be-

yond the walls for fear of an English invasion, and so
grew in *height*, but not in extent. In a somewhat
similar manner, to save the trouble of building new
churches, the existing Church of St. Giles was divided
into several parish churches, a minister was set over each
to look after the people, and each church was packed as
full as possible. Not only did galleries mar the architectural beauty of the church, but even with this additional
accommodation seats had to be placed in the passages.
To allow worshippers to reach the other seats, these
were let down on hinges after the rest of the congregation was seated. So little attention was paid, not only
to beauty, but even to ordinary cleanliness, that one
minister, who had not preached in St. Giles' for several
years, declared he recognised one of the cobwebs! The
Tolbooth seems to have held a proud pre-eminence
of ugliness over the High Church, the Little Church, and
the Old Church, but none comformed at all to modern
ideas of beauty or even seemliness. The High Church,
or choir, was the eastern part of the church, the
Tolbooth the south-west, the Old Church the middle and
south, and the Little Kirk, otherwise known as Haddo's
Hole, the north-west. The Little Kirk derived its
second name from the fact that Sir John Gordon of
Haddo was imprisoned in a room above it before he was
tried and executed in 1644. There seems no limit to
the unecclesiastical uses to which St. Giles' was put.
The Preston Aisle and part of the north transept were,
it will be seen from the above account, left unappro-
priated. We do not hear of the Preston Aisle ever
being used for business either of Church or State, but
the north transept was used as a police office till 1818.
The author of the *Traditions of Edinburgh* thus dis-
tinguishes the characteristics of the different churches:
'The High Church had a sort of dignified aristocratic
character, approaching somewhat to prelacy, and was
frequented only by sound church and state men, who

did not care so much for the sermon as for the gratifica-
tion of sitting in the same place with His Majesty's
Lords of Council and Session, and the magistrates of
Edinburgh, and who desired to be thought men of
sufficient liberality and taste to appreciate the prelections
of Blair. The old Church in the centre of the whole was
frequented by people who wished to have a sermon of
good divinity about three quarters of an hour long, and
who did not care for the darkness and dreariness of their
temple. The Tolbooth Church was the peculiar resort
of a set of rigid Calvinists from the Lawnmarket and
head of the Bow, termed "Towbuith Whigs," who loved
nothing but extempore evangelical sermons, and would
have considered it sufficient to bring the house down
about their ears, if the precentor had ceased, for one
verse, the old hillside fashion of reciting the lines of the
psalm before singing them.' Dr. Webster was long one
of the clergymen of this church, and deservedly admired
as a pulpit orator. Readers of 'Bonnie Dundee' remember how Scott in one phrase, 'the sanctified bends of
the Bow,' has brought before us these unbending Calvinists—the Towbuith Whigs—who had far more in
common with the wild western Whigs, or Cameronians,
than with the stately, respectable, and—they would have
said—Erastian frequenters of the High Church. It is
hardly necessary to add that the term 'High' had no
ecclesiastical significance.

It is a matter of surprise to some that the citizens
so long tolerated the condition of the church. Scott
refers to the ugliness of St. Cuthbert's of that day, but
makes no reference to the state of St. Giles'. Cockburn
seems to have realised that things were not all they
might be, but made no attempt to improve them. We
must, however, remember that the period at the end of
the eighteenth and beginning of the nineteenth centuries
is a byword for lack of architectural taste. Most of
the churches built at that time merit the rebuke dealt

out unsparingly by the Countess of Galloway to her minister : 'I gave you money for a church, and (relapsing into Doric) ye hae biggit a barn.' It is a well-known fact that it is easier to make an entirely new thing than to renovate and improve an old one, so if the new churches were barnlike in their lack of beauty, it is small wonder that St. Giles' continued in its unlovely condition without interference.

At last, however, people began to realise that something must be done. In 1817 a beginning was made when the 'Krames' were cleared away. These were small shops which were actually in the niches of the church, and which certainly did not improve the appearance of the exterior. When this beginning was made, it was not difficult to make people realise that the condition of the interior could no longer be tolerated. Government offered more than half of the estimated cost, and the design of an architect named Burn was accepted.

The desire to renovate the church was laudable in the extreme, but it is greatly to be regretted that, since restoration had been so long deferred, it did not come a few years later. Interest in the antique had, by 1829, been stimulated by two quite different causes : the prose and verse romances of Scott, and the beginning of the Oxford movement, as exemplified in Keble and others. But while interest was there, definite systematic study had hardly begun. Scott had caught the spirit of chivalry, but it is only necessary to compare his works with those of a true mediævalist like Rossetti to realise how far short he fell of an accurate knowledge of former days. In a similar way people had begun to realise that the condition of St. Giles' was a public scandal, but they had not yet sufficient knowledge to enable them to rectify that scandal. If the restoration had been deferred, even a few years, the increasing study of the principles of Norman and Gothic architecture would have enabled the

149

architect to produce a result in harmony with the intention of the founder, and above all would have prevented the destruction of parts of the original building,
which no amount of good taste or expense on the part of
succeeding generations could ever replace.

The improvements were carried out in the most
reckless manner imaginable. Two of the chapels of 1387
were demolished to improve the entrance to Parliament
Square. These were on the south-west side of the building, but two on the north side were also removed.
Daniel Wilson tells us that ' they formed originally very
picturesque features externally with their pointed gables,
and steep roofs theiket with stane, and with them also
the deep archway which had formerly given access to the
most ancient fragment of the Parish Church. The
eastmost of these chapels, which is now replaced by what
appears externally as the west aisle of the north transept,
was the only portion of the Church in which any of the
coloured glass remained, with which, doubtless, most of
its windows were anciently filled.' This was St. Eloi's
Chapel, and the present chapel occupies the site of the
former one.

In addition to the chapels and windows which were
swept away in the course of the restoration, the monument to the Earl of Moray was removed—it is hard to
say why. The brass tablet on it was, however, recovered,
and now adorns the monument recently erected to
Moray.

The internal arrangements of the church were not
greatly improved. The High Church, or choir, was
unaltered. It was decided to hold meetings of the
Assembly in the south part, but as the plan did not
work well, this was afterwards given over to the Old
Church. The nave rejoiced in the name of the New
North Church, and this name was afterwards changed to
West St. Giles'. The Tolbooth and Haddo's Hole
were no more heard of. The police office also vanished,

and was replaced by a large lobby belonging to all the congregations. The one mode of ingress was by a door in the north transept.

The exterior was restored 'as ruthlessly as the interior.' With the exception of the spire or 'crown' the outside was entirely altered. Moulding, pinnacles, carving— Norman and Gothic alike—were completely swept away and a uniform standard of modern unpicturesqueness was adopted. Fortunately the spire escaped the restorers. It is said by some to date from the twelfth century, but it was remodelled and considerably changed during the alterations which took place in the fifteenth century. It was again restored in 1648, but the restorers seem to have had sufficient wisdom to retain its original form. It was left untouched in 1829, and still remains many times restored, yet essentially the same. Its height is one hundred and sixty-one feet and its appearance is that of a crown. It needs little imagination to see the appropriateness of this emblem, the crowned church ruling and guarding the city which lies around it.

The bells of St. Giles' are worthy of attention. To many they are associated only with bringing in the New Year, but, as might be expected, they have an interesting history. The St. Mary bell was, it seems, disposed of in 1563, at a time when the zeal of the reformers was at its height. The great bell of St. Giles' is the best known alike in history and literature. Dr. Laing says it 'was cast in Flanders, and is described as having the arms of Guelderland upon different parts of it, together with figures of the Virgin and Child and other devices, and had the following Latin inscription: 'Honorabiles viri burgenses villae de Edinburch, in Scotia, hanc campanam fieri fecerunt Anno Dni MCCCCLVV (1460). Johs et Wilhelmus Hoerhen me fecerunt, ipsamque campanam Gyelis vocari voluerunt. Defunctos plango; vivos voco; fulmina frango.' Translation: 'The honourable men, burgesses of the city of Edinburgh, in Scotland, caused this bell to be made in the year of our Lord one thousand four hundred and sixty, Johannes and Wilhelm Hoerhen made me. And they determined that I should be called Giles' bell. I mourn the dead; I summon the living; I disperse thunder.' In addition to performing these useful functions it was also rung on occasions of great national moment, when it was necessary to get the citizens gathered together, as after the battle of Flodden. The inscription is not now visible, as, owing to an accident, the bell had to be recast. This bell is still used 'to call the living' to church, and on it the hours sound. Two smaller bells chime the half-hours and quarters. One old bell, which when discovered was guiltless of a clapper, is unaltered since pre-Reformation days. It may have been either the Vesper bell or the Ave bell. The inscription seems to favour the latter alternative. It is 'O Mater Dei, memento mei; anno DMIIII.' Translation: 'O Mother of God, remember me; 1504.' It has since been provided with a clapper, and is now used 'to summon the living' to the daily service, which is held every day at 3.30 P.M. It is now known as the Angelus bell of St. Giles'. But the chimes of St. Giles', which all inhabitants of Edinburgh know so well, are purely modern. However interesting the associations of the old bells may be, it cannot be denied that the peal of Harrington's tubular bells, which have lately been placed there, emits a more musical chime.

Although the restoration of 1829 left so much to be desired it does not seem to have occurred to any one for many long years to take the responsibility of beginning a movement for more suitable restoration. When that movement did come, the High Church, as being the most important, was the first to be restored. It was the High Church which was honoured by the presence of royalty, by the Lord High Commissioners, and by the magistrates. It was therefore fitting that the then Lord Provost, the late Dr. William Chambers, should have been the first to plan and afterwards to carry through this much needed restoration. He himself, in his 'Historical Sketch of St. Giles' Cathedral Church,' tells how the project first appealed to him. 'There and then, when seated in that elevated gallery close to the carved shields of the boy-prince James and his mother, the inestimable Mary of Gueldres, we conceived the idea of attempting a restoration of the building, and producing a church in which the people of Edinburgh might feel some pride—a shrine fitting for the devotional exercises of royalty.'

The project was first proposed in 1867, but was not seriously taken up till 1871, when a public meeting was held, a committee chosen, and Dr. Chambers appointed chairman. After much trouble and expense on the part of the committee and its chairman the High Church was opened for public worship on Sunday, 9th March 1873. This was a great step in the right direction, but it was only the first step. The Old Church had been abolished by Act of Parliament in 1870, so it was possible without detriment to vested interests to restore the southern aisles, *i.e.* the Preston, Chepman, and Moray Aisles. That this was done was owing entirely to the generosity of Dr. Chambers. Having done so much he was now anxious that the church should be made into one complete and beautiful whole, but the nave belonged to the congregation of the New North Church (West St. Giles'), and nothing could be done until it was provided for. An Act of Parliament passed in 1879 enacted that they should leave St. Giles' on payment of £10,500, which would enable them to build a new church. Subscriptions were obtained—with some difficulty—and then Dr. Chambers at his own expense restored the nave also, thereby completing this noble achievement.

It is hard to imagine St. Giles' as it must have been before the restoration, with galleries, old-fashioned pews, plaster pillars, etc. Dr. Chambers says the appearance of the Royal Pew itself was such that no one could look at it without being reminded of a four-post bed! This distressing state of affairs was finally put an end to in 1883, when the church assumed its present form. In the nave chairs have taken the place of narrow pews; the plaster has been removed, leaving the stone interior as it was originally intended to be; the unsightly galleries have been cleared away, and the church stands now unequalled in Edinburgh for beauty of architecture. It is, of course, easy to find fault, to say that it is not pure Gothic, that parts are not real antique but only a good imitation, and that it is hopelessly inferior to the beautiful English cathedrals. Much of that is true, but the fact remains that the patriotic generosity of a great Scotsman has rescued this cathedral church of St. Giles from a condition of almost unspeakable ugliness, and has restored it to its rightful appearance as the metropolitan church of the capital of Scotland. Those going to Sunday services at St. Giles' enter by the west door, but visitors or those going to the daily service go in by the north door, which is the entrance on the High Street side of the church. On the right-hand side as we go in is the Chapel of St. Eloi. This chapel has an interesting history. St. Eloi seems to have been the patron-saint of the Hammermen of Edinburgh, and at his altar the citizens who had followed Allan, Lord High Steward of Scotland, to the Holy Land dedicated the famous banner which was familiarly known as the Blue Blanket, but really bore the more euphonious title of the Banner of the Holy Ghost. This banner was bestowed on the citizens of Edinburgh by James III. in recognition of their loyalty to him. The wrought-iron screen in this chapel is the work of Skidmore, and is specially beautiful in design and workmanship, in order to do honour to the Hammermen of Edinburgh. The blue and gold medallions on the upper part of the screen are interesting, and the floor of inlaid marble and mosaics is well worth looking at. But

St Giles' Cathedral looking East

it must be confessed that many quite well-informed
people have somewhat hazy ideas about the Hammermen
of Edinburgh, and the great majority of visitors will probably be more interested in the monument to Argyle
than in the doings of these craftsmen. The stained-
glass window is filled with the arms of Argyle and
other Covenanting families, such as Dalhousie, Loudoun,
Eglinton, Leven, Lothian, etc.

This chapel has been much altered since the days of
the Hammermen. As has already been said, it suffered
greatly during the restoration of 1829. Its keystone
had a peculiarly eventful history. After some vicissitudes it came into the possession of Charles Kirkpatrick
Sharpe, then it passed to the Antiquarian Museum,
whence it was rescued, and now forms the centre of the
carved roof. Daniel Wilson thus describes it : ' It is
adorned with a richly sculptured boss formed of four
dragons with distended wings, each different in design,
the tails of which are gracefully extended so as to cover
the intersecting ribs of the groined roof. The centre
is formed by a large flower to which an iron hook is
attached; from whence, no doubt, anciently depended a
lamp over the altar of St. Eloi.'

Farther west than St. Eloi's Chapel, but still on the
north side of the church, we come to the Albany Aisle.
This was a chapel built by Robert, Duke of Albany, son
of Robert II., and Archibald Douglas, fourth Earl of
Douglas, Duke of Touraine, and Marshal of France, who
fell at the battle of Verneuil in 1424. The ' Black
Book ' of Scone tells how Douglas joined with Albany in
the imprisonment and subsequent murder at Falkland of
the Duke of Rothesay (son of Robert III.), who was the
nephew of Albany and the brother-in-law of Douglas,
having married his sister Marjorie. The arms of both
these noblemen appear on the centre pillar. Their arms
appear also on the modern floor on each side of the royal
arms of Scotland, the medallions being copied from old

156

seals. A screen of wrought iron shuts off the aisle from the rest of the church.

On the south side of the church the most westerly chapel or aisle is the Moray Aisle, so called because Regent Moray was buried there. It is larger than the other aisles, and is admirably adapted for the daily service which is held here. There are three windows, one to the late Mr. J. R. Findlay of the *Scotsman*. The second is to the memory of the late Major-General Wauchope, who led the Highland Brigade at Magersfontein and fell at the head of his men. The third window represents the assassination of the Regent, while the lower part shows John Knox preaching his funeral sermon in St. Giles'. This window bears the inscription 'In memory of the Regent Murray, presented by George Stuart, fourteenth Earl of Moray, 1881.' The Moray Aisle also contains a mural shrine dedicated to the Passion of Christ. This shrine, originally in one of the southern aisles, was moved in 1829 to the staircase. In 1879 it was removed to the Moray Aisle, where it may now be seen. It dates from the fifteenth century and has some really beautiful carving. Unfortunately, owing to its position below the window, the carving can only be seen with some difficulty. The carvings represent the crown of thorns, the scourge, the nails, etc., and are symbolic of the Passion. There is also a monument to Regent Moray. It is of Caen stone, and was presented by the then Earl of Moray in 1864. It is quite modern, but the old brass tablet—which has already been mentioned—forms part of the monument. It bears the arms and motto of the Regent, and is moreover adorned with allegorical figures like Religion and Justice, and also with a Latin epitaph composed by Buchanan in praise of the Regent. Near at hand there is also a monument to another great Scotsman—Robert Louis Stevenson. The visitor to St. Giles' is advised not to leave the Moray Aisle without examining the really beautiful embroidery which may be seen there, notably the frontal.

Like the Albany Aisle and St. Eloi's Chapel, the Moray Aisle is enclosed by a wrought-iron screen, the work of Skidmore. Unlike them it is raised considerably above the level of the nave. Outside the screen, but on the floor of the aisle, is a brass tablet which declares that 'near this spot a brave Scotchwoman Janet Geddes . . . struck the first blow in the great struggle for freedom of conscience.' Not far away is a plate let into a pillar: 'To James Hannay, D.D., Dean of this Cathedral . . . erected in happier times by his descendant.'

Brass tablets on the pillars near the organ commemorate Leighton and Gavin Douglas, Provost of St. Giles', Bishop of Dunkeld, son of the Earl of Angus, and 'a distinguished Scottish poet author of a celebrated metrical translation of Virgil.'

The next thing to be noted is the Chepman Aisle. Architecturally it is interesting, but to most people its chief interest is historical. It owes its name to 'the Scottish Caxton,' who is buried there. The arms of Chepman were discovered under the whitewash during the restoration of 1879. A beautiful carving of an eagle may also be seen. The eagle is, of course, the emblem of St. John, and the carving bears the words 'In principio,' the first two words of St. John's Gospel as translated in the Vulgate. There is also a brass tablet which bears the inscription: 'To the memory of Walter Chepman, designated the Scottish Caxton, who, under the auspices of James IV. and his Queen Margaret, introduced the art of printing into Scotland 1507; founded this aisle in honour of the King and Queen and their family 1513; and died in 1532; this tablet is gratefully inscribed by William Chambers, LL.D., 1879.' But interesting as Chepman is to historians and antiquarians it is not to him that the aisle which bears his name owes the interest which it has for the general public. Many people who are fairly well educated know little of the 'Scottish Caxton' beyond his name, some have never even heard of him. But surely the Scotsman does not live who does not know the 'Great Marquess' by name and reputation, and there are few who have not tolerably strong views about him, favourable, or the reverse. It was here that the remains of Montrose were reverently interred at the Restoration. In 1888 the Clan Graham erected a beautiful monument to his memory. The monument consists of an arch covering the recumbent figure of Montrose, which being in white marble shows up well against the black marble bier. The window is filled with the arms of the various branches of the Clan Graham and of the clans allied to it.

Close at hand is the Preston Aisle. It has a groined roof which Dr. Chambers considered the 'Gem of St. Giles'.' He even says, 'The roof of the Preston Aisle as now developed perhaps excels in beauty of groining anything of the kind in Great Britain or in the world.' Unquestionably it is a beautiful example of fifteenth-century work. A small recess is still visible which was completely covered up until the repairs. It is surmised that here the arm-bone of St. Giles was enshrined. Needless to say the Preston arms are prominently displayed in various parts of the aisle. The arms of Sir Patrick Hepburn of Hales—an ancestor of Queen Mary's Bothwell—may also be seen. The Royal Pew is situated here. It is seldom now occupied by royalty, but the Lord High Commissioner repairs here on the opening day of the Assembly to listen to a sermon from the retiring moderator, and here he sits on 'Assembly Sunday' when he comes in state to St. Giles'. Three monuments in the Preston Aisle are worth notice. John William, Earl of Dalhousie, and John Inglis, Lord Glencorse, are more interesting to Scotsmen than to outsiders, but the remaining monument is to a

man who is known throughout the English-speaking
world.

> 'In memory of ARTHUR PENRHYN STANLEY, D.D.
> Dean of Westminster and of the Bath
> Celebrated as a Churchman, Historian, and Divine.
> He loved Scotland and her Church and is therefore
> fitly commemorated here.
> Born Dec. 13, 1815 and died July 18, 1881.
> Charity never faileth.'

It is good to know that we have to some extent out-
lived the sectarian bitterness of the past, and that St.
Giles', which was ministered to by such uncompromising
supporters of ' Christ's Kirk and Covenant' as Balfour
and Henderson, can honour a great Churchman although
he belonged to the national Church across the border,
and not to the Church of Scotland. The difference of
the attitude of Dean Hannay and Dean Stanley towards
Scotland and her Church may possibly be a sign that as
the years go on our national Churches are gaining more
of that ' charity ' which ' never faileth.'

The choir of St. Giles' cannot boast of many objects of
interest. An old arched recess is claimed by some as the
monument to Napier of Merchiston, but it is at least two
centuries too old for that honour. It has, however, been
copied in the monument of the Napiers. The King's
Pillar is also interesting, and the windows, though modern,
are considered good representations of the antique. On
the north side of the choir is the Chambers Aisle, where
the brothers Robert and William Chambers are commemorated. On pillars near the north door are tablets
to three ministers of St. Giles': James Balfour, whose
ministry lasted from 1589 to 1613 and who 'refused to
accept Episcopacy,' John Craig the ex-Dominican, and
Alexander Henderson, ' Statesman, Scholar, Divine,' who
' framed the solemn League and Covenant, presided at
the deposition of the bishops, and sat in the Assembly of
Divines at Westminster.' He is best remembered by the

prominent part he took in framing the Confession of St. Giles'
Faith, especially the Shorter Catechism.

There are also many monuments to Scottish soldiers
who fell in India, Africa, the Soudan, etc.

But nothing in St. Giles' is more interesting or more
characteristic than the display of regimental colours,
frayed with age and torn or discoloured in many a hard-
fought battle. In our more peaceful days they tell us of
our ancestors who fought, not always wisely but always
bravely, and are silent witnesses of the noble deeds done
in the past by Scotsmen. While we are proud of these
tangible proofs of the courage of Scots in the past, we
cannot but rejoice that St. Giles' while still 'the soldier's
church' is also a living proof that national feuds have
long since been buried, and that Scotsmen may rejoice in
the gallantry and devotion shown by Scotsmen on both
sides in the civil wars. It is fitting that this cathedral
church, which stands as the representative of the gospel
of peace and goodwill, should contain tributes to Gavin
Douglas and Regent Moray, to Henderson and Leighton,
to Montrose and Argyle, to Jenny Geddes and Dean
Hannay, and that we may all unite in being proud of what
they dared and did for Scotland.

CHAPTER VII

PARLIAMENT CLOSE

PARLIAMENT CLOSE is a convenient expression for the various objects of interest in the immediate neighbourhood of St. Giles'. It would be more accurate but less convenient to divide the Parliament Close into the divisions of County Square and Parliament Square. Among the many relics of the past the ' Mercat Croce ' is surpassed in interest by none and equalled by few. But the interest is entirely that of association. It has been said with truth that in many of the most interesting parts of Edinburgh there is little to see, but a great deal to think about. Of nothing is this truer than of the Mercat Croce, unless it be the Heart of Midlothian, which is all that remains of the Old Tolbooth. The Cross is interesting as being mainly of ancient workmanship, and has a considerable interest for the antiquarian; but the greater part of its interest is unquestionably historical. Although most of the chief historical incidents connected with it have been already mentioned in earlier chapters, it may be well to indicate them briefly. The Cross seems to have existed in early times, but the first actual reference is in the reign of William the Lion, when we read, ' It is commandit by the King that the merchandises forsaid, and all other merchandises salbe presentit at the Mercat and Mercat Croce of burghis.' Here it is not actually said that Edinburgh had a ' Croce,' but from its size and importance we are justified in concluding

162

MERCAT CROSS

that this was the case. There is a probable reference
also in 1436, when some of the murderers of James I.
were 'mounted on a pillar in the Market Place' of
Edinburgh—in all probability, the pillar of the Cross
is the pillar referred to. We find the Cross explicitly
mentioned in a charter of St. Giles' Church dated 1447:
'ex parte occidentali fori et *crucis* dicti burgi inter

terram domini Wilhelmi Marschale et parte australi,'
etc. In the reign of James III. it became more important,
and from that time on was the scene of festivals, proclamations, and executions: in fact, of all public functions,
grave and gay. Wilson, in his *Memorials of Old Edinburgh*, says it was ' garnished at one period with rich
hangings and flowing with wine for the free use of the
populace, and at another overshadowed by the Maiden
and hung only with the reversed armorial bearings of
some noble victim of law or tyranny.'

The Cross seems to have been built in the prevailing
Gothic style of the day. It was fifteen feet high and
sixteen feet in diameter, and had four angular turrets
and a central pillar. Many people who are comparatively
ignorant of history, know about the Cross from Scott's
description of it in *Marmion* :—

> ' Dun-Edin's Cross, a pillar'd stone,
>   Rose on a turret octagon ;
>   (But now is razed that monument,
>   Whence royal edict rang,
>   And voice of Scotland's law was sent
>   In glorious trumpet-clang.
>   O ! be his tomb as lead to lead,
>   Upon its dull destroyer's head !—
>   A minstrel's malison is said).'

To return to James III. As has already been said, he
was greatly beloved by the citizens, who owed the ' Blue
Blanket' to his favour, and he repaid this by a constant
watchfulness over their interests which earned for him
the hatred of the nobles. We read that in 1477 he
ordered ' alsa all pietricks, pluvaris, capones, conyngs,
checkins and all other wyld foulis and tame to be
usit and sald about the Market Croce and in na other
place.'

In the reign of James IV. the Cross was the scene of
many interesting events. Wine flowed there on the
occasion of the King's marriage, but it had not always

such pleasant associations. Dunbar, in his 'Address to
the Merchants of Edinburgh,' abuses them for neglecting
municipal matters, and says:

> 'At your Hie Cross where gold and silk
> Suld be, there is but cruds and milk';

and his satire is equally pungent when directed against
the West-Country poet Kennedy in the 'Flyting':

> 'Thou bring'st the Carrick clay to Edinburgh corse.'

Leaving these 'flytings,' which were quite as often jest
as earnest, the Cross was the scene of the weird summons
to King James and his army to 'compeir' before 'Plat-
cok,' as has been related in an earlier chapter, along
with the order of the provost's deputy which was read
at the Cross after Flodden.

Sir David Lyndesay being 'Lord Lyon King at Arms'
was closely connected with the Cross, and it is not
surprising to find many references to it in his poems.
Knox's *History of the Reformation* is likewise full of
events which happened at this spot. It was here that
the will of James v. was read by Cardinal Beaton: 'This
was done on Munday at the Market Cross of Edinburgh.'
There is also an account of a skirmish in 1549 between
some French allies of the Queen-Regent and some of the
Reforming party, when, as Knox says, 'two of the French-
men were stricken down and the rest chased from the
Crosse to Nudris-winde heade' (Niddry's Wynd). In
1555 Knox was burned in effigy at the Cross, and the
same year 'a bigging of the Mercat Croce and rowme
thereof' was carried out.

The Cross seems to have been an expensive ornament
at this time. The following entries are to be found in
the accounts of the city treasurer:

> '1561. Item, the 24th day of Marche for ane chenzie
>   of iron to ye branx at ye Croce.

Item for imputtying of ye said chenzie and
ye led to ye mason.

'1562. Item, the laist day of Junii for ane lok to
ye brankis to brank ye sklates yt wantit
ye hand.'

Its varied history of proclamations, fights, feastings, and
punishments went merrily on. At Easter 1565, a priest
was punished for saying Mass at Holyrood. The following is Knox's description. He was 'invested with all
his garments upon him, and so carried to the Market
Crosse, where they set him on high, binding the chalice
in his hands, and himself fast tyed to the said cross,
where he tarried the space of one hour, during which
time the boyes served him with his Easter egges.' One
version declares that he was pelted to death, another
that he was rescued by 'the Provost Archibald Dowglas.'

It was at the Market Cross that Darnley declared he
was innocent of the murder of Rizzio, and here too
Bothwell was accused as the 'principall author, diviser
and actor of the cruell murther of the late King'
(Darnley). One Act which was proclaimed at the Cross
in this reign deserves special notice. It declared that it
was based 'upon the principles of indulgence of conscience and regard to freedom.' Chambers calls this
'the first British Act of Tolerations,' and maintains that
Mary and her advisers deserve the greatest credit for so
enlightened an Act. But Mary's downfall occurred soon
after, and James VI. was proclaimed at the Cross in July
1567, while the following month Moray was proclaimed
Regent. Lennox, Moray's successor, was furious with the
citizens for supplying Kirkaldy with food while he held the
Castle for Queen Mary. Accordingly he arranged to
have a proclamation at the Cross forbidding this practice :
'Bot or he [the pursuivant] culd cry his oyessis he wes
tane by the saidis capitanis suddartis the saidis lettres
tane fra him and he tane to the said castell.' Kirkaldy
replied by a counter-proclamation of a somewhat violent

character: 'If any gentleman undefamit of my qualitie and degree of his factioun or perteining to him will say the contrare hereof, bott I am ane trew Scottisman, I will say he will speak untrewlie and lies falselie in his throat,' etc. But neither brave deeds nor furious words could save Kirkaldy of Grange, and he was hanged at the Cross 'with his face to the sun,' as Knox had already predicted. Morton likewise was executed at the Cross, and here the dead bodies of the Earl of Gowrie and his brother were exposed to view, although the actual execution had taken place at Perth. The Cross played a prominent part in the various state entries James made into Edinburgh, notably on the occasion of his marriage. 'Thus she passed on to the Crosse, upon the topp whereof she had a psalm sung in verie good musicke before her coming to the church.' It was at the Cross that James's extraordinary banquet of reconciliation took place in 1587.

Even the Market Cross witnessed few more important events than the proclamation in 1603 of the death of Queen Elizabeth. It was fitting that this proclamation, with all its far-reaching consequences, should be the last event of importance connected with the old Cross. It was rebuilt in 1617 in honour of the visit of King James. A new 'bodie' was built, but the old pillar was erected on it, so the new Cross was heir to all traditions and associations of the old. The cost of this renovation was £448, 5s. 6d. (Scots). Arnot gives the following description of the Cross as it was till 1756: 'The building was an octagon of sixteen feet diameter, and about fifteen feet high; besides the pillar in the centre, at each angle there was an Ionick pillar, from the top of which a species of Gothick bastion projected; and between the columns there were modern arches. Upon the top of the arch fronting the Netherbow, the town's arms were cut in the shape of a medallion, in rude workmanship; over the other arches, heads also, cut in the shape of a medallion, are placed. These appear to be much older workmanship than the town's arms or any other part of the Cross. Four of these are preserved . . . they are in alto relievo ; the engraving is good, but the Gothick barbarity of the figures themselves bears the appearance of the lower empire. The entry to this building was by a door fronting the Netherbow, which gives access to a stair in the inside leading to a platform on the top of the building. From the platform rose a column consisting of one stone upwards of twenty feet high, and of eighteen inches diameter, spangled with thistles and adorned with a Corinthian capital, upon the top of which was a unicorn.'

James had no reason to complain of his welcome, and the same hospitality was extended to Charles I. on his visit in 1633. We read that on this occasion ' upon the Cross of the town was a show of panisks. Bacchus, crowned with ivy, bestrode a hogshead ; by him stood Silenus, Sylvanus, Pomona, Venus. Ceres in a straw-coloured mantle, embroidered with ears of corn, and a dressing of the same on her head, should have delivered a speech to the King, but was interrupted by Satyrs. She bore a scutcheon upon which was " Sustulit exutis vinclis ad sidera palmas," meaning by the King she was free of the great abuse of the tithes of this country.'

But although the Cross bore its part in the general rejoicing, its other function as a place of execution was never forgotten. Among the many victims both gentle and simple whose names have come down to us few are more interesting than Gilderoy, 'the red-haired lad.' Though not so famous historically as many other victims of law or tyranny, as the case might be, he is a favourite of the balladists, and has thus earned undying fame. Gilderoy's real name was Patrick Macgregor, and he was hanged for ' cattle lifting.' He seems to have resembled Rob Roy not only in his surname, but in his colouring (roy) and in his lawless propensities. He was hanged at

the same time as ten others, but, along with John Forbes,
had the distinction of being hanged on a higher gallows
than the others, and of having his head and hands fixed
on the city gates. One verse of a ballad in his honour
may be quoted :

> ' My love he was a brave man
>   As ever Scotland bred,
> Descended from a Highland clan,
>   A catheran to his trade.
> No woman then or woman kind
>   Had ever greater joy,
> Than we two when we lived alone,
>   I and my Gilderoy.'

Shortly after this the Civil War began, and executions
at the Cross became more and more frequent. Montrose
was executed there in 1650, although shortly before
Charles ii. had been proclaimed King of Scotland at this
same Mercat Croce of Edinburgh. Drastic measures
continued. Nicoll tells how, on February 1652, 'the
Royal Arms were pulled down and the crown that was
on the unicorn was hung upon the gallows by these
treacherous villains.' This seems strong language! He
also gives a painfully circumstantial account of the
punishment inflicted on ' Twa Englisches, for drinking
the Kingis helth.' He gives an equally detailed, but
less horrible, account of a punishment inflicted in 1655
on 'Mr. Patrick Maxwell, ane notorious decevar and
ane intelligencer, sumtyme for the Englisches, uther
tymes for the Scottis, and decevand both of thame.'

Besides criminals and political opponents, *bankrupts*
were punished at the Cross in a somewhat singular
manner. The order for this was passed by the Court of
Session in 1604 : 'The Lordis ordaine the Provest,
Bailleis, and Counsale of Edinburgh, to cause big ane
pillery of hewn stone near to the Mercat Croce of
Edinburgh, upon the heid thereof ane sait and place
to be maid quhairupon, in tyme cuming, sull be set all

169

dyvoris (bankrupts), wha sall sit thairon ane mercat day,
from ten hours in the morning quhill ane hour efter
dinner; and the saidis dyvoris, before thair libertie and
cuming furth of the tolbuith, upon thair awn chairges,
to cause mak or bring ane hat or bonnet of yellow
colour, to be worn be thame all the tyme of their
sitting on the said pillery and in all tyme thairefter,
swa lang as they remane and abide dyvoris.' This en-
actment was afterwards modified. In 1669 'The Lords
declare that the habite is to be a coat and upper garment,
which is to cover their cloaths, body and arms, whereof
the one half is to be of yellow and the other half of
a brown colour, and a cap or hood which they are to
wear on their head, party-coloured as said is conform
to a pattern delivered to the magistrates of Edinburgh
to be keeped in their Tolbooth.' The 'pillery' must
have been a severer ordeal than a modern bankruptcy
court, but perhaps on that account all the more efficacious.

Three proclamations at the Cross followed each other
in somewhat rapid succession. In 1654 Cromwell was
proclaimed Protector of England, Scotland, and Ireland,
in the presence of Monk and a considerable body of
soldiers which 'did compass the Mercat Croce of Edinburgh.' A banquet was held in honour of the great
event, and 'the same day at nicht there was great
preparation for fireworks, which was actit at the Mercat
Croce of Edinburgh betwixt nine and twelve hours in the
necht to the admiration of many people.' Cromwell
died in 1657, and Richard Cromwell was proclaimed
Protector in his stead, 'the mercat croce of Edinburgh
being richlie hung with tapestrie and with all takines
of joy.' But this did not prevent even greater 'takines
of joy' being visible when Charles II. was proclaimed in
1660. Nicoll says this event was celebrated with all
'solemnite requisite, by ringing of bells, setting out
of bail fires, sounding of trumpets, roaring of cannons,

touking of drums, dancing about the fires, and using
all uther taking of joy for the adornment and preferment
of thair native King to his crowne and native inheritance. Quhairat also thair wes much wyne spent, the
spoutes of the croce ryning and venting out abundance
of wyne placed their for that end, and the magistrates
and counsell of the town being present drinking the
King's helth and breking numbers of glasses'; and
farther, 'The Mercat Croce was briskit up with floweris
and grene bransches of treyis, and sum punzeones of
wyne layd on the heid of the Croce, with Bachus set
thairon, and his fellow servandis ministoring unto him,
quha drank lairglie, and distribute full glassis abun-
dantlie casting thame over among the pepile'; and also,
'Efter denner the Magistrates of Edinburgh come throw
the city to the Mercat Croce, quich was gairdit with
a great number of partizens, and thair drank the Kingis
helth upon thair kneyis, and at sindry uther pryme
pairtes of the citie; the nobles also and gentrie did
the lyke at sindry of the bone fyres of the Croce dansing
about thame and drinking thair wyne upon thair knees.'
These festivities involved considerable preparation; accordingly we find a Minute of Council, dated 11th May
1660, ordering 'that the treasurer cause John Scott and
Alexander Skirven prepare upon the Cross pipes of lead
and such other things necessary for running of wyne
at the spouts, and the treasurer to provide wine-glasses
and other necessaries for the said use, with dry con-
fections, with such others as shall be thought needful
and convenient, and sicklike, the treasurer shall provide
eight trumpeters.' Full advantage was taken of these
arrangements, and we read that 'thrie hundreth dosane
of glasses strewed the streets.' Among the various festivities at this time we may notice one: '1662—To wit
in July and August, thair wes sindrie commedois actit,
playing and dancing at the Croce of Edinburgh, upone
towis [ropes], done by strangeris, for quhich and for

droges sauld be thame, thai resavit much money, and
for dancing and volting upon a towe to the admiration
of many.' In striking contrast to these festivities were
the executions at the Cross. Nicoll tells us that 'Upone
the 13 day of Maij 1661, Sir Archibald Johnestoun
of Warystoun, lait Clerk Register, being forfalt in
this Parliament . . . the Lord Lyon King at airmes,
with four hiraldis and sex trumpetteris went to the
Mercat Croce of Edinburgh, and thair maid publict
intimation of his forfaltrie and treason, rave asunder
his airmes [*i.e.* coat of armes] and trampled thame under
thair feet, and kuist a number of thame over the Croce,
and affixt ane of thame upon the height of the great stane,
to remayne thair to the publict view of all beholderis.'

Shortly after, Rutherford's books *Lex Rex* and *The
Causes of God's Wrath* 'were brocht to the Mercat
Croce of Edinburgh and thair oppenlie brint in ane
fyre by the hand of the hangman.' Soon after this,
Argyle was executed at the Cross. While many of the
Covenanters suffered in the Grassmarket, the more
important of them were executed at the Cross, among
them Argyle himself; his son, the Earl of Argyle,
Rev. James Guthrie, Johnstone of Warriston, Hugh
M'Kail, Donald Cargill, and James Renwick.

In 1682 the Solemn League and Covenant was burned
at the Cross, and in 1689 there was another important
proclamation. The Estates 'statute and ordain that
William and Mary, King and Queen of England, France
and Ireland be forthwith proclaimed King and Queen
of Scotland at the Mercat Cross of Edinburgh by
the Lyon King at Arms or his Deputs, his Brethern
Heraulds, Macers and Pursevants, and at the Head-
Burghs of all the Shires, Stewartries, Bailliaries and
Regalities within the Kingdom by messengers at arms.'
In the account of the 'Union' negotiations which occurred nearly twenty years later, it is interesting to find
that one method which was used to recommend the

project to the citizens was the preaching of sermons at the Cross in favour of the Union. Many of the riots at the time of the Union raged round the Cross, but it became once more the scene of an important royal proclamation when, in 1745, Prince Charles Edward had his father proclaimed at the Cross as James VIII. of Scotland. It was at the Cross of Edinburgh that the Highland standards were ignominiously burned after Culloden. But the day of the ancient Cross was almost over. In 1756 it was decided to remove it, as the magistrates considered it obstructed the traffic. It is curious to read the different sentiments expressed on the subject of its removal. Scott's 'Malison' is one. One author speaks of 'the gross perversion of taste and the barbarous absence of all veneration that prevailed in the Scotland of the eighteenth century,' while another says: 'As the old Royalists used to break their glasses after drinking the King's health, so that they should never be used for meaner toasts—soon after the proclamation of the last of the old line of Kings the old Cross was broken up and removed.' We fear the magistrates of that day were guiltless of such loyalty to 'the King over the Water,' and we are quite sure these canny Scots would in any case have considered this extravagance loyalty run mad. It is a beautiful and poetic thought that, in spite of themselves, the city magnates paid this tribute to the old line of Kings, but we fear that the explanation of obstruction of traffic must suffice as the motive which actuated them. A lawyer called Walter Ross annexed some of the medallions and built them into a tower at St. Bernard's, Stockbridge. They afterwards passed into the possession of Scott, who had them built into his garden wall at Abbotsford, where they may still be seen. He also got possession of a stone basin, which he declared to be the veritable fountain which ran wine on occasions of national rejoicing. The pillar deserves some notice. There was an old

prophecy which declared that in time to come the
laverock would bring up its young at the foot of the
Mercat Cross, *i.e.* that the city would be totally destroyed. Though the spirit of the prediction remains—
as yet—unfulfilled, it was carried out to the letter.
Lord Somerville removed the pillar to his country-house
—Drum by name—and there in the depths of the
country the laverock did for more than a century bring
up her young at the foot of the Cross of Edinburgh.
The removal of the Cross caused great dissatisfaction
at the time. The night before its demolition a body
of enterprising young men appeared at the Cross and in
true bacchanalian style solemnly drank 'the dredgie
(dirge) of the auld Mercat Croce.' A poem was published
at this time entitled 'The last speech and dying words
of the Cross of Edinburgh, which was hanged, drawn
and quartered on Monday the 15th of March 1756,
for the horrid crime of being an encumbrance to the
street.' A few extracts of this may be given :—

> ' I was built up in Gothic times
>   And have stood several hundred reigns ;
>   Sacred my mem'ry and my name
>   For Kings and Queens I did proclaim.
>   I peace and war did oft declare,
>   And roused my country everywhere ;
>   On me great men have lost their lives,
>   And for a *maiden* left their wives.
>   Low rogues likeways oft got a peg
>   With turnip—or a rotten egg ; . . .
>
> When the intrepid matchless Charles
>   Came here with many Highland carles,
>   And o'er my top in public sight
>   Proclaimed aloud his Father's Right ;
>   From that day forth it was agreed
>   That I should as a Rebel bleed,
>   And at this time they think it meet
>   To snatch my fabric off the street,
>   Lest I should tell to them once more
>   The tale I told ten years before.'

In spite of the undercurrent of dissatisfaction, no one strongly opposed the proposal; and though many people lamented what had been done, and thought it would be desirable that the Cross should be restored, yet no one was sufficiently interested to undertake the trouble and expense which such restoration would involve. The site of the Cross was marked by the stones of the 'causey.' Business was still transacted 'at the Cross,' the furniture of people who were sold up was 'roupit at the Cross,' and Royal Proclamations were still made there. In 1885, however, Mr. Gladstone, then M.P. for Midlothian, restored the Cross at his own charges. The ancient pillar had been previously brought to Edinburgh, and was used in the structure of the new Cross. The eight medallions at Abbotsford were not available, so eight others were made bearing the following devices: 1. The Arms of the United Kingdom as quartered in Scotland. 2. The Arms of Scotland. 3. The Arms of England. 4. The Arms of Ireland. 5. The Arms of the City of Edinburgh copied from one of the medallions at Abbotsford. 6. The Arms of the Burgh of Canongate. 7. The Arms of the Town of Leith. 8. The Arms of the University of Edinburgh. The Arms of Mr. and Mrs. Gladstone likewise appear, also a Latin inscription written by Mr. Gladstone himself which may be seen on the Cross. It has been thus translated: 'Thanks to God, this ancient monument, the Cross of Edinburgh, which of old was set apart for public ceremonies, having been utterly destroyed by a misguided hand A.D. MDCCLVI, and having been avenged as well as lamented, in song alike noble and manful, by that great man Walter Scott, has now by favour of the Magistrates of the City been restored by William Ewart Gladstone, who claims, through both parents, a purely Scottish descent, 23rd November 1885.' If it cannot be claimed for the present Cross that its existence is as full of excitement as was that of its predecessors, it is still the

scene of all proclamations of importance. It was here
that Edward VII. was proclaimed on a snowy morning in
January 1901. On other occasions it stands reminding
us by its very presence of 'the brave days of old.'

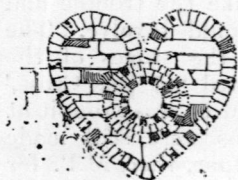

The Heart of Midlothian

Another relic of the past
quite near the Cross is the
pattern of a heart traced on
the pavement, which may be
seen just outside the west door
of St. Giles'. This is all that
remains of the old Tolbooth
of Edinburgh so familiar to
readers of the *Heart of Midlothian*. A prison has not
usually a cheerful aspect, but the Tolbooth seems
to have been specially awe-inspiring. One writer describes it as 'antique in form, gloomy and haggard in
aspect, its black stanchioned windows opening through
its dingy walls like the apertures of a hearse, it was
calculated to impress all beholders with a sense of what
was meant in Scottish law by the "squalor carceris."'
At the west end of the hall of the old Tolbooth was
hung a board containing verses which thus described
it:—

'A prison is a house of care,
　A place where none can thrive,
A touchstone true to try a friend,
　A grave for men alive.

Sometimes a place of right,
　Sometimes a place of wrong,
Sometimes a place for jades and thieves,
　And honest men among.'

Scott, writing about the time it was demolished, thus
describes it : 'The ancient prison . . . rears its ancient front
in the very middle of the High Street, forming, as it
were, the termination to a huge pile of buildings called

176

the Luckenbooths, which for some inconceivable reason our ancestors had jammed into the midst of the principal street of the town, leaving for passage a narrow street on the north; and on the south, into which the prison opens, a narrow crooked lane, winding betwixt the high and sombre walls of the Tolbooth, and the adjacent houses on one side, and the buttresses and

The Tolbooth

projections of the old Cathedral upon the other. To give some gaiety to this sombre passage (well known by the name of the Krames), a number of little booths or shops after the fashion of cobblers' stalls are plastered, as it were, against the Gothic projections and abutments, so that it seemed as if the traders had occupied with nests, bearing the same proportion to the building, every buttress and coign of vantage, as the martlett did in Macbeth's Castle. Of later years these booths have degenerated into mere toy-shops, where the little loiterers chiefly interested in such wares are tempted to linger, enchanted by the rich display of hobby-horses, babies, and Dutch toys, arranged in artful and gay confusion; yet half-scared by the cross looks of the withered pantaloons, or spectacled old lady, by whom these tempting stores are watched and superintended. But, in the times we write of, the hosiers, the glovers, the hatters, the mercers, the milliners, and all who dealt in the miscellaneous wares now termed haberdasher's goods, were to be found in this narrow alley.' It is curious to read Scott's description of the Krames in what he called modern days, and to realise how utterly things have changed since then.

M

In old charters the Tolbooth is described as the 'Pretorium burgi de Edinburgh.' Maitland mentions the tradition that it was originally the residence of the Provost of St. Giles' only to disprove it (or rather to try to disprove it), but the general consensus of opinion seems to be that it was connected in some way with the church. The site is an argument in favour of this supposition, and the style of architecture was in accordance with that usually employed for collegiate buildings connected with a church. All the evidence goes to prove that it was built in the reign of James III. about the time when St. Giles' was made into a collegiate church. We find some curious references to it in old charters, *e.g.* in 1477 James III. granted a charter to the town in which the market for corn and grain is ordered to be held 'fra the Tolbuth up to Libbertones Wynd.' The regulation brings us to the original meaning of the word 'Tolbooth,' viz. a tax-house. It is supposed that there was even an earlier building than the one which was taken down in 1817, and that it was this earlier building where parliaments were held in 1438, 1449, and 1459. In 1438 the name Tolbooth is used for the first time, 'the parleament of ane richt hie and excellent prince, and our soverane lorde, James the Secunde, by the grace of Gode King of Scotts, haldyn at Edinburgh, the begunyn in the Tolbuth of the samyn.' In 1561 Queen Mary issued a mandate : 'The Queiny's Majestie understanding that the Tolbuith of the Burgh of Edinburgh is ruinous and abill haistielie to dekay and fall doun, quhilk will be varray dampnable and skaythfull to the pepill dwelland thairabout . . . without heistie remeid be providit thairin. Thairfor her Heines ordinis ane masser to pass and charge the Provest, Baillies, and Counsale, to caus put workmen to the taking doun of the said Tolbuith with all possible diligence.' This order was considerably modified. The very oldest parts of the Tolbooth probably were taken down, but most of it

178

remained. A new building was, however, erected, standing close to St. Giles's Church, and quite apart from the older erection. The Tolbooth was divided into east and west ends, like a modern city.

The Tolbooth shared with the Netherbow Port the doubtful honour of being adorned with the heads of those executed for political offences. Among other celebrated victims it bore the heads of Morton in 1580, and of Montrose from 1650 to 1661, when the head of Argyle replaced it. The Tolbooth is, however, chiefly memorable as a prison, and it is remarkable in two ways —the number of celebrated persons who were confined there, and the number of even more celebrated escapes. Some of the entries are curious enough. '1662, June 10, Robert Binning for falsehood ; hanged with the false papers about his neck.' '1663, March 13, Alexander Kennedy, hanged for raising false bonds and writs.' 'Aucht Quakers, liberated certifying if again troubling the place, the next prison shall be the Correction House.' 'July 8, Katherine Reid, hanged for theft. July 8, Sir Archibald Johnstone of Warriston, treason. Hanged, his head cut off and placed on the Netherbow.' 'August 25, the Provost of Kirkcudbright, banished for keeping his house during a tumult.' '1728, October 25, John Gibson, forging a declaration 18th January 1727. His lug nailed to the Tron and dismissed.' The grammar, or rather want of grammar, in this last sentence is delightful. An exciting incident happened in the Tolbooth when James VI. was hearing the divorce case of the Laird of Craigmillar. James's reckless kinsman, the Earl of Bothwell, carried off one of the chief witnesses, and no one was able to interfere. It was here that the Countess of Abercorn was confined on the charge of being a 'Papist.' Her health suffered to such an extent that she was allowed to go to Bristol, and finally was sent home again in 1631, as we should say, on bail, as she was ordered to 'reset no Jesuits,' and to return if

necessary under a penalty of 5000 merks. It was in the
Tolbooth, too, that Mrs. Macleod, the skilful forger, was
shut up. In 1726 great excitement was caused in Edinburgh by a trial for forgery. A wealthy merchant named
Henderson was accused of having forged a bill for £58
on the Duchess of Gordon, which bill he had endorsed to
Mrs. Macleod, the wife of a Leith wigmaker. Henderson denied the charge, but witnesses whose testimony
was beyond suspicion swore that they had been present
when Henderson signed the bill. The Lord Advocate—
Duncan Forbes of Culloden—demanded Henderson's condemnation, and his death would inevitably have followed
had not a mere accident revealed the fact that Mrs.
Macleod had induced a workman called Household to
personate Henderson for that purpose. *Her* execution
followed as a matter of course, but she met her fate with
the most undaunted courage and died protesting her
innocence.

It has already been remarked that many celebrated
people escaped from the Tolbooth. It is a curious fact
that almost all of these were people of rank who doubtless made it worth while for the officials to assist them.
But, indeed, the Tolbooth cannot have been a very secure
' place for retaining evil-doers.' We actually read of
criminals taking refuge there from pursuit. Among
others who sought this extraordinary place of safety
were Mitchell, after his attempt to assassinate the Archbishop of St. Andrews, and Robert Ferguson, best known
by the sobriquet of ' the Plotter.' On both these occasions the city gates were closed and strict search was
made throughout the town, but naturally no one thought
of criminals taking refuge in prison, the place they—
presumably—wanted to avoid. Another instance was
that of a Jacobite gentleman who in 1746 was quietly
sheltering in the Tolbooth while the Highlands were
being searched by the King's agents for him.

One of the first recorded escapes was that of James

Gillon, a cordiner's servant, who joined in the frolic of 'Robin Hood and Lord of Inobedience' in 1561 after these sports had been forbidden by the magistrates and clergy of Edinburgh. For this he was condemned to be hanged—rather hard measure for such a venial offence. However, on the appointed day, the mob armed with spears, hand-guns, and axes, seized and imprisoned the Provost and two Bailies, broke up the gibbet, forced open the doors of the Tolbooth, and brought out the prisoner in triumph. In 1689 Lord Burleigh was carried out of the Tolbooth in a trunk. The porter who took him out was not in the secret and carried him head downwards, and, worse still, threw the trunk violently on the ground when asked by a friend to 'have a glass.' Lord Burleigh's shrieks startled the porter, who thereupon opened the box and found that the unhappy prisoner had fainted. The inevitable crowd speedily gathered and the City Guard promptly came up, with the result that Lord Burleigh soon afterwards was taken back to the Tolbooth. The Douglas *Peerage*, however, declares that he eventually escaped disguised in his sister's clothes—but some writers are rather doubtful of this second escape. The Tolbooth was also the scene of the attempted escape of Wilson and Robertson (the smugglers who were the original cause of the Porteous Riot), and the actual escape of some of their friends. They cut the iron bars of their window and covered the necessary noise by singing psalms. One of the prisoners escaped and Robertson wished to follow him. Wilson, however, insisted on going first. Being—as the *Caledonian Mercury* describes him—'a squat round man,' he stuck fast in the window and could neither go back nor forward. In this awkward position he was discovered by his gaolers, thus putting an end to all hope of escape either for himself or for Robertson. In an earlier chapter (Chapter III) we have already related the generous manner in which he finally effected Robertson's escape beneath the eyes of the soldiers and of the congregation of St. Giles'.

Another noted escape from the Tolbooth was that of Katherine Nairne, daughter of Sir Robert Nairne of Dunsinane. She had been married—when a girl of nineteen—to Ogilvie of Eastmilne, and was now imprisoned on the charge of having poisoned him, the reason alleged being that she was in love with his brother Patrick, a lieutenant in the Gordon Highlanders, who was her accomplice in the poisoning case. They were both tried and condemned, and Patrick Ogilvie was hanged in the Grassmarket in spite of the endeavours of his friends to procure his pardon. The execution of Katherine Nairne was deferred owing to the birth of her child,—and deferred to some purpose. Her nurse, Mrs. Shields, for some days pretended that she was suffering agonies from toothache, and went in and out of the Tolbooth with her face wrapped in flannel. One evening when the warders were accustomed to seeing her in this condition Katherine Nairne changed clothes with her, and appeared in the usual head-dress of shawls and flannels groaning from the agony of her toothache. So little was the disguise suspected that one of the warders jocosely slapped her back, called her 'a howling old Jezebel,' and hoped she would trouble him no longer. She escaped to James's Court, but in her perturbation she knocked at the wrong door—that of Lord Alva instead of that of her father's agent. She was recognised, and immediately a hue and cry was raised. She fled with great rapidity down a neighbouring close, and hid for some time quite near the Tolbooth in a cellar belonging to her uncle, an advocate, who afterwards became Lord Dunsinane. She was then taken to Dover by one of her uncle's clerks, who must have had an anxious journey, as, owing to her excessive frivolity, he was in constant dread of discovery. From Dover she escaped to the Continent, and from there she safely reached America, where she lived and died. She married again, and is said to have died 'surrounded by a numerous and attached family.' Mrs. Shields continued to practise her profession in Edinburgh till 1805, and was not averse to relating this romantic story which reflected so much credit on her own adroitness, though she always maintained ' there were other folks besides her could tell the same tale,' meaning that the Lord Advocate and other authorities were quite glad the prisoner should escape.

In 1770 Mungo Campbell escaped from the Tolbooth in a less auspicious manner—*i.e.* by committing suicide when under sentence of death.

The last of the escapes from the Tolbooth took place in 1783. James Hay, the son of a stabler in the Grassmarket, lay under sentence of death for stealing. His father visited him a few days before the date fixed for the execution, and produced some liquor which he invited the turnkey to share. When it was finished the turnkey went out for some more, and young Hay slipped out behind him, unnoticed by the tipsy turnkeys. He then fled to Greyfriars, climbed the wall and took refuge in ' Bluidy Mackenzie's ' mausoleum. The following advertisement appeared in the *Edinburgh Advertiser*, 24th November 1783 :—

'Escaped from the Tolbooth of Edinburgh, James Hay indicted for highway robbery, aged about 18 years, by trade a glazier, 5 feet 10 inches high, slender made, pale complexion, long visage, brown hair cut short, pitted a little in the face with the small-pox, speaks slow with a *hoar* in his tone and has a mole on one of his cheeks. The magistrates offer a reward of Twenty Guineas to any person who will apprehend and secure the said James Hay, to be paid by the City Chamberlain on the said James Hay being re-committed to the Tolbooth of this city.'

It was impossible for James Hay's father to attempt to communicate with his son, much less to supply him

183

with food as his every movement was carefully watched.
Yet if he was left to his own resources he would inevitably starve. Fortunately for himself he had been at
Heriot's Hospital, and when the schoolboys heard of his
plight they determined to help him. Abstract questions
of right and wrong never appeal much to schoolboys ;
esprit de corps, and any question touching the honour of
the school, emphatically do. Accordingly for six weeks
they supplied him with food, braving alike punishment from the authorities of the school or the law if
discovered, and the more intangible but equally real
terrors of supernatural visitors in the churchyard, as
their visits had to be paid at night. At the end of six
weeks Hay ventured out of his hiding-place and escaped
to England.

Howard visited the Tolbooth in 1782 and was greatly
distressed by its condition, which was indeed squalid in
the extreme. Arnot, in his *History of Edinburgh,* gives
an appalling picture of its horrors. In 1787 Howard
returned, and was much disappointed to find no improvement in this 'House of Care.' In 1817, however, the
magistrates decided not to 'mend' but to 'end' it, and
accordingly ordered it to be taken down. That, of
course, involved clearing away the Luckenbooths. The
Edinburgh of that day was delighted with the result.
A writer in the *Edinburgh Review* thus describes the
result of these proceedings : 'Now that the Luckenbooths have been safely carted to Leith Wynd (would
that it had been done some dozen years ago !) and the
Tolbooth—to the unutterable delight of the inhabitants
—is journeying quickly to Fettes Row, there to be transformed into common sewers and drains, the irregular
and grim visage of the Cathedral has been in a great
measure unveiled.' That this 'improvement' did not
commend itself so much to unprejudiced outsiders is
shown by Turner's well-known remark that 'the *old*
High Street of Edinburgh was only surpassed in Europe

by that of Oxford.' One part of the Tolbooth escaped the 'base uses' to which the other parts were put, viz. the old door, which was removed to Abbotsford by Sir Walter Scott. In a note written in 1830 he says: 'Last year, to complete the change, a tomtit was pleased to build her nest within the lock of the Tolbooth, a strong temptation to have committed a sonnet.' Of the old Tolbooth, so closely bound up with the life and history of the city, not a vestige now remains; a heart traced on the pavement near St. Giles' is the only visible reminder of 'The Heart of Midlothian.'

Another relic of bygone days, of which hardly a trace remains, is the St. Giles Churchyard. In olden days this extended from St. Giles' to the Cowgate, where it was bounded by a wall and the Chapel of the Holy Rood, built, Arnot tells us, 'in memory of Christ crucified.' This chapel remained till the end of the sixteenth century, when it was destroyed by the Reformers. One writer says that among those who lie in St. Giles' Churchyard are 'old citizens who remembered the long-haired King David passing forth with barking hound and twanging horn on that Rood-day in harvest which so nearly cost him his life; and how the fair Queen Margaret daily fed the poor at the Castle gate "with the tenderness of a mother"; those who had seen Randolph's patriots scale "the steep, the iron-belted rock," Count Guy of Namur's Flemish lances routed on the Burghmuir, and William Wallace mustering his bearded warriors by the Figgate-burn ere he marched to storm Dunbar.' There, too, lie those who helped to sustain the courage of Edinburgh after Flodden, who lived through the disasters of Solway Moss and Pinkie Cleugh, and who witnessed the Reformation and the sorrows of Queen Mary. But there the line stops, for, after the Reformation, the St. Giles Churchyard was hardly used at all. There are four epoch-making dates in its history. In 1496 the Provost of St. Giles' granted part of his glebe to increase the available space of the cemetery. In 1528 Walter Chepman, 'The Scottish Caxton,' endowed a chaplaincy for the Chapel of Holy Rood ; in 1559 the chapel was pulled down, and in 1562 its débris were used to build the new Tolbooth. The effect of this on the churchyard is not at once obvious, but a moment's reflection makes it clear. In olden days the churchyard was 'a haunt of ancient peace,' sloping down towards the south from the church to the chapel, lying towards the sun, and surrounded only by buildings dedicated to the service of God. But in later days belligerent litigants, chattering lackeys, and magnificent young nobles took the place of the old priests who formerly paced the quiet paths of 'God's Acre.' What wonder that men could hardly realise that this was consecrated ground, or that they speedily availed themselves of Queen Mary's charter, which, in 1566, granted the gardens of the Greyfriars monastery to be used by the citizens as a place of interment. The last notice we have of St. Giles Churchyard is painfully characteristic of its new character. Calderwood, describing the famous street tumult of 1596, says : ' The noblemen, barons and gentlemen that were in the kirk went forth at the alarum, and were likewise in their armes. The Earl of Mar and the Lord Halyrudhous went out to the barons and ministrie, conveened in the Kirkyard. Some hote speeches passt betwixt the Earl of Mar and the Lord Lindsey so that they could not be pacified for a long tyme.' Scenes like these are sufficient to account for the desertion of the churchyard in favour of the more secluded Greyfriars.

They are not, however, sufficient to account for the disgraceful fact that the churchyard soon became a public thoroughfare, and paving-stones covered over the last resting-place of many citizens of Edinburgh. It was here that John Knox was buried in 1572, in the presence of nobles and citizens, his epitaph pronounced by the Regent. Yet in the lifetime of many of those

who were present on that occasion the churchyard
became a thoroughfare and a promenade. If it is a
national reproach to us that we care
less than other nations for the seemly
ordering of churchyards, it is surely
true that nowhere, even in Scotland,
is there a greater scandal than this.
It does not make matters better—on
the contrary, rather worse—to reflect
that Blackfriars, the Kirk o' Field,
Trinity College, St. Roque's, and St.
Leonard's Churchyards all shared the
same fate. We understand that in all these places human
bones are still to be found by those who dig deeply.
The traditional grave of Knox is marked by a small stone
let into the pavement bearing the simple inscription :

John Knox's Grave

'I.K.
1572.'

Wilson, speaking of this, says : 'The churchyard has
long since been paved and converted into Parliament
Square, and all evidence of the spot lost. It cannot
but excite surprise that no effort should have been
made to preserve the remains of the Reformer from such
desecration, or to point out to posterity the site of
his resting-place. If the tradition mentioned by
Chambers may be relied upon, that his burial-place was
a few feet from the front of the old pedestal of King
Charles's statue, the recent change in the position of the
latter must have placed it directly over his grave,—
perhaps as strange a monument to the Great Apostle of
Presbyterianism as fancy could devise !' This statue
needs a few words of explanation. It represents the
Merry Monarch on horseback and was erected in his
honour in 1685. A correspondent of the *Caledonian
Mercury*, November 10, 1788, gives some useful information thereanent. 'The statue of Charles II. placed on
187

the spot intended for that of Cromwell, and superior to everything of the kind in Britain, is said by Maitland to have been erected at the expense of the citizens. If he means it was a contribution for the purpose, it is a mistake. The statue was placed by the Magistrates and Council. In the accounts of George Drummond, the Town Treasurer, in 1684-5, he charges £2580 Scots (£215 sterling), the contents of a bill of exchange drawn by " James Smith upon him, for the price of King Charles II. his statue." The bill seems to have come from Rotterdam.' In 1824 a serious fire broke out and destroyed a large part of Parliament Close. During the rebuilding of this, the statue of King Charles was deported to the Calton, and remained in durance vile for several years. Eventually, however, the statue was restored, with the addition of a pedestal and two marble tablets found among some rubbish in Parliament House, which tablets set forth Charles's virtues in no measured terms. It is rather odd that this statue should have escaped violence at the hands of the mob in 1688, but it can be accounted for by the fact that Charles himself was always popular with the common people, who expended their hatred on those who carried out his policy—on Lauderdale, Sharp, Dalzell, Grierson of Lag, and Claverhouse—with what justice students of history must decide. The statue remains here to the present day beside the grave of Knox, though R. L. Stevenson makes the characteristic remark that 'the King has his back turned, and as you look, seems to be trotting clumsily away from such a dangerous neighbour.'

Close by is Parliament House itself, once the scene of old Scottish Parliaments when Scotland *had* a Parliament, now that useful but unromantic institution, a Court of Law. It cannot claim great antiquity, for it was not built till 1639, but it can claim a great deal of historical and human interest. Shortly after it was finished in 1639 its eventful history began. Montrose in his covenanting days consulted with Loudon and Rothes and Lindsay on matters of policy, and in this very hall some years later he received sentence from his former allies. After Dunbar¦the unfamiliar figures of English soldiers haunted Parliament House. Their first duty was to guard the prisoners of war who were confined in the 'laigh Parliament House,' but they varied this monotonous task by holding forth in the Parliament Hall to the people who assembled to hear them. Possibly this relaxation made them careless in attending to their duty, certainly all the prisoners but two contrived to escape in May 1654. The following year Monk and some of the English Puritans were hospitably entertained to a banquet, and in 1660 another banquet was given, this time to the Duke of Albany and York, who along with his wife and daughters came to represent King Charles on the occasion of the Restoration. After the Restoration sadder associations follow. In the 'laigh Parliament House' the Privy Council met to try and condemn Covenanters and to put them to torture. This was the time when the Lord Advocate, Sir George Mackenzie of Rosehaugh, gained such unpleasant notoriety. Some of the Covenanters bore their sufferings in calm and heroic silence, others referred in unflattering terms to the King or his representatives. One of this latter class was Forman, who addressed General Dalzell as 'A Muscovia beast who used to roast men,' and referred to the Privy Council as 'bloody murderers and papists . . . charging all the Parliamenters . . . to put away that sinful man [the Duke of York] or else the judgments of God were ready to break upon the land.' The whole story may be found in Fountainhall's memoirs. It was in Parliament House that 'to the Lords of Convention twas Claverhouse spoke,' when he vainly attempted to recall them to their allegiance to King James, and it was here that the uncompromising Scottish Convention declared that King James had 'forfeited his crown.' Here too discussions waxed long and loud in

189

connection with the Darien affair. 1700 nearly saw the last of Parliament House, for it narrowly escaped destruction in the 'Great Fire' of that year. Duncan Forbes of Culloden, writing to his brother, gives a graphic account of its ravages. 'The Parliament House very hardly escapt, all registers confounded, clerks' chambers and processes in such a confusion that the lords and officers of state are just now met in Rosse's tavern in order to adjourning of the sessione, by reason of the dissorder. Few people are lost, if any at all; but there was neither heart nor hand left amongst them for saveing from the fyre, nor a drop of water in the cisterns; 20,000 hands flitting ther trash they knew not wher, and hardly 20 at work; these babells of ten and fourteen story high, are down to the ground, and their fall very terrible. Many rueful spectacles such as Crossrig, naked with a child under his oxter, hopping for his lyffe; the Fish Mercate and all from the Cowgate to Pett-streets Close, burnt; the Exchange, vaults and coal-cellars under the Parliament Close are still burning.'

In the minds of most people, however, old Parliament House is associated—as its name implies—with the meetings of the Scottish Parliament. In these prosaic days when little of old ceremonial survives, it is interesting to try and picture to ourselves the aspect of Edinburgh when it was the seat of the legislature instead of being merely the nominal capital of Scotland. Every year the ceremony called 'the Riding of Parliament' took place—that was the riding in state from Holyrood Palace to Parliament House. Arnot gives a graphic account of the procedure on the 6th of May 1703. The streets were cleared and guarded by the Scottish Horse, Grenadier Guards (who were nearest the Palace), the Scottish Foot Guards, the trained bands of the city, and the Guards of the Lord High Constable and of the Earl Marischal. The members of Parliament met at Holyrood and were called out by the Lord Clerk

Register, while the Lord Lyon King at Arms and the heralds sounded the trumpets. The order of the procession was as follows :—

Two mounted trumpeters with coats and banners, bareheaded.

Two pursuivants in coats and foot mantles, ditto.

Sixty-three Commissioners for burghs on horseback, two and two, each having a lackey on foot, the odd number walking alone.

Seventy-seven Commissioners for shires, mounted and covered, each having two lackeys on foot.

Fifty-one Lord Barons in their robes, riding two and two, each having a gentleman to support his train, and three lackeys on foot wearing above their liveries velvet coats with the arms of their respective Lords on the breast and back embossed on plate or embroidered in gold or silver.

Nineteen Viscounts as the former.

Sixty Earls as the former.

Four Trumpeters, two and two.

Four pursuivants, two and two.

The heralds, Islay, Ross, Rothesay, Albany, Snowdon and Marchmont in their tabards, two and two, bareheaded.

The Lord Lyon King at Arms, in his tabard, with chain, robe, bâton and foot mantle.

The Sword of State, borne by the Earl of Mar.

The Sceptre, borne by the Earl of Crawford.

THE CROWN
borne by the Earl of Forfar.

The purse and commission, borne by the Earl of Morton.

THE DUKE OF QUEENSBERRY, LORD HIGH COMMISSIONER,

with his servants, pages, and footmen.

Four Dukes, two and two.

Gentlemen bearing their trains and each having eight lackeys.

Six Marquises, each having six lackeys.

The Duke of Argyle, Colonel of the Horse Guards.

A Squadron of Horse Guards.

Three macers.   *Three macers.*

The Lord High Constable and the Earl Marischal received the Lord High Commissioner and led him to the throne. The Usher of the White Rod followed them, and then, with every token of honour, the Regalia were laid on the table. Such was the ceremony entitled riding in state. Shorn of much of its glory it still remains, though in a somewhat different form. Every year, on the occasion of the opening of the General Assembly, the Lord High Commissioner rides in state to St. Giles' and thence to the Assembly Hall. The ceremony has but a shadow of its former magnificence, yet 'the procession,' as it is called, has still considerable interest, and loyal citizens can never forget that the Lord High Commissioner is His Majesty's representative.

It was in the hall of Parliament House that those stirring debates took place on the subject of the Union, which have been described in an earlier chapter (Chapter III). Unquestionably, without bribery, the Union would never have been carried through; but, as Daniel Wilson remarks, 'happily for Scotland, English bribes outweighed the mistaken zeal of Scottish patriotism and Jacobitism united against the measure.' It cannot, however, have been pleasant for the recipients of the said bribes when the indefatigable Lockhart discovered and published the sum that each received. The following is the list :—The Lord High Commissioner (Queensberry) received £12,325; the Earl of Marchmont £1104, 15s. 7d.; the Duke of Athole and the Marquis of Tweeddale £1000; the Duke of Roxburgh and the Earl of Balcarres £500; the Earl of Seafield £490; the Earl of Cromarty, Lord Anstruther, Stewart of Castle Stewart, and Sir William Sharp £300; Lord Prestonhall, Lord Ormiston (Lord Justice-Clerk), the Duke of Montrose, the Earl of Dunmore, the Earl of Eglinton, the Earl of Kintore, and Mr. John Campbell £200; Lord Fraser, the Earl of Forfar, Sir Kenneth Mackenzie, the Earl of Glencairn, the Earl of Findlater, John Muir, Provost of Ayr, and Major Cunningham of

Eikate £100; Mr. Alexander Wedderburn £75; the
bearer of the Treaty of Union £60; Lord Cessnock,
Lord Forbes, and Lord Elibank £50; Coultrain, Provost
of Wigtown £25; and Lord Banff £11, 12s.: total
£20,540, 17s. 7d. Even Queensberry with his £12,325
hardly seems so contemptible as Lord Banff, selling what
he believed to be his country's liberty for £11, 12s.

Parliament House is now the scene of the sittings of the
Court of Session and of the High Court of Justiciary, and
is frequented by advocates instead of politicians. As we
enter the great hall, the faces of well-known lawyers look
down on us, and we realise that for most people the
associations of this hall have reference to Duncan Forbes
or Lord Monboddo, Scott, Cockburn, or Jeffrey, rather
than to Lord Belhaven, the Duke of Hamilton, 'Union'
Queensberry, or Lockhart of Carnwath. The aspect of
'Old Parliament House' is well known, both from
illustrations of old books and from the fact that it
appeared on the bank-notes of Sir William Forbes and
Co. It was built in the style so prevalent in the
seventeenth century, which appears in those parts of
Holyrood dating from that time. It abounded in
pinnacles and towers, and quaint devices and Latin
inscriptions. Over the main doorway the royal arms
were supported by Justice and Mercy. Above was the
inscription *Stant his felicia regna*, and below were the
words *Uni unionum*. The city arms were placed above
another doorway, and above them were the words *Dominus custodit introitum nostrum*. It is in connection with
the figure of Justice, referred to above, that a story is told
about Robertson of Kincraigie, a Jacobite laird, said by
some to be insane. If this is so, it must be confessed his
smartness of repartee might be useful to some who are
supposed to enjoy the full use of their faculties. On
being asked to go into the Parliament House by Henry
Erskine he promptly declined, adding, 'But I'll tell you
what, Harry: tak' in Justice wi' ye, for she has stood lang

at the door, and it wad be a treat for her to see the
inside like other strangers.' What a disquisition on the
distinction between law and equity is conveyed here by
the word 'stranger'! Justice no longer guards the door;
she, along with Mercy, was carted away as 'old rubbish'
during the renovations. The great hall is the chief
beauty of the present Parliament House. It is 120 feet
long by 50 feet wide and 60 feet high, and has a really
beautiful carved wood roof, not unlike that of Westminster Hall. Advocates in gowns and wigs pace up and
down, discussing business with agents, or conducting
friends round the sacred precincts, or discussing current
topics. What marvel that current topics are occasionally
'improved' out of recognition, or that tales about Edinburgh celebrities can usually be traced to Parliament
House!

The stained glass window which fills the south end of
the hall represents the founding of the College of Justice
by James v. in 1532. It must not be forgotten that the
College of Justice is to be kept quite distinct from its
present abode; it existed long before Parliament House,
and was only transferred there when that building was no
longer needed for its original purpose. The window,
which is handsome rather than beautiful, dates only
from 1868. It is said to have cost £2000. The side
windows show the arms of various legal luminaries.
There are some fine pictures by Raeburn and Sir Daniel
Macnee, and also some good examples of statuary—notably, Henry, first Viscount Melville, by Chantrey, and
Duncan Forbes of Culloden (Lord Advocate and finally
Lord President), by Roubiliac. Among others who are
represented, either by portrait or by statue, are Henry
Erskine, Henry Cockburn, Francis Jeffrey, and 'Bluidy
Mackenzie,' the only pre-Revolution worthy in this
picture gallery. It must be admitted, however, that to
the ordinary man and woman outside of Scotland Forbes
and Mackenzie are but names, while Jeffrey and Cockburn

are literary men whom they know about, but with whose works they are not closely acquainted. But at least two Scottish advocates are known intimately wherever the English language is spoken, and to lovers of literature it seems strange that there is no sign either by picture or by statue that Scott and Stevenson were members of the Faculty of Advocates. It must, however, be remembered that Stevenson was not noted for his success at the Bar, and if Scott is not represented here it is not because he is forgotten. His favourite seat at the fire is still shown, his statue is to be seen in the Advocates' Library, and some original manuscripts are a prized possession of this same library.

The three principal legal bodies have their respective libraries within the precincts of Parliament House. The Library of the Solicitors before the Supreme Courts is housed in a handsome building which is built of red stone and rises from the Cowgate. It is new, and, it must be confessed, somewhat uninteresting. The Signet Library, which possesses some valuable old books, is kept in the north-west portion of Parliament House. Most interesting of all is the Advocates' Library, which was founded by Sir George Mackenzie in the seventeenth century. It is kept in the Laigh Parliament House, where the Covenanters were 'put to the question.' This library, along with the Bodleian, the British Museum, and the Library of Trinity College, Dublin, is presented with a free copy of every book published. Naturally it has attained considerable dimensions, and is said to have over 400,000 books and manuscripts. Among the most interesting are the Confession of Faith, signed by James VI. (known as the 'King's Confession'), the Covenant, letters of James V., of Queen Mary, of Charles II. and of James II., a copy of St. Augustine which belonged to Georges d'Amboise, and many curious old black-letter editions of books, missals, and breviaries illuminated and transcribed by the patient labour of monks of bygone days. Some

195

of these seem strange possessions for a court of law,
but no one can deny the appropriateness of the Advocates'
Library possessing the original manuscript of *Waverley*.
A seated statue of 'The Shirra' bearing the words 'Sic
sedebat' completes the scene. We feel that it is he who
invested Parliament House with the interest that it has
for us. The advocates and judges of bygone days, Lord
Monboddo and Lord Hailes and Braxfield, the 'hanging
judge,' and all the rest, were famous men, and doubtless
served their generation according to their several abilities.
But it is not their ghosts who haunt the Court; we do
not see it peopled by them, but by Saddletree and Effie
Deans and 'Poor Peter Peebles' and Alan Fairford, and
the other creations of this wonderful man who well earned
his sobriquet of the 'Wizard of the North.'

John Knox's House

CHAPTER VIII

CASTLEHILL, THE LAWNMARKET, AND HIGH STREET

The Upper West Bow

THE High Street of Edinburgh was, as its name indicates, the chief thoroughfare of the ancient city. Strange as it seems to us now, it must have occupied the position in the Old Town that Princes Street does in the New. Relics of former greatness still survive, and it is not uncommon to find beautiful old oak panelling covered over with whitewash, both in the High Street and, still more, in the closes which open out of it. These closes were inhabited by the Scottish nobility who had their town-houses there; so if we compare the High Street to Princes Street we shall find the parallel to these even more dirty closes in Drumsheugh Gardens or Moray Place. Yet it is hard to realise that this street, from upper windows of whose houses are displayed clothes from 'the wash' in various stages of dilapidation, and which is now haunted by tribes of street arabs, was once considered an important feature

199

in the beauties of Edinburgh. Carlyle's characteristic description of Old Edinburgh is well known : ' a sloping high street and many side lanes, covering like some wrought tissue of stone and mortar, like some rhinoceros skin, with many a gnarled embossment, church steeple, chimney head, Tolbooth, and other ornament or indispensability, back and ribs of the slope.' The figure of a back-bone and ribs was too appropriate and too obvious not to have been adopted before Carlyle, but it is more widely known through him than it would otherwise have been. Less well-known and more flattering is the description of the High Street given by Taylor the ' water-poet,' who visited Edinburgh in 1618. ' The fairest and goodliest street mine eyes ever beheld, for I did never see or hear of a street of that length (which is half a mile from the Castle to a fair port they call the Nether bow), and from that port the Kenny Gate (Canongate) is one quarter of a mile, down to the King's Palace called Holyrood House, the buildings on each side of the way being all of squared stone, five, six, and seven storeys high, and many by-lanes and closes on each side of the way, wherein are gentlemen's houses, much fairer than the buildings in the High Street, for in the High Street the merchants and tradesmen do dwell, but the gentlemen's mansions and goodliest houses are obscurely founded on the aforesaid lanes. The walls are eight or ten feet thick, exceeding strong, not built for a day, a week, a month, or a year, but from antiquity to posterity—for many ages. There I found entertainment beyond expectation or merit; and there is fish, flesh, bread and fruit in such variety that I think I may offencelessly call it superfluity or satiety.' Braun Agrippinensis, writing in the sixteenth century, gives an equally favourable account. ' In this city there are two spacious streets, of which the principal one, leading from the Palace to the Castle, is paved with square stones. The city itself is not built of bricks, but of square freestones, and so stately is its appearance

200

that single houses may be compared to palaces. From the abbey to the castle there is a continued street, which, on both sides, contains a range of excellent houses, and the better sort are built of hewn stone.'

Notwithstanding these favourable testimonies, it cannot be denied that if the old High Street of Edinburgh was picturesque, it was also, according to modern notions, peculiar. We have already spoken of the Luckenbooths and the Krames, but these were far from being the only instances of outside traffic. Both the meat market and the fish market were held in the High Street until the reign of James v., and a flesh market was for long held at the Netherbow. Street riots were of common occurrence. 'Cleanse the Causeway' is the best known of these, but family feuds were responsible for a great many such struggles. It was in one of these that Sir Walter Scott of Buccleuch was killed. His death is thus referred to, in the *Lay of the Last Minstrel*:—

> 'Bards long shall tell,
> How Lord Walter fell!
> When startled burghers fled, afar,
> The furies of the Border war ;
> When the streets of high Dunedin
> Saw lances gleam, and falchions redden,
> And heard the slogan's deadly yell—
> Then the Chief of Branksome fell.'

The *Diurnal of Occurrents* gives a less poetical account of the 'tulzie.' '1551 in this zeir all wes at guid rest, exceptande the Laird of Cesfurde and Fernyhirst with thair complices slew Schir Walter Scott, laird of Balclewche, in Edinburgh, quha was ane valzeand, guid knycht.' Few things could throw more light on the disturbed state of the streets in olden days than the order 'Anent walpynnis[1] in Buithis,' which appears in the Burgh Records, March 4, 1552. 'It is statute and ordainit be the Provest, Bailies, and Counsall of this

[1] Weapons.

burgh, because of the greit slauchteris and utheris cum-
meris and tulzies done in tyme bygane within the burgh,
and apperendlie to be done gif na remeid be provydit
thairto; and for eschewing thairof;—that ilk manner of
persone, merchandis, craftismen, and all utheris occu-
pyaris of buthis, or chalmeris in the hie gait, outher
heych or laych, that they have lang valpynnis thairin, sic
as hand ex, Jedburgh staif, hawart jawalying, and siclyk
lang valpynnis, with knaip schawis and jakkis; and that
they come thairwith to the hie-gate incontinent efter the
commoun bell rynging.' In ordinary speech this order of
Council runs somewhat like this: 'Anent weapons in
booths.' ' It is statute and ordained by the Provost, Bailies
and Council of this burgh, because of the great slaughters
and other troubles and fights done in time past within
the burgh, and apparently to be done if no remedy
is provided for it and for preventing thereof, that
each manner of person, merchant, artisan, and all others
who occupied booths or chambers in the High Street,
either high or low, that they have long weapons therein,
such as hand axe, Jedburgh staff, strong javelin, and such
long weapons, also with " knaip schawis and jakkis," and
that they come with these to the High Street immediately after the common bell rings.'

Besides being more disturbed than is usual in modern
thoroughfares, the sanitation—or rather want of it—in
the High Street would not accord with modern ideas.
As Edinburgh increased, it grew in *height* not in extent,
and the present age which so deprecates 'overcrowding'
can hardly realise what that meant. In those days there
were no luxurious elevators to take tired people up and
down, and the turnpikes were steep and narrow. What
marvel that the inhabitants of the upper stories of these
ancient ' skyscrapers ' saved a long descent and a more
wearisome ascent by emptying the domestic débris out
on the street, warning foot passengers by a cry of ' Get

out o' the gait!' or—strange relic of the Franco-Scottish alliance—'Gardez l'eau.' This unpleasing custom was the origin of the old Scots proverb 'Jouk and let the jaw go by'—meaning, as far as its meaning can be expressed in English, 'Stand aside and let adverse circumstances pass.' Those who were students about 1830 have told how, in defiance of all police regulations, the old cry of 'gardey loo' was frequently heard and a sudden rush to the middle of the street ensued.

The High Street proper extends only from St. Giles' to the Netherbow, but the term is often used to include the continuation of the street which stretches up to the Castle, and is known as Castlehill and the Lawnmarket. On Castlehill may be seen a house where a cannon ball still remains which was fired from the Half-Moon battery during the siege of 1745. The house bears the date 1630, and the initials A.M. M.N. Passing through this building by a narrow wynd we reach an open court which in former days contained a handsome Gothic doorway giving access to a turnpike stair. Above the doorway was an ogee arch, in the tympanum of which was a coronet supported by two deerhounds, which are, says Chambers, 'the well-known supporters of the Duke of Gordon's arms.' Tradition declares that this was the town-house of the Dukes of Gordon, and it is interesting to find confirmation of this in the 'Disposition of House be Sir Robert Baird to William Baird his second son, 1694,' which speaks of 'All and hail that my lodging in the Castell Hill of Edinburgh formerly possessed by the Duchess of Gordon.' The Duchess here referred to was daughter of the Duke of Norfolk, and wife of that Duke of Gordon who held the Castle for King James in 1689. She withdrew for some time to a convent in Flanders, but after the death of the Duke she returned to her house in Edinburgh where she lived for sixteen years, till 1732. Her Jacobite principles remained unchanged, and in 1711 she caused considerable excitement by sending to the Dean and Faculty of Advocates 'a silver medal with the head of the Pretender on one side, and on the other the British Isles with the word "Reddite."' Some of the Whig members of the Faculty of Advocates wished to decline the gift, but they were in a decided minority. Only twelve out of seventy-five voted that it should be refused.

Although owned by the Duke of Gordon, the house is older than the dukedom. It was owned in 1570 by a man Patrick Edgar. As has already been indicated, it passed from the family of the Duke of Gordon to the Bairds of Newbyth, who kept it for several generations. Here was born in 1757 Sir David Baird, whose exploits in Mysore, especially at Seringapatam, are well known. Here, too, lived that Spartan old lady his mother. When she heard that Tippoo's prisoners were shut up in the dungeons of Mysore chained two and two, with the true Scottish propensity for veiling deep feeling with a joke, she ejaculated, 'Guid help the chield that's chained to oor Davie.' It is said that, when he returned, Baird visited his old home and found small boys in the garden busily engaged in trying to throw cabbage-stalks down the Grassmarket chimneys, and rejoicing mightily if they succeeded. Sir David begged the boys' father 'not to be angry; he and his brother,' he said, 'when living here, at the same age, had indulged in precisely the same amusement, the chimneys then, as now, being so provokingly open to attacks that there was no resisting the temptation.' In course of time the house changed owners again, passing from the Bairds of Newbyth to the Browns of Greenbank. It is from these same Browns that Brown's Close, which is one entrance to the house, derives its name.

In Boswell's Court there are some old houses. One of these has the common inscription, 'O Lord in Thee is al my Traist.' The armorial bearings are obliterated, and so is the date, which looks more like 1558 than anything else.

Castle-
hill, the
Lawn-
market,
and
High
Street

Near at hand was Webster's Close which commemorated Dr. Alexander Webster of the Tolbooth Church,
famous for inaugurating the Widows' Fund of the Church
of Scotland, famous also for his wit, his skill as a
raconteur, and his fondness for claret. Close by is the
Tolbooth Church where the General Assembly of the
Church of Scotland meets in May. On this site stood
the town-houses of the Marquis of Argyle and the Earl
of Cassilis, while on the spot now occupied by the
Outlook Tower dwelt the 'Laird of Cockpen,' so well
known to all lovers of Scottish song. The houses of
Lord Gray of Kinfauns, Lord Leven, and Lord Semple
(also celebrated in song), were near this spot. Just above
the Outlook Tower is Ramsay Lane, called after Allan
Ramsay, the poet, who lived there.

Below the Tower is the Free Church Assembly Hall.
The Assembly Hall forms one side of the Quadrangle,
New College (the Free Church Theological Hall) is on
the left, and the Free High Church is on the right.
The Quadrangle contains a statue of John Knox which
was unveiled in 1896. It is a strange coincidence which
led to a statue of John Knox being erected on the site
of the palace of Mary of Guise. This palace is said to
have been extremely beautiful, with fine stone work and
wood-carving, winding passages, and quaint stone stair-
cases. The doorway bore the inscription 'Laus honor
Deo,' with J. R., the initials of King James v. A shield
on the right-hand side of the door bore the monogram of
the Virgin Mary, while on the corresponding shield on
the left-hand side were carved the letters I. H. S. An
old oak door with exquisite carved panels may be seen
in the Museum of the Society of Antiquaries, but most
of the beautiful wood and stone carving was cleared away
to make room for this modern edifice. In the course
of removing this old house a secret chamber with a
sliding panel and spiral staircase was disclosed. This,
along with its nearness to the Castle, must have made

it a desirable residence for an unprotected woman in those troublous times. The situation must have been extremely beautiful, with gardens sloping down to the Nor' Loch, and with fine views of the Forth and the Highland hills. We are apt to forget the additional beauty and privacy given by the gardens to the better houses, but all, rich and poor alike, shared in the glorious view.

The two Assembly Halls are the boundary between the Castlehill and the Lawnmarket—so called, because in olden days merchants used to have rolls of cloth for sale here in little booths in the open street, giving the neighbourhood, as one writer says, ' an appearance of something between a busy country fair and an Indian camp. In olden days the Weigh-house or Butter Tron was the western boundary of the Lawnmarket. It seems to have been clumsy in the extreme, but it served useful purposes besides that for which it was originally designed. Built in 1352 on a site granted by David II., it was for long associated with royalty. It was here that Kings and Queens were received on entering the city—*e.g.* when Queen Mary arrived in Edinburgh in 1561 it was here that ' the cloud opynnit and the barne descendit doun as it had beene ane angell and deliuerit to her hienes the keyis of the toun, togidder with ane Bybill and ane Psalme Buik.' The Butter Tron also served as a convenient base of operations in attacking the Castle. It was used for this purpose by Cromwell in 1650, but when the Castle surrendered he destroyed the Butter Tron lest it should prove as serviceable to his enemies as it had been to himself. It was, however, rebuilt in 1660, and was again utilised in 1745 for attacking the Castle, this time without success.

One of the houses in Mylne's Court was also occupied by the Highlanders. The owner of the house, who was a strong supporter of the Hanoverian Government, expressed his sentiments towards his uninvited guests by

Mylne's Court

Castle-
hill, the
Lawn-
market,
and
High
Street

advertising for articles which he declared were missing.
Mylne's Court is said to have been the first example of the
modern square as opposed to the 'Close' which prevailed
in ancient days. It dates from 1690, but the close held
its own till long afterwards. Mylne's Court derives its
name from its architect, Robert Mylne, who was the last
of seven royal master-masons. His son built Blackfriars
Bridge, London, and afterwards became surveyor of
St. Paul's Cathedral.

A little to the east of Mylne's Court is James's Court,
which dates only from 1727, but is not without interesting associations. When David Hume left his house in

207

Jack's Land in the Canongate he came to James's Court, and there remained from 1762 to 1771. Here too lived Boswell, and here he welcomed Paoli the Corsican chief in 1771, and Dr Johnson in 1773. Possibly the treatment he had received in the White Horse Inn, Canongate, had proved too much for the temper of this great man; certainly he made a powerful, if hardly a favourable, impression on his hostess and her friends. Mrs. Boswell described him as 'a great brute.' The house where Boswell lived was burned down in 1858, and on its site now stand the Savings Bank and the offices of the Free Church. These are both entered from the Mound though they stretch back to James's Court and the Lawnmarket. On the same site stood some old closes now forgotten, in one of which lived Sir John Lauder, better known as Lord Fountainhall. It was he who, along with Lockhart and four others, defended Argyle in 1681. His memoirs throw some interesting sidelights on the history of that day. A granddaughter of Lord Fountainhall, who lived till 1838, described the room he usually sat in as 'a room covered with gilt leather and containing many huge presses and cabinets, one of which was ornamented with a death's head at the top.'

Near James's Court was Thomas Gladstone's Land, which is referred to in the time of Charles I., but is interesting chiefly because Thomas Gladstone was an ancestor of William Ewart Gladstone. The land still survives; it is No. 489 High Street.

Near this is Lady Stair's Close. It was named after Elizabeth, Countess of Stair, who in later life was known as a leader of Edinburgh fashion, but in earlier days had an exciting, if somewhat painful, history. When quite young she married James, Lord Primrose, who treated her badly in every way. Once she saw him in her mirror coming behind her, rapier in hand, with the evident intention of murdering her. She had only time to jump through the open window and escape to his mother's house and claim her protection. Naturally the unfortunate woman refused to return to her husband, who shortly after went abroad. The curious experience which Lady Primrose had during his absence is related by Scott in his short story *Aunt Margaret's Mirror*. Briefly, Lady Primrose saw in a magic mirror her brother interrupt a wedding where Lord Primrose was bridegroom. On the return of her brother from Rotterdam she discovered that not only were the facts correct, but she had seen the interrupted ceremony the very day and hour when it took place. Lord Primrose died in 1706, and suitors were not wanting to persuade Lady Primrose to change her name and estate. She declared, however, that she never would marry again, but Lord Stair won her consent by

Lady Stairs Close

O

stratagem. They married and would have been very happy, only Lord Stair was apt to indulge too freely in strong drink. Once when in this condition he struck her so violent a blow that her face was cut open. His horror when he discovered what he had done was so great that he promised never again to touch any drink that had not passed through her hands, and this vow he faithfully kept. After his death, which took place at Queensberry House, Canongate, in 1747, Lady Stair kept state in her little flat. A second-floor flat in the High Street seems to us a curious residence for a leader of fashion, but a leader of fashion Lady Stair undoubtedly was. She received only those people whose social position she considered beyond question, and admission to the circle of her acquaintances was greatly prized. She was the first lady in Edinburgh to keep a black servant. She seems to have been a stately old lady with a considerable opinion of her own importance ; but Lady Mary Wortley Montagu declares in her letters that she occasionally took hysterical fits,—poor woman, can we wonder thereat when we consider her matrimonial experiences ? Possibly she may have been hysterical on the celebrated occasion when she appeared at Holyrood and applied her forcible, if somewhat inelegant, expression to Lord Dundonald. Lady Stair died in Edinburgh in November 1759, twelve years after the death of her husband. Lady Stair's house has been restored by Lord Rosebery in honour of his collateral ancestress.

Baxter's Close will be for ever associated with Burns in the days when, as Cunningham relates, he had only ' his share of a deal table, a sanded floor, and a chaff bed at eighteenpence a week.' The house where he lodged may be reached from Lady Stair's Close, and it is on this close that the window of Burns's room looks out. The room was more comfortable than Allan Cunningham's description would suggest; it is large and airy, and panelled with wood. There is an interesting old house

Baxter's Close

here which has a carved lintel and a device of a shield, a cross and a crown, all evidently very old. The crown is placed above the shield, the cross, with a man leaning over it, above the crown; while above all in old lettering is the inscription: BLISSIT · BE · THE · LORD · IN · HIS · GIFTIS · FOR · NOV · AND · EVIR. Antiquaries believe that this stone is very old, perhaps older than any other stone or inscription in Edinburgh. The house itself is of comparatively modern date. Its most famous occupant was Martha White, only daughter of a wealthy citizen, who became Countess of Elgin and Kincardine, and governess to Princess Charlotte of Wales. Farther east are Wardrop's Close, which opens on James's Court, and a curious old opening called Paterson's Court. Near this was the house in Bank Street inhabited by David Bridges, nicknamed, as Professor Wilson tells, 'Director-General of the Fine Arts.' Near Lady Stair's Close on the opposite side of the Lawnmarket is Riddle's Court, which is associated with Hume and also with Bailie Macmorran, who was accidentally shot during the 'barring out' of the High School boys. The culprit, Sinclair by name, and some others were imprisoned, but in spite of the demands for vengeance on the part of Macmorran's relatives, they were all set free because their 'friends threatened death to all the people of Edinburgh if they did the child any harm, saying they were not wise who meddled with scholars, especially *gentlemen's sons.*' Sinclair lived and flourished, was created Sir William Sinclair of Mey, and became the ancestor of the Earls of Caithness. An old oak door may still be seen which is said to be the work of Macmorran. His house was the scene of a magnificent banquet given to the Duke of Holstein, brother of Queen Anne of Denmark. Other celebrated people who lived here are Lord Royston, Sir John Clerk of Penicuik, William Little of Craigmillar, and Sir Francis Grant of Cullen, so prominent in the Convention of 1789.

Castle-
hill, the
Lawn-
market,
and
High
Street

Macmorran's House
Riddle's Court

A well-known occupant of the neighbouring close,
which bears his name, was Deacon Brodie, whose burglaries
were suitably rewarded by his execution at the Cross.

On the site of the present Melbourne Place stood an
old house known as Robert Gourlay's House, which was
closely connected with many interesting historical events.
Robert Gourlay seems to have been a messenger-at-arms
belonging to the Abbey of Holyrood, which office he

213

owed to Adam Bothwell, Bishop of Orkney and Commendator of Holyrood. He seems to have enjoyed royal
favour in the reign of James VI., and to have used this
favour diplomatically in spite of the motto above his
door, 'O LORD IN THE IS MY TRAIST.' Apparently
this court favour brought the ill-will of Gourlay's
neighbours. We find a royal mandate granted by
King James in 1588, which runs thus: 'Lyke as ye
said Robert Gourlay and Helen Cruik, his spouse, has
raisit ane new biggin, and wark upon ye waste and
ground of their lands and houses foresaid, wherein they
are quarelled and troubled for enlarging and outputing
of ye east gavill and dyke . . . we therefor . . . give
and grant special liberty to accomplish the foresaid bigging.' Apparently this did not produce the desired
effect, for the next mandate was much more imperious in
tone, and speaks of the 'richt . . . quilk be all lawis
inviolable observit in tymes bygane has pertainit and
aught to pertene to us.' Robert Gourlay also obtained
notoriety in a manner he could well have dispensed with.
We read in Calderwood's *History*: 'About this time,
Robert Gourlay, an elder of the kirk of Edinburgh, was
ordeanned to mak his publict repentance in the kirk
upon Friday the 28th May (1574) for transporting wheat
out of the countrie.' The Regent, however, prevented
this sentence being carried out. In this house lodged
Sir William Durie, governor of Berwick during the siege
of the Castle in 1573. After the Castle fell, it was here
that Kirkaldy of Grange and the other prisoners were
brought; or, in the words of the *Diurnal of Occurrents,*
'The noblemen past to the said lieutennentis lugeing,
callit Gourlayes lugeing, thair to remayne quhill farder
aduertisement come fra the Quene of England.' In 1581
Morton was confined here previous to his execution; and
the following year this astonishing house, which alternated
between being a prison and a royal residence, was the
temporary home of the French Ambassador, M. de la

Motte Fénelon. Colonel Sempill and Lord Maxwell were imprisoned here for intriguing with the Catholics against King James vi., and in 1593 the King himself sought safety in this same house during one of the Earl of Bothwell's outbreaks. 'The 3rd of Apryle the King being ludgit in Robert Gourlay's ludging he came to the sermone and ther in presence of the haill peipill he promest to revenge God's cause to banische all the papists and he requystet the haill peiple to gang with him against Boduell, quha wes in Leith for the tyme.' This house was in 1637 sold to Sir Thomas Hope of Craighall, a zealous Covenanter. The legend that Robert Gourlay's house was the scene of 'the last sleep of Argyle' is quite unfounded. The house of such strong Covenanters as the Hopes would not have been considered a secure prison; and moreover, quite recently, the original warrant for the execution of Argyle was discovered, which proves beyond question that he was taken straight from the Tolbooth to the Market Cross. Robert Gourlay's house was the home of Sir George Lockhart, who was Lord Advocate and then Lord President of the Court of Session. Chiesley of Dalry considered himself aggrieved by one of Lockhart's decisions, and threatened vengeance. Speaking of his purpose to Sir James Stewart, an advocate, Stewart tried to dissuade him, saying, 'The very imagination of such a thing is a sin against God'; but Chiesley replied, 'Leave God and me alone; we have many things to reckon betwixt us, and we will reckon this too.' The Lord President was warned, but could not believe that Chiesley was in earnest. Nevertheless on Easter Sunday 1689 he followed Lockhart home from the High Church, and shot him in the back just as he was entering his house. Instead of manifesting any contrition Chiesley exclaimed, 'I am not wont to do things by halves, and now I have taught the President justice.' Chiesley was tortured and then hanged in chains. For many a long day his house at

215

Dalry was supposed to be haunted, and even courageous
people declined to visit the back kitchen after dusk, as
there was a tradition to the effect that Chiesley was
buried there in that unromantic spot. It was in vain
that those interested in bygone days tried to preserve
this interesting house from demolition. No amount of
persuasion seems to have had the smallest effect on the
Improvements Commission.

Beside Robert Gourlay's House was *Gosford's Close*,
containing the remains of a beautifully decorated house
belonging to the Augustinian Abbey of Cambuskenneth.
The Gothic carvings were specially noteworthy, and even
without written evidence there would have been little
difficulty in determining the character of the building.
But when we find a reference to ' all and haill these lands,
houses and stables, biggit and waste, lying within ye
tenements sometime pertaining to the Comendator and
Convent of Cambuskenneth,' its origin is proved beyond
a doubt. 'The building was in all likelihood,' says
Daniel Wilson, 'the town mansion of the abbot, with
a beautiful chapel attached to it, and may serve to
remind us how little idea we can form of the beauty
of the Scottish capital before the Reformation, adorned
as it was with so many churches and conventual buildings, the very sites of which are now unknown.' Over
this house was a lintel on which was carved a representation of the Crucifixion. The interior of this house was as
magnificent as the exterior. Kay says: 'The dining and
drawing rooms were spacious; indeed, more so than those
of any private modern house we have seen. The lobbies
were all variegated marble, and a splendid mahogany
staircase led to the upper story. Beneath the house
was a cellar containing a trap-door which opened into
a still lower cellar cut out of the rock.' Visions of the
Inquisition have suggested to some people that these
cellars were perhaps torture-chambers, but a greater
knowledge of old Edinburgh customs makes it almost

Castle-
hill, the
Lawn-
market,
and
High
Street

Gosford's Close

certain that they were used for receiving smuggled
goods. The Nor' Loch was a convenient method of
conveying these into Edinburgh in the days when, in
the words of Mr. Peter Plumdamas (vide *Heart of
Midlothian*), 'sic an host of idle English guagers and

217

excisemen as hae come down to vex and torment us,
that an honest man canna fetch sae muckle as a bit
anker o' brandy frae Leith to the Lawnmarket, but
he's like to be rubbit o' the very gudes he's bought
and paid for.' Gosford's Close ceased to be fashionable
with the advent of sedan chairs, as owing to the narrowness of the 'close' it was impossible for them to get
through.

Next Gosford's Close was *Libberton's Wynd*, which is
mentioned in a charter of James III. in 1477. In olden
days it was the principal thoroughfare to the High
Town from the suburb of Cowgate. In later days, however, the principal interest attaching to it centres round
'Johnnie Dowie's Tavern,' frequented by such representatives of the Muse as Robert Fergusson and Robert Burns.
Fergusson described it as a place

> 'Where couthy chields at e'enin' meet,
> Their bizzin' craigs and mou's to weet,
> And blythely gar auld care gae by
> Wi' blinkin' and wi' bleerin' eye.'

Burns along with his boon companions, Willie Nicol
(who 'brewed a peck of maut') and Allan Masterton,
was equally assiduous in his attendance, and there some
of his best-known songs were composed. But Libberton's
Wynd as well as Gosford's Close and Robert Gourlay's
House disappeared somewhere between 1825 and 1836
to make room for George IV. Bridge and the County
Buildings.

Dunbar's Close takes its name from Cromwell's Iron-
sides who lodged there after Dunbar. It contains some
old inscriptions of considerable interest, but they cannot
be inspected owing to the iron gate which shuts off the
close. It may be mentioned in passing that dwellers in
Old Edinburgh seem to have believed that mottoes, especially those containing the name of God, exercised a bene-
ficent influence on their house.

Byres Close, too, had some interesting carving, much of which has disappeared. Sir Patrick Walker of Coates removed it to Coates House. But the chief interest of Byres Close centres round the house of Adam Bothwell, Bishop of Orkney, Commendator of Holyrood. The house faced the High Street, but had at the back a garden terrace looking on the Nor' Loch. The front part of the house is completely modernised and rejoices in a new and uninteresting stone front, but the back presents much the same appearance as it did in the days of the time-serving bishop. An old stone stair leads up to the house. The back part is evidently very old, and its dormer windows bear inscriptions. Over one is the inscription 'Nihil est ex omni parte beatum.' We may say that this is only partially visible from the close, and to decipher even a little of it needs both good eyesight and the power of holding one's head in a far from comfortable position! Another window bears the inscription 'Laus ubique Deo,' while over a third is carved 'Feliciter infelix.' Even apart from its associations this house would have considerable interest, but when we think of Adam Bothwell himself and of his intimate connection with the tragedy of Mary's reign, we feel that we are indeed in 'Old Edinburgh.' Though a bishop, Adam Bothwell had no scruples about matrimony, and espoused Margaret Murray of Touchadam. He died peacefully in 1593; his laudatory epitaph has already been referred to in Chapter v. His son was created Lord Holyroodhouse in 1607. But in spite of all this prosperity, misfortunes came to the family of this unscrupulous prelate. The well-known ballad 'Lady Ann Bothwell's Lament' commemorates the sorrows of his beautiful daughter, and in the middle of the eighteenth century his family died out. There is now no record of him but the epitaph at Holyrood and this old house with its wealth of memories of Mary Stuart and her son, of Adam Bothwell and Lord Holyroodhouse and the hapless Lady Ann. This house

is also associated with 'the glorious days of auld, worthy,
faithfu' Provost Dick.' This was Sir William Dick of
Braid, a wealthy and patriotic Scot who flourished in the
seventeenth century. His wealth was considered so great
at that day that it became proverbial, reaching as it did
the sum of £200,000 sterling. Not only was there less
money in the country then, but general prices were lower,
and the purchasing power of this sum was much greater
than it would be at the present day. Readers of the
Heart of Midlothian will remember David Deans's reference to his wealth : ' And then folk might see men deliver
up their silver to the state's use, as if it had been as muckle
sclate stanes. My father saw them toom the sacks of
dollars out o' Provost Dick's window intill the carts that
carried them to the army at Dunse Law ; and if ye dinna
believe his testimony, there is the window itsell still
standing in the Luckenbooths—I think it's a claith
merchant's booth the day—at the airn stanchells, five
doors abune Gosford's Close.' Sir William Dick of Braid
—or Provost Dick, as he was more frequently called—was
a zealous Covenanter : in fact, the Scottish Covenanting
army would have been disbanded in 1641 had he not
come to the rescue with a timely gift of one hundred
thousand merks. But his horror of the English sectaries
was greater than his hatred of 'prelacy,' and he afterwards made over a sum of £20,000 to be spent for King
Charles. The English government thereupon forfeited
the remainder of his property, which amounted to £65,000.
He went to London to try to get back part of it, but was,
instead, imprisoned at Westminster, where he died in 1655,
his death being hastened, it was said, by the want of the
common necessaries of life. This somewhat rapid change
from great wealth to poverty and misfortune is illustrated
in a pamphlet called *The Lamentable Estate and Distressed Case of Sir William Dick*. 'It contains,' says
Scott, 'three copper-plates, one representing Sir William
on horseback, and attended with guards as Lord Provost

of Edinburgh, superintending the unloading of one of his rich argosies. A second exhibiting him as arrested, and in the hands of the bailiffs. A third presents him dead in prison. The tract is esteemed highly valuable by collectors of prints. The only copy I ever saw upon sale, was rated at £30.'

On the east side of this old house is *Advocates' Close*, which derived its name from Sir James Stewart of Goodtrees (Jamie Wylie, the Jacobites called him), Lord Advocate from 1692 till 1713, with the exception of a few months. His father was twice Provost

Advocates Close

of Edinburgh—in 1648, when Cromwell paid his first visit,
and afterwards ten years later. His son was an ardent
supporter of Revolution principles, hence the detestation
and ridicule of the Jacobites. He was, however, greatly
respected by the citizens of Edinburgh, and Wodrow tells
that, at his funeral in 1713, 'so great was the crowd that
the Magistrates were at the grave in the Greyfriars
Churchyard before the corpse was taken out of the
house at the foot of the Advocates' Close.' Sir James
Stewart's house was sold by his grandson in 1796 to
David Dalrymple, the future Lord Westhall. Advocates'
Close, though indebted for its name, in the first place, to
the fact that the Lord Advocate lived there, maintained
its right to the said name by being long a favourite
residence for advocates. Among those who lived there
—famous doubtless in their day, but now forgotten—
was Andrew Crosbie, who was rescued from oblivion by
Scott and introduced to the world as 'Counsellor Paulus
Pleydell.' The description of Advocates' Close in *Guy
Mannering* might have been written at the present day,
except that advocates do not now inhabit it. Andrew
Crosbie was a man of considerable force of character,
and seems to have been able to hold his own with Dr.
Johnson when that great man visited Edinburgh. Like
Pleydell he 'affected the manners of a former generation,'
but in course of time so far conformed to the fashion of
his own as to remove his residence from Advocates' Close
to St. Andrew Square. He was, however, reduced to
poverty by the failure of the Ayr Bank, and after his
death in 1784 his widow's only means of livelihood was
an annuity of £50 granted by the Faculty of Advocates.
Advocates' Close is also interesting as it contained the
first picture gallery in Edinburgh. This was the work
of John Scougal, a celebrated portrait painter who
flourished in the seventeenth century. It was he who
painted the well-known portrait of George Heriot, which
may still be seen at Heriot's Hospital. He was also

Castle-
hill, the
Lawn-
market,
and
High
Street

greatly in request as a
painter of ladies' por-
traits to add to family
picture galleries. It is
strange to think of the
'beauty and chivalry' of
Edinburgh frequenting
this dingy old close,
where no one would now
go willingly unless bent
on antiquarian pursuits
or district visiting.
Scougal was a cousin of
Patrick Scougal, who was
consecrated Bishop of
Aberdeen in 1664. The
painter died in 1730 at
the age of eighty-five,
having lived through
the Civil War, the execu-
tion of the King, the

Newel stairway
Advocates' Close

Protectorate, the Restoration, the Revolution, the ''15'
and the permanent settlement of the House of Hanover,
—a somewhat eventful lifetime. Advocates' Close has
some interesting inscriptions, among others—

'C. C. 1590
Blissit be God of al His Giftis,'

and

'C. C. H. B.
Spes alteræ vitæ 1590.'

Roxburghe Close (341 High Street) is said by tradition
to have contained the town-house of the Earl of Roxburghe. This seems probable, but cannot be definitely
proved. Most of the old houses have vanished, but the
house which is said to have belonged to the Earls of
Roxburghe still survives.

223

Like Roxburghe Close, *Warriston's Close* is sadly
modernised, though so late as 1868 it retained most of
its interesting old houses unchanged. In Warriston's Close
lived Lord Philiphaugh, whose fortitude was not great
enough to resist the torture of ' the boot,' and who
betrayed what he knew of the Ryehouse Plot. Here,
too, lived Johnston of Warriston, that grim upholder
of the Covenant, whose courage also failed at the prospect of an ignominious death. He took a prominent
part in drawing up the Covenant, and was intimate
with all the leading Covenanters, so his house must
have been frequented by men like Henderson, Argyle,
Rothes, Callander, Leslie, Monk, and—probably—Cromwell.   His mother was Elizabeth Craig, daughter of
Sir Thomas Craig of Riccarton. The following epitaph
shows the state of (cavalier) feeling at the time :—

> ' Deevil suell ye deathe,
>   And burste the lyke a tune,
>   That took away good Elspet Craige
>   And left ye knave her son.'

Warriston was connected—through the Craigs—with
Bishop Burnet, the historian. But Warriston's Close
was inhabited by a still more noted personage—John
Knox. It has been proved quite recently that it was
here he lived during those critical years when he ' dang
the pulpit to blads' in St. Giles', or expounded his
views to Queen Mary at Holyrood in such plain un-
varnished phrases. Warriston's Close now contains the
printing establishment of William and Robert Chambers.
Near Warriston's Close is *Writers' Court*, which contained
Clerihugh's, where Colonel Mannering and Dandie Din-
mont went ' into a dark alley, then up a dark stair,' to
seek for Pleydell. We feel we can sympathise with
Mannering, who could hardly conceive how a gentleman
of a liberal profession and good society, could choose such
a scene for social indulgence. Besides the miserable

entrance, the house itself seemed paltry and half ruinous. The passage in which they stood had a window to the close which admitted a little light during the day-time, and a villainous compound of smells at all times.' Clerihugh's seems to have been greatly frequented by Edinburgh citizens grave and gay, and one hears tales of the Town Council adjourning there to settle such weighty matters as the question of a new bell-rope. The name ' Writers' Court ' is due to the fact that the Signet Library was kept here until it was removed to its present location. Castle-hill, the Lawn-market, and High Street

No trace now remains of *Mary King's Close.* How it got its name is unknown. It seems to have suffered severely from plague during the great epidemic of 1645. Most of the inhabitants of the close died, and it was for long supposed that if the doors were opened the plague would again break out. Drummond of Hawthornden wrote an epigram which runs thus :—

> ' Turn, citizens, to God, repent, repent !
> And pray your bedlam frenzies may relent.
> Think not rebellion a trifling thing,
> This plague doth fight for Marie and the King.'

' Marie ' was, of course, Queen Henrietta Maria. But the associations of Mary King's Close cannot strictly be termed historical. No memories of gallant knights and beauteous dames linger around it, only horrible tales of witches and goblins. ' Those who had been foolhardy enough to peep through the windows after nightfall,' says one writer, ' saw the spectres of the long-departed denizens engaged in their wonted occupations ; headless forms danced through the moonlit apartments ; on one occasion a godly minister and two pious elders were scared out of their senses by the terrible vision of a raw head and blood-dripping arm, which protruded from the wall in this terrible street and flourished a sword above their heads.' There is the still more ghastly tale of Mr. and Mrs. Coltheart. These and other equally

P

gruesome stories are related at some length in a work
entitled *Satan's Invisible World Discovered*, by Mr. George
Sinclair, Professor of Moral Philosophy at Glasgow
University, and afterwards minister of Eastwood. This,
it will be remembered, was Wodrow's parish, and a love
of the marvellous seems to have haunted Eastwood Manse.

In the City Chambers may be seen the *Municipal
Museum*. It is well worth a visit, in spite of the fatigue
entailed by toiling up many long flights of stairs. Once
inside, however, the visitor feels amply repaid. There
is an extremely interesting collection of relics of various
kinds. A full description is out of the question, but a few
of the main objects of interest may be indicated. A panel
brought from an old house in the High Street, and a
painting by David Allan, 'the Scottish Hogarth,' will
appeal to those who are interested in Art. Most of the
relics, however, are historical. There are some letters of
Mary of Guise, and many letters of Queen Mary—one,
subscribed by the Queen and Bothwell, letting part of
the lands of Newhaven to Englishmen for the purpose
of making salt. There are also some of Burns's letters,
and the original manuscript of 'Scots wha hae.' Allan
Ramsay is also represented. There are political documents as well as literary, such as the warrant for Argyle's
execution in 1685, and the proclamation by the Duke of
Buccleuch and the Lord Provost in 1803, when the
citizens were in a panic lest 'Bony' should attack them.
The original stone of the Covenanters' grave in Greyfriars is also here; and, in curious contrast to this, the
Family Bible of Francis Brodie, father of the notorious
Deacon Brodie, whose birth is duly entered therein. In
fact, there is no limit to the curious relics of the past
which may be seen in this Museum.

Near the Royal Exchange, on the north side of the
street, is *Craig's Close*. It was here that Andro Hart,
the well-known Scottish printer, displayed his famous
printed Bible, Barbour's 'Bruce,' and the 'Psalms in

Scottish Meter.' He died in 1621, and two centuries later another lover of books, Provost Creech, took up his abode here, and here also dwelt Archibald Constable. There were some old houses with curious devices cut in stone, but they have now disappeared, though some of the stones are still to be seen in Princes Street Gardens.

Castle-hill, the Lawn-market, and High Street

In Craig's Close met the Cape Club, one of the most curious of old Edinburgh clubs. All the members bore more or less eccentric names, and each member, on being admitted, held the poker and took his oath as a Knight of the Cape, in the following terms :—

> 'I devoutly swear by this light
> To be a true and faithful knight,
> With all my might,
> Both day and night,
> So help me, Poker !'

The Cape Club is referred to in the memoirs of several writers, *e.g.* Dr. Carlyle of Inveresk, and also in Fergusson's poem 'Auld Reekie.'

To the east of Craig's Close is *Old Post Office Close*, and to the east of that the *Anchor Close*. Some of the old houses had a good deal of carving, and bore the familiar mottoes : 'O LORD IN THE IS AL MY TRAIST,' and 'THE LORD IS ONLY MY SVPORT.' But the chief claim which the old Anchor Close has on our interest is that it contained 'Dawny Douglas's Tavern.' 'Dawny' rejoiced in a wife who is described as 'a large fat woman in a towering head-dress, and large flowered silk gown, who bowed to every one passing.' 'Dawny' himself seems to have been small, delicate, and insignificant looking. It was here that the famous 'Crochallan Fencibles' met. Various explanations of the name have been given. One of the most reasonable is that 'Dawny' used to sing to his customers a Gaelic song entitled 'Cro Chalien,' or 'Colin's Cattle.' Various Scottish corps were being raised at this time : hence the humorous nickname of 'Fencibles.' Legend declared that Queen Mary

227

Anchor Close

had, at one time, held state in
this house, and there was even
a circumstantial tradition to
the effect that when she held
Council Meetings her crown
was placed in a niche in the
wall. We fear this tale must
be relegated to the mass of unauthenticated tradition about
Queen Mary. The room where
this was supposed to have
happened was called the Crown
Room, and the Crochallan
Fencibles dated their circulars
from 'Queen Mary's Council
Room.' They had, however,
a surer title to immortality
than this somewhat dubious
tale, in the fact that they are
closely connected with Burns.
Other famous men who fre-
quented the Anchor Close,
either for business or pleasure,
were Dr. Blair, Adam Fer-
guson, Adam Smith, Lord
Kames, Dr. Beattie, Lord
Monboddo, Dr. Robertson, Henry Mackenzie, Hume,
Black, Lord Hailes, and Arnot; but there is this
additional interest attaching to the connection of Burns
with the Anchor Close, that he celebrated the doings
of the Crochallan Fencibles both in prose and verse.
William Smellie, who introduced him to the Club, is
thus described :—

> 'Shrewd Willie Smellie to Crochallan came,
> The old cocked hat, the grey surtout the same ;
> His bristling beard just rising in its might,
> 'Twas four long nights and days to shaving night.'

Smellie's printing office was situated in the Anchor Close, and it was here that many of the above-mentioned celebrities came to see about getting their works printed. Until this printing office was cleared away to make room for Cockburn Street, many interesting relics might be seen, notably the desk at which these and other famous men revised their proofs, and the stool on which Burns sat when engaged in the same occupation. The inscription stated that it was ' the stool on which Burns sat while correcting the proofs of his poems, from December 1786 to April 1787.' Another house in the Anchor Close had the distinction of possessing—so far as is known—the only interior doorway in Edinburgh which rejoiced in a legend. The words were

Castle-
hill, the
Lawn-
market,
and
High
Street

AUGUSTA . AD . USUM . AUGUSTA
W. F.   B. G.

W. F. stands for William Fowler, a well-known Edinburgh citizen, the author, it is generally supposed, of the poem called *The Triumph of Death*. B. G. are presumably his wife's initials, but no one quite knows what the rest of the legend was supposed to convey. In the Anchor Close, too, lived Sir Alexander Ogilvie, one of the Commissioners of the Treaty of Union, better known as Lord Forglen.

Quite near stood the house inhabited by Alexander, ninth Earl of Eglinton, and the beautiful Countess Susannah, whose charms we have dwelt on in a previous chapter (Chapter V). Afterwards this house became known as Fortune's Tavern, and, later still, it was the residence of the Lord High Commissioner during the sitting of the General Assembly. A little further east is *Fleshmarket Close*, where Henry Dundas (afterwards Viscount Melville) lived, in the third story, when he first began to practise as an advocate. On every hand we find sites of interesting scenes, but alas! modern ' improvements ' have ruthlessly swept away most of these relics of Old Edinburgh. The great fire of 1824 was, however, quite as destructive, and wrought havoc far and near. On one of the closes which escaped this fire was bestowed the appropriate name of Salamander Land. There is an unauthenticated tradition that Defoe lived here when in Edinburgh, but it is at least doubtful. The *Old Fishmarket Close*, on the other side of the High Street, was, however, unquestionably the home of George Heriot, and also of Lord President Dundas, the father of Henry Dundas, Lord Melville. The deemster, or public hangman, also had his abode here—a strange, incongruous collection of residents !

A relic of Old Edinburgh which perished in the great fire was the Old Assembly Room, which was in *Old Assembly Close*. Assemblies were first held in the West Bow, but about 1720 were removed to this more fashionable locality. Here Goldsmith came in 1753, and was not over delighted with this specimen of a Scottish ball, and here 'famed Miss Nicky Murray' held undisputed sway. There, more than a century earlier, lived Lord President Durie, who was carried off so unceremoniously by Will Armstrong and kept in durance until the lawsuit, then under consideration, was decided in favour of the Earl of Traquair, Armstrong's patron. It is to this tale the ballad ' Christie's Will ' in the Border Minstrelsy owes its origin. It begins thus :—

> ' Traquair he has ridden up Chapelhope,
> And sae has he down by the Grey Mare's Tail ;
> But he never stinted his light gallop
> Till he spiered for Christie's Will.'

This close was long known as Lord Durie's Close.

Covenant Close has a variety of associations. In it the Covenant was signed when it was renewed in 1649 ; here lived Macqueen of Braxfield, ' the Hanging Judge ' —the prototype of ' Weir of Hermiston,' and to turn from history to literature, here ' Nanty Ewart ' lodged when he studied Divinity at the University of Edinburgh. It is a curious commentary on the vicissitudes of history that the house which witnessed the renewal of the Covenant degenerated in course of time into a tavern and an oyster-shop.

Burnet's Close is interesting as the home of Dr. Hugh Blair—whose *Rhetoric* is well known to students—and of Lord Auchinleck, the father of James Boswell. It is probable that the future biographer was born here.

More interesting still is *Bell's Wynd*, which contained 'The Clamshell Turnpike,' the house of George Crichton, Bishop of Dunkeld and Abbot of Holyrood. This was afterwards 'my Lord Home's lugeing,' where Mary and Darnley took refuge on returning to Edinburgh in 1566. Holyrood was so closely associated with the awful tragedy of Rizzio's murder that even Mary's courage was not equal to returning there. Accordingly we read in the *Diurnal of Occurrents*, 'Upon the xviij day of the said moneth of March our soueranis lord and ladie accumpanyt with twa thousand horsemen come to Edinburgh, and lugeit not in thair palice of Halyrudhouse, bot lugeit in my Lord Home's lugeing callit the auld biscop of Dunkell his lugeing, anent the salt trone in Edinburgh : and the lordis being with thame for the tyme, wes lugeit round about thame within the said burgh.' Bell's Wynd has other associations. There in a flat, three stories up, lived the father of the 'Admirable Crichton.' It was, moreover, noted for the fact that books were published here, and also that here the art of periwig-making flourished. One building in Bell's Wynd passed through some curious vicissitudes. It was first a meeting-place for the Incorporations of Wrights and Weavers (Deacon Brodie was at one time Convener of the Wrights), then a Congregational Church, and finally a Children's Shelter.

Close beside Bell's Wynd was the *Black Turnpike*, the town-house of the Provost, Sir Simon Preston. There

Mary was imprisoned after Carberry Hill. It stood a
little to the west of the Tron Church, on the site of
what is now Hunter Square. Maitland describes it as ' a
magnificent edifice which, were it not partly defaced by a
wooden front, would appear to be perhaps the most sumptuous building in Edinburgh.' The date of the Black
Turnpike is a matter of some doubt. Some zealous
antiquaries declare that it was built by King Kenneth III.,
who was killed 994 A.D. Above the door was the motto
—singularly inappropriate to Queen Mary's enforced
visit—' PAX . INTRANTIBUS . SALUS . EXEUNTIBUS . 1674.'
Obviously, however, parts of the house must have been
much older if Queen Mary was imprisoned there in
1567.

The west side of Hunter's Square occupies the site of
Kennedy's Close, where George Buchanan died on 28th
September 1582—just a month after the appearance of
his *History*. When on his deathbed he discovered that
there was not sufficient money to pay for his funeral, he
ordered his servants to divide what there was among the
poor, adding cynically, ' that if the City did not choose
to bury him, they might let him lie where he was.'
The City ' did choose to bury him ' the following day in
Greyfriars Churchyard. In 1701 the Town Council
directed that a ' through-stane ' should mark the spot
where his house stood ; but if this was done, no trace of
it now remains. The ' Town Guard ' blocked the street
just in front of the Black Turnpike, and had many
interesting associations, and many temporary prisoners
who were guilty of nothing more than dining too well !
But in 1785 this, like so many other memorials of the
past, was pulled down in order to ' improve ' the High
Street and make it modern.

The *Tron Church* dates only from the reign of Charles I.,
and though interesting historically, cannot be termed
beautiful architecturally. It is known to most people as
the spot where the crowd assembles ' to bring in the New

Year,' but it has other and more respectable associations. The word 'Tron' means a beam for weighing merchandise. The weigh-house, or Butter Tron, has already been referred to; this was known as the 'Salt Tron,' to distinguish it. It was the scene of some curious occurrences; *e.g.*, when the news came of the landing of Charles II. in 1650, Nicoll tells us, 'All signes of joy was manifested in a speciall maner in Edinburgh, by setting furth of bailfyres, ringing of belles, sounding of trumpettis, dancing almost all that night through the streitis. The puir kaill wyfes at the Tron sacrificed thair mandis and creillis, and the verie stoolis thai sat upon to the fyre.' Some people have suggested that as Jenny Geddes was one of the Tron kail wives, her famous stool was one of those which came to an untimely end, but one ingenious writer declares that such a good churchwoman as Jenny would be sure to have a 'Sunday best' stool! Certainly her loyalty was not at fault, for the *Caledonian Mercury* gives a circumstantial account of the bonfire made by 'the immortal Jenet Geddis, Princesse of the Trone Adventurers,' to celebrate the Restoration ten years later. At this point the North and South Bridges meet and cross the High Street at right angles. Continuing eastwards there are many interesting old closes to engage our attention, and the sites of many more.

One of the most westerly of these closes was Halkerston's Wynd, of which no trace now remains. It is interesting, however, to note its site, both because of the gallant defence made there against the English, and also because it was one of the principal approaches to the town.

The first opening we come to on the south side of the street east of the Tron is *Niddry Street*. Its principal interest centres round the romantic story of Lady Grange. She was the daughter of Chiesley of Dalry who shot Lord President Lockhart. Her husband, a Judge of the Court of Session, seemed to have been concerned in some

233

Jacobite plot which Lady Grange discovered. Lord
Grange was meditating her removal, when she hastened
her fate by reminding him she was Chiesley's daughter.
This threat induced him, with the help of Lord Lovat,
to abduct the unfortunate lady and send her to St.
Kilda.

Lord Lovat's widow lived in *Dickson's Close*, the next
opening to Niddry Street. Her house was long known
as Lady Lovat's Land. Walter Chepman, the printer,
was another inhabitant of this old house. David Allan,
the artist (called by some 'the Scottish Hogarth '), also
lived in Dickson's Close.

On the north side of the street was *The Cap and
Feather Close*, where Fergusson was born, but of it not a
trace remains. 'At the sign of the Mercury opposite to
Niddry's Wynd,' Allan Ramsay carried on business as
bookseller, editor, and, of course, author, until in 1725
he removed to the Luckenbooths.

On the south side of the street, just opposite North
Gray's Close, are *Cant's Close*, and, further east, *Strichen's
Close*. Cant's Close once was the home of ecclesiastical
dignitaries. Sir William Crichton of that ilk, Lord
High Chancellor of Scotland, founded a collegiate church
at Crichton in 1448, and the prebendaries seem to have
lived mainly in Cant's Close.

Strichen's Close, as it is now called, was known first as
Durie's Close, then as Rosehaugh Close, and then by its
present name. This close was the town residence of the
Abbot of Melrose. It was a pleasant, secluded spot, with
a garden which stretched down to the Cowgate and even
extended to the Pleasance. The last Abbot of Melrose
who lived here was Andrew Durie, who gave his name to
the close. His death was hastened—so Knox tells us—
by his horror and dismay at the sacking of St. Giles'. The
next important resident was Sir George Mackenzie of
Rosehaugh, King's Advocate in the reigns of Charles II.
and James II. Sir George is said to have been of a kindly

Allan Ramsay's shop

disposition, and he was unquestionably a warm patron of
literature. He was the friend of Dryden, and the
founder of the Advocates' Library. None of these
things, however, could mitigate the detestation in which
he was held by the common people as the instrument of
the hated English Government—a detestation which
found vent in the unpleasant nickname of ' Bluidy Mackenzie.' It is said that he looked on his wife with much
the same mixture of fear and detestation with which he
himself was regarded by the Covenanters. His house
was on the left-hand side at the foot of the close. The
last man to give his name to the close was Alexander
Fraser of Strichen, afterwards Lord Strichen. Besides
these, a host of interesting people lived in Strichen's Close
—among them Walter Chepman.

Next to Strichen's Close is *Blackfriars Street*, which
has many historical associations. It derives its name
from the Dominican or Black Friars belonging to the
monastery founded by Alexander ii. in 1230. Ecclesiastical dwellers were not lacking even in later days. At
the south end near the Cowgate stood the palace of
James Beaton, Archbishop of St. Andrews, afterwards
inhabited by his better-known nephew the Cardinal.
Another Archbishop of St. Andrews, who, like Cardinal
Beaton, was murdered by his political enemies, is
connected with Blackfriars Street. Archbishop Sharp was
just getting into his coach at the head of the Wynd when
a fanatic called Mitchell—a friend, by the way, of the
notorious Major Weir—fired at the Archbishop and
missed him, but dangerously wounded Honeyman,
Bishop of Orkney. The turbulent Earl of Bothwell—
Francis Stewart—stabbed Sir William Stewart here,
and here the Hamiltons gathered together for the
' bruilzie' of ' Cleanse the Causey.' The Regent
Morton had a house in Blackfriars Wynd, and here
lived William St. Clair, Earl of Orkney, who founded
Roslin Chapel. The state he kept was more ' royal '

236

than that of many of the Scottish kings. We are told that he used dishes of gold and silver, and that his wife, Margaret Douglas, had seventy-five gentlewomen, fifty-three of these being daughters of Scottish nobles ; and all, says Hay, 'cloathed in velvets and silks, and with their chains of gold and other pertinents, togither with two hundred rideing gentlemen who accompanied her in all her journeys. She had carried before her, when she wente to Edinburgh, if it were darke, eighty lighted torches. Her lodgeing was att the foot of Black-friar Wynde, so that in a word, none matched her in all the countrey, save the Queen's Majesty.' Lord Home, who received Mary and Darnley in the Clamshell Turnpike, had also a house in Blackfriars Wynd, and to it he retired when he was released in 1575. *The Diurnal of Occurrents* states : 'Upon the secund day of Junij Alexander Lord Home was relevit out of the Castell of Edinburgh and wardit in his awne lugeing in the heid of the Frier Wynd, quha was caryt thairto in ane bed, be ressone of his great infirmitie of seiknes.' Perhaps the fact we dwell on most as we stand in this once quaint, now modern, street, is that Queen Mary passed up it on her way back to Holyrood after visiting Darnley at the Kirk o' Field, while Bothwell only avoided meeting her by hastening down a neighbouring close.

On the north side of the street stands *Carrubber's Close*, which has curiously mixed associations. It was used as a meeting-place for Jacobite Episcopalians who refused to include the names of the Elector of Hanover and his family in their prayers. In this close lived Captain Matthew Henderson, who was described by Burns as 'a gentleman who held the patent for his honours immediately from Almighty God.' In Carrubber's Close Allan Ramsay attempted to start his theatre, which was, however, closed by order of the magistrates. This theatre was named in derision 'St. Andrew's Chapel,' and has been attended by people of various persuasions. A speculative club called the Pantheon met there in 1775. In 1778 Dr. Wyse lectured on Natural Philosophy, and among the various sects represented there are ' Bereans' (founded by Mr. John Barclay), Rowites, Irvingites, Secession, Relief, and Roman Catholics—a curious mixture even for a theatre ! Carrubber's Close Mission Hall is not situated in Carrubber's Close proper. It is a house very considerably to the east, with several intervening closes—North Gray's Close, Morrison's Close, Bailie Fyfe's Close, Paisley Close, and Chalmers'Close being among the number. The foundation-stone was laid by D. L. Moody. It must be confessed that the architecture is somewhat out of harmony with the houses of Old Edinburgh. Just east of Carrubber's Close is *Bishop's Close*, where Henry Dundas, Lord Melville, was born. It derived its name from John Spottiswoode, Archbishop of St. Andrews, who seems to have lived there in his later years. Another resident was Lady Jane Douglas, who lived there while the Douglas Case was in progress, and was visited there in 1752 by the Lord Advocate, Lord Prestongrange, so well known to readers of *Catriona*. It is said that in old days no one lived in Bishop's Land who did not keep liveried servants. *Tempora mutantur !* North Gray's Close has some interesting old carvings.

On the same side of the High Street are several closes of only moderate interest. The thistle above *Morrison's Close* seems to be quite modern, but there is an old coat-of-arms above the entrance to Bailie Fyfe's Close which repays investigation. *Paisley Close* has no special historical interest, but there is a curious tale connected with the ' Heave awa'' Coffee and Public-House (No. 99 High Street) close beside it. In 1861 the house on this site fell and killed over thirty people. One young man who feared that the rescue party might think it useless to persevere, exclaimed, ' Heave awa', chaps, I 'm no deid yet !'

A little to the east of this, on the south side, is *South Gray's Close*, where the Earl of Buchan lived, and where Lord Erskine and his brother, the Dean of Faculty, were born, and the Earls of Selkirk had their town-house. Here lived that Lord Daer whose revolutionary and litigious tendencies seem to have been equally extreme.

Far more interesting is *Hyndford's Close*. The Earls of Stirling lived here. The close might also claim the Earls of Selkirk as residents, for their house had two entrances—one from South Gray's Close, and one from Hyndford's Close; and the town-house of the Earls of Hyndford gave its name to the close. Among the residents were Lady Maxwell of Monreith and her three daughters, Catherine, Jane, and Eglantine (or Eglintoun, —called after the beautiful Susannah). So little accommodation was there in Old Edinburgh that their laces and 'best clothes' were hung up to dry in the passage outside the dining-room door, while plainer things were hung on a pole outside the window—a fashion which is still followed in that neighbourhood, though not by ladies of quality. Lady Maxwell's daughters were known as 'the three romps of Monreith.' In the *Traditions of Edinburgh* we find an interesting account of their doings. 'So easy and familiar were the manners of the great, fabled to be so still and decorous, that Miss Eglantine, afterwards Lady Wallace, used to be sent across the street to the Fountain Well for water to make tea. Lady Maxwell's daughters were the wildest romps imaginable. An old gentleman who was their relation, told me that the first time he saw these beautiful girls was in the High Street, when Miss Jane (afterwards Duchess of Gordon) was riding upon a sow, while Miss Eglantine thumped lustily behind with a stick!' The same high spirit which prompted this unconventional amusement led in later days to the raising of the Gordon Highlanders. That, and the fact that she was the hostess of Burns, are, even more than her beauty, the Duchess's titles to fame.

239

Ayndford's Close

Another well-known resident in Hyndford's Close was Dr. Daniel Rutherford, Professor of Botany, discoverer of gas, and uncle of Scott,—to many this constitutes his best claim to celebrity. It is told, as an instance of the defective postal arrangements of those days, that one of his sisters died two days and the other nine days after him without hearing of his death! There was one curious circumstance about his house. The stair of the neighbouring house was so narrow that it was impossible to carry a coffin down it. It had accordingly what was called a *servitude* on Dr. Rutherford's house—*i.e.* the inhabitants had the right of carrying the coffin through a passage into Dr. Rutherford's house and down his stair, which was of somewhat larger dimensions. Another well-known resident was Lady Balcarres, whose daughter, Lady Anne Lindsay, wrote 'Auld Robin Gray.' Scott used to visit here as a boy, and forty years later he wrote to Lady Anne: 'I remember the *locale* of Hyndford's Close perfectly, even to the Indian screen with harlequin and columbine. . . . I suppose the Close, once too clean to soil the hem of your ladyship's garments, is now a resort for the lowest mechanics—so wears the world away. . . . It is, to be sure, more picturesque to lament the desolation of towers on hills and haughs than the degradation of an Edinburgh Close: but I cannot help thinking on the simple and cosie retreats where worth and talent, and elegance to boot, were often nestled, and which now are the resort of misery, filth, poverty and vice.' In her 'simple and cosie retreat' Lady Balcarres entertained a good deal. Her guests were mainly Jacobites, and were always spoken of and announced by their full rank, in contemptuous disregard of acts of attainder.

Fountain Close is a little to the east of Hyndford's Close. Some people think it was so named from the 'Endmylie's Well,' which is so often referred to. William Powrie, one of Bothwell's assistants in Darnley's murder,

Q

John Knox's Room

said that when they heard the explosion 'thai past away togidder out at the Frier Yet, and sinderit when thai came to the Cowgate, pairt up the Blackfrier Wynd and pairt up the Cloiss which is under the Endmylie's Well.' Bassendyne the printer lived here, and here the great folio Bible was published in 1570. Another resident of Fountain Close was Adam Fullarton, who helped to condemn those tradesmen who were guilty of 'Playing at Robin Hude.'

Opposite Fountain Close is a house which is popularly known as John Knox's House, although it has been practically proved that John Knox could not possibly have lived there. Mr. Robert Miller has stated, as the result of his investigation of town records and other historical documents, that at the time John Knox was supposed to have inhabited this house, it belonged to John Mossman, a strong Roman Catholic and follower of Queen Mary. It is sad to give up the window where Knox preached to the people, and the corner where he sat when he narrowly escaped a bullet, but truth must be followed at all costs. There is, however, this consolation: that if the house had not been supposed to be John Knox's it would not have been preserved in this careful way, and although it probably is not John Knox's house, it is such a house as he *might* have lived in, and it gives an excellent idea of a sixteenth-century dwelling. It is open from 10 to 5 daily (admission 6d.), and is well worth a visit.

On the south side of the High Street are *Tweeddale Court* and *World's End Close.*

In Tweeddale Court was the town-house of the Marquis of Tweeddale. It passed afterwards into the hands of the British Linen Company, and it was when it was used as a bank that the mysterious murder of Begbie, the bank porter, occurred. It eventually came into the possession

The Netherbow Port.

of Oliver and Boyd, the well-known publishers, who still retain it.

World's End Close has a curious name, and has an equally curious appearance. It has strange associations with Sir James Stanfield, Lady Lawrence, Lady Huntingdon, and Falconer, the author of 'The Shipwreck.'

The old Netherbow Port, which was the eastern boundary of Edinburgh, no longer stands, but the narrowness of the street clearly shows its site. It was the scene of many a struggle from the days when the invading English tried to force their way in, till its last invasion, when Lochiel's Highlanders slipped through, in 1745. The old 'Port' was rebuilt soon after the Union of the Crowns, and that building disappeared about the time the North Bridge was built. The Netherbow itself exists no longer—though its clock is now prominent on the Dean Orphan Hospital—but a representation of it is carved on a neighbouring house, and this is all that is left of the ancient division between Old Edinburgh and

243

the burgh of Canongate.   No visible barrier divides them
now. The fact is not uncharacteristic of Edinburgh.
What can be seen is only a suggestion of what must be
seen in the 'mind's eye' before Old Edinburgh can live
again before us in all its magnificence and squalor,
its stateliness and turbulence, its palaces and turnpike stairs, its romance and old-world charm, so
different from the steady uninteresting level of modern
respectability.

CHAPTER IX

IN considering Old Edinburgh we are met on every hand by the fact that the interest of these old palaces, closes, chapels, etc., is almost entirely historical, and their influence on the Edinburgh of to-day is practically non-existent. It is far otherwise with the University which, along with Parliament House, has set its mark on Edinburgh. Take away these two institutions, and you not only deprive Edinburgh of her most famous sons, you also remove the two factors which are most efficacious in moulding the life of the Edinburgh of to-day. By a curious irony of fate Edinburgh, whose glories are so largely connected with the past, possesses a University which not only is the youngest of the Scottish Universities, but which stands alone in being post-Reformation, and so owes nothing directly to the Roman Church. St. Andrews University was founded in 1411, Glasgow in 1450, and Aberdeen in 1494. Edinburgh University was not even thought of, till the Town Council in 1561 decided that ' colleges for learning and upbringing of youth ' would be a suitable way of spending ecclesiastical revenues. In 1562 they asked Queen Mary for the site of the Kirk o' Field. In 1564 the word ' University ' is first used in their minutes. The Kirk o' Field was granted in 1566, but the Council had first to buy off the ' Provost ' at a cost of 300 merks. After a good deal of negotiation, King James in 1582 again granted the Kirk o' Field : hence the name by which the University was for long known,

'Academia Jacobi Sexti.' Wearied probably by this long delay, the Council seem to have been in no hurry to build, for the following year they were informed that the grant would be resumed if the building did not begin at once. The actual building must have been done with considerable speed, for that same year 1583 we find a 'Regent' appointed—Robert Rollock by name. The Principal's salary has improved since those days. Robert Rollock received £40 Scots (£3, 6s. 8d.) per annum, with board and lodging for himself, and one servant, and also the fees of 'the bairns.' What would be the feelings of the present University students if they were so described? The students cannot, however, have been exactly 'bairns,' for they seem to have had a fairly heavy Arts curriculum, made harder by the fact that 'the Scots tongue' was not allowed, all lecturing, etc., being in Latin. Those modern students who groan at the prospect of a nine o'clock class may be thankful they did not attend the University in 'the good old days,' when classes began at six in winter and five in summer! Gradually the functions of the University were extended. About the end of the seventeenth century Medical Classes were begun, and in 1693 Carstares got funds for additional Divinity Classes. Queen Anne founded the Chair of Public Law in 1707, and Civil Law and Scots Law were added by the Town Council shortly afterwards. It seems to have been a plain, uninteresting building, with three quadrangles and a lofty bell-tower. The class-rooms and the houses of the professors occupied the southern quadrangle; from it a flight of steps led to the more picturesque western court containing the students' quarters. The eastern quadrangle contained the library. There was a handsome gateway directly opposite the College Wynd; the main entrance therefore was on the north side. Principal Robertson declared that a stranger might suppose the University was an almshouse, but could not imagine it was a seat of learning. People began to realise that this scandal must be put a stop to, and in 1789 the foundation-stone of the present 'Old University' was laid. Cockburn gives a graphic account of the ceremony, which he witnessed from the top of the Old Infirmary buildings. In 1874 the New University was begun. The Act of 1889 made considerable changes in the University curriculum, and threw open University degrees to women.

The present University is a solid block, bounded on the east by the South Bridge, on the north by Chambers Street, and on the south by College Street. The entrance from South Bridge bears the following inscription :—' Academia Jacobi VI., Scotorum Regis Anno post Christum Natum, MDLXXXII. Instituta. Annoque MDCCLXXXIX. renovari coepta ; Regnante Georgio III., Principe Munificentissimo : Urbis Edinensis Praefecto, Thoma Elder, Academiae Primario, Gulielmo Robertson, Architecto, Roberto Adam.'

The dome and cupola surmounted by the golden figure of Youth bearing the torch of Knowledge is 153 feet high, and adds greatly to the appearance of the building. Inside and out the Old University is solid, massive, and severe. Yet to most students the quadrangle suggests thoughts the reverse of serious. Is it not there that students seek relaxation between classes? is it not the scene of snowball-fights? Do not the torchlight processions start there? Above all, is it not the scene of those exciting battles at the rectorial elections when the Brewster statue and the fountain are carefully barricaded, and the quadrangle is strewn with yellow, red, and blue paint, mingled with ancient eggs and other electioneering ammunition? This ceremony of the rectorial election is an interesting one, apart from the incidents to which it sometimes gives rise. The Lord Rector sits in the University Court, and, along with an assessor chosen by himself, represents the students and guards their interests. Excitement is given to the contest by the fact that, although the duties of the Lord Rector are in no way political, the rectorial candidates are always chosen by the two political associations in the University, and the election proceeds on political lines. Some of the more famous men who have held this office are Gladstone, Carlyle, Lord Derby, Lord Hartington, Lord Rosebery, Lord Robertson, Lord Balfour of Burleigh, and Lord Dufferin. The present (1906) Lord Rector is Mr. Haldane, Secretary of State for War, who is also a graduate of this University. The University owns a large and valuable library. It is said to contain two hundred thousand volumes, and is still increasing, as new books are constantly added to it. It was begun by Clement Littel, increased by the books of Drummond of Hawthornden, and since then has received many valuable bequests of money and books, notably those of the late David Laing. There are, moreover, some interesting original manuscripts and autograph letters—such as the correspondence between Elizabeth and James after the execution of Queen Mary,—and some beautifully illuminated books, the work of the old monks. The library hall itself is worth seeing. One historical relic which may be seen here is the table where Napoleon had his meals at St. Helena, and the small hole burned by the end of his cigar is still visible. The tale is told of a practical, unimaginative countrywoman who gazed at the table, and, unmoved by historical associations, ejaculated: 'It's a braw table yet!' The librarian is Mr. Alexander Anderson, whose poems are so widely known both in this country and America under the pseudonym of 'Surfaceman.'

The Faculties of Arts, Law, and Divinity hold their classes in the Old University, and some medical classes are also held here. But the great majority of medical classes are held in the New University overlooking the Meadows and in convenient proximity to the Royal Infirmary.

The
University,
Cowgate,
and
Grass-
market

On the other side of the New University is the M'Ewan Hall, with its beautiful frescoes, where the great University functions take place —such as graduation ceremonials and the Lord Rector's address. This was the gift of the Member at that time for Central Edinburgh —Mr. M'Ewan.

Adjoining th'e M'Ewan Hall is the Students' Union.[1] Modern as these buildings are, the whole neighbourhood teems with historical association. Close at hand is Potterrow, the home of Mrs. Maclehose—Burns's Clarinda. In Charles Street was born Francis Jeffrey, and 18 Buccleuch Place was where Sydney Smith, Brougham and Jeffrey met to found the *Edinburgh Review* and ' cultivate literature on a little oatmeal.' As for George Square the number of its famous inhabitants is too great to be more than referred to. In No. 25 Scott's boyhood and student days were spent; in No. 5 lived Admiral Lord Duncan, the victor of Camperdown; while Sir Ralph Abercromby lived in No. 27—now the Church of Scotland Deaconess Training Home. George Square is fitly included in a chapter dealing with the University, for it is rapidly being given over to students' residences. The Congregational Theological Hall is here. No. 14 is

Potter Row

[1] Since the above was written, a Women Students' Union has been opened in Lothian Street.

inhabited by Divinity students; while the Muir Hall
(No. 12) and the Masson Hall (No. 31) are halls of
residence for women students—Medical and Arts respec-
tively. It is strange to look back to the days when the
first inhabitants ventured out to George Square, then
considered the depths of the country. We are told that
on dark nights the inhabitants of George Square used to
fortify themselves with whisky before leaving Edinburgh
on their perilous journey.

There are some other buildings to be considered
which may fairly claim connection with the University.
Returning to Chambers Street we pass the Darien Press,
which recalls the old Darien House. In Chambers Street
we find traces (hardly more) of Brown Square, which was
the first attempt of Old Edinburgh to break away from
its narrow closes. The house of Saunders Fairford is
supposed to have stood on the site of the present Dental
Hospital. Readers of *Redgauntlet* find it hard, however,
to conjure up visions of 'Green Mantle' in the present
changed surroundings. The Heriot-Watt College is
interesting educationally. The medical work of Edinburgh students is not all done at the New University.
The College of Surgeons in Nicolson Street is another
door into the medical profession, though its degree is
not prized so highly as the University degrees of M.B.,
Ch.B. The Medical College for Women is situated in
Chambers Street, has a course of study entitling those who
attend it to graduate either at the College or the University. The Museum of Science and Art, situated in
Chambers Street, must not be omitted, and, when visitors
have some time at their disposal, is worth visiting.

Near at hand is Guthrie Street, which was better
known as College Wynd. One house in this Wynd had
considerable celebrity. Joseph Black and Keith of
Ravelston lived there, and there Scott was born. Several
of Scott's brothers and sisters died, and his father decided
to go to healthier quarters in George Square. Readers

250

The
Univer-
sity,
Cowgate,
and
Grass-
market

College Wynd

of *Redgauntlet* will remember how Saunders Fairford,
who greatly resembled the elder Scott, removed to
Brown Square on account of the delicate health of
Alan.   When Chambers Street, then known as North
College Street, was built, the Scotts' house was bought to
make room for modern improvements.   The tale is told
that Scott, relating this to a friend, said his father had
got a very good price for the house ; whereupon the
friend remarked that it might have been more profitable
to retain the house as a show-place for visitors.   'Ay !

251

Ay!' replied Sir Walter, 'that is very well; but I am
afraid I should have required to be dead first, and that
would not have been so comfortable, you know!' An
unauthenticated tradition declares that Goldsmith lived
in College Wynd when he took out medical classes at
the University. Whether this was the case or not, it is
certain he must have passed up and down it many times.

The foot of Guthrie Street takes us into the Cowgate.
A little to the south of the Canongate and parallel
to it is South Back Canongate. It is squalid and uninteresting, and has few associations. Where St. Mary
Street divides the Canongate from the High Street,
it also divides South Back Canongate from the Cowgate.
The Cowgate, however, does not rise along with the
High Street, and by the time it reaches the Grassmarket
—its western boundary—it is very considerably below the
level of the High Street. It is now noted mainly for old-
clothes shops, and it is strange to look at the dingy, dirty
street and recall the terms in which Alexander of Alesse
described it about 1530, when he said that in it 'were
the palaces belonging to the princes of the land, where
nothing was humble or rustic, but everything magnificent.' 'The Palaces of the Cowgate' was a common
term in olden days; now the phrase could only be used
in the bitterest irony. The Cowgate was originally a
fashionable suburb, and was not at first surrounded by a
wall. After Flodden the inhabitants were panic-stricken
by the danger, and the new 'Flodden' wall was built so as
to take in the Cowgate. Many are the associations of the
Cowgate; perhaps the best-known personage connected
with it is Thomas Hamilton, first Earl of Haddington,
President of the Court of Session, and Secretary of State
for Scotland,—best known, in spite of his dignities, by
the nickname bestowed on him by King Jamie, 'Tam o'
the Coogait.' He was so immensely rich that he was
supposed to have discovered the Philosopher's Stone.
King James was extremely anxious to know the secret of

his wealth. 'Tam o' the Coogait' said the secret consisted of strict adherence to two simple rules, viz. 'Never put off till to-morrow what can be done to-day; nor ever trust to another's hand what your own can execute.' It was this personage who caused King James such consternation by arranging a marriage between his son and a daughter of the Earl of Mar, whereupon the King ejaculated : 'The Lord haud a grip o' me ! If Tam o' the Coogait's son marry Jock o' Sclates' daughter, what's to come o' *me* ? '

Many of the most interesting associations of the Cowgate centre round streets or wynds which have already been dealt with. Blackfriars Street, Niddry Wynd, and many others run down from the High Street to the Cowgate. The Horse Wynd, however, being on the south side of the Cowgate, has no connection with the High Street. Lord Kennet, Lord Stuart, Lord Covington, and Lord Minto were among the most famous residents in this Wynd. The best known of all was, however, Catherine, Countess of Galloway, who appears in the 'Ridotto of Holyrood House'—a satirical poem written by three fashionable ladies, which deals with the manners and morals of their friends in a manner 'more plain than pleasant.' The Countess is there described as

'A lady well known by her airs,
Who ne'er goes to revel but after her prayers.'

She was a very stately, ceremonious old lady, and always insisted on taking out her coach and six even though she was only going a short distance. Indeed, it used to be said—probably with some slight exaggeration—that 'the leaders were sometimes at the door she was going to, when she was stepping into the carriage at her own door'!

There is a perfect wealth of memories connected with the Cowgate. The old High School Wynd ran down into it, bringing to mind the famous men who attended the High School—Scott, Cockburn, Jeffrey, Brougham,

High School Wynd

and a host of others. It was down the High School Wynd that the students came—on rowdiness intent (one thing at least is unchanged in Edinburgh!)—when they burned the Pope in effigy during the residence of the Duke of York at Holyrood.

The Pleasance conjures up curious associations by its very name, so unlike the reality. In old deeds the Convent is sometimes spoken of as 'Dearenough.' To some modern readers the district of Pleasance is associated mainly with the adventures of Cleg Kelly, though to others Jeanie Deans and Reuben Butler are more attractive. In a little cottage at St. Leonards dwelt David Deans and his daughters. Near the Park is the district of Dumbiedykes, and through the Cowgate Port Reuben Butler left Edinburgh the morning after the execution of Porteous.

The Free Library rises from the Cowgate, though it is entered from George IV. Bridge. It is built on the site of Sir Thomas Hope's house, which is described as 'All and Haill that great Lodging or Tenement of Land, high and laigh, back and fore, under and above, . . . pertaining to Sir Thomas Hope of Craighall, His Majesty's Advocate, and which tenement was built by him . . . and lyes in the said burgh of Edinburgh, upon the North side of the King's high street, there called the Cowgate, towards Magdalen Chappel.' The house seems to have been very fine, and to have contained various mottoes, among them 'TECUM HABITA' and 'AT HOSPES HUMO'— the latter an anagram on Thomas Hope if the name be spelt Huope.

The 'Magdalen Chappel' will be treated in a later chapter, but an interesting relic of ancient days still survives in the Tailors' Hall. Above the door is a tablet which bears the insignia of the tailors—a pair of shears—and the following words :—

> 'ALMIGHTIE GOD WHO FOUNDED BUILT AND GROUND
> THIS WORK WITH BLESSINGS MAK IT TO ABOUND.'

255

There are also sundry other mottoes in different parts of the building. The Earl of Rothes and the Earl of Loudon interviewed the Covenanting leaders here in 1638, and Cromwell's Scottish Commission met here eighteen years later. But there are lighter associations connected with the Tailors' Hall. When the actors left Carrubber's Close they sought refuge here, one of the pieces performed being Allan Ramsay's *Gentle Shepherd*. A house at the corner of the Cowgate and Candlemaker Row was the first home of Henry Brougham's parents.

There are several other houses in the Cowgate which are well worth investigation, but their associations are not specially interesting historically.

Passing from the Cowgate into the Grassmarket, we find ourselves in a broad, open space which seems to have remained practically unchanged for a couple of centuries. Many are the associations of the Grassmarket, yet there is disappointingly little to see. The 'Cunzie Nook' seems to have been at the foot of Candlemaker Row. In the south-west corner of the Grassmarket stood the Franciscan Monastery, or the Monastery of the 'Greyfriars.' On the south side is a narrow passage known as the Vennel, which is well worth a visit, for here may be seen a fragment of the Flodden Wall, the hurried building clearly shown by the lack of care in the workmanship. The Vennel is extremely steep, and many tales are told about it. It was here that Henry Erskine crept down on his knees one frosty day to avoid slipping, when his ministerial friend Mr. Lothian ejaculated : 'Oh! man, what a sicht for sair e'en the Parliament Hoose missed that morning!' The Vennel impressed itself also on Mr. Lothian's small son who, on being asked what was meant by 'the slippery paths of youth' in Addison's hymn, gave the unexpected explanation : 'It's the Vennel, father, in grand sklyin' trim when the kirk is comin' oot, and mother says "Oh! John, dinna slide!"'

256

The
Univer-
sity,
Cowgate,
and
Grass-
market

The West Bow

The famous West Bow gave access to the Grassmarket
on the north-east. It is unnecessary to recount the
many entries which were made into the town by this
route. James IV. and V., Mary of Guise, Queen Mary

herself, James VI. and his bride, Anne of Denmark,
Charles I., Cromwell, and James VII. are among the
many who have done so. Near the West Bow lived
Major Weir the Wizard, who was said to have a magic
stick, and to have careered about in a fiery chariot invisible to all beholders. Here too lived Provost Stewart, at
whose house Prince Charlie was nearly captured making
a hairbreadth escape by a secret door.

At the south-west side was the West Port. Just outside this gate was the little burgh of Wester Portsburgh,
which has been described as 'the trade suburb of old
Edinburgh, as the Royal Burgh of Canongate outside
the Netherbow Port was its Court suburb.' The curious
customs of this little burgh are charmingly told by Miss
Dunlop in her paper ' Anent Wester Portsburgh.' Early
last century the West Port had an unpleasant notoriety
on account of the murders of Burke and Hare. When all
is said, the fact remains that the Grassmarket is mainly
interesting because of the executions which took place
there. The stones on the causeway still mark the place
where the gallows stood. Criminals of higher rank were
executed at the Cross, but plainer people were hanged in
the Grassmarket : hence the expression so common among
the Covenanters, ' to glorify God in the Grassmarket.'
It was here that most of them suffered, and their memory
still haunts the place. It was in the Grassmarket, too,
that the smuggler Wilson was hanged in 1736. Dr.
Carlyle gives a vivid account of the proceedings, which
might well impress him, as a young man sitting at the
window where he had hoped to be was among those
accidentally killed by the soldiers. Finally, it was in
the Grassmarket that Captain John Porteous was hanged
on a dyer's pole.

In modern days the Grassmarket has been less notorious,
but not less interesting ; for in the Corn Exchange orators
like Gladstone and Disraeli have thrilled crowds by their
eloquence. No longer do men die for ' the good cause,'

but statesmen who sacrifice time and strength in the service of the country, and keep our flag flying, are no unworthy successors of the men who gave up their lives for their Faith.

The Lower Bow

CHAPTER X

WE have already, in previous chapters, referred to the fact that Old Edinburgh abounded in churches, chapels, and other ecclesiastical houses. In some cases these are still in existence, but of the great majority not a trace remains. One writer mentions the following as being a few of the churches of old Edinburgh dedicated in whole or in part to the Virgin Mary : 'The Abbey Church of Holyrood, founded in honour of the Holy Cross, the Blessed Virgin and all Saints ; Trinity College Church in honour of the Holy Trinity, the ever blessed and glorious Virgin Mary, etc. ; the large Collegiate Church of St. Mary in the Fields ; St. Mary's Chapel and Nunnery in St. Mary's Wynd ; St. Mary's Chapel, Niddry's Wynd ; the Virgin Mary's Chapel, Portsburgh ; the Hospital of Our Lady, Leith Wynd ; the Chapel and Convent of St. Mary de Placentia in the Pleasance ; the great church at Leith of old styled St. Mary's Chapel, and the Collegiate Church of Restalrig.' Although they all possess considerable interest, we do not propose to discuss these churches. In addition to the Abbey of Holyrood and the Cathedral Church of St. Giles', which we have already dwelt on at some length (Chapters IV. and V.), we believe that the ecclesiastical buildings of greatest general interest are the Churches of St. Cuthbert, Trinity College, and Greyfriars, and the Magdalene Chapel. St. Cuthbert's derives its name from the famous

Scottish Border Saint who flourished in the seventh century. He was Prior of Old Melrose, and many churches in the south of Scotland are named after him —notably Glencairn, Sorn, and Kirkcudbright (the Kirk of St. Cuthbert). But his later years were spent at Lindisfarne, and when he died in 687 he was buried in the church which afterwards became Durham Cathedral, and which is another 'St. Cuthbert's.' In very early days we hear of a church on the site of the present St. Cuthbert's—probably at first a mere hut of wattles. Chalmers says : 'The Church of St. Cuthbert is unquestionably ancient, perhaps as old as the age which followed the demise of the worthy Cuthbert, towards the end of the seventh century.' Some claim that St. Giles' is older than St. Cuthbert's, while Archbishop Eyre says that 'St. Cuthbert's is the oldest foundation of any Church in Scotland.' It is unprofitable to discuss which can claim the greater antiquity; it is sufficient to say that both are very old, and that in early days the function of St. Giles' was to supply ordinances to the Castle, while St. Cuthbert's was responsible for the rest of Edinburgh. We find references to St. Cuthbert's in charters of David I., by which we learn that the chapelries of Corstorphine and Liberton belonged to it. It seems, indeed, to have had many dependencies, including the Virgin Mary's Chapel, Portsburgh, St. Roque's and St. John's Chapel on the Boroughmuir. St. John's Chapel became afterwards the Convent of St. Catherine of Siena, and the name is preserved in Sciennes Road. St. Mary of Placentia was another dependency of St. Cuthbert, and that name is preserved in the district of Pleasance. St. Ninian's Chapel, Pleasance, and the Chapel of St. Mary and St. James, Newhaven ; the Chapel of Mounthorby (connected with the Knights Templar) and the Chapel and Hospital of St. Leonards, also belonged to St. Cuthbert's. St. Cuthbert's was very rich and powerful in the reign of David I., and may be taken as representing the Culdee Church of that day.

Distressed by some of the irregularities of the Culdees,
David did his best to raise the rival power of Rome.
Accordingly he made St. Cuthbert's into a vicarage under
the Abbey of Holyrood. Although St. Cuthbert's never
again rose above the status of a parish church, it regained
much of its old wealth and importance. It is a signi-
ficant fact that at the present day, on investigating
the origin of Edinburgh churches, in nine cases out of
ten the answer will be, 'A *quoad sacra* taken off St.
Cuthbert's.'

We read that in 1487 a certain William Towers gave
an endowment amounting to fourteen merks annually for
the Chaplain of St. Anne's Altar, while Alexander Currie,
vicar of Haddington, made a similar provision for the
altar of Holy Trinity. In 1560 'St. Cuthbert's under
the Castle' fared better than many other churches.
The altars and 'images' were removed, but the outward
form of the church remained unchanged. In 1589 a
new 'loft' was added, and also—what sounds strange to
modern ears—a 'pillar of repentance for offenders.' It
was repaired again in 1623, but suffered severely at the
hands of Cromwell's soldiers. Cromwell, with his customary disregard for sacred things, converted the church
into barracks, and his soldiers seem to have destroyed
everything they could lay hands on. In 1772 it was
decided to build a new church, which was finished in
1775. It was this which was the object of Scott's satire
in his well-known remark, that St. John's was like a
pretty child's toy, and St. Cuthbert's like the ugly pack-
ing-case. The present church was opened on 11th July
1894. It is a solid and imposing structure, and it is
interesting to note that the old tower has been retained.

St. Cuthbert's can boast of some famous men among its
ministers. The first reformed minister was William
Harlaw, and his colleague, appointed in 1578, was
Robert Pont, who was Superintendent of Moray, Provost
of Trinity College, a Lord of Session, and five times

Moderator of the General Assembly. When the church was demolished in 1774, 'a heart enclosed in lead and filled with perfumes' was discovered, and was supposed to belong to Mr. Pont. One of his colleagues, Richard Dickson, contributed largely to the *Second Book of Discipline*, and published a book on 'Sacrilege.' One of the best known of the St. Cuthbert's ministers was Alexander Williamson, who rejoiced in a large supply of wives, no fewer than seven. This ecclesiastical Henry VIII. was turned out of St. Cuthbert's in 1665 on account of his Covenanting principles, but returned at the Revolution of 1688. His successor was the famous Neil M'Vicar, who prayed for King George when Prince Charlie held the city. Dr. David Dickson, who is commemorated by a piece of sculpture built into the tower; Sir Henry Wellwood Moncreiff of Tullibole; Dr. Paul, and Dr. Veitch were St. Cuthbert's ministers of a later date. The present ministers, Dr. Macgregor and Dr. Wallace Williamson, are well known beyond the bounds of Scotland. With the exception of St. Giles', St. Cuthbert's is the only parish church in Edinburgh which has a daily service. It is held in the choir at five o'clock. As is to be expected, many famous people are buried in St. Cuthbert's Churchyard, among them the Rev. David Williamson, the Nisbets of Dean, Napier of Merchiston, the inventor of logarithms, and Thomas De Quincey, author of *Confessions of an Opium Eater*.

Another important ecclesiastical foundation is the Magdalene Chapel at the west end of the Cowgate. It was founded in 1503 by 'Janet Rynd, relict, executrix, and only intromissatrix with the guds and gear of umquhil Michael Macquhan.' The charter goes on to say: 'Therefore wit ye me, To the praise and honour of Almighty God and of his mother the Blissed Virgin Mary, and of Mary Magdallen and of the haill celestial court to have erected and edified ane certain chapell and hospital-house, lyeing in the burgh of Edinburgh, upon the

MAGDALENE CHAPEL

South side of the King's high street, called the Cowgate, for habitation of the aforesaid chaplain and poor.' The Magdalene Chapel was the scene of occurrences which would greatly have surprised Janet Rynd could she have foreseen them. In 1560 John Craig came to Scotland. He was a Dominican Monk who had turned Protestant, and had been condemned to be burned. He escaped, however, the day before the auto-da-fé, and after living at Bologna and Vienna returned to Scotland. As he had completely forgotten his native language, he preached Latin sermons in the Magdalene Chapel. It was this same John Craig who, in St. Giles', 'proclaimed' Queen Mary and Bothwell. The Chapel was also used as a meeting-place for the General Assembly in 1578. Melville tells us: 'The Generall Assemblie conveinit at Edinbruche in Apryll 1578 in the Magdalen Chapell. Mr. Andrew Melvill was chosin Moderator, whar was concludit, That Biscopes suld be callit be thair awin names or be the names of *Breither* in all tyme coming, and that lordlie name and authority banissed from the Kirk of God, quhilk hes bot a Lord Chryst Jesus.' In this Chapel the National Covenant was got ready, as it was conveniently near Greyfriars Churchyard. In 1661 the body of Argyle was brought here, while his head was fixed to the Tolbooth. Here the body lay some days until it was removed to Kilmun. After these various vicissitudes the Chapel is now used by the Edinburgh Medical Mission.

The Chapel is small, but apart even from its historical associations has some interesting features. The arms of the Hammermen of Edinburgh with the Hammer and Crown are still there, and curiously wrought iron which was hammered out by them. The tomb of Janet Rynd is here, with an inscription in Gothic letters which is far from easy to decipher. It is covered by a wooden slab forming part of the floor, but the slab is always raised to allow visitors to see it. The glass is extremely interesting, as it is almost the only specimen in Scotland of pre-Reformation glass. Below are the arms of the founder, while above are the royal arms of Scotland and the Guise arms. The royal arms of Scotland are surrounded by a wreath of thistles, while the arms of Mary of Guise are encircled by a laurel wreath. The colouring of the royal arms is considered a good example of the skill of the pre-Reformation craftsmen.

A small room opening out of the chapel contains a clock belonging to the Hammermen of Edinburgh, and some of the chairs used at the General Assembly held here. They are old and worm-eaten and look extremely fragile, though every care is taken to preserve them. The sword of Argyle is also shown, and the table where his headless body was laid after his execution. These relics of bygone days have a curiously effective setting in this little Chapel away from the bustle of modern life. It is easier to fancy oneself back in Old Edinburgh than in some of the other 'sights' where modernity is painfully in evidence.

Another ecclesiastical relic is Trinity College Church, or, to give it its correct designation, 'The Collegiate Church of the Holy Trinity.' It was dedicated 'to the honour and praise of the Holy Trinity, to the ever blessed and glorious Virgin Mary, to Saint Ninian the Confessor, and to all the Saints and elect people of God,' and was founded in 1462 by Mary of Gueldres who was the Queen Dowager. She died the following year, and was buried, Lesley tells us, 'in the Queen's College besyde Edinburgh, quhilk sche herself foundit, biggit, and dottit.'[1]   Endowment was provided for 'a provost, eight prebends, and two singing boys,' and it was also appointed that 'whenever any of the said Prebendaries shall read Mass, he shall after the same in his sacerdotal habiliments, repair to the tomb of the foundress with a sprinkler, and there devoutly read over the *De Profundis*, together with the *Fidelium*, and an exhortation to excite the people to devotion.'   In addition to the ecclesiastical functionaries, provision was also made for thirteen poor bedesmen, on condition that they prayed for the soul of the foundress.   It is interesting to read that 'the saidis Beidsmen sall prepair and mak ilk ane of yame on yair awin expensis ane blew gown conform to the first Foundation.'   The Reformation naturally made considerable changes in a foundation of this kind.   In 1567 Moray made over the church and buildings to the Provost, Sir Simon Preston—the same who lived at the Black Turnpike, and who was Queen Mary's gaoler there. This transference of authority necessitated new regulations for 'the beidmen and hospitularies now present and to cum.'   After the town took up this, it became customary for private citizens to make provision for its inmates : for example, Katherine Norwell, widow of Bassendyne the printer, left 'to everie ane of the pure folkis in the Hospitall of the Trinitie College, and of the Toun College of the west end of the College Kirk, iijs. iiijd.'

The curious old paintings (referred to in Chapter V.) which may be seen in the Holyrood Portrait Gallery are supposed to have formed the altarpiece of the original Trinity College Church.   There is another link between Holyrood and Trinity College.   Mary of Gueldres was originally buried in the church which she founded, but in 1842 her remains were removed to Holyrood, where they now rest in the Royal Vault.   Trinity College was

---

[1] Built and endowed.

situated in Leith Wynd. But Leith Wynd had to be
sacrificed to the exigencies of the North British Railway,
and the old church was pulled down in 1848. The stones
were, however, carefully marked, and rebuilt after years
of delay in exactly the same relative positions; so, though
the site of Trinity College Church is different, part of it
bears the same appearance as in the days of Mary of
Gueldres. A plan of the old church may be seen in the
vestry. It is adorned with curious carving and quaint
old gargoyles, and should on no account be omitted by
any one going round the 'sights' of Edinburgh. A
curious effect is produced if we look through and past the
modern part of the church to the beautiful Gothic building shut off by two fine arches which seem strangely out
of keeping with the modern addition. The very fact that
only a part can be seen through those wonderful arches
gives an effect of mystery which must be seen to be
realised. The church stands in Jeffrey Street, but may
also be reached from the High Street by Chalmers' Close.[1]

Better known to the majority of 'sightseers' than either
the Magdalene Chapel or Trinity College Church is Greyfriars Churchyard. The Monastery of the 'Greyfriars'
was founded by James I. It stood in the Grassmarket,
but the gardens or 'yairds' occupied the site of the
present graveyard. As has already been told in Chapter
VII., when St. Giles' Churchyard became too crowded
Queen Mary granted the request of the magistrates and
bestowed this open space on the town—'swa that the air
within oure said towne may be the mair puire and clene.'
It is strange that this churchyard, which to us suggests
everything ancient and venerable, was considered a sort of
new cemetery in 1562.

The two churches of Old and New Greyfriars cannot
claim remote historical interest, though Old Greyfriars is
able to boast of some famous men among its ministers. Dr.
Robertson, ' our historian of Scotland, of the Continent,

[1] It may be seen on Saturdays after 2 p.m.

and of America,'—whom Colonel Mannering did not hear
—was one of these. Dr. Robertson's colleague, Dr.
Erskine, was a well-known man in his day; and in later
days Old Greyfriars has numbered among its ministers
Dr. Robert Lee and Dr. Robert Wallace. Greyfriars
was the church attended by the Scotts, and it was on the
way home from church that Sir Walter Scott (then a
young man) first got to know the beautiful Miss Stuart
by offering her his umbrella.

The great interest of Greyfriars, however, centres
round its graves. The Covenanters here are greatly
in evidence. That flat stone where the Covenant was
signed is still pointed out by the attendant. One may
also see the grave of Alexander Henderson who preached
in Greyfriars on this occasion, and who was largely
responsible for the Shorter Catechism. The long alley
to the north was where the twelve hundred Covenanting
prisoners after Bothwell Brig were shut up for five weary
months. Lastly, the ' Martyrs' Monument ' is one of the
most prominent objects of interest in Greyfriars. The
verse on the tomb cannot exactly be commended as a
literary effort, but the prose unadorned conveys information which is sufficiently startling without any outside aids
to impressiveness—namely, that there were ' one way and
another, murdered and destroyed for the same cause,
about eighteen thousand, of whom were executed at
Edinburgh about a hundred noblemen and gentlemen,
ministers and others.' Many of these were buried in the
churchyard of the ' West Kirk ' (St. Cuthbert's), but ' the
most of them lie here.' This is not the place to consider
the merits of the case. Doubtless there were faults on
both sides; but we may well be thankful that we live in
happier days, when it would be utterly impossible that
eighteen thousand persons should die for any religious or
political cause in less than thirty years. The list begins
with Argyle, who was executed in 1661, and ends with
Renwick in 1688. In the words of R. L. Stevenson,

GREYFRIARS CHURCHYARD

whose essay on Greyfriars is a constant joy to those
who read it, 'there stands a monument dedicated in
uncouth Covenanting verse to all who lost their lives in
that contention. There is no moorsman shot in a snow-
shower beside Irongray or Co'monell, there is not one of
the two hundred who were drowned off the Orkneys, nor
so much as a poor, over-driven Covenanting slave in the
American plantations, but can lay claim to a share in
that Memorial, and, if such things interest just men
among the shades, can boast he has a monument on earth
as well as Julius Cæsar or the Pharaohs.'

At some distance from the 'Martyrs' Monument,' but
within this same hospitable all-embracing graveyard of
Greyfriars, is the grave of Sir George Mackenzie of Rosehaugh, King's Advocate under Charles II., founder of the
Advocates' Library, 'author of some pleasing sentiments
on toleration,' and the 'Bluidy Mackenzie' of the Covenanters. The Heriot boys used to 'snatch a fearful joy'
by daring the late King's Advocate to appear:—

> 'Bluidy Mackenzie, come oot if ye daur,
> Lift the bolt and draw the bar,'

269

they shouted through the grating, rushing off to safety
the moment their defiance was delivered. 'But,' says
Stevenson, 'Sir George had other affairs on hand, and the
author of an essay on toleration continued to sleep peacefully among the many whom he so intolerantly helped to
slay.' It was in Mackenzie's tomb that James Hay took
refuge in 1783, and was supplied with food by the other
Heriot boys, as, fortunately for himself, he too was a
'Herioter.'

Of famous Scots buried in Greyfriars there is no end.
A strange incongruous mixture they are:—Regent
Morton, Porteous, Sir Thomas Hope of Craighall, John
Mylne the Master Mason, Duncan Forbes of Culloden,
the Fowlis of Ravelston, the Byres of Coates, the Chies-
leys of Dalry, the Littles of Craigmillar, and the Prim-
roses—ancestors of Lord Rosebery—are among those who
lie there. Literature is well represented in the person
of George Buchanan, Henry Mackenzie ('The Man of
Feeling'), M'Crie the historian, Principal Robertson,
Allan Ramsay, Duncan Ban Macintyre, and many others.
The father of George Heriot lies not far from the
Martyrs' Monument, while the elder Scott is buried in
the eastern side of the churchyard. Space fails to tell
of the principals and professors of the University, and
the Lords of Session and advocates who have found a last
resting-place here. A list of the most famous people may
be seen at the gate.

On the south side of Greyfriars is Heriot's Hospital,
an enduring proof of the generosity of 'Jingling Geordie,'
and of the love he bore his native town even when far
away from it.

But, as we stand in this 'infelix campus,' we feel that
here, in the presence of her mighty dead, we really are in
the heart of Old Edinburgh. The strange mingling of
different persuasions and avocations does but make it
more characteristic of the town; as we think of the long
procession of soldiers, literary men, musicians, architects,

tradesmen, advocates, judges, ministers, Royalists and Covenanters, we seem actually to be transported to those bygone days, to realise their hopes and fears, the great principles of loyalty and of freedom for which they gladly laid down their lives; and while regarding those who differ from us with a larger charity than was possible in the 'Killing Time,' we gain an inspiration to serve our country and our generation as faithfully, as unselfishly, and as loyally, as did these gallant Scotsmen of another day.

Calton Hill shewing the monuments to Dugald Stewart & Nelson

CHAPTER XI

SOME LITERARY MEN OF OLD EDINBURGH

WHEN we think of literary men in Old Edinburgh, one of the earliest figures we see is that of GAVIN DOUGLAS, the learned Provost of St. Giles', the translator of Virgil, afterwards Bishop of Dunkeld, who lived between 1475 and 1522.

> 'More pleased that, in a barbarous age,
> He gave rude Scotland Virgil's page ;
> Than that beneath his rule he held
> The Bishopric of fair Dunkeld.'

He lived, as we have seen, in the Prebends' Close, south of the church, on one side of the old graveyard. In the nether kirkyard, as has been already mentioned, was the Chapel of the Holy Rood, founded by WALTER CHEPMAN, the first printer in Scotland ; and not very far away, in a close at the Netherbow, lived, a little later, THOMAS BASSENDYNE, who will always be remembered on account of the beautiful folio Bible which he printed in 1574. These Bibles are very rare, and are known as Bassendyne's Bibles to this day.

DUNBAR, the author of the *Thrissill and the Rois*, was constantly in Edinburgh about this time with the court, and his descriptions of the life and manners of the King's 'Hie Street' are extremely vivid :—

> 'At your Hie Cross where gold and silk
> Suld be there are but cruds and milk,
> And at your Tron but cockle and wilk,
> Panches puddings for Jock and Jame.'

s

It is generally thought that he was killed at Flodden; certainly he is never heard of after that date.

A little further west than the Prebends' Close was the dwelling of the Littels of Liberton. CLEMENT LITTEL, advocate, bequeathed his library to the town, and it formed the nucleus of the University Library. The present Free Library is built very near the site of Clement Littel's house.

SIR DAVID LYNDSAY must have been often in Edinburgh when he was attached to the court of James IV., and also when he was 'Usher' of the little prince, who became King James V. when little more than a year old. James, in later years, knighted him and made him Lyon King at Arms. He occupied the place in Scottish poetry of the 'people's poet,' which Burns afterwards held, and his poems preserve for us the manners and feelings of the time. His satirical poems, directed against the vices and frivolity of the priests, are said to have 'done more for the Reformation than all the sermons of Knox.'

In the earlier days of Queen Mary's reign GEORGE BUCHANAN was her reader and tutor. In one of Randolph's letters we hear of Mary reading daily after dinner with Maister George Buchanan 'somewhat of Lyvie.' At this time he greatly admired the Queen's ability, and in testimony thereof dedicated to her his fine metrical Latin version of the Psalms. It was about this time she made him a pensioner of the Abbey of Crossraguel. He wrote poems celebrating her marriage to Darnley, and the birth of the prince; but went finally over to the side of Moray, by whose influence he was appointed, in 1566, Principal of St. Leonard's College in St. Andrews, and there he wrote his *History*, in which he condemned the unhappy Queen in no measured terms. It has been said, though never proved, that he wrote the Casket Letters. He certainly accompanied Moray to England to give evidence against the Queen. It gives a curious glimpse into the history of the time to hear that in 1567, shortly after Mary was imprisoned in Lochleven, Buchanan was, though a layman, appointed Moderator of the General Assembly. Part of the 'deliverance' was as follows: 'This present has offered some better occasion than in times byegane, and has begun to tread Satan under foot.'

No one can pass along the High Street or enter St. Giles' without thinking of JOHN KNOX and the part he played in the Reformation. We realise how true Randolph's words were: 'The voice of that one man is able, in an hour, to put more life in us than six hundred trumpets.' He had had a stormy and stirring life from the days when he bore 'a twa-handed sword' before 'Maister' George Wishart, when he was shut up in the Castle of St. Andrews with his 'bairns,' sons of the Lairds of Ormiston and Longniddry, and when he rowed in the French galley a prisoner, and once when tossing on the waves saw, with wistful eyes, the Cathedral of St. Andrews and the Tower of St. Rule in the distance. Then came long years when he lived in England and on the Continent, years in which he gathered knowledge of men and affairs. He was fifty-four when the Reformation took place, and for more than ten years he preached in St. Giles', with short intervals of absence, twice every Sunday and thrice during the week. It was of his pulpit in St. Giles', now in the Antiquarian Museum, that he said: 'I am in the place where I must speak the truth, and the truth I will speak, impugn it who so list.' Some of his notable sermons were those preached against Queen Mary, for which she afterwards took him to task at Holyrood. Another famous sermon was that on the death of Moray, when the corpse lay on a bier in the church; and his last sermon, also well known, was preached at the induction of his colleague, Mr. Lawson. He wrote as strenuously as he worked and preached; and his *History* is valuable, though much of the wording of it jars upon modern ears.

Some
Literary
Men of
Old
Edin-
burgh

The Parish Schools which John Knox initiated, and which for centuries have provided education for the 'bairns' of broad Scotland, are a lasting memorial to his zeal for education. If he had been permitted to carry out the complete scheme given in the *Book of Discipline*, there would have been a school in every parish, and a grammar-school in every town; and these 'primary' and 'secondary' schools were to be so arranged as to link them on to the Universities. But the greed of the nobles and the apathy of the people were fatal to the scheme in its entirety.

Nearly a century after the days of Knox and the troublous times of the Reformation, the saintly LEIGHTON, another Presbyterian minister and man of letters, may be seen passing along the busy High Street—at first when he paid occasional visits to the city from the leafy shades of Newbattle Park and Manse, and afterwards when he was Principal of the University. One of Old Edinburgh's own students, he went abroad afterwards, as so many young Scotsmen did, and studied at Douay, where he lived for some time with relatives.

He was presented to the parish of Newbattle in 1641, and laboured there for eleven years. It has been said of him—'a purer, humbler, holier spirit than Robert Leighton's never tabernacled in Scottish clay.' In 1652 he gave up his charge, and later on became Principal of Edinburgh University, where he remained for ten years. His continental studies and experiences had given him a breadth of view which made the narrowness of many of his co-Presbyters very painful to him. In 1662 he was urged to accept a bishopric, and chose that of Dunblane, because 'it was small and poor.' He found, to his grief, that Episcopalians were as intolerant as Presbyterians. Sick at heart owing to the cruelty that prevailed, he twice journeyed to London to implore of the King personally to adopt milder measures. Much was promised, but nothing was done. In 1670 he was made Archbishop of Glasgow, and accepted the office only that he might carry out measures 'for the comprehension of Presbyterians.' Finding this a hopeless task, he resigned his office in 1673 and retired to Sussex, where he spent his last days in peaceful study. His commentary on St. Peter is full of deep spiritual teaching, and is probably the best known of all his works.

In 1684, the year that Leighton died, WILLIAM CARSTARES, who had been, like him, first a student of Edinburgh University, and who was to be also, in later years, its Principal, was tortured (probably in the Laigh Parliament House) to make him reveal secrets connected with the Rye House Plot. The torture was in vain, and he was finally allowed to return to Holland, where he had been living before as a Professor at Utrecht. He was on terms of intimate friendship with William of Orange, who said of him, 'I have known Carstares long and well, and know him to be an honest man.' He came from Holland with William, and was afterwards appointed Chaplain for Scotland to the King and Queen. His great influence with William was used in the service of the Church of Scotland, and owing to this he was popularly called 'Cardinal Carstares.' He was appointed Principal of Edinburgh University in 1704, was presented to Greyfriars Church the same year, and in the following eleven years was four times Moderator of the General Assembly. He died in 1715, and to this day his wisdom, scholarship, and piety are held in remembrance. The story is told that when he was laid to rest in Greyfriars Churchyard two of the many mourners were deeply affected; they turned out to be two Episcopalian clergymen who had been long supported by him, sturdy Presbyterian though he was.

In the early years of the eighteenth century the vexed question of the Union filled the minds of the people, and the busy pen of LOCKHART OF CARNWATH describes the scene and the various actors in it. In 1717 a

Ramsay's first shop
sign of the Mercury

young man ALLAN RAMSAY opened a shop as a wig-maker at the sign of the Mercury in a timber-fronted land opposite the head of Niddry's Wynd, which survived till a very recent period. He was a great 'club' man, and his earliest poems were pro-duced for the diversion of the members of his club. By and by these poems were printed, and it be-came quite a popular thing to send to the wig-shop for a penny sheet con-taining the latest poem.

Many of the names most famous in that day at the bar, in the pulpit, judges and professors, were friends of 'honest Allan.' In 1725 he brought out his *Tea-table Miscellany of Scottish Songs.* Books were added to the wig-shop, and he boasts that he 'thatches the outside and lines the inside of the head of many a douce citizen, and baithways gathers in the cash.' While the poet was still at the sign of the Mercury, he wrote *The Gentle Shepherd*, and dedicated it to Susannah, Countess of Eglinton. Some years afterwards he presented her with the original manuscript, and for many years it was preserved in the library of Auchinleck House.

The great charm of *The Gentle Shepherd* was its absolute truth to Nature, and its simplicity: hence it found its way at once into the hearts of the people. There were few Lowland homes, gentle or simple, that did not possess a copy of it, and it stood on many a cottage window-sill, beside Boston's *Fourfold State* and *Crook in the Lot*, a sure test of its hold on the hearts

278

of the people. About the date of the second edition
Ramsay moved to the end shop of the Luckenbooths
looking east down the High Street, and here he started
a lending library and regular book-shop. Many famous
people visited the shop in the Luckenbooths, and looked
out on the crowds who surrounded the 'Cross' every fine
afternoon or took a stroll on the 'plainstanes.' When
dinner was at midday, and assemblies and concerts
began at five or six o'clock, the early afternoon was the
time when all were abroad. 'This habit of congregating
at the Cross of Edinburgh was common to all classes : the
lawyer met his clients, the citizen made of it his Rialto
to talk business or civic gossip with his brother traders,
and there the beau, ready dressed for the assembly in
scarlet waistcoat, lace ruffles and scarf, buckles, wig, and
cocked hat, showed himself off to an admiring or envious
crowd.'

Among those who visited Allan Ramsay's shop in the
Luckenbooths was the poet GAY, described as 'a pleasant-
looking little man in a tye wig,' and Smollett, spoken of
by a contemporary as 'a very handsome man and a good
talker.' Gay and Ramsay were great friends, and had
many discussions about Scotch words and phrases, and
also about the allusions to national customs in *The Gentle
Shepherd*.

By the time SMOLLETT came to Edinburgh, the Cross
was gone, though, he says, 'it may still be seen in my
Lord Somerville's garden.' Smollett at this time lived
with his sister, Mrs. Telfer, in St. John Street—then a
very aristocratic quarter. Lord Monboddo, who is best
remembered by his persistent assertion that man was
evolved from the ape, lived here also. His picture may
be seen on the stairs leading from the Signet Library.
He was very hospitable, and Lord Cockburn describes his
suppers as 'the most Attic in his day. Beautiful flowers
decorated the table ; he had the finest of wines, and sweet
odours as well as light were diffused by his lamps. His

279

Smollett's House

lovely daughter 'Bess' Burnet was the belle of many an
assembly and concert. She was admired by Burns, both
for her looks and manners, and he mourned for her early
death in the elegy beginning :

> 'Life ne'er exulted in so rich a prize
>   As Burnet—lovely from her native skies,
>   Nor envious death so triumphed in a blow,
>   As that which laid the accomplished Burnet low.'

280

Some
Literary
Men of
Old
Edin-
burgh

The Earl of Aboyne also lived in St. John Street, and
the Countess of Hyndford, who was compared by Charles
Kirkpatrick Sharpe to the bearded Countess in *Don
Quixote*. Sharpe's mother, Mrs. Sharpe of Hoddam,
was a beautiful woman who inherited much of the beauty
and ability of her grandmother, Susannah, Countess of
Eglinton. She frequently met Smollett as Miss Renton,
and in *Humphrey Clinker* we hear that Jerry Milford
' had the honour to dance with the charming Miss
R. . .n at the Hunters' Ball, and fell a victim to her
bright eyes.' Smollett knew the Renton family intimately, as one of Mrs. Sharpe's sisters married his
nephew.

By the time BURNS visited Edinburgh in 1786, ' honest
Allan's ' shop in the Luckenbooths had passed into the
hands of Mr. William Creech, who had been tutor to the
Earl of Glencairn, Burns's patron. A brilliant circle
frequented the shop—David Hume, John Home, Dugald
Stewart, Henry Mackenzie, Adam Smith, Dr. Blair, and
many others. Creech was twice Lord Provost of Edinburgh, and it was he who put a stop to the gruesome
custom of the ' Deid Chack,' a repast of which the
magistrates had always been in the habit of partaking
after they had witnessed an execution. Creech died in
1815, and two years afterwards, in 1817, the Luckenbooths were swept away. In the days before Flodden,
Dunbar wrote of the Luckenbooths that ' it hald the
licht fra' its Paroche Kirk,' and its old walls survived to
see the rejoicings for Waterloo.

One of the most brilliant figures in the eighteenth
century—the ' Augustan age of Scotland,' as it has been
called—was DAVID HUME, the historian, of the family of
Hume of Ninewells. He was very friendly with Dr.
Carlyle of Inveresk, and in that well-known minister's
autobiography we get many glimpses of him. As has
been mentioned before, he lived in Riddle's Court, then
in Jack's Land, where most of his *History* was written, and

281

then in James's Court. Soon after moving there he went
to France as Secretary of the Embassy, and wrote from
Paris to his friend Adam Ferguson,
'I wish twice or thrice every day
for my easy chair and my retreat
at James's Court.' He returned
to Edinburgh in 1766 for a few
months, but went to London as
Under-Secretary of State. At
length in 1769 he returned to Edinburgh, to settle down for the rest
of his life. After his return he
wrote to Adam Smith at Kirkcaldy
from his room with its windows
looking across the Firth of Forth:
'I am glad to have come within
sight of you and have a view of
Kirkcaldy, but I wish also to be within speaking terms of
you.'

Chimney & Gable,
Riddles Close

This is Dr. Carlyle's opinion of him, and it is specially
interesting as given by an intimate friend and contemporary : 'He was a man of great knowledge and of a
most social and benevolent temper. He was branded with
the name of atheist on account of the attacks on revealed
religion in his works. He was professedly a sceptic, but
not an atheist. Along with much learning and fine
taste, he had the greatest simplicity of mind and manners
I ever knew. I never believed that these sceptical
principles had laid hold on his mind, but thought his
books were written from affectation and love of vainglory.
Robertson, John Home and I all lived in the country, and
came only occasionally to town. Supper being the
fashionable meal, we, by cadies, assembled our friends to
meet us in a tavern at nine o'clock ; and a fine time it was
when we could collect David Hume, Adam Smith, Adam
Ferguson, Lord Elibank, and Drs. Blair and Jardine on
an hour's warning. One night David Hume came in

rather late. He pulled the door-key from his pocket and said his maid Peggy had given it to him so that she need not sit up for him; for, quoth she, when the honest fellows came in from the country he never got home till after one o'clock.'

He used to regale his friends in his flat in James's Court with supper, which consisted of the favourite 'roasted hens' or 'mince collops,' good French claret, and sometimes punch. When the new town began to arise beyond the Nor' Loch he built a house for himself at the south-west corner of St. Andrew Square, which may still be seen. The street leading southward to Princes Street had not yet got a name, but Miss Nancy Ord, one of the Chief Baron's daughters, got a workman to paint on the corner-stone of Hume's house 'St. David Street,' where it remains to this day. Tradition goes on to tell that when his maid went out in the morning she was horror-stricken to see such liberties taken with her master's name, but Hume himself laughed and said to her, 'Never heed; many a better man has been made a saint before now.'

We get many glimpses of the coterie who were at supper in the tavern. ADAM SMITH, who lived with his old mother in Kirkcaldy while he wrote his great work *The Wealth of Nations*, was much beloved by all his friends. He was very absent, and a curious story is told regarding his habit of talking and laughing to himself when he was walking on the street. Two market-women one day looked at him with surprise and compassion, thinking he was 'daft.' 'Hegh, sir!' said one with a sigh; while the other replied, 'Ay, and he's weel pit on,' evidently thinking it remarkable that such a well-dressed lunatic should be at large.

ADAM FERGUSON was another of the party. As a young man he was chaplain of the 42nd (Black Watch), and at Fontenoy, disregarding the injunction of his commanding officer to keep in the rear with the surgeons, he took part, broadsword in hand, in the fiery onslaught of the Highlanders, which was described by the French themselves as 'the Highland furies rushing upon them with more violence than a sea driven by a tempest.'

His military service made Ferguson turn his mind to the study of war, and gave great clearness to his account of battles in his *History of Rome*. He finally became Professor of Philosophy, and though always dignified in manner was full of humour among his friends. Lord Elibank was, we are told, 'enlightened and profound, with a mind that embraced a great variety of subjects. He was most original in conversation, beloved and admired by all.' He had been a lieutenant-colonel in the army, and was a Jacobite.

DR. HUGH BLAIR was minister of the High Church, and was made Professor of Rhetoric in the University. His sermons were admired for their polished style, and his church was crowded with people of position and high rank. George III. read and admired his published sermons, and gave Dr. Blair a pension of £200 a year.

ROBERTSON, the future historian and Principal of the University, was at this time minister of Gladsmuir; CARLYLE of Inveresk, and JOHN HOME of Athelstaneford. All these ministers were famous in Church matters, and their names appear in many vehement controversies of the day; but John Home will always be remembered as the author of the tragedy of *Douglas*, which created so much stir not only in the literary but also in the ecclesiastical world. It may be mentioned in passing that a sentence from Dr. Carlyle's autobiography throws a curious light on the customs of these days. He says: 'Blair and Robertson having been bred at a time when playing cards was thought to be a sin, and every one thought it certainly an indecorum in clergymen, they could neither of them play at golf or bowls, far less at cards or backgammon, and on that account were very unhappy when staying at the houses of friends in rainy weather.'

284

Some
Literary
Men of
Old
Edin-
burgh

In 1754 Lady Dalkeith, then living at Dalkeith Palace, had At Homes, or 'public days' as they were called then, twice a week. At that time there was quite a rage among the aristocracy in England for private theatricals, and Lady Dalkeith proposed to have a play for the entertainment of her visitors on these public days. It was represented to her, however, that this would give great offence, so she at once gave up the idea.

The young minister of Athelstaneford had written a good deal of poetry, and a classical play which was not successful. He now chose the patriotic theme of Douglas and founded it on the ballad of 'Gil Morrice.' Encouraged by Sir Gilbert Elliot, who read the various acts of the tragedy as they were written, he finished it. On a snowy morning in February he set out on his Galloway nag 'Piercy' to try the fortunes of his tragedy in London. Half a dozen of his brethren in the Merse [1] accompanied him to give him a 'convoy,' and one of them thus describes their expedition: 'Our bard had the tragedy in the pocket of his great-coat; this we thought an unsafe mode of carrying his precious treasure, which we thought enough of, but hardly foresaw that it was to be pronounced a perfect tragedy by the best judges.' Finally they got the loan of a leather bag used for the conveyance of Synod papers from Mr. Landreth, minister of Simprin and Synod Clerk, and so, with some delays, went with him part of the way and saw him fairly started. Garrick, however, would not accept *Douglas*, much to Home's disappointment. About a year after, in 1756, it was brought out in Edinburgh, under the patronage of the Duke of Argyle, Lord Milton, Sir Gilbert Elliot, and others. It had unbounded success, and many people who had never been in a theatre before, went to hear the 'popular Scottish tragedy of *Douglas*.' Ill-natured gossip declared that Dr. Carlyle and Dr.

[1] Berwickshire.

Blair had even assisted at a rehearsal, and Edinburgh
society was in a ferment.

The grandmother of Charles Kirkpatrick Sharpe, Lady
Susan Renton, was at the first performance, and Mr.
Sharpe used to tell that when the mournful air of 'Gil
Morrice' was played before the curtain went up most of
the ladies were in tears. The prologue was a favourite
piece for recitation in Edinburgh for many long years.
It contained the famous lines :—

> 'Douglas, a name through all the world renowned,
> A name that rouses like the trumpet sound,
> Oft have your fathers, prodigal of life,
> A Douglas followed through the bloody strife.
> Hosts have been known at that dread name to yield,
> And, Douglas dead, his name hath won the field.'

'My name is Norval,' and other parts of the play, were
also frequently recited. The former piece, we have heard,
was a 'stock' recitation at parish schools all over the
south of Scotland till the days of School Boards.

Though the general public were charmed with *Douglas*,
its production gave great offence to many ministers. The
Presbyteries of Edinburgh and Glasgow in particular
took up the matter vehemently, and in the end Home
resigned his parish and lived as a private gentleman.
The minister of Liberton was suspended from his office
for six weeks because he had gone to see the play,
and Dr. Carlyle of Inveresk was 'libelled' by the
Presbytery.

When Mrs. Siddons came to Edinburgh, about thirty
years later, in 1784, the important sittings of the
General Assembly had to be fixed for the days when the
great actress was not taking any part, as so many
members of Assembly thronged to see her. This shows
what a change had taken place in public opinion in a
comparatively short space of time.

David Hume and John Home were very great friends
—the only things they ever disputed about were John

Home's preference for claret to port, and the spelling of their name, as Home is always pronounced Hume in Scotland. Claret had always been much more used in Scotland than England owing to the old connection between Scotland and France, and when a ship came into Leith with a cargo of claret a cart was sent round the town with a hogshead as an advertisement, and any one could get a good-sized jugful for sixpence. John Home wrote a famous epigram on claret at the time the heavy duty was imposed upon it. Old people tell us that this epigram was often quoted at dinner tables for at least the first half of the nineteenth century :—

Some
Literary
Men of
Old
Edin-
burgh

> 'Firm and erect the Caledonian stood,
>   Old was his mutton, and his claret good ;
>   "Let him drink port," the English statesman cried,
>   He drank the poison, and his spirit died.'

David Hume lived, as we have seen, in James's Court on the Castle Hill. When he migrated to the New Town, James Boswell rented his house, and Dr. Johnson visited him there in 1773. We are indebted to the recollections of Mrs. Sharpe for some of the details of this visit. Mrs. Boswell, who was a Montgomery by birth, a connection of the Eglinton family, a clever, high-bred woman, naturally did not at all approve of Dr. Johnson's domineering manner towards her husband. Her remark with regard to him is well known : 'I have often seen a man leading a bear, but never before a bear leading a man.' Mrs. Sharpe gives an amusing account of a tea-party given at this time by Mr. and Mrs. Boswell in honour of Johnson. Margaret, Duchess of Douglas, was of the party 'in all her diamonds.' Dr. Johnson decribes her as an old lady 'who talks very broad Scotch with a paralytic voice.' Nevertheless we hear that the Doctor devoted himself to her the whole evening. 'Boswell,' we are told, 'had to act as interpreter, and had frequently to translate some of the gaucheries of the

287

Duchess, who could be uncommonly vulgar, into palat-
able commonplaces for his guest.' It may be remarked
here, as a curious fact in connection with Hume's house,
that both the dining-room and drawing-room had a tiny
oratory attached, so common in the older houses in Edinburgh, where the master of the house could retire for private devotions. There were at this time many other famous
men in Edinburgh among the 'literati,' as they called themselves, and one or two of these may be specially mentioned.
HENRY ERSKINE, whose bright and piercing eyes look out
at us from Raeburn's famous portrait, was noted for his
brilliant wit. DUGALD STEWART was famed as a philosopher; and DR. BLACKLOCK, the blind poet, who by his
kindly aid saved Burns from leaving Scotland, is an
example of intellect triumphing over bodily infirmity.
BURNS, by Dr. Blacklock's advice, came to Edinburgh in
1786, soon after the Kilmarnock edition of his poems
had been published, and lodged with his friend Rich-
mond, a writer's clerk, in the house of Mrs. Carfrae,
Baxter's Close. He became the fashion, and visited at
that time all the best society of Edinburgh. We get
two views of him from different standpoints. Mrs.
Cockburn describes him as ' the ploughman poet who
receives adulation with native dignity, and is the very
figure of his profession—strong and coarse—but has a
most enthusiastic heart of love. I fear he may be
spoiled, if he can spoil; but he keeps his simple manners
and is quite sober. No doubt he will be at the Hunters'
Ball to-morrow, which has made all women and milliners
mad.'

Then Scott tells us, in his own inimitable way, of the
only time they ever met. It was at Adam Ferguson's
house, when Scott was a boy of fifteen, that he met
Burns. It was on that occasion that Burns was touched
by the print of the dying soldier, and Scott was able to
tell him that the verse describing the picture was written
by Langhorne. Scott thus describes him: ' His con-

Some
Literary
Men of
Old
Edin-
burgh

versation showed perfect self-confidence, without pre-
sumption. Among the men who were the most learned
of their time and country he expressed himself with
perfect firmness, but without forwardness. When he
differed in opinion he did not hesitate to express it
firmly, but modestly.'

The great WIZARD OF THE NORTH himself permeates
every part of Edinburgh. If we walk through Guthrie
Street we stop and construct again in memory the old
'College Wynd' where he was born. When we pass
through George Square we see No. 25, the house his
father moved into from the College Wynd, and where the
boy Walter moved to and fro to the High School—not
far away in those days—and later on to the University.
We can picture the father, 'a very handsome man,' whose
habits and characteristics are quaintly brought before us
in Scott's own account of Alan Fairford's father in *Redgauntlet*; and the mother, of whom he had such tender
thoughts, who kept Walter's first poem in her desk, and
who looked with pride and joy on the silver taper-stand
he bought for her with the first fee he got at the Bar.
We see him getting up, in the days when he was studying
for the Bar, at seven in the morning, and trudging off to
read with William Clerk (the original of Darsie Latimer)
who then lived at the west end of Princes Street.
Then in later years, after he married and settled down in
39 Castle Street, we hear of merry dinner-parties there,
and we cannot forget the well-known story of the 'busy
hand,' seen from the back windows of George Street, writing steadily on far into the night, and dropping sheet
after sheet of MSS. on the floor. What a vivid picture we
get of him in Dr. John Brown's paper on 'Pet Marjorie,'
hurrying along to Charlotte Street against a stinging
wind and a grey sky 'onding o' snaw'; getting hold of
his wee woman and wrapping her in his plaid, bringing
her triumphantly home with him for hours of fun and
frolic. The old house of Ravelston, too, with its old-

T

PAUL'S WARK

world garden, its roses, its beech hedges, its greenery and peace, has many associations with him.

His grand-aunt Mrs. Keith, who was Johanna Swinton of Swinton, 'a childhood's friend' of Mrs. Patrick Cockburn, lived there, and he visited her frequently as a boy. By the fireside in winter, or in the sunny, peaceful garden in summer, she told him stories of Border raids and bygone days. After she passed away he said of her: ' Much tradition, and that of the best, has died with this excellent old lady, whose spirits, *cleanliness*, and freshness of mind and body, made old age lovely and desirable.'

Sir Walter Scott had another friend, Mistress Anne Murray Keith, who has sometimes been mistaken for Mrs. Keith of Ravelston. She also related to him many old legends and family traditions, such as the original story of the *Bride of Lammermoor*. We are told in *The Lives of the Lindsays* that it was Anne Keith who playfully said, in reference to the authorship of the Waverley Novels,' D' ye think I dinna ken my ain groats amang ither folks' kail.'

She was the original of Mrs. Bethune Baliol, who is so delightfully depicted in the *Chronicles of the Canongate*. He heard from her the descriptions of manners and events far back beyond her own time, which she, in turn, had heard from her forebears.

'She would describe how Fletcher of Salton spoke; how Graham of Claverhouse danced; what were the jewels worn by the Duchess of Lauderdale, and how she came by them, till I could not help telling her I thought

290

Some
Literary
Men of
Old
Edin-
burgh

her some kind of fairy. . . . I will frankly admit, she
said, that I have heard so much of the years which immediately succeeded the Revolution, that I sometimes con-
fuse the vivid descriptions fixed on my memory by the
animated recitation of others for things which I myself
have actually witnessed. I caught myself but yesterday
describing to Lord M—— the riding of the last Scottish
Parliament with as much minuteness as if I had seen it,
as my mother did, from the balcony in front of my Lord
Moray's lodging in the Canongate.'

The cottage at Lasswade can still be seen where he and
his young wife spent two or three happy summers, and
where Wordsworth and his sister Dorothy visited them.
Ashestiel and Abbotsford do not come into the sphere of
Edinburgh reminiscences, but few people will visit Parliament House and the Court of Session, or see his statue
in the Advocates' Library, without feeling that he is the
'genius loci.' His early essays at poetry, his collecting of
Border Minstrelsy, his poems of *Marmion, Lady of the
Lake, Lay of the Last Minstrel*, and then the prose writings of the 'Great Unknown,' are all matters of common
knowledge. So, alas! too are the monetary troubles of
his later years, and his brave efforts to free himself from
them. The Castle and the Scott Monument are almost
the first distinctive features of Edinburgh which the
traveller recognises, and as he travels over Scotland,
north or south, he realises more and more the glamour
Scott has cast over his own beloved town and land. A girl
of sixteen, who, as an old lady, was well known to the
writer, came up from Ayrshire to be present at a conversa-
zione given at the opening of the Picture Gallery on the
'Earthen' Mound, as it was frequently called in those
days. A grey-haired, lame gentleman, whose name she
did not catch when she was introduced to him, walked
about with her uncle and herself for a long time. She
thought him a most genial man, brimming over with
funny stories and witty remarks about all the company,

but she only discovered on her way home that she had
spent a great part of the evening in Scott's company.

With Scott's name are associated a wide circle of kindred spirits in Parliament House. JEFFREY, COCKBURN,
HORNER, and BROUGHAM formed a notable group. They
were all born in Edinburgh, all educated at the High
School, all passed for the Bar. Brougham, after treading the floor of the Parliament House for seven years, went
to London, joined the English Bar, and finally went into
Parliament. Jeffrey married early and had a singularly
happy married life. His home, a third flat in Buccleuch
Place, will always be remembered as the place where the
idea of the *Edinburgh Review* originated, and the
occasion is thus described by Sydney Smith : 'One day
we happened to meet in Buccleuch Place, the elevated
residence of Mr. Jeffrey. I proposed we should set up
a Review; this was acceded to with acclamation. I was
appointed Editor, and remained long enough in Edinburgh to edit the first number of the *Edinburgh Review*.' The time was ripe for something of the kind; the
mental upheaval which had attended the great events of
the French Revolution, the ability of the young men then
in Edinburgh, the fall of old systems, and, it must be admitted, the vehemence of party politics, all opened the
way for something new and vigorous.

During the first year of the *Review's* existence Sydney
Smith thus writes to Mr. Constable, the publisher : 'It
is notorious that all the Reviews are the organs either of
party or publishers. I have therefore no manner of
doubt but that an able, intrepid, and independent Review
would be useful to the public and profitable to those
engaged in it.'

The first number appeared in October 1802, and contained articles by Smith, Horner, Brougham, and Jeffrey.
One by Jeffrey on the 'Influence of the French Revolution' began the work. The effect, we are told, was
'electrical,' and for many years the *Edinburgh Review*,

whose motto, as originally suggested by its promoters, was, 'We cultivate literature on a little oatmeal,' was a power in literature. The little band of friends was looked on at first with a good deal of suspicion, but a few received them kindly and encouraged them in their literary projects. Among these were Henry Mackenzie, the Rev. Archibald Alison, Dr. James Gregory, and Scott. The last, however, was afterwards considerably alienated by the extreme Whig principles of the *Review*. Cockburn says of himself and his friends that, though they were hard students, yet they were always ready for a 'saunter, a discussion, or a hilarious supper,' in which respects the present generation of young advocates at Parliament House can doubtless follow in their footsteps.

Bonaly Tower, near Colinton, where Cockburn spent his later years, is inseparably associated with him. His literary fame rests chiefly on his *Life of Jeffrey* and his own graphic *Memorials*. He rose to be Solicitor-General when Jeffrey was Lord Advocate, and finally became a Judge. Horner went to the English Bar, where, as we have seen, Brougham followed him and rose to be Lord Chancellor; but Jeffrey was the life and soul of the group, and for many happy years his home at Craigcrook, sheltered by the wooded slopes of Corstorphine Hill, was the centre of literary life in Edinburgh. The friends of the present owners of Craigcrook can still see the turret-room which was Jeffrey's library, the chair he used, and the bowling-green upon which so many friendly contests were held on summer Saturdays, but the 'glorious yellow roses' which then clothed the garden wall are now all gone.

With the early years of the Nineteenth Century, life in *Old* Edinburgh comes to a close, and not only life but letters underwent a complete change.

A word, however, may be said about the 'Blackwood' group in literature. CHRISTOPHER NORTH (John Wilson), LOCKHART—Scott's son-in-law and biographer, the father of 'Hugh Littlejohn,' for whom the *Tales of a Grand-*

father were written,—JAMES HOGG, the Ettrick Shepherd, author of *Bonny Kilmeny* ; WILLIAM EDMONDSTOUNE
AYTOUN, Wilson's son-in-law, who wrote the *Lays of
the Scottish Cavaliers* and *Bothwell*,—all these distinguished men made up a brilliant coterie who kept
up the reputation of Edinburgh as a literary centre far
on into the nineteenth century.

These jottings on 'Some Literary Men in Old Edinburgh' may be fitly concluded by a brief reference to
ROBERT LOUIS STEVENSON, the child of the New Town
of Edinburgh, and of the later decades of the Victorian
era.   The house in Howard Place in which he was born
can still be seen, and not far away is the pleasant home
in Heriot Row where he spent much of his childhood
and youth.   That house, 17 Heriot Row, is full of bright
recollections to those who had the good fortune to be
welcomed by the genial host and hostess, Stevenson's
father and mother.   The latter used to point out in
the pleasant sunny drawing-room the large old-fashioned
sofa where the future author played, while his father
and mother sat chatting by the fire, as he tells us in
'The Land of Storybooks':—

> ' At evening, when the lamp is lit,
> Around the fire my parents sit :
> They sit at home and talk and sing,
> And do not play at anything.
>
> Now with my little gun I crawl
> All in the dark, along the wall,
> And follow round the forest track,
> Away behind the sofa back.
>
> I see the others far away,
> As if in firelit camp they lay ;
> And I, like to an Indian scout,
> Around their party prowl about.'

Here too was the window from which the child and
his devoted nurse, Alison Cunningham, familiarly known

as 'Cummie,' used to watch nightly for 'Leerie' lighting the lamps:—

> 'My tea is nearly ready, and the Sun has left the sky,
> It's time to take the window to see Leerie going by ;
> For every night at tea-time, and before you take your seat,
> With lantern and with ladder, he comes posting up the street.
> But I, when I am stronger and can choose what I'm to do,
> Oh ! Leerie, I'll go round at nights and light the lamps with
>   you.'

All who know and love his *Child's Garden of Verses*, and *Memories and Portraits*, will take a special interest in the manse at Colinton, his mother's early home, where he spent many happy days of childhood with the numerous cousins of a large connection, and with his grandfather, Dr. Balfour of Colinton, whose personality he brings so vividly before us in 'The Manse.' Even yet the manse may be seen, 'still as a dream,' the trees, the shady walks, the stream foaming or still, as may be, and the 'garden with flower-plots lying warm in sunshine, laurels, and a great yew making elsewhere a pleasing horror of shade, the sound of water everywhere and the sound of mills':—

> 'The river, on from mill to mill,
>   Flows past our childhood's garden still,
> But ah ! we children, never more
>   Shall watch it from the water door.'

We can walk out to Swanston by Fairmilehead and think of the friendly gauger who played on the flute 'Over the hills and far away,' and so reach the 'hamlet of twenty cottages, in the woody fold of a green hill.' For years Mr. and Mrs. Stevenson lived much at Swanston to benefit the health of their delicate boy, and in his writings there are many allusions to it and to the scenery of the Pentland Hills. As we look at the familiar scene now, many word-pictures come into our minds : the old gardener and 'the garden in the lap of the hill, with its rocks overgrown with clematis, its

295

shadowy walks, and the splendid breadth of champaign that one saw from the north-west corner.' John Todd, 'the oldest herd on the Pentlands, with his flocks and his dogs, who knew neither rest nor sleep except by snatches; in the grey of the summer morning and already far up the hill, he would wake the "toun" with the sound of his shoutings, and in the lambing time his cries were not yet silenced late at nights.' We see the cottages with their shining interiors, the green or scarred hillsides, the frosty winter nights, the still summer days, the silent dawns. It was not till he was gone that people realised the brave patience with which he had struggled against feeble health and enforced exile, nor was the steady toil fully estimated which perfected the style and grace of diction which so eminently characterise his writings. Many of these descriptions were written far from Scotland, and perhaps for that very reason are instinct with a pathos which touches the heart of the reader, especially if he too is a 'kindly Scot' in far lands.

This is how he writes of the grey city of his birth from Vailima in the Southern Seas :—

'There is no Edinburgh emigrant far or near from China to Peru, but he or she carries some lively pictures of the mind, some sunset behind the Castle cliffs, some snow scene, some maze of city lamps, indelible in the memory and delightful to study in the intervals of toil.'

> 'Under the wide and starry sky
>   Dig a grave, and let me lie ;
> Glad did I live, and gladly die,
>   And I laid me down with a will.
>
> This be the verse you grave for me :
>   Here he lies where he longed to be ;
> Home is the sailor, home from sea,
>   And the hunter home from the hill.'

(Engraved on the tomb of Robert Louis Stevenson at Vailima.)

CHAPTER XII

WHEN visitors come to Edinburgh, and from the hotels in Princes Street look across the green valley to the rugged cliffs of the Castle and the irregular roofs of high houses which mark the line of the High Street and Lawnmarket, it is difficult for them to realise what Edinburgh was like in olden days. Then noble families lived in all the closes opening off the High Street; there were palaces in the Cowgate; the Canongate was a court suburb; the Nor' Loch filled the valley now occupied by the Waverley Station and Princes Street Gardens; Princes Street was a somewhat lonely pathway known as the Lang Gait; and Leith was a seaport two miles from Edinburgh.

If it is difficult to realise these outward changes, it is far more difficult to get a clear idea of the great changes which have taken place in manners, customs, and modes of life in Edinburgh—indeed, all over Scotland, during the last two hundred years.

From the Union of the Crowns to the Union of the Parliaments the old city, though despoiled of its royal denizens, and shorn of the gay functions and spectacles of the days of the Stuarts, had still much to brighten it. The mere presence of the 145 Lords and 160 Commoners who attended the sittings of the Scottish Parliament must have made a prodigious difference in a small city such as Edinburgh was then. It was not merely

the members themselves, but their families and retainers
who helped to make trade brisk, and to crowd the
High Street and the Canongate. There are still to
be seen Lady Stair's Close, Lord President Hyndford's
Close, the Duke of Gordon's house, my Lord Seton's
'ludging,' the Marquis of Huntly's house, the Earl of
Selkirk's house, Queensberry House, Moray House, etc. etc.

The situation of Edinburgh, perched on a hill and
confined by its walls and gates within narrow limits,
led, as we have seen, to the building of immensely
high houses arranged in flats,—at that time so strange
to our English neighbours. These houses at first had
gardens and orchards behind them, which are mentioned
in many old documents; in time these were built upon,
and hence came the 'closes' leading north and south
from both sides of the High Street, and the 'courts,'
which are chiefly behind the Lawnmarket houses. The
old winding 'turnpike' or 'scale' staircase in many
instances still remains, with low-browed archway surmounted by a carved motto or text, and heavy old door
studded with nails. In one or two instances the remains
of a hammered iron grating shuts off an inner court.
In a house of ten or twelve stories there were a large
number of families, of the most diverse social conditions.
High up in the garrets lived poor tradespeople, or
mechanics; descending gradually came better-class shop-
keepers, ministers or professors, old dowagers, 'sma'
gentry,' lawyers, advocates, Lords of Session, noblemen.
In the cellars and one or two of the lower flats lived
Highland chairmen, caddies, and sweeps. An anecdote
is told of a Scotch laird who went up to London after
the Union. He was offered rooms on the ground floor,
which he refused, and indignantly retorted that 'he
hadna' leeved a' his days on a sixth flat to be pit on
the grun' noo.' These flats were very cramped and
small, but in early days the best parlour or 'hall'
possessed a box bed, and the family bedroom was also

298

used as a sitting-room. We are told that Bruce of Kennet, an advocate of good family, lived in a flat in the Lawnmarket which had three rooms and a kitchen, for which he paid £11. One room was the 'Lady's,' probably a parlour, the other his study and consulting-room, and the third the bedroom. The nurse and children slept in the study, their beds being removed during the day, while the cook slept in the kitchen under the dresser! When he was raised to the Bench and became Lord Kennet, they removed to a larger house in Horse Wynd.

A traveller in 1697 says, 'there were turned up beds in nearly all the best rooms in Edinbro houses, they were so small.' Can we wonder that lawyers and their clients, merchants and their customers, one friend 'treating' another, adjourned to taverns when the accommodation in private houses was so scanty?

The staple food for dinner in town and country was barley-broth, called and spelled *broath*. It was made of beef, generally salt, and was thickened with barley. In those days there were no barley-mills, so the barley was bruised in a mortar and then rubbed in a coarse cloth to husk it. Cabbage was also largely used, as other vegetables were little cultivated. In some old books we read of *cabbie-claw*,[1] codfish dressed with a sauce made of horse radish and eggs. Friar's chicken was a dish which had descended from monastery cooks, and was considered a dainty. It was made of chicken cut in pieces and cooked with eggs and parsley and cinnamon. Cockie-leekie was then, as now, a favourite dish, and was reserved for company. It was made with a well-fed young cock, boiled with leeks and prunes, which seem to point to a French origin. Roast meat was very little used; pigeons and moorfowl were roasted on the spit or baked in 'pot ovens,' which may be seen to this day in herds' houses in the moorland solitudes of Dumfriesshire and Galloway.

---

[1] Probably from *cabillaud*, French for cod.

Knives and spoons were used at table, but, up to the
time of the Union, forks were rarely provided. The
ordinary dinner-knife was called by the odd name of a
Jockteleg, from its inventor, 'Jacques de Liége.' When
the use of forks became more common, people of any
position always carried a leather case with a knife and
fork, and sometimes also a spoon. At the end of a meal
these were carefully wiped, put in the case, and returned
to the owner's pocket. A favourite present to a young
lady of quality was a silver knife and fork which could
be carried in her reticule. The silver fruit-knives dear
to the hearts and pockets of our great-grandmothers
were a survival of this custom. Silver cups, or 'tassies'
as they were called, were used by the better classes,
and pewter drinking-cups by working people. Burns
uses this word in his well-known song:

> 'Gae bring to me a pint o' wine,
> And fill it in a silver tassie.'

If a Scotch pint (two quarts) is meant, the tassie must
have been a capacious one. Even in the eighteenth
century glasses were very little used. A Border laird
of these days, Armstrong of Sorbie, remarked that 'it
was a better warl' whan there were fewer glasses and
mair bottles.'

In reading history the changes of the dinner hour in
different generations are very curious. In the fourteenth
century kings and nobles dined at eleven o'clock, and
supped at five. Mary Queen of Scots when she lived
at Holyrood dined at one o'clock, and we read that
she was at supper, between five and six on 9th March
1566, when Rizzio was murdered.

In the eighteenth century in Edinburgh, one was
the common dinner hour for all, 'gentle or simple';
by the beginning of the nineteenth century it had crept
on to two or even three o'clock; and from 1850 onwards,
for a good many years, 4.30 or five was a very usual

dinner hour. Now, dinner is really what was our ancestors' supper. In the eighteenth century people began the day much earlier, as in the days of small dark rooms, lighted merely by candles, people liked to get the benefit of all the daylight they could. The men of the house had a morning dram, over which they said ' grace'; breakfast was between seven and eight, and consisted of porridge, collops of beef or mutton, oatcakes or barley bannocks, washed down by draughts of strong ale.

The midday dinner was generally all put on the table at once. To show how much used ' broath' was, Mrs. Calderwood of Polton remarks in a letter from London, in 1756, 'I thought I had not got a dinner since I left home, for want of broath.'

Wooden trenchers were used in earlier days; then pewter plates, deep or shallow ' broath plates,' and ' flesh plates,' came into common use. Specimens of these may be seen at St. Mary's College, St. Andrews. They were used by the students when they dined in the Old Hall with its beautiful carved oak table and chairs, and when they lived in the curious little rooms which can still be seen.

As every small farmer and crofter paid part of his rent in 'kain' hens, boiled fowls were often added to the salt beef of which the 'broath' was made. The frequent appearance of these 'kain' hens was not appetising, and the story is told of an Episcopalian who said the best way to keep Lent would be to live entirely upon 'kain' hens. This seems a strange custom; but we remember in our childish days talking to a very old farmer in Upper Nithsdale whose grandfather paid part of his rent in this very way. Potatoes were little known, and not much used. Turnips, or 'neeps,' and 'cabadge' were in great request for broth. Ale and claret were largely drunk at meals; the latter came from France to Leith, and was sold for one shilling per quart or 'chopin,' as it was usually termed.

After dinner came the 'four hours,' corresponding
to afternoon tea. At this meal ladies drank sweet ale
or wine (before tea came in), and ate slices of wheaten
bread or sweet cakes of sorts. The day was wound up
by supper—a solid meal, frequently consisting of 'hens'
again, or mince collops. We read of suppers where
the guests were regaled with 'roasted hens and claret
wine.'

Tea was almost unknown till 1720, but after that
gradually crept into use. We are told that it was
sold at the Luckenbooths by a goldsmith at 16s. per
pound for green tea, and 30s. for Bohea, while chocolate
only cost 3s. 6d. Many forces combined to fight against
the custom of drinking tea. The doctors pronounced
that it caused 'tremblings, vapours, and similar ailments.'
Old-fashioned people decried it as a foolish innovation,
and Lord President Forbes called it 'a vile drug.' A
Highland laird complained : 'I used to be asked if I had
had my "morning" (draught); I am now asked if I have
had my tea!'

People had not very polished manners in Old Edinburgh, for we read that every one took their bones of
poultry or game in their fingers and picked them. In
Traditions of Edinburgh there is an amusing account
of the Duchess of Queensberry (Prior's Kitty) shrieking
with horror when she saw the knives of her guests at
Queensberry House conveying the food to their mouths.
She sent a spoon and fork on a salver to them, and
insisted that they should be used! From *Rules of
Good Deportment* we learn that it was very bad
manners to leave any wine in the cup which had to
be passed to the next guest.

These days seem to have been a strange mixture of
formal, indeed rigid, decorum, and a certain lawlessness
which found an outlet in curious directions, such as the
oyster suppers which Captain Topham graphically describes in 1774. A large and brilliant company were

302

assembled in a cellar eating oysters and drinking porter. He sat 'awaiting a repast which never arrived.' Afterwards came a bowl of brandy punch, and somewhat lively conversation, and finally they 'all began to dance reels, their favourite dance, which they perform with great agility and perseverance.'

The language used by some of the ladies would be considered remarkable nowadays, and even in the later days of Sir Walter Scott, Pet Marjorie with the utmost simplicity uses expressions in her poems, for the sake of rhyme, which would astound a High School mistress. Lord Cockburn gives graphic pictures in his *Memorials* of some of these ladies of olden days. Two of these may be taken as specimens of the contrast alluded to. Sophia or 'Suphy' Johnston was an original; she was of good family, daughter of a Fife laird, but had not been taught even to read or write. As a woman she taught herself to read, and then read incessantly. Lord Cockburn describes her thus: 'Her dress was always the same—a man's hat out of doors, and often within; a cloth covering like a man's great-coat, buttoned from the chin to the ground, worsted stockings, and strong shoes with brass clasps. In this raiment she sat at any table, amidst the aristocracy of the land, respected and liked, for her talk was intelligent and racy, rich in old anecdote and spiced with sarcasm. Sitting with her back to the light in an arm-chair by the fire in the Niddrie drawing-room, with her great-coat and hat, her dark wrinkled face and firm pursed mouth, her two feet flat on the floor, showing her substantial shoes, the book very near the eyes, if the quick ear overheard any presumptuous folly, be it from solemn gentleman or fine lady, down went the volume, up the spectacles: "That's surely great nonsense, sir," though she had never seen him before.'

Lady Anne Lindsay writes of her that she was 'Amazonian,' sang a man's song in a bass voice, and

303

was a 'droll ingenious fellow.' In contrast to 'Suphy,'
let us take Lord Cockburn's description of Lady Don
and Mrs. Rochead of Inverleith. They had both been
beauties of the minuets and ladies of ceremonies at the
Assemblies, and each carried her peculiar grace and
air to the verge of the grave. 'Except Mrs. Siddons,
no one could sit down like the lady of Inverleith.
She would sail in like a ship from Tarshish, with fan,
ear-rings, falling sleeves, scent-bottle, hoop and train,
managing all this with as much ease as a swan its
plumage. She would then take possession of a sofa
and cover the whole of it with her bravery. Lady Don
was still more highly bred, and her venerable beauty,
white hair, soft hands sparkling with gems, kind heart
and gentle voice account for the love by which her
old age was surrounded.' He goes on to tell that these
ladies both sat in the Tron Church, and a group of
bystanders always formed to watch the stately majesty
with which one descended from her sedan chair and
the other from her coach.

Many old annals tell of the dignity of great ladies,
and the state they kept from the days of Charles II. to the
end of the eighteenth century. The Duchess of Buccleuch,
Monmouth's widow, claimed royal honours, sat under a
canopy, and was served by pages on their knees. The
beautiful Elizabeth Gunning, when Duchess of Hamilton,
always walked to dinner with the Duke before all their
guests. They sat together at the head of the table, and
only drank wine with earls and countesses. The same
lady, when Duchess of Argyle, ignored Boswell at her
own table, when he and Johnson were entertained by the
Duke at Inverary.

The description of the hoop and train of the Lady of
Inverleith reminds us of the vagaries of ladies' dress in
bygone days. Hoops were worn four and a half yards
wide, the petticoats were trimmed with gold and silver
lace, and the train was of silk or velvet. The gowns had

Social
Life and
Customs
in Edin-
burgh in
Olden
Days

long waists, the shoes high heels, and hair powder was almost universally used. The hair was curled on the forehead and patches were worn. The usual head-dress was of ribbons and Flanders lace, and ladies everywhere wore green paper fans about two feet long, attached to their waists by a ribbon. These served as parasols (which were then unknown) when walking out.

A distinguishing feature of dress in Old Edinburgh was the plaid of fine wool or silk tartan which ladies wore wrapped about the head and shoulders, and which served to muffle the face on occasion. The magistrates remonstrated against this custom, but in vain. Plaids were also much worn in church, and there are many traces in the records of Church Courts of rules made against this fashion. The Kirk Session of Kinghorn in 1645 denounced 'the uncomelieness of women coming to the church on Sabbath with plaids about their heads, which provocks sleeping in the time of sermone without being espied.' Nearly half a century later, in the Parish Church of St. Andrews, intimation was made from the pulpit 'discharging weamen's playdes from their heids in the church,' and appointing the beadle to go 'throw the Kirk with ane lang rod and take doun their playdes fram their heids,' but in spite of official injunctions plaids were in common use for fifty years longer. In 1750 the plaid ceased to be worn in this manner among the better classes; short cloaks called 'capuchins,' and the 'calash,' a collapsible silk hood, were the mode. The latter as garden head-gear came down to the days of our great-grandmothers; formerly it was worn over the powdered hair dressed high on the head.

From the days of Queen Anne till far on into the eighteenth century gentlemen wore wigs. At various periods the Ramillies wig and the full-dress perruque were all the fashion; also 'tied hair' was worn for some time. Wigs were an expensive article of dress, costing from one guinea to six or seven.

U

The coats had no collars, but had wide full skirts, sometimes distended with buckram; square cuffs and three-cornered laced hats were generally worn.

Early in the eighteenth century home-made linen was coarse and poor, and the younger men, we hear, insisted on having 'fine Hollands,' which at that period cost 6s. an ell. Mrs. Fletcher (sister-in-law of Andrew Fletcher), who was an excellent spinner, began to consider whether it would not be possible to make this fine 'Hollands' in Scotland. The story goes that she set out on an expedition to Holland accompanied by two mechanics in the guise of men-servants, found out the secret of the weaving of fine linen, came home and successfully started its manufacture near Salton, thereby reducing the price and bringing it within reach of all. Much in the same way Lady Bargarran and her clever daughters commenced making linen thread at Bargarran House, near Paisley. A friend who had been in Holland gave them some hints, and in 1725 the newspapers announced that the Bargarran thread was put up in papers on which was printed their coat-of-arms, ' to prevent people being imposed upon by other thread.' Thus was laid the foundation of the Glasgow and Paisley thread industry.

With the improvement in spinning and weaving, Scotland soon began to be famous for its fine 'naperie,' as bed and table-linen was called in these days. In a few linen-presses of the present day may still be found webs of old homespun linen, fine sheets with button-holes to slip over the bleaching pegs, and table-cloths and table-napkins which have the peculiar soft, satiny texture which is the special characteristic of table-linen made of home-spun thread and woven on the old handlooms.

In connection with the subject of napery Miss Dunlop tells an anecdote (in *Wester Portsburgh*) about the little orphan Countess of Sutherland who was, in later years, known as the 'Countess Duchess.' She was living at Leven Lodge, then a country house, with her grandmother,

Lady Alva. One day when she was playing with some little friends on Bruntsfield Links she happened to see a weaver who worked for her grandmother. He was bringing in from the village where he lived twenty-four tea-towels, with initials and crest, for a customer. Tea-towels —just small napkins—were then used to protect the satin or brocade skirts at the 'four hours.' The little Countess examined the man's burden and saw that the crest was the swan—the crest of the Wemyss family; and immediately announced that she was going to learn to spin, and then she would have 'tea-towels' with the 'Great Cat'—her own crest—on them. After sundry objections from her guardian, she got a little ebony wheel with silver mountings, duly learned to spin, and after a time got her own tea-towels. When, in 1785, she was going to marry Lord Trentham, the pattern of the crest and coronet was borrowed from the weaver to mark her 'wedding providing.'

During the end of the seventeenth and a considerable part of the eighteenth centuries Sunday was kept with an austerity only equalled by the Pilgrim Fathers. This has been generally attributed to Presbyterian influence, but old records show that it was kept as rigidly when Episcopacy held sway. On Saturday evening everything was made ready for the next day, even to the shaving of the 'gudeman.' On Sunday morning the church bells rang at six o'clock to warn every one to get up at once, so as to have family prayers (or 'exercises') and breakfast over in time to get to the forenoon service, which was at nine or ten o'clock. It may be mentioned in passing that in some country places the ringing of the church bell at eight and again at ten o'clock is still called the 'warning' bell. The service lasted two hours. In the interval the people went home, frequently had exercises (which were conducted by the chaplain in aristocratic families), and whatever food they had was cold. A traveller in these days writes: 'I arrived at Kirkcudbright on Saturday night. Next day

the landlord told me that they never dress a dinner on
Sunday, so I must either take up with bread and butter
and a fresh egg, or fast till after the evening service, when
they never fail to have a hot supper.' In country
districts the laird had often a room adjoining the pew in
the ' breist o' the laft,' which was invariably given to the
laird's family. In this room they and their friends had a
cold collation, also a fire, which must have been a luxury,
as churches were not heated then. This practice was
held in abhorrence by the Episcopalians, one of whom
thus spoke of it : ' a profaneness unheard of in antiquity,
and only worthy of the age we live in.' The rest of the
congregation, if far from their homes, adjourned to the
alehouse. In the afternoon there was another long
service ; in the evening the children and servants were
catechised, there was a hot supper at eight, and family
worship closed the day.

Christmas, or Yule, as it was generally termed, and its
observances were regarded as ' superstitious,' and the
goose was even called a ' superstitious ' bird, while many
stern old people did not hesitate to call this holiday
time the ' daft days.'

It may be asked, if the services were so tedious why did
people attend them ? *Now*, if services were too lengthy,
the hearers would simply absent themselves, but *then* a
rigid system of supervision was exercised (in which civil
and religious authorities supported each other) in a
manner which could hardly be credited if it were not so
well authenticated. ' Seizers ' were regularly appointed
who went about and seized any one not at church, or
' vaguing' on the street, and reported him or her to
the Kirk Session. They peeped through windows and
peered about the wynds and up the turnpike stairs, and
the streets were so deserted that we are told lamps were
not lighted on Sunday evenings. Woe betide the barber
who tried to carry home a customer's wig on a Sabbath
morning. The unfortunate minister of New Machar was

libelled by his Presbytery in 1735 for 'powdering his wig on the Sabbath day.' Traces of these old customs lingered far on into the early part of the nineteenth century. Window blinds were drawn down on Sunday, hot dinners were rare, 'walking out' for the sake of exercise was highly disapproved of, and the catechising of children and servants on the Sunday evening was regularly carried on.

In a farmhouse in Upper Nithsdale, well known to the writer, the farmer, his wife and family, went regularly into the kitchen on Sunday evening. A 'grand fire' of peats was blazing, and every one employed on the farm sat in a wide circle round the fire. There were some questions asked in the first place about the sermons heard at church, and then part of the Shorter Catechism and a certain number of Paraphrases were repeated by every one in turn. It gives us a glimpse of the patriarchal ways of an older generation to think of the kindly old man thus leading all around him in the ways of pleasantness and paths of peace.

The awe with which children regarded their parents, and the strict discipline to which they were subjected, seems strange to us. In the *Lives of the Lindsays*, Lady Anne Lindsay gives a curious account of the large family of children (of whom she was one of the elders) setting out in solemn procession to escape from their home because their mother, Lady Balcarres, dealt out such hard measure to them in the way of punishments. Lady Anne writes : 'Everything was done by authority, and correction.' Miss Mure of Caldwell and other writers speak in the same way; and in Miss Ferrier's book *Marriage* one of the characters says : 'In my grandfather's time ilka master o' a family had his ain seat in his ain hoose ; ay, and sat wi' his hat on afore the best in the land ; an' had his ain dish and was aye helpit first, an' keepit up his authority as a man should dae. Pawrents were pawrents then.'

309

Young people in those days stood in the presence of their parents, and only spoke when they were spoken to; but by slow degrees all this passed away.

In the matter of outdoor amusements gentlemen fared better than ladies two hundred years ago. They had golf and archery, horse-racing on Leith sands, and cock-fighting. Strange to say, even the ministers never objected to this pastime, probably because they had been familiar with it from childhood. Strolling companies performed plays at rare intervals, but there were no theatres before 1764. Dancing and music therefore were the chief amusements of the town. The Assemblies were held at first in the West Bow, and later in the Old Assembly Close. Here all the beauty and fashion of Edinburgh were in the habit of meeting. There was a hall where the sedan chairs were brought in, and the fair ladies descended. Across the gulf of time, we still seem to see the scene so graphically portrayed by Oliver Goldsmith, and also by Mrs. Cockburn. The latter writes thus of one Assembly: ' Never was so handsome an Assembly. There were seven sets, one all quality ladies and all handsome; one called the Maiden Set, for they admitted no married woman; and one was called the ' Heartsome Set,' led off by Lady Christian Erskine. In this set was Miss Suphy Johnstone.' One cannot help wondering if, in these earlier days, she wore the greatcoat and man's hat spoken of by Lord Cockburn. Oliver Goldsmith, being a stranger, took rather a jaundiced view of the entertainment. ' One end of the room,' he says, ' is taken up by ladies who sit dismally by themselves; at the other stand their pensive partners to be, but no more inter-course between them than between two countries at war.'

Miss Nicky Murray, sister of Lord Mansfield, was Lady Directress at this time. She made all the arrangements and introductions, and her word was law. It is told of her that when a young lady was introduced to her, her reply was ' Miss —— of *what*? ' for she considered it *de rigueur*

310

that all young ladies presented to her should be ' of that
ilk,' or have some other territorial designation. The Directress sat in a high chair and called upon several couples to
dance minuets, then came country dances. One can imagine
the young Irishman in his ' sky blew sattin' and Genoa
' velvett' and ' hatt' with silver lace, looking longingly at
the merry girls in the Heartsome Set. He tells his friend
Bob Bryanston about the broad Scotch of these young
ladies, ' which so well becomes a pretty mouth. Teach
one of your young ladies to pronounce " Whoar will I
gang" with becoming wideness of mouth, and I 'll lay my
life they will wound every hearer.' He alludes in the
same letter to ' my Lord Kilcoubry, a glover who attended
in the lobby to supply the gentlemen with gloves.' This
was the sixth Lord Kirkcudbright, the representative of
the ancient family of MacLellans, whose ruined ivy-clad
castle still stands in the centre of the town of Kirkcudbright, on the site of the monastery of the Grey Friars.
They were strong Jacobites and had lost all their patri-
mony in the Stuart cause : hence the glover's shop. It
has been supposed that he was the prototype of Davie
Ramsay in the *Fortunes of Nigel,* of whom King James
says : ' Ye see that a man of richt gentle blood may lay
by his gentry yet ken whare to find it when he has
occasion. He hangs his sword on the cleek, lays his
beaver on the shelf, pits his pedigree in his pocket,
and gangs doucely and cannily about his craft ; but
let him be transposed into a bien merchant, out he
pulls his pedigree, on he buckles his sword, gives his
beaver a brush and cocks it in the face of all creation.'

These Assemblies began about five and stopped at eleven.
As the bells of St. Giles' rung out the hour, Miss Nicky
waved her fan, the fiddlers stopped playing, and the dance
was at an end.

Music was much loved and cultivated even in these old
days. So far back as 1694 ' a citizen named Beck erected
a Concert of Music.' Some time before 1728 a number

Social
Life and
Customs
in Edin-
burgh in
Olden
Days

of gentlemen who played harpsichord and violin formed
a weekly club at the Cross Keys kept, as Arnot tells us,
' by one Steil, a great lover of music and a good singer of
Scots songs.' At these weekly concerts sonatas and con-
certos by Corelli were played, also Handel's overtures.
From 1728 this Musical Society held its meetings in St.
Mary's Chapel which stood in Niddry's Wynd. It was
founded by Elizabeth, Countess of Ross, in 1505. It
belonged to the Corporations of St. Mary's Chapel
(Wrights and Masons), and was used for meetings of
various kinds. In 1745 an entertainment was given by
Lord Drummore (Hew Dalrymple), who was at that time
Governor of the Musical Society, to the Prince of Hesse,
who came over with six thousand mercenaries to fight
against the Jacobites. The Prince, we are told, was not
only a lover of music, but a good performer on an enormous 'cello. When Lord Drummore died, ten years later,
a concert was given in honour of his memory, when all the
distinguished company were dressed in deepest mourning.

In 1762 St. Cecilia's Hall rose at the corner of Niddry's
Wynd and the Cowgate. It was built by Robert Mylne,
after the model of the opera at Parma; the orchestra
was at the north end, and there was a fine organ. It was
an oval hall seated for five hundred persons. In the
centre was an open space used for promenading in the
intervals of the music ; the seats rose gradually on either
side, the audience thus facing each other ; the hall pronounced ' the best and most beautiful concert room
ever seen.' The concerts were arranged by a set of
directors, and were given weekly. The best instrumental music was performed, but Scotch music was also
largely represented. Every year an oratorio, generally
by Handel, was performed, principally by professional
singers, but assisted by distinguished amateurs. A supper
in Fortune's Tavern to the directors and their friends
wound up this entertainment.

The Earl of Kellie was one of the best known of these

amateurs; he was a very fine violinist, and with his violin led the orchestra at the weekly concerts. His jovial, rubicund countenance, big wig, white satin waistcoat and richly embroidered suit, were long remembered as features of the concerts. He was not only a performer but a composer. He composed six overtures for the St. Cecilia Orchestra, and his cousin, Charles Kirkpatrick Sharpe, edited Lord Kellie's minuets and songs and dedicated them to his mother, Mrs. Sharpe.

It is told of the Earl of Kellie that, when no other instrument was available, he was an excellent performer on the Jew's-harp, and in private houses made it discourse most excellent music.

Lords Haddington and Colville were also distinguished amateurs, and played on the violin and 'cello; while Sir Gilbert Elliot is said to have introduced the German flute into Scotland. General Middleton not only played the flute admirably, but occasionally sang ' humorous songs' to the accompaniment of the key and tongs!

Gilbert Innes of Stow and a number of other well-known Edinburgh gentlemen sang in these 'Orchestral Concerts,' and it was frequently remarked how well our national music was rendered.

George Thomson, who died in 1851 at the age of ninety-four, wrote : ' Let us call to mind some of the lovely faces at these concerts — Jane Maxwell, Duchess of Gordon; "Bess" Burnet ; Miss Halket of Pitferran, who married Count Lally Tollendal ; Miss Hay of Hayston ; Miss Jardine ; Miss Kinloch of Gilmerton, and Miss Murray of Lintrose, known as the Flower of Strathmore, of whom Burns wrote :

> " Blithe, blithe, and merry was she,
> Blithe was she but and ben :
> Blithe by the banks of Ern,
> And blithe in Glenturit glen,"

and many more.'

Lord Cockburn writes thus about St. Cecilia's Hall:

'There have I myself seen most of our literary and fashionable gentlemen with side-curls, frills, ruffles, and silver buckles; our stately matrons stiffened in their hoops and gorgeous satin; and our beauties with high-heeled shoes, powdered hair, and lofty headdress. All this was in the Cowgate, the last retreat nowadays of destitution and disease.'

From old books and memoirs we get a vivid picture of the love of music in these times. Captain Topham in his letters gives the following description of the musical taste of residents in Edinburgh: 'The degree of attachment to music in this country exceeds belief. It is not only the principal entertainment, but it is the constant topic of conversation, and here it is necessary not only to be a lover of music, but to be possessed of a knowledge of the science in order to make oneself agreeable to society.'

We also get glimpses into the entertainments in private houses when great ladies had their 'four hours,' and gave their guests 'tea, plumb cake and sugar biskits.' With a wide stretch of imagination we can see the lace, the powdered heads, and the brocade of the ladies; the velvet coats, the ruffles, and the laced 'hatts' of the men; we can almost hear the excellence of the music and singing, and we can picture to ourselves Lady Anne Lindsay, sitting quietly in a corner, perhaps behind the 'Indian screen' in her mother's house in Hyndford's Close, listening to her own song of 'Auld Robin Gray.' Or it may be Mrs. Cockburn, when she was the young wife of Patrick Cockburn, listening in some distinguished gathering of legal luminaries to her version of the 'Flowers of the Forest.' Or again, it might be Miss Jean Elliot of Minto listening to *her* version of the same song, for we must never forget that all these ladies hid the fact that they had written these poems as if it had been a crime.

At these parties might also have been seen Lord Binning, Hamilton of Bangour, and Sir John Clerk of Penicuik, who all wrote lyrics. Hamilton of Bangour

Social
Life and
Customs
in Edin-
burgh in
Olden
Days

wrote 'The Braes of Yarrow,' and Sir John Clerk 'Merry
may the Maid be that marries the Miller.' The latter
was an ardent admirer of Susannah Kennedy before she
became Countess of Eglinton. When the young beauty
was first brought to Edinburgh by her father, an old
cavalier, she was a girl of eighteen. John Clerk, then
an advocate, fell deeply in love with her, but lacking
courage 'to put his fortune to the touch' by word of
mouth, he sent her a flute as a present. When she
attempted to play on it, no sound came, and on unscrew-
ing the flute a paper dropped out with a 'declaration'
in poetry. The story of her marriage to the Earl of
Eglinton has been already told in connection with Jack's
Land. She was universally considered the most charming
woman of her time ; and even when her seven handsome
daughters were grown up, George II. pronounced her the
most beautiful woman he had ever seen.

The changes which have taken place in the last
hundred years have been greater, in some respects, than
in the century preceding ; but what marks the change from
the eighteenth to the nineteenth century is the extraordinary change in manners and habits, and in the whole
social life of Edinburgh—a change largely owing to the
expansion of the city. A verse of a favourite song by
Sir Alexander Boswell of Auchinleck, which was frequently sung at the close of these old entertainments,
may be given as an appropriate finale to this brief sketch
of some outstanding features of Social Life in Edinburgh
in these bygone days :—

> 'The auld maun speak, the young maun hear,
> Be canty, but be gude and leal,
> Your ain ills aye hae hert to bear,
> Anither's aye hae hert to feel.
> So ere I set, I'll see you shine,
> I'll see your triumph ere I fa',
> My parting breath shall boast you mine,
> Gude nicht, an' joy be wi' ye a'.'

APPENDIX

ITINERARY

THE account of Edinburgh given in the preceding chapters has been more historical than descriptive. This method, though it possesses many advantages in describing a city like Edinburgh, affords no guidance to the tourist as to the order in which he should visit the various objects of interest. It has, therefore, been thought desirable to give a short itinerary. Although no break in the route is indicated, it is not suggested that the visitor should try to see everything in one day. This would only result in great confusion of mind, and, where a longer visit is impossible, strangers are not recommended to attempt more than the Castle and Holyrood with the intervening streets and closes. We think, however, that it will be well to give the itinerary as a continuous whole, so that visitors may, according to the time at their disposal, decide on the amount of ground to be covered each day.

The west end of Princes Street is a convenient starting-place. If we make our way along Castle Terrace, and, turning to the left, toil uphill past Johnston Terrace, we shall soon reach the Castle. A full description of it is to be found on pp. 86-102. Leaving the Castle behind us, we find ourselves in Castlehill. The Duke of Gordon's House is on our right (pp. 203-4). Farther east is Boswell's Court (p. 204), and beyond it are the two Assembly Halls—that belonging to the Church of Scotland being on our right, while the Free Church Assembly Hall is on our left (pp. 205-6).

We now enter the Lawnmarket. On our left-hand side we find Mylne's Court (pp. 206-7), James's Court (pp. 207-8), and Lady Stair's Close (pp. 208-10); while on our right are Riddle's Court (p. 212), and Brodie's Close (p. 213). We now enter the High Street proper. On our left are Dunbar's

Close (p. 218), Byres' Close (pp. 219-21), Advocates' Close (pp. 221-3), Roxburghe Close (p. 223), Warriston's Close (p. 224), and Writers' Court (pp. 224-5). To the east of Writers' Court is the Municipal Museum (p. 226). On the right-hand side are the County Buildings, St. Giles' (pp. 139-61), and Parliament Square with its wealth of memories (pp. 162-96). The heart, marking the site of the old Tolbooth (pp. 176-85), is to be seen near the west door of St. Giles', while the original site of the Cross is marked on the pavement to the east of the church by an octagonal figure. The Cross itself (pp. 162-76) must not be overlooked. The letters I.K., marking the grave of John Knox (p. 187), are a little to the west of the statue of Charles II. which is in the centre of Parliament Square. Parliament House, the Courts of Justice, the Advocates' Library and the Signet Library, all open off this interesting Square.

On the north side of the High Street may be seen Craig's Close (p. 226), Old Post Office Close (p. 227), Anchor Close (pp. 227-9), and Fleshmarket Close (p. 229). On the south side are Old Fishmarket Close (p. 230), Old Assembly Close (p: 230), Morrison's Close, and Paisley Close, while John Knox's House (admission sixpence) (pp. 242-3), is a little farther east. On our right are South Gray's Close (p. 239), Hyndford's Close (pp. 239-41), Fountain Close (pp. 241-2), Tweeddale Court (p. 243), and World's End Close (p. 243). Jeffrey Street and St. Mary Street mark the limits alike of the High Street and of the ancient city of Edinburgh.

The first thing we notice in the Canongate is Morocco Land (pp. 133-5). Playhouse Close (p. 133) on the right, and New Street (p. 133) on the left, are interesting. Jack's Land (pp. 130-3) on the north side is almost opposite St. John Street (p. 130) and Moray House (pp. 128-30). The Churchyard and Tolbooth of Canongate (pp. 126-8) are on our left, while Huntly House with its curious timber-fronted gables is on our right. The back of Huntly House overlooks Bakehouse Close (p. 124), which contains Acheson House (p. 124). Farther east is Queensberry House (pp. 123-4), while on the other side of the street are Golfers' Land (p. 123), and—a little farther down—the site of 'my Lord Seton's ludging in the Canongate' (pp. 121-2). A little to the east is White Horse Close

(p. 121), and then we find ourselves in front of Holyrood
(pp. 103-118). After investigating the Palace and Chapel and
—if time permits—taking a stroll in the King's Park, the
visitor is advised to walk up the South Back Canongate.
At St. Mary Street the South Back Canongate becomes the
Cowgate (pp. 252-6). Many of the old houses are interesting,
and the Magdalene Chapel (pp. 263-5) must on no account be
omitted. There is no charge for admission, but a small
gratuity should be given to the attendant.

The visitor should then go up Candlemaker Row, at the
head of which may be seen the monument to 'Greyfriars
Bobbie.' Greyfriars Churchyard (pp. 267-71) is on our right.
On the left Chambers Street with its fine museum leads to
the University (Old Buildings) (pp. 245-8). On leaving the
University the visitor should walk along College Street.
Potterrow, the home of Burns's 'Clarinda,' runs down from
this street. At the end of College Street may be seen
the M'Ewan Hall, which was presented to the University
by the ex-M.P. for Central Edinburgh. The hall is very
fine, the frescoes being specially beautiful. Adjoining it
are the University Union, the New University buildings, and
the Royal Infirmary. At the back of the Union is George
Square (p. 249), and beyond that Buccleuch Place (p. 249).
Returning to George Square, the visitor should leave it by
the Middle Meadow Walk and proceed along Lauriston
Place. Having passed Heriot's Hospital (founded by
'Jingling Geordie') he should turn down Heriot Place, a
lane leading into the Vennel (p. 256), which, in its turn,
leads to the Grassmarket (pp. 256-9). He should then take
his course along King's Stables Road and will soon arrive
once more at the west end of Princes Street.

The trams marked Braid Hills Road will take him for one
penny to the Boroughmuir (p. 34), now entirely covered
with houses, while a few minutes' walk along the tramway
line will bring him to Morningside Parish Church, where
he will see the 'Bore Stone' (p. 34). If he has time, a
walk along Colinton Road will be found interesting, for
he will then see Merchiston Castle, the home of Napier of
Merchiston, the inventor of logarithms. It is now a large
boys' school, noted, among other things, for its prowess in

athletics. From the end of Colinton Road a tramway car takes the visitor back to Princes Street.

He should now walk along this fine street until he reaches the Mound, where may be seen the Scottish National Gallery, and, in the season, the Royal Scottish Academy. A little farther east is the Scott Monument, which should be visited, and, if possible, ascended. At the east end of Princes Street are the General Post Office, on the one side, and, on the other, the Register House, with an equestrian statue of Wellington in front. Proceeding along Waterloo Place he passes, on his right, the Calton Jail, which has been mistaken by strangers for the Castle. On his left is the Calton Hill, from which there is a magnificent view of the Forth and the East Lothian coast. He should then retrace his steps as far as St. David Street (p. 283), which leads to Queen Street, where he may visit the Scottish Portrait Gallery and Antiquarian Museum. He should go westward along Queen Street, taking care not to miss the charming views of Fife which are visible at the cross streets. He proceeds by St. Colme Street, Ainslie Place, Great Stuart Street and Randolph Crescent, and then, turning to the right, finds himself on the famous Dean Bridge. On one side lies the little village of Dean, which is being rapidly absorbed by the advancing town, yet retains many of its own peculiarities. There are many interesting old houses here, notably one which was formerly inhabited by the mother of the Colonel Gardiner who fell at Preston-pans. In many of these houses oak panelling is concealed by whitewash, and relics of past splendour are mingled incongruously enough with present squalor. But the character of the village is rapidly changing. These interesting but insanitary houses are being swept away, and their place taken by model dwellings which are clean, comfortable, and, in some cases, picturesque. The other side of the Dean Bridge looks past the stately houses of Moray Place on the right and Eton Terrace on the left, over the green turf of the gardens and the foliage of the trees surrounding St. Bernard's Well to the blue waters of the Firth of Forth and the still bluer hills of Fife.

This completes the itinerary of Edinburgh, but there are

many places of interest in the neighbourhood which should
be visited if possible. The Forth Bridge (nine miles) may
be reached either by train or by coach. The trains start
from Waverley Station, and those going by train take
tickets to Dalmeny. The coaches start from Princes Street.
The drive is both pleasant and interesting, as the road passes
close to Craigcrook (p. 293), crosses Cramond Bridge (where
King James v. was helped by Jock Howieson), and runs
alongside the park walls of Dalmeny, which belongs to Lord
Rosebery. Visitors are taken round the bridge in a steam
launch, and can have lunch or tea at the Hawes Inn, which
is mentioned in *The Antiquary.*

Craigmillar Castle has many associations with Queen
Mary, and is, moreover, an interesting old ruin. It is quite
near Duddingston, a station on the Suburban Railway.
Suburban trains start from Waverley.

Dalkeith Palace (open on Wednesdays and Saturdays) is
interesting in many ways, both on account of its fine collection of historical portraits, and also because of the avenue
of ' beheaded ' trees which the Duchess of Monmouth sacrificed in memory of her husband. Newbattle Abbey, a mile
away, which has some wonderful old trees, may be visited
the same day. Dalkeith is the station for the Palace, but
Eskbank—half a mile away—has a greater variety of trains.

Roslin (seven miles) should not be omitted ; its chapel with
the famous ' Prentice Pillar ' is well worth seeing. The
visitor might drive out by coach from Princes Street ; after
seeing the chapel and the ruins of the castle he should
walk down the woodland path in the valley of the Esk,
which passes Hawthornden, with its memories of Drummond
and Ben Jonson. This path will bring him out at Polton
Station where he will get a train for Edinburgh.

Linlithgow (fifteen miles) is full of tragic memories. It
was here that Queen Margaret sat and lamented her
husband's reckless folly which led to Flodden. It was
here, too, that Margaret's granddaughter, Mary Stuart, was
born. Linlithgow, like Holyrood and Edinburgh Castle, is
full of memories of the most beautiful and hapless Princess
of the Stuart line.

INDEX

Printed by T. and A. CONSTABLE, Printers to His Majesty
at the Edinburgh University Press

A CATALOGUE OF BOOKS PUBLISHED BY METHUEN AND COMPANY: LONDON 36 ESSEX STREET W.C.

CONTENTS

MARCH 1906

A CATALOGUE OF

MESSRS. METHUEN'S
PUBLICATIONS

Colonial Editions are published of all Messrs. METHUEN's Novels issued at a price above 2s. 6d., and similar editions are published of some works of General Literature. These are marked in the Catalogue. Colonial editions are only for circulation in the British Colonies and India.

An asterisk denotes that a book is in the Press.
I.P.L. represents Illustrated Pocket Library.
S.Q.S. represents Social Questions Series.

PART I.—GENERAL LITERATURE

Abbot (Jacob). See Little Blue Books.

Abbott (J. H. M.). Author of 'Tommy Cornstalk.' AN OUTLANDER IN ENGLAND: BEING SOME IMPRESSIONS OF AN AUSTRALIAN ABROAD. *Second Edition. Cr. 8vo. 6s.*
A Colonial Edition is also published.

Acatos (M. J.). See Junior School Books.

Adams (Frank). JACK SPRATT. With 24 Coloured Pictures. *Super Royal 16mo. 2s.*

Adeney (W. F.), M.A. See Bennett and Adeney.

Æschylus. See Classical Translations.

Æsop. See I.P.L.

Ainsworth (W. Harrison). See I.P.L.

Alderson (J. P.). MR. ASQUITH. With Portraits and Illustrations. *Demy 8vo. 7s. 6d. net.*
A Colonial Edition is also published.

Aldis (Janet). MADAME GEOFFRIN, HER SALON, AND HER TIMES. With many Portraits and Illustrations. *Second Edition. Demy 8vo. 10s. 6d. net.*
A Colonial Edition is also published.

Alexander (William), D.D., Archbishop of Armagh. THOUGHTS AND COUNSELS OF MANY YEARS. *Demy 16mo. 2s. 6d.*

Alken (Henry). THE NATIONAL SPORTS OF GREAT BRITAIN. With descriptions in English and French. With 51 Coloured Plates. *Royal Folio. Five Guineas net.* The Plates can be had separately in a Portfolio. *£3, 3s. net.*
See also I.P.L.

Allen (Jessie). See Little Books on Art.

Allen (J. Romilly), F.S.A. See Antiquary's Books.

Almack (E.). See Little Books on Art.

Amherst (Lady). A SKETCH OF EGYPTIAN HISTORY FROM THE EARLIEST TIMES TO THE PRESENT DAY. With many Illustrations. *Demy 8vo. 10s. 6d. net.*

Anderson (F. M.). THE STORY OF THE BRITISH EMPIRE FOR CHILDREN. With many Illustrations. *Cr. 8vo. 2s.*

Anderson (J. G.), B.A., Examiner to London University, NOUVELLE GRAMMAIRE FRANÇAISE. *Cr. 8vo. 2s.*

EXERCICES DE GRAMMAIRE FRANÇAISE. *Cr. 8vo. 1s. 6d.*

Andrewes (Bishop). PRECES PRIVATAE. Edited, with Notes, by F. E. BRIGHTMAN, M.A., of Pusey House, Oxford. *Cr. 8vo. 6s.*

Anglo=Australian. AFTER-GLOW MEMORIES. *Cr. 8vo. 6s.*
A Colonial Edition is also published.

Aristophanes. THE FROGS. Translated into English by E. W. HUNTINGFORD, M.A. *Cr. 8vo. 2s. 6d.*

Aristotle. THE NICOMACHEAN ETHICS. Edited, with an Introduction and Notes, by JOHN BURNET, M.A., Professor of Greek at St. Andrews. *Cheaper issue. Demy 8vo. 10s. 6d. net.*

Ashton (R.). See Little Blue Books.

Atkins (H. G.). See Oxford Biographies.

Atkinson (C. M.). JEREMY BENTHAM. *Demy 8vo. 5s. net.*

Atkinson (T. D.). A SHORT HISTORY OF ENGLISH ARCHITECTURE. With over 200 Illustrations. *Fcap. 8vo. 3s. 6d. net.*

*A GLOSSARY OF TERMS USED IN ENGLISH ARCHITECTURE. Illustrated. *Fcap. 8vo. 3s. 6d. net.*

Auden (T.), M.A., F.S.A. See Ancient Cities.

Aurelius (Marcus). See Standard Library and W. H. D. Rouse.

Austen (Jane). See Little Library and Standard Library.

Aves (Ernest). See Books on Business.

Bacon (Francis). See Little Library and Standard Library.

Baden=Powell (R. S. S.), Major-General. THE DOWNFALL OF PREMPEH. A Diary of Life in Ashanti, 1895. Illustrated. *Third Edition. Large Cr. 8vo. 6s.*
A Colonial Edition is also published.
THE MATABELE CAMPAIGN, 1896. With nearly 100 Illustrations. *Fourth Edition. Large Cr. 8vo. 6s.*
A Colonial Edition is also published.

*****Bagot (Richard). THE LAKE OF COMO. *Cr. 8vo. 3s. 6d. net.*

Bailey (J. C.), M.A. See Cowper.

Baker (W. G.), M.A. See Junior Examination Series.

Baker (Julian L.), F.I.C., F.C.S. See Books on Business.

Balfour (Graham). THE LIFE OF ROBERT LOUIS STEVENSON. *Second Edition. Two Volumes. Demy 8vo. 25s. net.*
A Colonial Edition is also published.

Bally (S. E.). See Commercial Series.

Banks (Elizabeth L.). THE AUTO-BIOGRAPHY OF A 'NEWSPAPER GIRL.' *Second Edition. Cr. 8vo. 6s.*
A Colonial Edition is also published.

Barham (R. H.). See Little Library.

Baring (The Hon. Maurice). WITH THE RUSSIANS IN MANCHURIA. *Third Edition. Demy 8vo. 7s. 6d. net.*
A Colonial Edition is also published.

Baring=Gould (S.). THE LIFE OF NAPOLEON BONAPARTE. With over 450 Illustrations in the Text, and 12 Photogravure Plates. *Gilt top. Large quarto. 36s.*
THE TRAGEDY OF THE CÆSARS. With numerous Illustrations from Busts, Gems, Cameos, etc. *Fifth Edition. Royal 8vo. 10s. 6d. net.*
A BOOK OF FAIRY TALES. With numerous Illustrations by A. J. GASKIN. *Second Edition. Cr. 8vo. Buckram. 6s.*
OLD ENGLISH FAIRY TALES. With numerous Illustrations by F. D. BEDFORD. *Second Edition. Cr. 8vo. Buckram. 6s.*
A Colonial Edition is also published.
THE VICAR OF MORWENSTOW. Revised Edition. With a Portrait. *Cr. 8vo. 3s. 6d.*
DARTMOOR: A Descriptive and Historical Sketch. With Plans and numerous Illustrations. *Cr. 8vo. 6s.*
THE BOOK OF THE WEST. Illustrated. *Two volumes. Vol. I. Devon. Second Edition. Vol. II. Cornwall. Second Edition. Cr. 8vo. 6s. each.*
A BOOK OF NORTH WALES. Illustrated. *Cr. 8vo. 6s.*
A BOOK OF SOUTH WALES. Illustrated. *Cr. 8vo. 6s.*
A BOOK OF BRITTANY. Illustrated. *Cr. 8vo. 6s.*
A BOOK OF THE RIVIERA. Illustrated. *Cr. 8vo. 6s.*
A Colonial Edition is also published.

*****THE RHINE. Illustrated. *Cr. 8vo. 6s.*
A BOOK OF GHOSTS. With 8 Illustrations by D. MURRAY SMITH. *Second Edition. Cr. 8vo. 6s.*
A Colonial Edition is also published.
OLD COUNTRY LIFE. With 67 Illustrations. *Fifth Edition. Large Cr. 8vo. 6s.*
A GARLAND OF COUNTRY SONG: English Folk Songs with their Traditional Melodies. Collected and arranged by S. BARING-GOULD and H. F. SHEPPARD. *Demy 4to. 6s.*
SONGS OF THE WEST: Folk Songs of Devon and Cornwall. Collected from the Mouths of the People. By S. BARING-GOULD, M.A., and H. FLEETWOOD SHEPPARD, M.A. New and Revised Edition, under the musical editorship of CECIL J. SHARP, Principal of the Hampstead Conservatoire. *Large Imperial 8vo. 5s. net.*
See also Little Guides and Half-Crown Library.

Barker (Aldred F.). See Textbooks of Technology.

Barnes (W. E.), D.D. See Churchman's Bible.

Barnett (Mrs. P. A.). See Little Library.

Baron (R. R. N.), M.A. FRENCH PROSE COMPOSITION. *Second Edition. Cr. 8vo. 2s. 6d. Key, 3s. net.* See also Junior School Books.

Barron (H. M.), M.A., Wadham College, Oxford. TEXTS FOR SERMONS. With a Preface by Canon SCOTT HOLLAND. *Cr. 8vo. 3s. 6d.*

Bartholomew (J. G.), F.R.S.E. See C. G. Robertson.

Bastable (C. F.), M.A. See S.Q.S.

Batson (Mrs. Stephen). A BOOK OF THE COUNTRY AND THE GARDEN. Illustrated by F. CARRUTHERS GOULD and A. C. GOULD. *Demy 8vo. 10s. 6d.*
A CONCISE HANDBOOK OF GARDEN FLOWERS. *Fcap. 8vo. 3s. 6d.*

Batten (Loring W.), Ph.D., S.T.D. THE HEBREW PROPHET. *Cr. 8vo. 3s. 6d. net.*

Beaman (A. Hulme). PONS ASINORUM; OR, A GUIDE TO BRIDGE. *Second Edition. Fcap. 8vo. 2s.*

Beard (W. S.). See Junior Examination Series and Beginner's Books.

Beckford (Peter). THOUGHTS ON HUNTING. Edited by J. OTHO PAGET, and Illustrated by G. H. JALLAND. *Second Edition. Demy 8vo. 6s.*

Beckford (William). See Little Library.

Beeching (H. C.), M.A., Canon of Westminster. See Library of Devotion.

Begbie (Harold). MASTER WORKERS. Illustrated. *Demy 8vo. 7s. 6d. net.*

Behmen (Jacob). DIALOGUES ON THE SUPERSENSUAL LIFE. Edited by BERNARD HOLLAND. *Fcap. 8vo. 3s. 6d.*

Belloc (Hilaire). PARIS. With Maps and Illustrations. *Cr. 8vo.* 6s.

*MARIE ANTOINETTE. With many Portraits and Illustrations. *Demy 8vo.* 12s. 6d. net.
A Colonial Edition is also published.

Bellot (H. H. L.), M.A. THE INNER AND MIDDLE TEMPLE. With numerous Illustrations. *Crown 8vo.* 6s. net.
See also L. A. A. Jones.

Bennett (W. H.), M.A. A PRIMER OF THE BIBLE. *Third Edition. Cr. 8vo.* 2s. 6d.

Bennett (W. H.) and Adeney (W. F.). A BIBLICAL INTRODUCTION. *Third Edition. Cr. 8vo.* 7s. 6d.

Benson (Archbishop) GOD'S BOARD: Communion Addresses. *Fcap. 8vo.* 3s. 6d. net.

Benson (A. C.), M.A. See Oxford Biographies.

Benson (R. M.). THE WAY OF HOLINESS: a Devotional Commentary on the 119th Psalm. *Cr. 8vo.* 5s.

Bernard (E. R.), M.A., Canon of Salisbury. THE ENGLISH SUNDAY. *Fcap. 8vo.* 1s. 6d.

Bertouch (Baroness de). THE LIFE OF FATHER IGNATIUS. Illustrated. *Demy 8vo.* 10s. 6d. net.
A Colonial Edition is also published.

Betham-Edwards (M.). HOME LIFE IN FRANCE. Illustrated. *Fourth Edition. Demy 8vo.* 7s. 6d. net.
A Colonial Edition is also published.

Bethune-Baker (J. F.), M.A. See Handbooks of Theology.

Bidez (M.). See Byzantine Texts.

Biggs (C. R. D.), D.D. See Churchman's Bible.

Bindley (T. Herbert), B.D. THE OECUMENICAL DOCUMENTS OF THE FAITH. With Introductions and Notes. *Cr. 8vo.* 6s.

Binns (H. B.). THE LIFE OF WALT WHITMAN. Illustrated. *Demy 8vo.* 10s. 6d. net.
A Colonial Edition is also published.

Binyon (Laurence). THE DEATH OF ADAM, AND OTHER POEMS *Cr. 8vo.* 3s. 6d. net.

*WILLIAM BLAKE. In 2 volumes. *Super Royal Quarto.* £1, 1s. each.
Vol. I.—THE BOOK OF JOB.

Birnstingl (Ethel). See Little Books on Art.

Blackmantle (Bernard). See I.P.L.

Blair (Robert). See I.P.L.

Blake (William). See I.P.L. and Little Library.

Blaxland (B.), M.A. See Library of Devotion.

Bloom (T. Harvey), M.A. SHAKESPEARE'S GARDEN. Illustrated. *Fcap. 8vo.* 3s. 6d. ; *leather,* 4s. 6d. net.
See also Antiquary's Books.

Blouet (Henri). See Beginner's Books.

Boardman (T. H.), M.A. See Textbooks of Science.

Bodley (J. E. C.), Author of 'France.' THE CORONATION OF EDWARD VII. *Demy 8vo.* 21s. net. By Command of the King.

Body (George), D.D. THE SOUL'S PILGRIMAGE : Devotional Readings from his writings. Selected by J. H. BURN, B.D., F.R.S.E. *Pott 8vo.* 2s. 6d.

Bona (Cardinal). See Library of Devotion.

Boon (F. C.). See Commercial Series.

Borrow (George). See Little Library.

Bos (J. Ritzema). AGRICULTURAL ZOOLOGY. Translated by J. R. AINSWORTH DAVIS, M.A. With 155 Illustrations. *Cr. 8vo. Third Edition.* 3s. 6d.

Botting (C. G.), B.A. EASY GREEK EXERCISES. *Cr. 8vo.* 2s. See also Junior Examination Series.

Boulton (E. S.), M.A. GEOMETRY ON MODERN LINES. *Cr. 8vo.* 2s.

Boulton (William B.). THOMAS GAINSBOROUGH With 40 Illustrations. *Second Ed. Demy 8vo.* 7s. 6d. net.
SIR JOSHUA REYNOLDS, P.R.A. With 49 Illustrations. *Demy 8vo.* 7s. 6d. net.

Bowden (E. M.). THE IMITATION OF BUDDHA : Being Quotations from Buddhist Literature for each Day in the Year. *Fifth Edition. Cr. 16mo.* 2s. 6d.

Boyle (W.). CHRISTMAS AT THE ZOO. With Verses by W. BOYLE and 24 Coloured Pictures by H. B. NEILSON. *Super Royal 16mo.* 2s.

Brabant (F. G.), M.A. See Little Guides.

Bradley (J. W.). See Little Books on Art.

Brailsford (H. N.). MACEDONIA Illustrated. *Demy 8vo.* 12s. 6d. net.

Brodrick (Mary) and Morton (Anderson). A CONCISE HANDBOOK OF EGYPTIAN ARCHÆOLOGY. Illustrated. *Cr. 8vo.* 3s. 6d.

Brooke (A. S.), M.A. SLINGSBY AND SLINGSBY CASTLE. Illustrated. *Cr. 8vo.* 7s. 6d.

Brooks (E. W.). See Byzantine Texts.

Brown (P. H.), LL.D., Fraser Professor of Ancient (Scottish) History at the University of Edinburgh. SCOTLAND IN THE TIME OF QUEEN MARY. *Demy 8vo.* 7s. 6d. net.

Browne (Sir Thomas). See Standard Library.

Brownell (C. L.). THE HEART OF JAPAN. Illustrated. *Third Edition. Cr. 8vo.* 6s. ; *also Demy 8vo.* 6d.
A Colonial Edition is also published.

Browning (Robert). See Little Library.

Buckland (Francis T.). CURIOSITIES OF NATURAL HISTORY. Illustrated by H. B. NEILSON. *Cr. 8vo.* 3s. 6d.

Buckton (A. M.) THE BURDEN OF ENGELA: a Ballad-Epic. *Second Edition. Cr. 8vo.* 3s. 6d. net.

EAGER HEART: A Mystery Play. *Fourth Edition. Cr. 8vo.* 1s. net.

Budge (E. A. Wallis). THE GODS OF THE EGYPTIANS. With over 100 Coloured Plates and many Illustrations. *Two Volumes. Royal 8vo.* £3, 3s. net.

Bull (Paul), Army Chaplain. GOD AND OUR SOLDIERS. *Second Edition. Cr. 8vo.* 6s.
A Colonial Edition is also published.

Bulley (Miss). See S.Q.S.

Bunyan (John). THE PILGRIM'S PROGRESS. Edited, with an Introduction, by C. H. FIRTH, M.A. With 39 Illustrations by R. ANNING BELL. *Cr. 8vo.* 6s.
See also Library of Devotion and Standard Library.

Burch (G. J.), M.A., F.R.S. A MANUAL OF ELECTRICAL SCIENCE. Illustrated. *Cr. 8vo.* 3s.

Burgess (Gelett). GOOPS AND HOW TO BE THEM. Illustrated. *Small 4to.* 6s.

Burke (Edmund). See Standard Library.

Burn (A. E.), D.D., Rector of Handsworth and Prebendary of Lichfield.
See Handbooks of Theology.

Burn (J. H.), B.D. See Library of Devotion.

Burnand (Sir F. C.). RECORDS AND REMINISCENCES. With a Portrait by H. v. HERKOMER. *Cr. 8vo. Fourth and Cheaper Edition.* 6s.
A Colonial Edition is also published.

Burns (Robert), THE POEMS OF. Edited by ANDREW LANG and W. A. CRAIGIE. With Portrait. *Third Edition. Demy 8vo, gilt top.* 6s.

Burnside (W. F.), M.A. OLD TESTAMENT HISTORY FOR USE IN SCHOOLS. *Cr. 8vo* 3s. 6d.

Burton (Alfred). See I.P.L.

Butler (Joseph). See Standard Library.

Caldecott (Alfred), D.D. See Handbooks of Theology.

Calderwood (D. S.), Headmaster of the Normal School, Edinburgh. TEST CARDS IN EUCLID AND ALGEBRA. In three packets of 40, with Answers. 1s. each. Or in three Books, price 2d., 2d., and 3d.

Cambridge (Ada) [Mrs. Cross]. THIRTY YEARS IN AUSTRALIA. *Demy 8vo.* 7s. 6d.
A Colonial Edition is also published.

Canning (George). See Little Library.

Capey (E. F. H.). See Oxford Biographies.

Careless (John). See I.P.L.

Carlyle (Thomas). THE FRENCH REVOLUTION. Edited by C. R. L. FLETCHER, Fellow of Magdalen College, Oxford. *Three Volumes. Cr. 8vo.* 18s.

THE LIFE AND LETTERS OF OLIVER CROMWELL. With an Introduction by C. H. FIRTH, M.A., and Notes and Appendices by Mrs. S. C. LOMAS. *Three Volumes. Demy 8vo.* 18s. net.

Carlyle (R. M. and A. J.), M.A. See Leaders of Religion.

*****Carpenter (Margaret).** THE CHILD IN ART. Illustrated. *Cr. 8vo.* 6s.

Chamberlin (Wilbur B.). ORDERED TO CHINA. *Cr. 8vo.* 6s.
A Colonial Edition is also published.

Channer (C. C.) and Roberts (M. E.). LACEMAKING IN THE MIDLANDS, PAST AND PRESENT. With 16 full-page Illustrations. *Cr. 8vo.* 2s. 6d.

Chapman (S. J.). See Books on Business.

Chatterton (Thomas). See Standard Library.

Chesterfield (Lord), THE LETTERS OF, TO HIS SON. Edited, with an Introduction by C. STRACHEY, and Notes by A. CALTHROP. *Two Volumes. Cr. 8vo.* 12s.

*****Chesterton (G. K.).** DICKENS. With Portraits and Illustrations. *Demy 8vo.* 7s. 6d. net.
A Colonial Edition is also published.

Christian (F. W.). THE CAROLINE ISLANDS. With many Illustrations and Maps. *Demy 8vo.* 12s. 6d. net.

Cicero. See Classical Translations.

Clarke (F. A.), M.A. See Leaders of Religion.

Cleather (A. L.) and Crump (B.). RICHARD WAGNER'S MUSIC DRAMAS: Interpretations, embodying Wagner's own explanations. *In Four Volumes. Fcap 8vo.* 2s. 6d. each.
VOL. I.—THE RING OF THE NIBELUNG.
VOL. II.—PARSIFAL, LOHENGRIN, and THE HOLY GRAIL.
VOL. III.—TRISTAN AND ISOLDE.

Clinch (G.). See Little Guides.

Clough (W. T.). See Junior School Books.

Coast (W. G.), B.A. EXAMINATION PAPERS IN VERGIL. *Cr. 8vo.* 2s.

Cobb (T.). See Little Blue Books.

Cobb (W. F.), M.A. THE BOOK OF PSALMS: with a Commentary. *Demy 8vo.* 10s. 6d. net.

Coleridge (S. T.), SELECTIONS FROM. Edited by ARTHUR SYMONS. *Fcap. 8vo.* 2s. 6d. net.

Collingwood (W. G.). See Half-Crown Library.

Collins (W. E.), M.A. See Churchman's Library.

Colonna. HYPNEROTOMACHIA POLIPHILI UBI HUMANA OMNIA NON NISI SOMNIUM ESSE DOCET ATQUE OBITER PLURIMA SCITU SANE QUAM DIGNA COMMEMORAT. An edition limited to 350 copies on handmade paper. *Folio. Three Guineas net.*

Combe (William). See I.P.L.

Cook (A. M.), M.A. See E. C. Marchant.

Cooke=Taylor (R. W.). See S.Q.S.

Corelli (Marie). THE PASSING OF THE GREAT QUEEN : *Fcap. 4to. 1s.*

A CHRISTMAS GREETING. *Cr. 4to. 1s.*

Corkran (Alice). See Little Books on Art.

Cotes (Rosemary). DANTE'S GARDEN. With a Frontispiece. *Second Edition. Fcap. 8vo. 2s. 6d.; leather, 3s. 6d. net.*

BIBLE FLOWERS. With a Frontispiece and Plan. *Fcap. 8vo. 2s. 6d. net.*

Cowley (Abraham). See Little Library.

Cowper (William), THE POEMS OF. Edited with an Introduction and Notes by J. C. BAILEY, M.A. Illustrated, including two unpublished designs by WILLIAM BLAKE. *Demy 8vo. 10s. 6d. net.*

Cox (J. Charles), LL.D., F.S.A. See Little Guides, The Antiquary's Books, and Ancient Cities.

Cox (Harold), B.A. See S.Q.S.

Crabbe (George). See Little Library.

Craigie (W. A.). A PRIMER OF BURNS. *Cr. 8vo. 2s. 6d.*

Craik (Mrs.). See Little Library.

Crashaw (Richard). See Little Library.

Crawford (F. G.). See Mary C. Danson.

*Cross (J. A.). A LITTLE BOOK OF RELIGION. *Fcap. 8vo. 2s. 6d. net.*

Crouch (W.). BRYAN KING. With a Portrait. *Cr. 8vo. 3s. 6d. net.*

Cruikshank (G.). THE LOVING BALLAD OF LORD BATEMAN. With 11 Plates. *Cr. 16mo. 1s. 6d. net.*

Crump (B.). See A. L. Cleather.

Cunliffe (Sir F. H. E.), Fellow of All Souls' College, Oxford. THE HISTORY OF THE BOER WAR. With many Illustrations, Plans, and Portraits. *In 2 vols. Quarto. 15s. each.*

A Colonial Edition is also published.

Cunynghame (H.), C.B., See Connoisseur's Library.

Cutts (E. L.), D.D. See Leaders of Religion.

Daniell (G. W.), M.A. See Leaders of Religion.

Danson (Mary C.) and Crawford (F. G.). FATHERS IN THE FAITH. *Fcap. 8vo. 1s. 6d.*

Dante. LA COMMEDIA DI DANTE. The Italian Text edited by PAGET TOYNBEE, M.A., D.Litt. *Cr. 8vo. 6s.*

THE PURGATORIO OF DANTE. Translated into Spenserian Prose by C. GORDON WRIGHT. With the Italian text. *Fcap. 8vo. 2s. 6d. net.*

See also Paget Toynbee, Little Library and Standard Library.

Darley (George). See Little Library.

D'Arcy (R. F.), M.A. A NEW TRIGONOMETRY FOR BEGINNERS. *Cr. 8vo. 2s. 6d.*

Davenport (Cyril). See Connoisseur's Library and Little Books on Art.

*Davey (Richard). THE PAGEANT OF LONDON With 40 Illustrations in Colour by JOHN FULLEYLOVE, R. I. *In Two Volumes. Demy 8vo. 7s. 6d. net.* Each volume may be purchased separately.

VOL. I.—TO A.D. 1500.

VOL. II.—A.D. 1500 TO 1900.

Davis (H. W. C.), M.A., Fellow and Tutor of Balliol College, Author of 'Charlemagne.' ENGLAND UNDER THE NORMANS AND ANGEVINS : 1066-1272. With Maps and Illustrations. *Demy 8vo. 10s. 6d. net.*

Dawson (A. J.). MOROCCO. Illustrated *Demy 8vo. 10s. 6d. net.*

Deane (A. C.). See Little Library.

Delbos (Leon). THE METRIC SYSTEM. *Cr. 8vo. 2s.*

Demosthenes. THE OLYNTHIACS AND PHILIPPICS. Translated by OTHO HOLLAND. *Cr. 8vo. 2s. 6d.*

Demosthenes. AGAINST CONON AND CALLICLES. Edited by F. DARWIN SWIFT, M.A. *Fcap. 8vo. 2s.*

Dickens (Charles). See Little Library and I.P.L.

Dickinson (Emily). POEMS. *Cr. 8vo. 4s. 6d. net.*

Dickinson (G. L.), M.A., Fellow of King's College, Cambridge. THE GREEK VIEW OF LIFE. *Fourth Edition. Cr. 8vo. 2s. 6d.*

Dickson (H. N.), F.R.Met. Soc. METEOROLOGY. Illustrated. *Cr. 8vo. 2s. 6d.*

Dilke (Lady). See S.Q.S.

Dillon (Edward). See Connoisseur's Library and Little Books on Art.

Ditchfield (P. H.), M.A., F.S.A. THE STORY OF OUR ENGLISH TOWNS. With an Introduction by AUGUSTUS JESSOPP, D.D. *Second Edition. Cr. 8vo. 6s.*

OLD ENGLISH CUSTOMS: Extant at the Present Time. *Cr. 8vo. 6s.* See also Half-crown Library.

Dixon (W. M.), M.A. A PRIMER OF TENNYSON. *Second Edition. Cr. 8vo. 2s. 6d.*

ENGLISH POETRY FROM BLAKE TO BROWNING. *Second Edition. Cr. 8vo. 2s. 6d.*

Dole (N. H.). FAMOUS COMPOSERS. With Portraits. *Two Volumes. Demy 8vo. 12s. net.*

Doney (May). SONGS OF THE REAL. *Cr. 8vo. 3s. 6d. net.* A volume of poems.

Douglas (James). THE MAN IN THE PULPIT. *Cr. 8vo. 2s. 6d. net.*

Dowden (J.), D.D., Lord Bishop of Edinburgh. See Churchman's Library.

Drage (G.). See Books on Business.

Driver (S. R.), D.D., D.C.L., Canon of Christ Church, Regius Professor of Hebrew in the University of Oxford. SERMONS ON SUBJECTS CONNECTED WITH THE OLD TESTAMENT. *Cr. 8vo.* 6s.
See also Westminster Commentaries.

Dry (Wakeling). See Little Guides.

Dryhurst (A. R.). See Little Books on Art.

Duguid (Charles). See Books on Business.

Dunn (J. T.)., D.Sc., and **Mundella** (V. A.). GENERAL ELEMENTARY SCIENCE. With 114 Illustrations. *Second Edition. Cr. 8vo.* 3s. 6d.

Dunstan (A. E.), B.Sc. See Junior School Books and Textbooks of Science.

Durham (The Earl of). A REPORT ON CANADA. With an Introductory Note. *Demy 8vo.* 4s. 6d. net.

Dutt (W. A.). A POPULAR GUIDE TO NORFOLK. *Medium 8vo.* 6d. net.
THE NORFOLK BROADS. With coloured Illustrations by FRANK SOUTHGATE. *Cr. 8vo.* 6s. See also Little Guides.

Earle (John), Bishop of Salisbury. MICROCOSMOGRAPHIE, or A PIECE OF THE WORLD DISCOVERED. *Post 16mo.* 2s net.

Edmonds (Major J. E.), R.E.; D.A.Q.-M.G. See W. Birkbeck Wood.

Edwards (Clement). See S.Q.S.

Edwards (W. Douglas). See Commercial Series.

Egan (Pierce). See I.P.L.

Egerton (H. E.), M.A. A HISTORY OF BRITISH COLONIAL POLICY. New and Cheaper Issue. *Demy 8vo.* 7s. 6d. net.
A Colonial Edition is also published.

Ellaby (C. G.). See The Little Guides.

Ellerton (F. G.). See S. J. Stone.

Ellwood (Thomas), THE HISTORY OF THE LIFE OF. Edited by C. G. CRUMP, M.A. *Cr. 8vo.* 6s.

Epictetus. See W. H. D. Rouse.

Erasmus. A Book called in Latin ENCHIRIDION MILITIS CHRISTIANI, and in English the Manual of the Christian Knight.
From the edition printed by Wynken de Worde, 1533. *Fcap. 8vo* 3s. 6d. net.

Fairbrother (W. H.), M.A. THE PHILOSOPHY OF T. H. GREEN. *Second Edition. Cr. 8vo.* 3s. 6d.

Farrer (Reginald). THE GARDEN OF ASIA. *Second Edition. Cr. 8vo.* 6s.
A Colonial Edition is also published.

***Fea** (Allan). BEAUTIES OF THE SEVENTEENEH CENTURY. With 100 Illustrations. *Demy 8vo.* 12s. 6d. net.

FELISSA; OR, THE LIFE AND OPINIONS OF A KITTEN OF SENTIMENT. With 12 Coloured Plates. *Post 16mo.* 2s. 6d. net.

Ferrier (Susan). See Little Library.

Fidler (T. Claxton), M.Inst. C.E. See Books on Business.

Fielding (Henry). See Standard Library.

Finn (S. W.), M.A. See Junior Examination Series.

Firth (C. H.), M.A. CROMWELL'S ARMY: A History of the English Soldier during the Civil Wars, the Commonwealth, and the Protectorate. *Cr. 8vo.* 6s.

Fisher (G. W.), M.A. ANNALS OF SHREWSBURY SCHOOL. Illustrated. *Demy 8vo.* 10s. 6d.

FitzGerald (Edward). THE RUBAIYAT OF OMAR KHAYYÁM. Printed from the Fifth and last Edition. With a Commentary by Mrs. STEPHEN BATSON, and a Biography of Omar by E. D. ROSS. *Cr. 8vo.* 6s. See also Miniature Library.

***FitzGerald** (H. P.). A CONCISE HANDBOOK OF CLIMBERS, TWINERS, AND WALL SHRUBS. Illustrated. *Fcap. 8vo.* 3s. 6d. net.

Flecker (W. H.), M.A., D.C.L., Headmaster of the Dean Close School, Cheltenham. THE STUDENT'S PRAYER BOOK. THE TEXT OF MORNING AND EVENING PRAYER AND LITANY. With an Introduction and Notes. *Cr. 8vo.* 2s. 6d.

Flux (A. W.), M.A., William Dow Professor of Political Economy in M'Gill University, Montreal. ECONOMIC PRINCIPLES. *Demy 8vo.* 7s. 6d. net.

Fortescue (Mrs. G.). See Little Books on Art.

Fraser (David). A MODERN CAMPAIGN; OR, WAR AND WIRELESS TELEGRAPHY IN THE FAR EAST. Illustrated. *Cr. 8vo.* 6s.
A Colonial Edition is also published.

Fraser (J. F.). ROUND THE WORLD ON A WHEEL. With 100 Illustrations. *Fourth Edition Cr. 8vo.* 6s.
A Colonial Edition is also published.

French (W.), M.A. See Textbooks of Science.

Freudenreich (Ed. von). DAIRY BACTERIOLOGY. A Short Manual for the Use of Students. Translated by J. R. AINSWORTH DAVIS, M.A. *Second Edition. Revised. Cr. 8vo.* 2s. 6d.

Fulford (H. W.), M.A. See Churchman's Bible.

C. G., and F. C. G. JOHN BULL'S ADVENTURES IN THE FISCAL WONDERLAND. By CHARLES GEAKE. With 46 Illustrations by F. CARRUTHERS GOULD. *Second Edition. Cr. 8vo.* 1s. net.

***Gallaher** (D.) and **Stead** (D. W.). THE COMPLETE RUGBY FOOTBALLER. With an Account of the Tour of the New Zealanders in England. With Illustrations. *Demy 8vo.* 10s. 6d. net.

Gallichan (W. M.). See Little Guides.

Gambado (Geoffrey, Esq.). See I.P.L.

Gaskell (Mrs.). See Little Library and Standard Library.

Gasquet, the Right Rev. Abbot, O.S.B. See Antiquary's Books.

George (H. B.), M.A., Fellow of New College, Oxford. BATTLES OF ENGLISH HISTORY. With numerous Plans. *Fourth Edition.* Revised, with a new Chapter including the South African War. *Cr. 8vo.* 3s. 6d.

A HISTORICAL GEOGRAPHY OF THE BRITISH EMPIRE. *Second Edition. Cr. 8vo.* 3s. 6d.

Gibbins (H. de B.), Litt.D., M.A. INDUSTRY IN ENGLAND: HISTORICAL OUTLINES. With 5 Maps. *Fourth Edition. Demy 8vo.* 10s. 6d.

A COMPANION GERMAN GRAMMAR. *Cr. 8vo.* 1s. 6d.

THE INDUSTRIAL HISTORY OF ENGLAND. *Eleventh Edition.* Revised. With Maps and Plans. *Cr. 8vo.* 3s.

ENGLISH SOCIAL REFORMERS. *Second Edition. Cr. 8vo.* 2s. 6d.

See also Commercial Series and S.Q.S.

Gibbon (Edward). THE DECLINE AND FALL OF THE ROMAN EMPIRE. A New Edition, edited with Notes, Appendices, and Maps, by J. B. BURY, M.A., Litt.D., Regius Professor of Greek at Cambridge. *In Seven Volumes. Demy 8vo. Gilt top,* 8s. 6d. each. *Also, Cr. 8vo.* 6s. each.

MEMOIRS OF MY LIFE AND WRITINGS. Edited by G. BIRKBECK HILL, LL.D. *Demy 8vo, Gilt top.* 8s. 6d. *Also Cr. 8vo.* 6s.

See also Standard Library.

Gibson (E. C. S.), D.D., Lord Bishop of Gloucester. See Westminster Commentaries, Handbooks of Theology, and Oxford Biographies.

Gilbert (A. R.). See Little Books on Art.

Gloag (M.). See K. Wyatt.

Godfrey (Elizabeth). A BOOK OF REMEMBRANCE. Edited by. *Fcap. 8vo.* 2s. 6d. net.

Godley (A. D.), M.A., Fellow of Magdalen College, Oxford. LYRA FRIVOLA. *Third Edition. Fcap. 8vo.* 2s. 6d.

VERSES TO ORDER. *Second Edition. Fcap. 8vo.* 2s. 6d.

SECOND STRINGS. *Fcap. 8vo.* 2s. 6d.

Goldsmith (Oliver). THE VICAR OF WAKEFIELD. *Fcap. 32mo.* With 10 Plates in Photogravure by Tony Johannot. *Leather,* 2s. 6d. net. See also I.P.L. and Standard Library.

Goodrich=Freer (A.). IN A SYRIAN SADDLE. *Demy 8vo.* 7s. 6d. net.

A Colonial Edition is also published.

Goudge (H. L.), M.A., Principal of Wells Theological College. See Westminster Commentaries.

Graham (P. Anderson). See S.Q.S.

Granger (F. S.), M.A., Litt.D. PSYCHOLOGY. *Third Edition. Cr. 8vo.* 2s. 6d.

THE SOUL OF A CHRISTIAN. *Cr. 8vo.* 6s.

Gray (E. M'Queen). GERMAN PASSAGES FOR UNSEEN TRANSLATION. *Cr. 8vo.* 2s. 6d.

Gray (P. L.), B.Sc. THE PRINCIPLES OF MAGNETISM AND ELECTRICITY: an Elementary Text-Book. With 181 Diagrams. *Cr. 8vo.* 3s. 6d.

Green (G. Buckland), M.A., late Fellow of St. John's College, Oxon. NOTES ON GREEK AND LATIN SYNTAX. *Cr. 8vo.* 3s. 6d.

Green (E. T.), M.A. See Churchman's Library.

Greenidge (A. H. J.), M.A. A HISTORY OF ROME: During the Later Republic and the Early Principate. *In Six Volumes. Demy 8vo.* Vol. I. (133-104 B.C.). 10s. 6d. net.

Greenwell (Dora). See Miniature Library.

Gregory (R. A.). THE VAULT OF HEAVEN. A Popular Introduction to Astronomy. Illustrated. *Cr. 8vo.* 2s. 6d.

Gregory (Miss E. C.). See Library of Devotion.

Greville Minor. A MODERN JOURNAL. Edited by J. A. SPENDER. *Cr. 8vo.* 3s. 6d. net.

Grubb (H. C.). See Textbooks of Technology.

Guiney (Louisa I.). HURRELL FROUDE: Memoranda and Comments. Illustrated. *Demy 8vo.* 10s. 6d. net.

Gwynn (M. L.). A BIRTHDAY BOOK. New and cheaper issue. *Royal 8vo.* 5s. net.

Hackett (John), B.D. A HISTORY OF THE ORTHODOX CHURCH OF CYPRUS. With Maps and Illustrations. *Demy 8vo.* 15s. net.

Haddon (A. C.), Sc.D., F.R.S. HEADHUNTERS BLACK, WHITE, AND BROWN. With many Illustrations and a Map. *Demy 8vo.* 15s.

Hadfield (R. A.). See S.Q.S.

Hall (R. N.) and Neal (W. G.). THE ANCIENT RUINS OF RHODESIA. Illustrated *Second Edition, revised. Demy 8vo.* 10s. 6d. net.

A Colonial Edition is also published.

Hall (R. N.). GREAT ZIMBABWE. With numerous Plans and Illustrations. *Second Edition. Royal 8vo.* 21s. net.

Hamilton (F. J.), D.D. See Byzantine Texts.

Hammond (J. L.). CHARLES JAMES FOX. *Demy 8vo.* 10s. 6d.

Hannay (D.). A SHORT HISTORY OF THE ROYAL NAVY, Illustrated. *Two Volumes. Demy 8vo.* 7s. 6d. each. Vol. I. 1200-1688.

Hannay (James O.), M.A. THE SPIRIT AND ORIGIN OF CHRISTIAN MONASTICISM. *Cr. 8vo.* 6s.

THE WISDOM OF THE DESERT. *Fcap. 8vo.* 3s. 6d. net.

Hare (A. T.), M.A. THE CONSTRUCTION OF LARGE INDUCTION COILS. With numerous Diagrams. *Demy 8vo.* 6s.

Knowling (R. J.), M.A., Professor of New Testament Exegesis at King's College, London. See Westminster Commentaries.

Lamb (Charles and Mary), THE WORKS OF. Edited by E. V. LUCAS. Illustrated. *In Seven Volumes. Demy 8vo. 7s. 6d. each.*

THE LIFE OF. See E. V. Lucas. See also Little Library.

Lambert (F. A. H.). See Little Guides.

Lambros (Professor). See Byzantine Texts.

Lane-Poole (Stanley). A HISTORY OF EGYPT IN THE MIDDLE AGES. Fully Illustrated. *Cr. 8vo. 6s.*

Langbridge (F.), M.A. BALLADS OF THE BRAVE : Poems of Chivalry, Enterprise, Courage, and Constancy. *Second Edition. Cr. 8vo. 2s. 6d.*

Law (William). See Library of Devotion and Standard Library.

Leach (Henry). THE DUKE OF DEVON-SHIRE. A Biography. With 12 Illustrations. *Demy 8vo. 12s. 6d. net.*
A Colonial Edition is also published.

***Le Braz (Anatole).** THE LAND OF PARDONS. Translated by FRANCES M. GOSTLING. Illustrated in colour. *Crown 8vo. 6s.*

Lee (Captain L. Melville). A HISTORY OF POLICE IN ENGLAND. *Cr. 8vo. 3s. 6d. net.*

Leigh (Percival). THE COMIC ENGLISH GRAMMAR. Embellished with upwards of 50 characteristic Illustrations by JOHN LEECH. *Post 16mo. 2s. 6d. net.*

Lewes (V. B.), M.A. AIR AND WATER. Illustrated. *Cr. 8vo. 2s. 6d.*

***Lewis (Mrs. Gwynn).** A CONCISE HANDBOOK OF GARDEN SHRUBS. Illustrated. *Fcap. 8vo. 3s. 6d. net.*

Lisle (Fortunéede). See Little Books on Art.

Littlehales (H.). See Antiquary's Books.

Lock (Walter), D.D., Warden of Keble College. ST. PAUL, THE MASTER-BUILDER. *Second Edition. Cr. 8vo. 3s. 6d.*

THE BIBLE AND CHRISTIAN LIFE. *Cr. 8vo. 6s.*
See also Leaders of Religion and Library of Devotion.

Locker (F.). See Little Library.

Longfellow (H. W.). See Little Library.

Lorimer (George Horace). LETTERS FROM A SELF-MADE MERCHANT TO HIS SON. *Fourteenth Edition. Cr. 8vo. 6s.*
A Colonial Edition is also published.

OLD GORGON GRAHAM. *Second Edition. Cr. 8vo. 6s.*
A Colonial Edition is also published.

Lover (Samuel). See I. P. L.

E. V. L. and **C. L. G.** ENGLAND DAY BY DAY : Or, The Englishman's Handbook to Efficiency. Illustrated by GEORGE MORROW. *Fourth Edition. Fcap. 4to. 1s. net.*

Lucas (E. V.). THE LIFE OF CHARLES LAMB. With numerous Portraits and Illustrations. *Third Edition. Two Vols. Demy 8vo. 21s. net.*
A Colonial Edition is also published.

A WANDERER IN HOLLAND. With many Illustrations, of which 20 are in Colour by HERBERT MARSHALL. *Fifth Edition. Cr. 8vo. 6s.*
A Colonial Edition is also published.

THE OPEN ROAD : a Little Book for Wayfarers. *Ninth Edition. Fcap. 8vo. 5s. ; India Paper, 7s. 6d.*

THE FRIENDLY TOWN : a Little Book for the Urbane. *Second Edition. Fcap. 8vo. 5s. ; India Paper, 7s. 6d.*

Lucian. See Classical Translations.

Lyde (L. W.), M.A. See Commercial Series.

Lydon (Noel S.). See Junior School Books.

Lyttelton (Hon. Mrs. A.). WOMEN AND THEIR WORK. *Cr. 8vo. 2s. 6d.*

M. M. HOW TO DRESS AND WHAT TO WEAR. *Cr. 8vo. 1s. net.*

Macaulay (Lord). CRITICAL AND HISTORICAL ESSAYS. Edited by F. C. MONTAGUE, M.A. *Three Volumes. Cr. 8vo. 18s.*
The only edition of this book completely annotated.

M'Allen (J. E. B.), M.A. See Commercial Series.

MacCulloch (J. A.). See Churchman's Library.

MacCunn (Florence A.). MARY STUART. With over 60 Illustrations, including a Frontispiece in Photogravure. *Demy 8vo. 10s. 6d. net.*
A Colonial Edition is also published. See also Leaders of Religion.

McDermott (E. R.). See Books on Business.

M'Dowall (A. S.). See Oxford Biographies.

Mackay (A. M.). See Churchman's Library.

Magnus (Laurie), M.A. A PRIMER OF WORDSWORTH. *Cr. 8vo. 2s. 6d.*

Mahaffy (J. P.), Litt.D. A HISTORY OF THE EGYPT OF THE PTOLEMIES. Fully Illustrated. *Cr. 8vo. 6s.*

Maitland (F. W.), LL.D., Downing Professor of the Laws of England in the University of Cambridge. CANON LAW IN ENGLAND. *Royal 8vo. 7s. 6d.*

Malden (H. E.), M.A. ENGLISH RECORDS. A Companion to the History of England. *Cr. 8vo. 3s. 6d.*

THE ENGLISH CITIZEN : HIS RIGHTS AND DUTIES. *Third Edition. Cr. 8vo. 1s. 6d.*

A SCHOOL HISTORY OF SURREY. Illustrated. *Cr. 8vo. 1s. 6d.*

Marchant (E. C.), M.A., Fellow of Peterhouse, Cambridge. A GREEK ANTHOLOGY. *Second Edition. Cr. 8vo. 3s. 6d.*

Marchant (C. E.)), M.A., and **Cook (A. M.),** M.A. PASSAGES FOR UNSEEN TRANSLATION. *Third Edition. Cr. 8vo. 3s. 6d.*

Marlowe (Christopher). See Standard Library.

Marr (J. E.), F.R.S., Fellow of St John's College, Cambridge. THE SCIENTIFIC STUDY OF SCENERY. *Second Edition.* Illustrated. *Cr. 8vo. 6s.*

AGRICULTURAL GEOLOGY. Illustrated. *Cr. 8vo. 6s.*

Marvell (Andrew). See Little Library.

Masefield (John). SEA LIFE IN NELSON'S TIME. Illustrated. *Cr. 8vo. 3s. 6d. net.*

*ON THE SPANISH MAIN. With Portraits and Illustrations. *Demy 8vo. 10s. 6d. net.*
A Colonial Edition is also published.

Maskell (A.). See Connoisseur's Library.

Mason (A. J.), D.D. See Leaders of Religion.

Massee (George). THE EVOLUTION OF PLANT LIFE: Lower Forms. Illustrated. *Cr. 8vo. 2s. 6d.*

Massinger (P.). See Standard Library.

Masterman (C. F. G.), M.A. TENNYSON AS A RELIGIOUS TEACHER. *Cr. 8vo. 6s.*

*Matheson (Hon. E. F.). COUNSELS OF LIFE. *Fcap. 8vo. 2s. 6d. net.*

May (Phil). THE PHIL MAY ALBUM. *Second Edition.* 4to. 1s. net.

Mellows (Emma S.). A SHORT STORY OF ENGLISH LITERATURE. *Cr. 8vo. 3s. 6d.*

Methuen (A. M. S.). THE TRAGEDY OF SOUTH AFRICA. *Cr. 8vo. 2s. net.* Also *Cr. 8vo. 3d. net.*
A revised and enlarged edition of the author's 'Peace or War in South Africa.'

ENGLAND'S RUIN: DISCUSSED IN SIXTEEN LETTERS TO THE RIGHT HON. JOSEPH CHAMBERLAIN, M.P. *Seventh Edition. Cr. 8vo. 3d. net.*

Michell (E. B.). THE ART AND PRACTICE OF HAWKING. With 3 Photogravures by G. E. LODGE, and other Illustrations. *Demy 8vo. 10s. 6d.*

Millais (J. G.). THE LIFE AND LETTERS OF SIR JOHN EVERETT MILLAIS, President of the Royal Academy. With many Illustrations, of which 2 are in Photogravure. *New Edition. Demy 8vo. 7s. 6d. net.*
A Colonial Edition is also published.

*Millin (G. F.). PICTORIAL GARDENING. Illustrated. *Cr. 8vo. 3s. 6d. net.*

Millis (C. T.), M.I.M.E. See Textbooks of Technology.

Milne (J. G.), M.A. A HISTORY OF ROMAN EGYPT. Fully Illustrated. *Cr. 8vo. 6s.*

Milton (John), THE POEMS OF, BOTH ENGLISH AND LATIN, Compos'd at several times. Printed by his true Copies.
The Songs were set in Musick by Mr. HENRY LAWES, Gentleman of the Kings Chappel, and one of His Majesties Private Musick.
Printed and publish'd according to Order.
Printed by RUTH RAWORTH for HUMPHREY MOSELEY, and are to be sold at the signe of the Princes Armes in Pauls Churchyard, 1645,
See also Little Library Standard Library, and R. F. Towndrow.

Minchin (H. C.), M.A. See R. Peel.

Mitchell (P. Chalmers), M.A. OUTLINES OF BIOLOGY. Illustrated. *Second Edition. Cr. 8vo. 6s.*

Mitton (G. E.). JANE AUSTEN AND HER TIMES. With many Portraits and Illustrations. *Second Edition. Demy 8vo. 10s. 6d. net.*
A Colonial Edition is also published.

'**Moil (A.).**' See Books on Business.

Moir (D. M.). See Little Library.

Money (L. G. Chiozza). RICHES AND POVERTY *Second Edition Demy 8vo. 5s. net.*

Montaigne. See C. F. Pond.

Moore (H. E.). See S. Q. S.

Moran (Clarence G.). See Books on Business.

More (Sir Thomas). See Standard Library.

Morfill (W. R.), Oriel College, Oxford. A HISTORY OF RUSSIA FROM PETER THE GREAT TO ALEXANDER II. With Maps and Plans. *Cr. 8vo. 3s. 6d.*

Morich (R. J.), late of Clifton College. See School Examination Series.

*Morris (J.). THE MAKERS OF JAPAN. With many portraits and Illustrations. *Demy 8vo. 12s. 6d. net.*
A Colonial Edition is also published.

Morris (J. E.). See Little Guides.

Morton (Miss Anderson). See Miss Brodrick.

THE MOTOR YEAR-BOOK FOR 1906. With many Illustrations and Diagrams. *Demy 8vo. 7s. 6d. net.*

Moule (H. C. G.), D.D., Lord Bishop of Durham. See Leaders of Religion.

Muir (M. M. Pattison), M.A. THE CHEMISTRY OF FIRE. Illustrated. *Cr. 8vo. 2s. 6d.*

Mundella (V. A.), M.A. See J. T. Dunn.

Munro (R.), LL.D. See Antiquary's Books.

Naval Officer (A). See I. P. L.

Neal (W. G.). See R. N. Hall.

Newman (J. H.) and others. See Library of Devotion.

Nichols (J. B. B.). See Little Library.

Nicklin (T.), M.A. EXAMINATION PAPERS IN THUCYDIDES. *Cr. 8vo. 2s.*

Nimrod. See I. P. L.

Norgate (G. Le G.). SIR WALTER SCOTT. Illustrated. *Demy 8vo. 7s. 6d. net.*

Norregaard (B. W.). THE GREAT SIEGE : The Investment and Fall of Port Arthur. Illustrated. *Demy 8vo.* *10s. 6d. net.*

Northcote (James), R.A. THE CONVERSATIONS OF JAMES NORTHCOTE, R.A., AND JAMES WARD. Edited by ERNEST FLETCHER. With many Portraits. *Demy 8vo.* *10s. 6d.*

Norway (A. H.). NAPLES. With 25 Coloured Illustrations by MAURICE GREIFFENHAGEN. A New Edition. *Cr. 8vo.* *6s.*

Novalis. THE DISCIPLES AT SAIS AND OTHER FRAGMENTS. Edited by Miss UNA BIRCH. *Fcap. 8vo.* *3s. 6d.*

Oldfield (W. J.), Canon of Lincoln. A PRIMER OF RELIGION. *Fcap 8vo.* *2s. 6d.*

Oliphant (Mrs.). See Leaders of Religion.

Oman (C. W. C.), M.A., Fellow of All Souls', Oxford. A HISTORY OF THE ART OF WAR. Vol. II.: The Middle Ages, from the Fourth to the Fourteenth Century. Illustrated. *Demy 8vo.* *10s. 6d. net.*

Ottley (R. L.), D.D. See Handbooks of Theology and Leaders of Religion.

Overton (J. H.). See Leaders of Religion.

Owen (Douglas). See Books on Business.

Oxford (M. N.), of Guy's Hospital. A HANDBOOK OF NURSING. *Third Edition.* *Cr. 8vo.* *3s. 6d.*

Pakes (W. C. C.). THE SCIENCE OF HYGIENE. Illustrated. *Demy 8vo.* *15s.*

Palmer (Frederick). WITH KUROKI IN MANCHURIA. Illustrated. *Third Edition.* *Demy 8vo.* *7s. 6d. net.*
A Colonial Edition is also published.

Parker (Gilbert). A LOVER'S DIARY. *Fcap. 8vo.* *5s.*

Parkes (A. K.). SMALL LESSONS ON GREAT TRUTHS. *Fcap. 8vo.* *1s. 6d.*

Parkinson (John). PARADISI IN SOLE PARADISUS TERRESTRIS, OR A GARDEN OF ALL SORTS OF PLEASANT FLOWERS. *Folio.* *£4, 4s. net.*

Parmenter (John). HELIO-TROPES, OR NEW POSIES FOR SUNDIALS, 1625. Edited by PERCIVAL LANDON. *Quarto.* *3s. 6d. net.*

Parmentier (Prof. Leon). See Byzantine Texts.

Pascal. See Library of Devotion.

Paston (George). SOCIAL CARICATURES IN THE EIGHTEENTH CENTURY. *Imperial Quarto.* *£2, 12s. 6d. net.* See also Little Books on Art and I.P.L.

Paterson (W. R.) (Benjamin Swift). LIFE'S QUESTIONINGS. *Cr. 8vo.* *3s. 6d. net.*

Patterson (A. H.). NOTES OF AN EAST COAST NATURALIST. Illustrated in Colour by F. SOUTHGATE. *Second Edition.* *Cr. 8vo.* *6s.*

NATURE IN EASTERN NORFOLK. A series of observations on the Birds, Fishes, Mammals, Reptiles, and stalk-eyed Crustaceans found in that neighbourhood, with a list of the species. With 12 Illustrations in colour, by FRANK SOUTHGATE. *Second Edition. Cr. 8vo.* *6s.*

Peacock (N.). See Little Books on Art.

Pearce (E. H.), M.A. ANNALS OF CHRIST'S HOSPITAL. Illustrated. *Demy 8vo.* *7s. 6d.*

Peel (Robert), and **Minchin (H. C.),** M.A. OXFORD. With 100 Illustrations in Colour. *Cr. 8vo.* *6s.*

Peel (Sidney), late Fellow of Trinity College, Oxford, and Secretary to the Royal Commission on the Licensing Laws. PRACTICAL LICENSING REFORM. *Second Edition.* *Cr. 8vo.* *1s. 6d.*

Peters (J. P.), D.D. See Churchman's Library.

Petrie (W. M. Flinders), D.C.L., LL.D., Professor of Egyptology at University College. A HISTORY OF EGYPT, FROM THE EARLIEST TIMES TO THE PRESENT DAY. Fully Illustrated. *In six volumes. Cr. 8vo.* *6s. each.*

VOL. I. PREHISTORIC TIMES TO XVITH DYNASTY. *Fifth Edition.*
VOL. II. THE XVIITH AND XVIIITH DYNASTIES. *Fourth Edition.*
VOL. III. XIXTH TO XXXTH DYNASTIES.
VOL. IV. THE EGYPT OF THE PTOLEMIES. J. P. MAHAFFY, Litt.D.
VOL. V. ROMAN EGYPT. J. G. MILNE, M.A.
VOL. VI. EGYPT IN THE MIDDLE AGES. STANLEY LANE-POOLE, M.A.

RELIGION AND CONSCIENCE IN ANCIENT EGYPT. Illustrated. *Cr 8vo.* *2s. 6d.*

SYRIA AND EGYPT, FROM THE TELL EL AMARNA TABLETS. *Cr. 8vo.* *2s. 6d.*

EGYPTIAN TALES. Illustrated by TRISTRAM ELLIS. *In Two Volumes. Cr. 8vo.* *3s. 6d. each.*

EGYPTIAN DECORATIVE ART. With 120 Illustrations. *Cr. 8vo.* *3s. 6d.*

Phillips (W. A.). See Oxford Biographies.

Phillpotts (Eden). MY DEVON YEAR. With 38 Illustrations by J. LEY PETHYBRIDGE. *Second and Cheaper Edition. Large Cr. 8vo.* *6s.*

UP ALONG AND DOWN ALONG. Illustrated by CLAUDE SHEPPERSON. *Cr. 4to.* *5s. net.*
A volume of poems.

Pienaar (Philip). WITH STEYN AND DE WET. *Second Edition. Cr. 8vo.* *3s. 6d.*
A Colonial Edition is also published.

Plarr (Victor G.) and Walton (F. W.). A SCHOOL HISTORY OF MIDDLESEX. Illustrated. *Cr. 8vo.* *1s. 6d.*

Plato. See Standard Library.

Plautus. THE CAPTIVI. Edited, with an Introduction, Textual Notes, and a Commentary, by W. M. LINDSAY, Fellow of Jesus College, Oxford. *Demy 8vo.* 10s. 6d. *net.*

Plowden-Wardlaw (J. T.), B.A., King's College, Cambridge. See School Examination Series.

Pocock (Roger). A FRONTIERSMAN. *Third Edition. Cr. 8vo.* 6s.
  A Colonial Edition is also published.

Podmore (Frank). MODERN SPIRITUALISM. *Two Volumes. Demy 8vo.* 21s. *net.*
  A History and a Criticism.

Poer (J. Patrick Le). A MODERN LEGIONARY. *Cr. 8vo.* 6s.
  A Colonial Edition is also published.

Pollard (Alice). See Little Books on Art.

Pollard (A. W.). OLD PICTURE BOOKS. Illustrated. *Demy 8vo.* 7s. 6d. *net.*

Pollard (Eliza F.). See Little Books on Art.

Pollock (David), M.I.N.A. See Books on Business.

Pond (C. F.). A DAY BOOK OF MONTAIGNE. Edited by. *Fcap. 8vo.* 3s. 6d. *net.*

Potter (M. C.), M.A., F.L.S. A TEXT-BOOK OF AGRICULTURAL BOTANY. Illustrated. *Second Edition. Cr. 8vo.* 4s. 6d.

Power (J. O'Connor). THE MAKING OF AN ORATOR. *Cr. 8vo.* 6s.

Pradeau (G.). A KEY TO THE TIME ALLUSIONS IN THE DIVINE COMEDY. With a Dial. *Small quarto.* 3s. 6d.

Prance (G.). See Half-Crown Library.

Prescott (O. L.). ABOUT MUSIC, AND WHAT IT IS MADE OF. *Cr. 8vo.* 3s. 6d. *net.*

Price (L. L.), M.A., Fellow of Oriel College, Oxon. A HISTORY OF ENGLISH POLITICAL ECONOMY. *Fourth Edition. Cr. 8vo.* 2s. 6d.

Primrose (Deborah). A MODERN BŒOTIA. *Cr. 8vo.* 6s.

Pugin and **Rowlandson.** THE MICROCOSM OF LONDON, OR LONDON IN MINIATURE. With 104 Illustrations in colour. *In Three Volumes. Small 4to.* £3, 3s. *net.*

'Q' (A. T. Quiller Couch). See Half-Crown Library.

Quevedo Villegas. See Miniature Library.

G.R. and **E.S.** THE WOODHOUSE CORRESPONDENCE. *Cr. 8vo.* 6s.
  A Colonial Edition is also published.

Rackham (R. B.), M.A. See Westminster Commentaries.

Randolph (B. W.), D.D. See Library of Devotion.

Rannie (D. W.), M.A. A STUDENT'S HISTORY OF SCOTLAND. *Cr. 8vo.* 3s. 6d.

Rashdall (Hastings), M.A., Fellow and Tutor of New College, Oxford. DOCTRINE AND DEVELOPMENT. *Cr. 8vo.* 6s.

Rawstorne (Lawrence, Esq.). See I.P.L.

*Raymond (Walter). A SCHOOL HISTORY OF SOMERSETSHIRE. Illustrated. *Cr. 8vo.* 1s. 6d.

A Real Paddy. See I.P.L.

Reason (W.), M.A. See S.Q.S.

Redfern (W. B.), Author of ' Ancient Wood and Iron Work in Cambridge,' etc. ROYAL AND HISTORIC GLOVES AND ANCIENT SHOES. Profusely Illustrated in colour and half-tone. *Quarto,* £2, 2s. *net.*

Reynolds. See Little Galleries.

*Rhodes (W. E.). A SCHOOL HISTORY OF LANCASHIRE. Illustrated. *Cr. 8vo.* 1s. 6d.

Roberts (M. E.). See C. C. Channer.

Robertson (A.), D.D., Lord Bishop of Exeter. REGNUM DEI. The Bampton Lectures of 1901. *Demy 8vo.* 12s. 6d. *net.*

Robertson (C. Grant), M.A., Fellow of All Souls' College, Oxford, Examiner in the Honours School of Modern History, Oxford, 1901-1904. SELECT STATUTES, CASES, AND CONSTITUTIONAL DOCUMENTS, 1660-1832. *Demy 8vo.* 10s. 6d. *net.*

Robertson (C. Grant) and **Bartholomew (J. G.),** F.R.S.E., F.R.G.S. A HISTORICAL AND MODERN ATLAS OF THE BRITISH EMPIRE. *Demy Quarto.* 4s. 6d. *net.*

Robertson (Sir G. S.), K.C.S.I. See Half-Crown Library.

Robinson (A. W.), M.A. See Churchman's Bible.

Robinson (Cecilia). THE MINISTRY OF DEACONESSES. With an Introduction by the late Archbishop of Canterbury. *Cr. 8vo.* 3s. 6d.

Robinson (F. S.). See Connoisseur's Library.

Rochefoucauld (La). See Little Library.

Rodwell (G.), B.A. NEW TESTAMENT GREEK. A Course for Beginners. With a Preface by WALTER LOCK, D.D., Warden of Keble College. *Fcap. 8vo.* 3s. 6d.

Roe (Fred). ANCIENT COFFERS AND CUPBOARDS: Their History and Description. Illustrated. *Quarto.* £3, 3s. *net.*
OLD OAK FURNITURE. With many Illustrations by the Author, including a frontispiece in colour. *Demy 8vo.* 10s. 6d. *net.*

Rogers (A. G. L.), M.A. See Books on Business.

Roscoe (E. S.). ROBERT HARLEY, EARL OF OXFORD. Illustrated. *Demy 8vo.* 7s. 6d.
  This is the only life of Harley in existence. See also Little Guides.

Rose (Edward). THE ROSE READER. Illustrated. *Cr. 8vo. 2s. 6d. Also in 4 Parts. Parts I. and II. 6d. each; Part III. 8d.; Part IV. 10d.*

*Rouse (W. H. D.). WORDS OF THE ANCIENT WISE : Thoughts from Epictetus and Marcus Aurelius. Edited by. *Fcap. 8vo. 3s. 6d. net.*

Rowntree (Joshua). THE IMPERIAL DRUG TRADE. *Second Edition. Cr. 8vo. 5s. net.*

Rubie (A. E.), D.D. See Junior School ooks.

Russell (W. Clark). THE LIFE OF ADMIRAL LORD COLLINGWOOD. With Illustrations by F. BRANGWYN. *Fourth Edition. Cr. 8vo. 6s.*
A Colonial Edition is also published.

St. Anslem. See Library of Devotion.

St. Augustine. See Library of Devotion.

St. Cyres (Viscount). See Oxford Biographies.

St. Francis of Assisi. See Standard Library.

'Saki' (H. Munro). REGINALD. *Second Edition. Fcap. 8vo. 2s. 6d. net.*

Sales (St. Francis de). See Library of Devotion.

Salmon (A. L.). A POPULAR GUIDE TO DEVON. *Medium 8vo. 6d. net.* See also Little Guides.

Sargeant (J.), M.A. ANNALS OF WESTMINSTER SCHOOL. Illustrated. *Demy 8vo. 7s. 6d.*

Sathas (C.). See Byzantine Texts.

Schmitt (John). See Byzantine Texts.

Scott (A. M.). WINSTON SPENCER CHURCHILL. With Portraits and Illustrations. *Cr. 8vo. 3s. 6d.*
A Colonial Edition is also published.

Seeley (H. G.), F.R.S. DRAGONS OF THE AIR. Illustrated. *Cr. 8vo. 6s.*

*Selincourt (E. de). A DAY BOOK OF KEATS. *Fcap. 8vo. 3s. 6d. net.*

Sells (V. P.), M.A. THE MECHANICS OF DAILY LIFE. Illustrated. *Cr. 8vo. 2s. 6d.*

Selous (Edmund). TOMMY SMITH'S ANIMALS. Illustrated by G. W. ORD. *Fourth Edition. Fcap. 8vo. 2s. 6d.*

Settle (J. H.). ANECDOTES OF SOLDIERS. *Cr. 8vo. 3s. 6d. net.*
A Colonial Edition is also published.

Shakespeare (William).
THE FOUR FOLIOS, 1623; 1632; 1664; 1685. Each *Four Guineas net,* or a complete set, *Twelve Guineas net.*
Folios 3 and 4 are ready.
Folio 2 is nearly ready.

The Arden Shakespeare.
Demy 8vo. 2s. 6d. net each volume.
General Editor, W. J. CRAIG. An Edition of Shakespeare in single Plays. Edited with a full Introduction, Textual Notes, and a Commentary at the foot of the page.

HAMLET. Edited by EDWARD DOWDEN, Litt.D.

ROMEO AND JULIET. Edited by EDWARD DOWDEN, Litt.D.

KING LEAR. Edited by W. J. CRAIG.

JULIUS CAESAR. Edited by M. MACMILLAN, M.A.

THE TEMPEST. Edited by MORETON LUCE.

OTHELLO. Edited by H. C. HART.

TITUS ANDRONICUS. Edited by H. B. BAILDON.

CYMBELINE. Edited by EDWARD DOWDEN.

THE MERRY WIVES OF WINDSOR. Edited by H. C. HART.

A MIDSUMMER NIGHT'S DREAM. Edited by H. CUNINGHAM.

KING HENRY V. Edited by H. A. EVANS.

ALL'S WELL THAT ENDS WELL. Edited by W. O. BRIGSTOCKE.

THE TAMING OF THE SHREW. Edited by R. WARWICK BOND.

TIMON OF ATHENS. Edited by K. DEIGHTON.

MEASURE FOR MEASURE. Edited by H. C. HART.

*TWELFTH NIGHT. Edited by MORETON LUCE.

THE MERCHANT OF VENICE. Edited by C. KNOX POOLER.

*TROILUS AND CRESSIDA. Edited by K. DEIGHTON.

The Little Quarto Shakespeare. Edited by W. J. CRAIG. With Introductions and Notes. *Pott 16mo. In 40 Volumes. Leather, price 1s. net each volume.* Mahogany Revolving Book Case. *10s. net.* See also Standard Library.

Sharp (A.). VICTORIAN POETS. *Cr. 8vo. 2s. 6d.*

Sharp (Cecil). See S. Baring-Gould.

Sharp (Mrs. E. A.). See Little Books on Art.

Shedlock (J. S.) THE PIANOFORTE SONATA. *Cr. 8vo. 5s.*

Shelley (Percy B.). ADONAIS ; an Elegy on the death of John Keats, Author of 'Endymion,' etc. Pisa. From the types of Didot, 1821. *2s. net.*

Sheppard (H. F.), M.A. See S. Baring-Gould.

Sherwell (Arthur), M.A. See S.Q.S.

Shipley (Mary E.). AN ENGLISH CHURCH HISTORY FOR CHILDREN. With a Preface by the Bishop of Gibraltar. With Maps and Illustrations. Part I. *Cr. 8vo. 2s. 6d. net.*

Sichel (Walter). DISRAELI : A Study in Personality and Ideas. With 3 Portraits. *Demy 8vo. 12s. 6d. net.*
A Colonial Edition is also published.
See also Oxford Biographies.

Sime (J.). See Little Books on Art.

Simonson (G. A.). FRANCESCO GUARDI. With 41 Plates. *Imperial 4to.* £2, 2s. net.

Sketchley (R. E. D.). See Little Books on Art.

Skipton (H. P. K.). See Little Books on Art.

Sladen (Douglas). SICILY: The New Winter Resort. With over 200 Illustrations. *Second Edition. Cr. 8vo.* 5s. net.

Small (Evan), M.A. THE EARTH. An Introduction to Physiography. Illustrated. *Cr. 8vo.* 2s. 6d.

Smallwood (M. G.). See Little Books on Art.

Smedley (F. E.). See I.P.L.

Smith (Adam). THE WEALTH OF NATIONS. Edited with an Introduction and numerous Notes by EDWIN CANNAN, M.A. *Two volumes. Demy 8vo.* 21s. net.
See also English Library.

Smith (Horace and James). See Little Library.

Smith (H. Bompas), M.A. A NEW JUNIOR ARITHMETIC. *Crown 8vo.* 2s. 6d.

Smith (R. Mudie). THOUGHTS FOR THE DAY. Edited by. *Fcap. 8vo.* 3s. 6d. net.

Smith (Nowell C.). See W. Wordsworth.

Smith (John Thomas). A BOOK FOR A RAINY DAY: Or Recollections of the Events of the Years 1766-1833. Edited by WILFRED WHITTEN. Illustrated. *Demy 8vo.* 12s. 6d. net.

Snell (F. J.). A BOOK OF EXMOOR. Illustrated. *Cr. 8vo.* 6s.

Snowden (C. E.). A HANDY DIGEST OF BRITISH HISTORY. *Demy 8vo.* 4s. 6d.

Sophocles. See Classical Translations.

Sornet (L. A.). See Junior School Books.

South (Wilton E.), M.A. See Junior School Books.

Southey (R.). ENGLISH SEAMEN. Edited by DAVID HANNAY.
Vol. I. (Howard, Clifford, Hawkins, Drake, Cavendish). *Second Edition. Cr. 8vo.* 6s.
Vol. II. (Richard Hawkins, Grenville, Essex, and Raleigh). *Cr. 8vo.* 6s.
See also Standard Library.

Spence (C. H.), M.A. See School Examination Series.

Spooner (W. A.), M.A. See Leaders of Religion.

*Staley (Edgcumbe). THE GUILDS OF FLORENCE. Illustrated. *Royal 8vo.* 21s. net.

Stanbridge (J. W.), B.D. See Library of Devotion.

'Stancliffe.' GOLF DO'S AND DONT'S. *Second Edition. Fcap. 8vo.* 1s.

Stead (D. W.). See D. Gallaher.

Stedman (A. M. M.), M.A.
INITIA LATINA: Easy Lessons on Elementary Accidence. *Eighth Edition. Fcap. 8vo.* 1s.

FIRST LATIN LESSONS. *Ninth Edition. Cr. 8vo.* 2s.

FIRST LATIN READER. With Notes adapted to the Shorter Latin Primer and Vocabulary. *Sixth Edition revised.* 18mo. 1s. 6d.

EASY SELECTIONS FROM CÆSAR. The Helvetian War. *Second Edition* 18mo. 1s.

EASY SELECTIONS FROM LIVY. The Kings of Rome. 18mo. *Second Edition.* 1s. 6d.

EASY LATIN PASSAGES FOR UNSEEN TRANSLATION. *Tenth Edition Fcap. 8vo.* 1s. 6d.

EXEMPLA LATINA. First Exercises in Latin Accidence. With Vocabulary. *Third Edition. Cr. 8vo.* 1s.

EASY LATIN EXERCISES ON THE SYNTAX OF THE SHORTER AND REVISED LATIN PRIMER. With Vocabulary. *Tenth and Cheaper Edition, re-written. Cr. 8vo.* 1s. 6d. *Original Edition.* 2s. 6d. KEY, 3s. net.

THE LATIN COMPOUND SENTENCE: Rules and Exercises. *Second Edition. Cr. 8vo.* 1s. 6d. With Vocabulary. 2s.

NOTANDA QUAEDAM: Miscellaneous Latin Exercises on Common Rules and Idioms. *Fourth Edition. Fcap. 8vo.* 1s. 6d. With Vocabulary. 2s. Key, 2s. net.

LATIN VOCABULARIES FOR REPETITION: Arranged according to Subjects. *Thirteenth Edition. Fcap. 8vo.* 1s. 6d.

A VOCABULARY OF LATIN IDIOMS. 18mo. *Second Edition.* 1s.

STEPS TO GREEK. *Second Edition, revised.* 18mo. 1s.

A SHORTER GREEK PRIMER. *Cr. 8vo.* 1s. 6d.

EASY GREEK PASSAGES FOR UNSEEN TRANSLATION. *Third Edition, revised. Fcap. 8vo.* 1s. 6d.

GREEK VOCABULARIES FOR REPETITION. Arranged according to Subjects. *Fourth Edition. Fcap. 8vo.* 1s. 6d.

GREEK TESTAMENT SELECTIONS. For the use of Schools. With Introduction, Notes, and Vocabulary. *Fourth Edition. Fcap. 8vo.* 2s. 6d.

STEPS TO FRENCH. *Seventh Edition.* 18mo. 8d.

FIRST FRENCH LESSONS. *Seventh Edition, revised. Cr. 8vo.* 1s.

EASY FRENCH PASSAGES FOR UNSEEN TRANSLATION. *Fifth Edition, revised. Fcap. 8vo.* 1s. 6d.

EASY FRENCH EXERCISES ON ELE-
MENTARY SYNTAX. With Vocabu-
lary. *Fourth Edition. Cr. 8vo. 2s. 6d.*
KEY. *3s. net.*

FRENCH VOCABULARIES FOR RE-
PETITION : Arranged according to Sub-
jects. *Twelfth Edition. Fcap. 8vo. 1s.*
See also School Examination Series.

Steel (R. Elliott), M.A., F.C.S. THE
WORLD OF SCIENCE. With 147
Illustrations. *Second Edition. Cr. 8vo. 2s. 6d.*
See also School Examination Series.

Stephenson (C.), of the Technical College,
Bradford, and **Suddards (F.)** of the
Yorkshire College, Leeds. ORNAMEN-
TAL DESIGN FOR WOVEN FABRICS.
Illustrated. *Demy 8vo. Third Edition.*
7s. 6d.

Stephenson (J.), M.A. THE CHIEF
TRUTHS OF THE CHRISTIAN
FAITH. *Cr. 8vo. 3s. 6d.*

Sterne (Laurence). See Little Library.

Sterry (W.). M.A. ANNALS OF ETON
COLLEGE. Illustrated. *Demy 8vo. 7s. 6d.*

Steuart (Katherine). BY ALLAN
WATER. *Second Edition. Cr. 8vo. 6s.*

Stevenson (R. L.) THE LETTERS OF
ROBERT LOUIS STEVENSON TO
HIS FAMILY AND FRIENDS.
Selected and Edited by SIDNEY COLVIN.
Sixth Edition. Cr. 8vo. 12s.
LIBRARY EDITION. *Demy 8vo. 2 vols. 25s. net.*
A Colonial Edition is also published.

VAILIMA LETTERS. With an Etched
Portrait by WILLIAM STRANG. *Fifth
Edition. Cr. 8vo. Buckram. 6s.*
A Colonial Edition is also published.

THE LIFE OF R. L. STEVENSON. See
G. Balfour.

Stevenson (M. I.). FROM SARANAC
TO THE MARQUESAS. Being Letters
written by Mrs. M. I. STEVENSON during
1887-8. *Cr. 8vo. 6s. net.*
A Colonial Edition is also published.

LETTERS FROM SAMOA. Edited and
arranged by M. C. BALFOUR. With many
Illustrations. *Cr. 8vo. 6s. net.*

Stoddart (Anna M.). See Oxford Biographies.

Stokes (F. G.), B.A. HOURS WITH
RABELAIS. From the translation of SIR
T. URQUHART and P. A. MOTTEUX. With
a Portrait in Photogravure. *Cr. 8vo. 3s. 6d.*
net.

Stone (S. J.). POEMS AND HYMNS.
With a Memoir by F. G. ELLERTON,
M.A. With Portrait. *Cr. 8vo. 6s.*

Storr (Vernon F.), M.A., Lecturer in
the Philosophy of Religion in Cambridge
University ; Examining Chaplain to the
Archbishop of Canterbury; formerly Fellow
of University College, Oxford. DEVELOP-
MENT AND DIVINE PURPOSE *Cr.
8vo. 5s. net.*

Straker (F.). See Books on Business.

Streane (A. W.), D.D. See Churchman's
Bible.

Stroud (H.), D.Sc., M.A. See Textbooks of
Science.

Strutt (Joseph). THE SPORTS AND
PASTIMES OF THE PEOPLE OF
ENGLAND. Illustrated by many engrav-
ings. Revised by J. CHARLES COX, LL.D.,
F.S.A. *Quarto. 21s. net.*

Stuart (Capt. Donald). THE STRUGGLE
FOR PERSIA. With a Map. *Cr. 8vo. 6s.*

Sturch (F.)., Staff Instructor to the Surrey
County Council. MANUAL TRAINING,
DRAWING (WOODWORK). Its Prin-
ciples and Application, with Solutions to
Examination Questions, 1892-1905, Ortho-
graphic, Isometric and Oblique Projection.
With 50 Plates and 140 Figures. *Foolscap.*
5s. net.

Suckling (Sir John). FRAGMENTA
AUREA: a Collection of all the Incom-
parable Peeces, written by. And published
by a friend to perpetuate his memory.
Printed by his own copies.
Printed for HUMPHREY MOSELEY, and
are to be sold at his shop, at the sign of the
Princes Arms in St. Paul's Churchyard, 1646.

Suddards (F.). See C. Stephenson.

Surtees (R. S.). See I.P.L.

Swift (Jonathan). THE JOURNAL TO
STELLA. Edited by G. A. AITKEN. *Cr.
8vo. 6s.*

Symes (J. E.), M.A. THE FRENCH
REVOLUTION. *Second Edition. Cr. 8vo.*
2s. 6d.

Sympson (E. M.), M.A., M.D. See Ancient
Cities.

Syrett (Netta). See Little Blue Books.

Tacitus. AGRICOLA. With Introduction
Notes, Map, etc. By R. F. DAVIS, M.A.,
Fcap. 8vo. 2s.
GERMANIA. By the same Editor. *Fcap.
8vo. 2s.* See also Classical Translations.

Tallack (W.). HOWARD LETTERS AND
MEMORIES. *Demy 8vo. 10s. 6d. net.*

Tauler (J.). See Library of Devotion.

Taunton (E. L.). A HISTORY OF THE
JESUITS IN ENGLAND. Illustrated.
Demy 8vo. 21s. net.

Taylor (A. E.). THE ELEMENTS OF
METAPHYSICS. *Demy 8vo. 10s. 6d. net.*

Taylor (F. G.), M.A. See Commercial Series.

Taylor (I. A.). See Oxford Biographies.

Taylor (T. M.), M.A., Fellow of Gonville
and Caius College, Cambridge. A CON-
STITUTIONAL AND POLITICAL
HISTORY OF ROME. *Cr. 8vo. 7s. 6d.*

Tennyson (Alfred, Lord). THE EARLY
POEMS OF. Edited, with Notes and
an Introduction, by J. CHURTON COLLINS,
M.A. *Cr. 8vo. 6s.*

IN MEMORIAM, MAUD, AND THE
PRINCESS. Edited by J. CHURTON
COLLINS, M.A. *Cr. 8vo. 6s.* See also
Little Library.

Terry (C. S.). See Oxford Biographies.

Terton (Alice). LIGHTS AND SHADOWS IN A HOSPITAL. *Cr. 8vo. 3s. 6d.*

Thackeray (W. M.). See Little Library.

Theobald (F. V.), M.A. INSECT LIFE. Illustrated. *Second Ed. Revised. Cr. 8vo. 2s. 6d.*

Thompson (A. H.). See Little Guides.

Tileston (Mary W.). DAILY STRENGTH FOR DAILY NEEDS. *Twelfth Edition. Medium 16mo. 2s. 6d. net.* Also an edition in superior binding, 6s.

Tompkins (H. W.), F.R.H.S. See Little Guides.

Towndrow (R. F.). A DAY BOOK OF MILTON. Edited by. *Fcap. 8vo. 3s. 6d. net.*

Townley (Lady Susan). MY CHINESE NOTE-BOOK With 16 Illustrations and 2 Maps. *Third Edition. Demy 8vo. 10s. 6d. net.*
A Colonial Edition is also published.

*Toynbee (Paget), M.A., D.Litt. DANTE IN ENGLISH LITERATURE. *Demy 8vo. 12s. 6d. net.*
See also Oxford Biographies.

Trench (Herbert). DEIRDRE WED and Other Poems. *Cr. 8vo. 5s.*

Trevelyan (G. M.), Fellow of Trinity College, Cambridge. ENGLAND UNDER THE STUARTS. With Maps and Plans. *Second Edition. Demy 8vo. 10s. 6d. net.*

Troutbeck (G. E.). See Little Guides.

Tyler (E. A.), B.A., F.C.S. See Junior School Books.

Tyrell-Gill (Frances). See Little Books on Art.

Vardon (Harry). THE COMPLETE GOLFER. Illustrated. *Seventh Edition. Demy 8vo. 10s. 6d. net.*
A Colonial Edition is also published.

Vaughan (Henry). See Little Library.

Voegelin (A.), M.A. See Junior Examination Series.

Waddell (Col. L. A.), LL.D., C.B. LHASA AND ITS MYSTERIES. With a Record of the Expedition of 1903-1904. With 2000 Illustrations and Maps. *Demy 8vo. 21s. net.*
*Also Third and Cheaper Edition. With 155 Illustrations and Maps. *Demy 8vo. 10s. 6d. net.*

Wade (G. W.), D.D. OLD TESTAMENT HISTORY. With Maps. *Third Edition. Cr. 8vo. 6s.*

Wagner (Richard). See A. L. Cleather.

Wall (J. C.). DEVILS. Illustrated by the Author and from photographs. *Demy 8vo. 4s. 6d. net.* See also Antiquary's Books.

Walters (H. B.). See Little Books on Art

Walton (F. W.). See Victor G. Plarr.

Walton (Izaac) and **Cotton (Charles).** See I.P.L., Standard Library, and Little Library.

Warmelo (D. S. Van). ON COMMANDO. With Portrait. *Cr. 8vo. 3s. 6d.*
A Colonial Edition is also published.

Warren-Vernon (Hon. William), M.A. READINGS ON THE INFERNO OF DANTE, chiefly based on the Commentary of BENVENUTO DA IMOLA. With an Introduction by the Rev. Dr. MOORE. In Two Volumes. *Second Edition. Cr. 8vo. 15s. net.*

Waterhouse (Mrs. Alfred). WITH THE SIMPLE-HEARTED: Little Homilies to Women in Country Places. *Second Edition. Small Pott 8vo. 2s. net.* See also Little Library.

Weatherhead (T. C.), M.A. EXAMINATION PAPERS IN HORACE. *Cr. 8vo. 2s.* See also Junior Examination Series.

Webb (W. T.). See Little Blue Books.

Webber (F. C.). See Textbooks of Technology.

Wells (Sidney H.). See Textbooks of Science.

Wells (J.), M.A., Fellow and Tutor of Wadham College. OXFORD AND OXFORD LIFE. *Third Edition. Cr. 8vo. 3s. 6d.*
A SHORT HISTORY OF ROME. *Sixth Edition.* With 3 Maps. *Cr. 8vo. 3s. 6d.*
See also Little Guides.

'Westminster Gazette' Office Boy (Francis Brown). THE DOINGS OF ARTHUR. *Cr. 4to. 2s. 6d. net.*

Wetmore (Helen C.). THE LAST OF THE GREAT SCOUTS ('Buffalo Bill'). Illustrated. *Second Edition. Demy 8vo. 6s.*
A Colonial Edition is also published.

Whibley (C). See Half-crown Library.

Whibley (L.), M.A., Fellow of Pembroke College, Cambridge. GREEK OLIGARCHIES: THEIR ORGANISATION AND CHARACTER. *Cr. 8vo. 6s.*

Whitaker (G. H.), M.A. See Churchman's Bible.

White (Gilbert). THE NATURAL HISTORY OF SELBORNE. Edited by L. C. MIALL, F.R.S., assisted by W. WARDE FOWLER, M.A. *Cr. 8vo. 6s.* See also Standard Library.

Whitfield (E. E.). See Commercial Series.

Whitehead (A. W.). GASPARD DE COLIGNY. Illustrated. *Demy 8vo. 12s. 6d. net.*

Whiteley (R. Lloyd), F.I.C., Principal of the Municipal Science School, West Bromwich. AN ELEMENTARY TEXT-BOOK OF INORGANIC CHEMISTRY. *Cr. 8vo. 2s. 6d.*

Whitley (Miss). See S.Q.S.

Whitten (W.). See John Thomas Smith.

Whyte (A. G.), B.Sc. See Books on Business.

Wilberforce (Wilfrid). See Little Books on Art.

Wilde (Oscar). DE PROFUNDIS. *Sixth Edition. Cr. 8vo. 5s. net.*
A Colonial Edition is also published.

Wilkins (W. H.), B.A. See S.Q.S.

Wilkinson (J. Frome). See S.Q.S.

*****Williams (A.).** PETROL PETER: or Mirth for Motorists. Illustrated in Colour by A. W. MILLS. *Demy 4to. 3s. 6d. net.*

Williamson (M. G.). See Ancient Cities.

Williamson (W.). THE BRITISH GARDENER. Illustrated. *Demy 8vo. 10s. 6d.*

Williamson (W.), B.A. See Junior Examination Series, Junior School Books, and Beginner's Books.

Willson (Beckles). LORD STRATHCONA: the Story of his Life. Illustrated. *Demy 8vo. 7s. 6d.*
A Colonial Edition is also published.

Wilmot-Buxton (E. M.). MAKERS OF EUROPE. *Cr. 8vo. Fifth Ed. 3s. 6d.*
A Text-book of European History for Middle Forms.

THE ANCIENT WORLD. With Maps and Illustrations. *Cr. 8vo. 3s. 6d.*
See also Beginner's Books.

Wilson (Bishop.). See Library of Devotion.

Wilson (A. J.). See Books on Business.

Wilson (H. A.). See Books on Business.

Wilton (Richard), M.A. LYRA PASTORALIS: Songs of Nature, Church, and Home. *Pott 8vo. 2s. 6d.*

Winbolt (S. E.), M.A. EXERCISES IN LATIN ACCIDENCE. *Cr. 8vo. 1s. 6d.*

LATIN HEXAMETER VERSE: An Aid to Composition. *Cr. 8vo. 3s. 6d.* KEY, *5s. net.*

Windle (B. C. A.), D.Sc., F.R.S. See Antiquary's Books, Little Guides and Ancient Cities.

Winterbotham (Canon), M.A., B.Sc., LL.B. See Churchman's Library.

Wood (J. A. E.). See Textbooks of Technology.

Wood (J. Hickory). DAN LENO. Illustrated. *Third Edition. Cr. 8vo. 6s.*
A Colonial Edition is also published.

Wood (W. Birkbeck), M.A., late Scholar of Worcester College, Oxford, and **Edmonds (Major J. E.)**, R.E., D.A.Q.-M.G. A HISTORY OF THE CIVIL WAR IN THE UNITED STATES. With an Introduction by H. SPENSER WILKINSON. With 24 Maps and Plans. *Demy 8vo. 12s. 6d. net.*

Wordsworth (Christopher). See Antiquary's Books.

*****Wordsworth (W.).** THE POEMS OF. With Introduction and Notes by NOWELL C. SMITH, Fellow of New College, Oxford. *In Four Volumes. Demy 8vo. 5s. net each.* See also Little Library.

Wordsworth (W.) and Coleridge (S. T.). See Little Library.

Wright (Arthur), M.A., Fellow of Queen's College, Cambridge. See Churchman's Library.

Wright (C. Gordon). See Dante.

Wright (J. C.). TO-DAY. *Fcap. 16mo. 1s. net.*

Wright (Sophie). GERMAN VOCABULARIES FOR REPETITION. *Fcap. 8vo. 1s. 6d.*

Wrong (George M.), Professor of History in the University of Toronto. THE EARL OF ELGIN. Illustrated. *Demy 8vo. 7s. 6d. net.*
A Colonial Edition is also published.

Wyatt (Kate) and Gloag (M.). A BOOK OF ENGLISH GARDENS. With 24 Illustrations in Colour. *Demy 8vo. 10s. 6d. net.*

Wylde (A. B.). MODERN ABYSSINIA. With a Map and a Portrait. *Demy 8vo. 15s. net.*
A Colonial Edition is also published

Wyndham (George). THE POEMS OF WILLIAM SHAKESPEARE. With an Introduction and Notes. *Demy 8vo. Buckram, gilt top. 10s. 6d.*

Wyon (R.). See Half-crown Library.

Yeats (W. B.). AN ANTHOLOGY OF IRISH VERSE. *Revised and Enlarged Edition. Cr. 8vo. 3s. 6d.*

Young (Filson). THE COMPLETE MOTORIST. With 138 Illustrations *Fifth Edition. Demy 8vo. 12s. 6d. net.*
A Colonial Edition is also published.

Young (T. M.). THE AMERICAN COTTON INDUSTRY: A Study of Work and Workers. *Cr. 8vo. Cloth, 2s. 6d.; paper boards, 1s. 6d.*

Zimmern (Antonia). WHAT DO WE KNOW CONCERNING ELECTRICITY? *Fcap. 8vo. 1s. 6d. net.*

Ancient Cities

General Editor, B. C. A. WINDLE, D.Sc., F.R.S.

Cr. 8vo. 4s. 6d. net.

CHESTER. By B. C. A. Windle, D.Sc. F.R.S. Illustrated by E. H. New.

SHREWSBURY. By T. Auden, M.A., F.S.A. Illustrated.

CANTERBURY. By J. C. Cox, LL.D., F.S.A. Illustrated.

*EDINBURGH. By M. G. Williamson. Illustrated by Herbert Railton.

*LINCOLN. By E. Mansel Sympson, M.A., M.D. Illustrated by E. H. New.

*BRISTOL. By Alfred Harvey. Illustrated by E. H. New.

Antiquary's Books, The

General Editor, J. CHARLES COX, LL.D., F.S.A.

A series of volumes dealing with various branches of English Antiquities; comprehensive and popular, as well as accurate and scholarly.

Demy 8vo. 7s. 6d. *net.*

ENGLISH MONASTIC LIFE. By the Right Rev. Abbot Gasquet, O.S B. Illustrated. *Third Edition.*

REMAINS OF THE PREHISTORIC AGE IN ENGLAND. By B. C. A. Windle, D.Sc., F.R.S. With numerous Illustrations and Plans.

OLD SERVICE BOOKS OF THE ENGLISH CHURCH. By Christopher Wordsworth, M.A., and Henry Littlehales. With Coloured and other Illustrations.

CELTIC ART. By J. Romilly Allen, F.S.A. With numerous Illustrations and Plans.

ARCHÆOLOGY AND FALSE ANTIQUITIES. By R. Munro, LL.D. Illustrated.

SHRINES OF BRITISH SAINTS. By J. C. Wall. With numerous Illustrations and Plans.

THE ROYAL FORESTS OF ENGLAND. By J. C. Cox, LL.D., F.S.A. Illustrated.

THE MANOR AND MANORIAL RECORDS. By Nathaniel J. Hone. Illustrated.

*SEALS. By J. Harvey Bloom. Illustrated.

Beginner's Books, The

Edited by W. WILLIAMSON, B.A.

EASY FRENCH RHYMES. By Henri Blouet. Illustrated. *Fcap. 8vo.* 1s.

EASY STORIES FROM ENGLISH HISTORY. By E. M. Wilmot-Buxton, Author of 'Makers of Europe.' *Cr. 8vo.* 1s.

EASY EXERCISES IN ARITHMETIC. Arranged by W. S. Beard. *Fcap. 8vo.* Without Answers, 1s. With Answers, 1s. 3d.

EASY DICTATION AND SPELLING. By W. Williamson, B.A. *Fourth Edition. Fcap. 8vo.* 1s.

Business, Books on

Cr. 8vo. 2s. 6d. *net.*

A series of volumes dealing with all the most important aspects of commercial and financial activity. The volumes are intended to treat separately all the considerable industries and forms of business, and to explain accurately and clearly what they do and how they do it. Some are Illustrated. The first volumes are—

PORTS AND DOCKS. By Douglas Owen.

RAILWAYS. By E. R. McDermott.

THE STOCK EXCHANGE. By Chas. Duguid. *Second Edition.*

THE BUSINESS OF INSURANCE. By A. J. Wilson.

THE ELECTRICAL INDUSTRY: LIGHTING, TRACTION, AND POWER. By A. G. Whyte, B.Sc.

THE SHIPBUILDING INDUSTRY: Its History, Science, Practice, and Finance. By David Pollock, M.I.N.A.

THE MONEY MARKET. By F. Straker.

THE BUSINESS SIDE OF AGRICULTURE. By A. G. L. Rogers, M.A.

LAW IN BUSINESS. By H. A. Wilson.

THE BREWING INDUSTRY. By Julian L. Baker, F.I.C., F.C.S.

THE AUTOMOBILE INDUSTRY. By G. de H. Stone.

MINING AND MINING INVESTMENTS. By 'A. Moil.'

THE BUSINESS OF ADVERTISING. By Clarence G. Moran, Barrister-at-Law. Illustrated.

TRADE UNIONS. By G. Drage.

CIVIL ENGINEERING. By T. Claxton Fidler, M.Inst. C.E. Illustrated.

THE IRON TRADE. By J. Stephen Jeans. Illustrated.

MONOPOLIES, TRUSTS, AND KARTELLS. By F. W. Hirst.

THE COTTON INDUSTRY AND TRADE. By Prof. S. J. Chapman, Dean of the Faculty of Commerce in the University of Manchester. Illustrated.

*THE COAL INDUSTRY. By Ernest Aves. Illustrated.

Byzantine Texts

Edited by J. B. BURY, M.A., Litt.D.

A series of texts of Byzantine Historians, edited by English and foreign scholars.

ZACHARIAH OF MITYLENE. Translated by F. J. Hamilton, D.D., and E. W. Brooks. *Demy 8vo. 12s. 6d. net.*

EVAGRIUS. Edited by Léon Parmentier and M. Bidez. *Demy 8vo. 10s. 6d. net.*

THE HISTORY OF PSELLUS. Edited by C. Sathas. *Demy 8vo. 15s. net.*

ECTHESIS CHRONICA. Edited by Professor Lambros. *Demy 8vo. 7s. 6d. net.*

THE CHRONICLE OF MOREA. Edited by John Schmitt. *Demy 8vo. 15s. net.*

Churchman's Bible, The

General Editor, J. H. BURN, B.D., F.R.S.E.

A series of Expositions on the Books of the Bible, which will be of service to the general reader in the practical and devotional study of the Sacred Text.

Each Book is provided with a full and clear Introductory Section, in which is stated what is known or conjectured respecting the date and occasion of the composition of the Book, and any other particulars that may help to elucidate its meaning as a whole. The Exposition is divided into sections of a convenient length, corresponding as far as possible with the divisions of the Church Lectionary. The Translation of the Authorised Version is printed in full, such corrections as are deemed necessary being placed in footnotes.

THE EPISTLE OF ST. PAUL THE APOSTLE TO THE GALATIANS. Edited by A. W. Robinson, M.A. *Second Edition. Fcap. 8vo. 1s. 6d. net.*

ECCLESIASTES. Edited by A. W. Streane, D.D. *Fcap. 8vo. 1s. 6d. net.*

THE EPISTLE OF ST. PAUL THE APOSTLE TO THE PHILIPPIANS. Edited by C. R. D. Biggs, D.D. *Second Edition. Fcap 8vo. 1s. 6d. net.*

THE EPISTLE OF ST. JAMES. Edited by H. W. Fulford, M.A. *Fcap. 8vo. 1s. 6d. net.*

ISAIAH. Edited by W. E. Barnes, D.D. *Two Volumes. Fcap. 8vo. 2s. net each.* With Map.

THE EPISTLE OF ST. PAUL THE APOSTLE TO THE EPHESIANS. Edited by G. H. Whitaker, M.A. *Fcap. 8vo. 1s. 6d. net.*

Churchman's Library, The

General Editor, J. H. BURN, B.D., F.R.S.E.

THE BEGINNINGS OF ENGLISH CHRISTIANITY. By W. E. Collins, M.A. With Map. *Cr. 8vo. 3s. 6d.*

SOME NEW TESTAMENT PROBLEMS. By Arthur Wright, M.A. *Cr. 8vo. 6s.*

THE KINGDOM OF HEAVEN HERE AND HEREAFTER. By Canon Winterbotham, M.A., B.Sc., LL.B. *Cr. 8vo. 3s. 6d.*

THE WORKMANSHIP OF THE PRAYER BOOK: Its Literary and Liturgical Aspects. By J. Dowden, D.D. *Second Edition. Cr. 8vo. 3s. 6d.*

EVOLUTION. By F. B. Jevons, M.A., Litt.D *Cr. 8vo. 3s. 6d.*

THE OLD TESTAMENT AND THE NEW SCHOLARSHIP. By J. W. Peters, D.D. *Cr. 8vo. 6s.*

THE CHURCHMAN'S INTRODUCTION TO THE OLD TESTAMENT. By A. M. Mackay, B.A. *Cr. 8vo. 3s. 6d.*

THE CHURCH OF CHRIST. By E. T. Green, M.A. *Cr. 8vo. 6s.*

COMPARATIVE THEOLOGY. By J. A. MacCulloch. *Cr. 8vo. 6s.*

Classical Translations

Edited by H. F. FOX, M.A., Fellow and Tutor of Brasenose College, Oxford.

Crown 8vo.

A series of Translations from the Greek and Latin Classics, distinguished by literary excellence as well as by scholarly accuracy.

ÆSCHYLUS—Agamemnon, Choephoroe, Eumenides. Translated by Lewis Campbell, LL.D. *5s.*

CICERO—De Oratore I. Translated by E. N. P. Moor, M.A. *3s. 6d.*

CICERO—Select Orations (Pro Milone, Pro Mureno, Philippic II., in Catilinam). Translated by H. E. D. Blakiston, M.A. *5s.*

CICERO—De Natura Deorum. Translated by F. Brooks, M.A. *3s. 6d.*

[*Continued.*

CLASSICAL TRANSLATIONS—*continued.*

CICERO—De Officiis. Translated by G. B. Gardiner, M.A. 2s. 6d.

HORACE—The Odes and Epodes. Translated by A. D. Godley, M.A. 2s.

LUCIAN—Six Dialogues (Nigrinus, Icaro-Menippus, The Cock, The Ship, The Parasite, The Lover of Falsehood) Translated by S.

T. Irwin, M.A. 3s. 6d.

SOPHOCLES—Electra and Ajax. Translated by E. D. A. Morshead, M.A. 2s. 6d.

TACITUS—Agricola and Germania. Translated by R. B. Townshend. 2s. 6d.

THE SATIRES OF JUVENAL. Translated by S. G. Owen. 2s. 6d.

Commercial Series

Edited by H. DE B. GIBBINS, Litt. D., M.A.

Crown 8vo.

A series intended to assist students and young men preparing for a commercial career, by supplying useful handbooks of a clear and practical character, dealing with those subjects which are absolutely essential in the business life.

COMMERCIAL EDUCATION IN THEORY AND PRACTICE. By E. E. Whitfield, M.A. 5s.
 An introduction to Methuen's Commercial Series treating the question of Commercial Education fully from both the point of view of the teacher and of the parent.

BRITISH COMMERCE AND COLONIES FROM ELIZABETH TO VICTORIA. By H. de B. Gibbins, Litt. D., M.A. *Third Edition.* 2s.

COMMERCIAL EXAMINATION PAPERS. By H. de B. Gibbins, Litt. D., M.A. 1s. 6d.

THE ECONOMICS OF COMMERCE, By H. de B. Gibbins, Litt. D., M.A. *Second Edition.* 1s. 6d.

A GERMAN COMMERCIAL READER. By S. E. Bally. With Vocabulary. 2s.

A COMMERCIAL GEOGRAPHY OF THE BRITISH EMPIRE. By L. W. Lyde, M.A. *Fourth Edition.* 2s.

A COMMERCIAL GEOGRAPHY OF FOREIGN NATIONS. By F. C. Boon, B.A. 2s.

A PRIMER OF BUSINESS. By S. Jackson, M.A. *Third Edition.* 1s. 6d.

COMMERCIAL ARITHMETIC. By F. G. Taylor, M.A. *Fourth Edition.* 1s. 6d.

FRENCH COMMERCIAL CORRESPONDENCE. By S. E. Bally. With Vocabulary. *Third Edition.* 2s.

GERMAN COMMERCIAL CORRESPONDENCE. By S. E. Bally. With Vocabulary. *Second Edition.* 2s. 6d.

A FRENCH COMMERCIAL READER. By S. E. Bally. With Vocabulary. *Second Edition.* 2s.

PRECIS WRITING AND OFFICE CORRESPONDENCE. By E. E. Whitfield, M.A. *Second Edition.* 2s.

A GUIDE TO PROFESSIONS AND BUSINESS. By H. Jones. 1s. 6d.

THE PRINCIPLES OF BOOK-KEEPING BY DOUBLE ENTRY. By J. E. B. M'Allen, M.A. 2s.

COMMERCIAL LAW. By W. Douglas Edwards. *Second Edition.* 2s.

Connoisseur's Library, The

Wide Royal 8vo. 25s. *net.*

A sumptuous series of 20 books on art, written by experts for collectors, superbly illustrated in photogravure, collotype, and colour. The technical side of the art is duly treated. The first volumes are—

MEZZOTINTS. By Cyril Davenport. With 40 Plates in Photogravure.

PORCELAIN. By Edward Dillon. With 19 Plates in Colour, 20 in Collotype, and 5 in Photogravure.

MINIATURES. By Dudley Heath. With 9 Plates in Colour, 15 in Collotype, and 15 in Photogravure.

IVORIES. By A. Maskell. With 80 Plates in Collotype and Photogravure.

ENGLISH FURNITURE. By F. S. Robinson. With 160 Plates in Collotype and one in Photogravure. *Second Edition.*

*EUROPEAN ENAMELS. By H. CUNYNGHAME, C.B. With many Plates in Collotype and a Frontispiece in Photogravure.

Devotion, The Library of

With Introductions and (where necessary) Notes.

Small Pott 8vo, cloth, 2s. ; leather, 2s. 6d. net.

These masterpieces of devotional literature are furnished with such Introductions and Notes as may be necessary to explain the standpoint of the author and the obvious difficulties of the text, without unnecessary intrusion between the author and the devout mind.

THE CONFESSIONS OF ST. AUGUSTINE. Edited by C. Bigg, D.D. *Fifth Edition.*

THE CHRISTIAN YEAR. Edited by Walter Lock, D.D. *Third Edition.*

THE IMITATION OF CHRIST. Edited by C. Bigg, D.D. *Fourth Edition.*

A BOOK OF DEVOTIONS. Edited by J. W. Stanbridge. B.D. *Second Edition.*

LYRA INNOCENTIUM. Edited by Walter Lock, D.D.

A SERIOUS CALL TO A DEVOUT AND HOLY LIFE. Edited by C. Bigg, D.D. *Second Edition.*

THE TEMPLE. Edited by E. C. S. Gibson, D.D. *Second Edition.*

A GUIDE TO ETERNITY. Edited by J. W. Stanbridge, B.D.

THE PSALMS OF DAVID. Edited by B. W. Randolph, D.D.

LYRA APOSTOLICA. By Cardinal Newman and others. Edited by Canon Scott Holland and Canon H. C. Beeching, M.A.

THE INNER WAY. By J. Tauler. Edited by A. W. Hutton, M.A.

THE THOUGHTS OF PASCAL. Edited by C. S. Jerram, M.A.

ON THE LOVE OF GOD. By St. Francis de Sales. Edited by W. J. Knox-Little, M.A.

A MANUAL OF CONSOLATION FROM THE SAINTS AND FATHERS. Edited by J. H. Burn, B.D.

THE SONG OF SONGS. Edited by B. Blaxland, M.A.

THE DEVOTIONS OF ST. ANSELM. Edited by C. C. J. Webb, M.A.

GRACE ABOUNDING. By John Bunyan. Edited by S. C. Freer, M.A.

BISHOP WILSON'S SACRA PRIVATA. Edited by A. E. Burn, B.D.

LYRA SACRA : A Book of Sacred Verse. Edited by H. C. Beeching, M.A., Canon of Westminster.

A DAY BOOK FROM THE SAINTS AND FATHERS. Edited by J. H. Burn, B.D.

HEAVENLY WISDOM. A Selection from the English Mystics. Edited by E. C. Gregory.

LIGHT, LIFE, and LOVE. A Selection from the German Mystics. Edited by W. R. Inge, M.A.

AN INTRODUCTION TO THE DEVOUT LIFE. By St. Francis de Sales. Translated and Edited by T. Barns, M.A.

Methuen's Standard Library

In Sixpenny Volumes.

THE STANDARD LIBRARY is a new series of volumes containing the great classics of the world, and particularly the finest works of English literature. All the great masters will be represented, either in complete works or in selections. It is the ambition of the publishers to place the best books of the Anglo-Saxon race within the reach of every reader, so that the series may represent something of the diversity and splendour of our English tongue. The characteristics of THE STANDARD LIBRARY are four :—1. SOUNDNESS OF TEXT. 2. CHEAPNESS. 3. CLEARNESS OF TYPE. 4. SIMPLICITY. The books are well printed on good paper at a price which on the whole is without parallel in the history of publishing. Each volume contains from 100 to 250 pages, and is issued in paper covers, Crown 8vo, at Sixpence net, or in cloth gilt at One Shilling net. In a few cases long books are issued as Double Volumes or as Treble Volumes.

The following books are ready with the exception of those marked with a †, which denotes that the book is nearly ready :—

THE MEDITATIONS OF MARCUS AURELIUS. The translation is by R. Graves.

THE NOVELS OF JANE AUSTEN. In 5 volumes. VOL. I.—Sense and Sensibility.

ESSAYS AND COUNSELS and THE NEW ATLANTIS. By Francis Bacon, Lord Verulam.

†RELIGIO MEDICI and URN BURIAL. By Sir Thomas Browne. The text has been collated by A. R. Waller.

THE PILGRIM'S PROGRESS. By John Bunyan.

REFLECTIONS ON THE FRENCH REVOLUTION. By Edmund Burke.

†THE ANALOGY OF RELIGION, NATURAL AND REVEALED. By Joseph Butler, D.D.

[*Continued.*

THE STANDARD LIBRARY—*continued.*

THE POEMS OF THOMAS CHATTERTON. In 2 volumes.
  †Vol. I.—Miscellaneous Poems.
  †Vol. II.—The Rowley Poems.
†VITA NUOVA. By Dante. Translated into English by D. G. Rossetti.
TOM JONES. By Henry Fielding. Treble Vol.
CRANFORD. By Mrs. Gaskell.
THE HISTORY OF THE DECLINE AND FALL OF THE ROMAN EMPIRE. By Edward Gibbon. In 7 double volumes.
  Vol. V. is nearly ready.
  The Text and Notes have been revised by J. B. Bury, Litt.D., but the Appendices of the more expensive edition are not given.
†THE VICAR OF WAKEFIELD. By Oliver Goldsmith.
THE POEMS AND PLAYS OF OLIVER GOLDSMITH.
THE WORKS OF BEN JONSON.
  †Vol. I.—The Case is Altered. Every Man in His Humour. Every Man out of His Humour.
  The text has been collated by H. C. Hart.
THE POEMS OF JOHN KEATS. Double volume. The Text has been collated by E. de Selincourt.
ON THE IMITATION OF CHRIST. By Thomas à Kempis.
  The translation is by C. Bigg, DD., Canon of Christ Church.
A SERIOUS CALL TO A DEVOUT AND HOLY LIFE. By William Law.
THE PLAYS OF CHRISTOPHER MARLOWE.
  †Vol. I.—Tamburlane the Great. The Tragical History of Dr. Faustus.
THE PLAYS OF PHILIP MASSINGER.
  †Vol. I.—The Duke of Milan.

THE POEMS OF JOHN MILTON. In 2 volumes.
  Vol. I.—Paradise Lost.
THE PROSE WORKS OF JOHN MILTON.
  Vol. I.—Eikonoklastes and The Tenure of Kings and Magistrates.
SELECT WORKS OF SIR THOMAS MORE.
  Vol. I.—Utopia and Poems.
THE REPUBLIC OF PLATO. Translated by Sydenham and Taylor. Double Volume. The translation has been revised by W. H. D. Rouse.
THE LITTLE FLOWERS OF ST. FRANCIS. Translated by W. Heywood.
THE WORKS OF WILLIAM SHAKESPEARE. In 10 volumes.
  VOL. I.—The Tempest; The Two Gentlemen of Verona; The Merry Wives of Windsor; Measure for Measure; The Comedy of Errors.
  VOL. II.—Much Ado About Nothing; Love's Labour's Lost; A Midsummer Night's Dream; The Merchant of Venice; As You Like It.
  VOL. III.—The Taming of the Shrew; All's Well that Ends Well; Twelfth Night; The Winter's Tale.
  Vol. IV.—The Life and Death of King John; The Tragedy of King Richard the Second; The First Part of King Henry IV.; The Second Part of King Henry IV.
  †Vol. V.—The Life of King Henry V.; The First Part of King Henry VI.; The Second Part of King Henry VI.
THE LIFE OF NELSON. By Robert Southey.
†THE NATURAL HISTORY AND ANTIQUITIES OF SELBORNE. By Gilbert White.

Half-Crown Library
Crown 8vo.   2s. 6d. net.

THE LIFE OF JOHN RUSKIN. By W. G. Collingwood, M.A. With Portraits. *Sixth Edition.*
ENGLISH LYRICS. By W. E. Henley. *Second Edition.*
THE GOLDEN POMP. A Procession of English Lyrics. Arranged by A. T. Quiller Couch. *Second Edition.*
CHITRAL: The Story of a Minor Siege. By Sir G. S. Robertson, K.C.S.I. *Third Edition.* Illustrated.

STRANGE SURVIVALS AND SUPERSTITIONS. By S. Baring-Gould. *Third Edition.*
YORKSHIRE ODDITIES AND STRANGE EVENTS. By S. Baring-Gould. *Fourth Edition.*
ENGLISH VILLAGES. By P. H. Ditchfield, M.A., F.S.A. Illustrated.
A BOOK OF ENGLISH PROSE. By W. E. Henley and C. Whibley.
THE LAND OF THE BLACK MOUNTAIN. Being a Description of Montenegro. By R. Wyon and G. Prance. With 40 Illustrations.

Illustrated Pocket Library of Plain and Coloured Books, The
Fcap 8vo.   3s. 6d. net each volume.

A series, in small form, of some of the famous illustrated books of fiction and general literature. These are faithfully reprinted from the first or best editions without introduction or notes. The Illustrations are chiefly in colour.

COLOURED BOOKS

OLD COLOURED BOOKS. By George Paston. With 16 Coloured Plates. *Fcap. 8vo.* 2s. *net.*
THE LIFE AND DEATH OF JOHN MYTTON, ESQ.

By Nimrod. With 18 Coloured Plates by Henry Alken and T. J. Rawlins. *Third Edition.*

[*Continued.*

THE LIFE OF A SPORTSMAN. By Nimrod. With 35 Coloured Plates by Henry Alken.

HANDLEY CROSS. By R. S. Surtees. With 17 Coloured Plates and 100 Woodcuts in the Text by John Leech.

MR. SPONGE'S SPORTING TOUR. By R. S. Surtees. With 13 Coloured Plates and 90 Woodcuts in the Text by John Leech.

JORROCKS' JAUNTS AND JOLLITIES. By R. S. Surtees. With 15 Coloured Plates by H. Alken.

This volume is reprinted from the extremely rare and costly edition of 1843, which contains Alken's very fine illustrations instead of the usual ones by Phiz.

ASK MAMMA. By R. S. Surtees. With 13 Coloured Plates and 70 Woodcuts in the Text by John Leech.

THE ANALYSIS OF THE HUNTING FIELD. By R. S. Surtees. With 7 Coloured Plates by Henry Alken, and 43 Illustrations on Wood.

THE TOUR OF DR. SYNTAX IN SEARCH OF THE PICTURESQUE. By William Combe. With 30 Coloured Plates by T. Rowlandson.

THE TOUR OF DOCTOR SYNTAX IN SEARCH OF CONSOLATION. By William Combe. With 24 Coloured Plates by T. Rowlandson.

THE THIRD TOUR OF DOCTOR SYNTAX IN SEARCH OF A WIFE. By William Combe. With 24 Coloured Plates by T. Rowlandson.

THE HISTORY OF JOHNNY QUAE GENUS: the Little Foundling of the late Dr. Syntax. By the Author of 'The Three Tours.' With 24 Coloured Plates by Rowlandson.

THE ENGLISH DANCE OF DEATH, from the Designs of T. Rowlandson, with Metrical Illustrations by the Author of 'Doctor Syntax.' *Two Volumes.*

This book contains 76 Coloured Plates.

THE DANCE OF LIFE: A Poem. By the Author of 'Doctor Syntax.' Illustrated with 26 Coloured Engravings by T. Rowlandson.

LIFE IN LONDON: or, the Day and Night Scenes of Jerry Hawthorn, Esq., and his Elegant Friend, Corinthian Tom. By Pierce Egan. With 36 Coloured Plates by I. R. and G. Cruikshank. With numerous Designs on Wood.

REAL LIFE IN LONDON: or, the Rambles and Adventures of Bob Tallyho, Esq., and his Cousin, The Hon. Tom Dashall. By an Amateur (Pierce Egan). With 31 Coloured Plates by Alken and Rowlandson, etc. *Two Volumes.*

THE LIFE OF AN ACTOR. By Pierce Egan. With 27 Coloured Plates by Theodore Lane, and several Designs on Wood.

THE VICAR OF WAKEFIELD. By Oliver Goldsmith. With 24 Coloured Plates by T. Rowlandson.

THE MILITARY ADVENTURES OF JOHNNY NEWCOME. By an Officer. With 15 Coloured Plates by T. Rowlandson.

THE NATIONAL SPORTS OF GREAT BRITAIN. With Descriptions and 51 Coloured Plates by Henry Alken.

This book is completely different from the large folio edition of 'National Sports' by the same artist, and none of the plates are similar.

THE ADVENTURES OF A POST CAPTAIN. By A Naval Officer. With 24 Coloured Plates by Mr. Williams.

GAMONIA: or, the Art of Preserving Game; and an Improved Method of making Plantations and Covers, explained and illustrated by Lawrence Rawstorne, Esq. With 15 Coloured Plates by T. Rawlins.

AN ACADEMY FOR GROWN HORSEMEN: Containing the completest Instructions for Walking, Trotting, Cantering, Galloping, Stumbling, and Tumbling. Illustrated with 27 Coloured Plates, and adorned with a Portrait of the Author. By Geoffrey Gambado, Esq.

REAL LIFE IN IRELAND, or, the Day and Night Scenes of Brian Boru, Esq., and his Elegant Friend, Sir Shawn O'Dogherty. By a Real Paddy. With 19 Coloured Plates by Heath, Marks, etc.

THE ADVENTURES OF JOHNNY NEWCOME IN THE NAVY. By Alfred Burton. With 16 Coloured Plates by T. Rowlandson.

THE OLD ENGLISH SQUIRE: A Poem. By John Careless, Esq. With 20 Coloured Plates after the style of T. Rowlandson.

*THE ENGLISH SPY. By Bernard Blackmantle. With 72 Coloured Plates by R. Cruikshank, and many Illustrations on wood. *Two Volumes.*

PLAIN BOOKS

THE GRAVE: A Poem. By Robert Blair. Illustrated by 12 Etchings executed by Louis Schiavonetti from the original Inventions of William Blake. With an Engraved Title Page and a Portrait of Blake by T. Phillips, R.A.

The illustrations are reproduced in photogravure.

ILLUSTRATIONS OF THE BOOK OF JOB. Invented and engraved by William Blake.

These famous Illustrations—21 in number—are reproduced in photogravure.

ÆSOP'S FABLES. With 380 Woodcuts by Thomas Bewick.

[Continued

ILLUSTRATED POCKET LIBRARY OF PLAIN AND COLOURED BOOKS—*continued.*

WINDSOR CASTLE. By W. Harrison Ainsworth. With 22 Plates and 87 Woodcuts in the Text by George Cruikshank.

THE TOWER OF LONDON. By W. Harrison Ainsworth. With 40 Plates and 58 Woodcuts in the Text by George Cruikshank.

FRANK FAIRLEGH. By F. E. Smedley. With 30 Plates by George Cruikshank.

HANDY ANDY. By Samuel Lover. With 24 Illustrations by the Author.

THE COMPLEAT ANGLER. By Izaak Walton and Charles Cotton. With 14 Plates and 77 Woodcuts in the Text.
This volume is reproduced from the beautiful edition of John Major of 1824.

THE PICKWICK PAPERS. By Charles Dickens. With the 43 Illustrations by Seymour and Phiz, the two Buss Plates, and the 32 Contemporary Onwhyn Plates.

Junior Examination Series

Edited by A. M. M. STEDMAN, M.A. *Fcap. 8vo.* 1s.

This series is intended to lead up to the School Examination Series, and is intended for the use of teachers and students, to supply material for the former and practice for the latter. The papers are carefully graduated, cover the whole of the subject usually taught, and are intended to form part of the ordinary class work. They may be used *vivâ voce* or as a written examination.

JUNIOR FRENCH EXAMINATION PAPERS. By F. Jacob, M.A.

JUNIOR LATIN EXAMINATION PAPERS. By C. G. Botting, B.A. *Third Edition.*

JUNIOR ENGLISH EXAMINATION PAPERS. By W. Williamson, B.A.

JUNIOR ARITHMETIC EXAMINATION PAPERS. By W. S. Beard. *Second Edition.*

JUNIOR ALGEBRA EXAMINATION PAPERS. By S. W. Finn, M.A.

JUNIOR GREEK EXAMINATION PAPERS. By T C. Weatherhead, M.A.

JUNIOR GENERAL INFORMATION EXAMINATION PAPERS. By W. S. Beard.

*A KEY TO THE ABOVE. *Crown 8vo.* 3s. 6d. net.

JUNIOR GEOGRAPHY EXAMINATION PAPERS. By W. G. Baker, M.A.

JUNIOR GERMAN EXAMINATION PAPERS. By A. Voegelin, M.A.

Junior School-Books

Edited by O. D. INSKIP, LL.D., and W. WILLIAMSON, B.A.

A series of elementary books for pupils in lower forms, simply written by teachers of experience.

A CLASS-BOOK OF DICTATION PASSAGES. By W. Williamson, B.A. *Eleventh Edition.* *Cr. 8vo.* 1s. 6d.

THE GOSPEL ACCORDING TO ST. MATTHEW. Edited by E. Wilton South, M.A. With Three Maps. *Cr. 8vo.* 1s. 6d.

THE GOSPEL ACCORDING TO ST. MARK. Edited by A. E. Rubie, D.D. With Three Maps. *Cr. 8vo.* 1s. 6d.

A JUNIOR ENGLISH GRAMMAR. By W. Williamson, B.A. With numerous passages for parsing and analysis, and a chapter on Essay Writing. *Third Edition. Cr. 8vo.* 2s.

A JUNIOR CHEMISTRY. By E. A. Tyler, B.A., F.C.S. With 78 Illustrations. *Second Edition. Cr. 8vo.* 2s. 6d.

THE ACTS OF THE APOSTLES. Edited by A. E. Rubie, D.D. *Cr. 8vo.* 2s.

A JUNIOR FRENCH GRAMMAR. By L. A. Sornet and M. J. Acatos. *Cr. 8vo.* 2s.

ELEMENTARY EXPERIMENTAL SCIENCE. PHYSICS by W. T. Clough, A.R.C.S. CHEMISTRY by A. E. Dunstan, B.Sc. With 2 Plates and 154 Diagrams. *Third Edition. Cr. 8vo.* 2s. 6d.

A JUNIOR GEOMETRY. By Noel S. Lydon. With 276 Diagrams. *Second Edition. Cr. 8vo.* 2s.

*A JUNIOR MAGNETISM AND ELECTRICITY. By W. T. Clough. Illustrated. *Cr. 8vo.* 2s. 6d.

ELEMENTARY EXPERIMENTAL CHEMISTRY. By A. E. Dunstan, B.Sc. With 4 Plates and 109 Diagrams. *Cr. 8vo.* 2s.

A JUNIOR FRENCH PROSE COMPOSITION. By R. N. Baron, M.A. *Cr. 8vo.* 2s.

THE GOSPEL ACCORDING TO ST. LUKE. With an Introduction and Notes by William Williamson, B.A. With Three Maps. *Cr. 8vo.* 2s.

Leaders of Religion

Edited by H. C. BEECHING, M.A., Canon of Westminster. *With Portraits.*
Cr. 8vo. 2s. net.

A series of short biographies of the most prominent leaders of religious life and thought of all ages and countries.

CARDINAL NEWMAN. By R. H. Hutton.
JOHN WESLEY. By J. H. Overton, M.A.
BISHOP WILBERFORCE. By G. W. Daniell, M.A.
CARDINAL MANNING. By A. W. Hutton, M.A.
CHARLES SIMEON. By H. C. G. Moule, D.D.
JOHN KEBLE. By Walter Lock, D.D.
THOMAS CHALMERS. By Mrs. Oliphant.
LANCELOT ANDREWES. By R. L. Ottley, D.D. *Second Edition.*
AUGUSTINE OF CANTERBURY. By E. L. Cutts, D.D.

WILLIAM LAUD. By W. H. Hutton, M.A. *Third Edition.*
JOHN KNOX. By F. MacCunn. *Second Edition.*
JOHN HOWE. By R. F. Horton, D.D.
BISHOP KEN. By F. A. Clarke, M.A.
GEORGE FOX, THE QUAKER. By T. Hodgkin, D.C.L. *Third Edition.*
JOHN DONNE. By Augustus Jessopp, D.D.
THOMAS CRANMER. By A. J. Mason, D.D.
BISHOP LATIMER. By R. M. Carlyle and A. J. Carlyle, M.A.
BISHOP BUTLER. By W. A. Spooner, M.A.

Little Blue Books, The

General Editor, E. V. LUCAS.

Illustrated. Demy 16mo. 2s. 6d.

A series of books for children. The aim of the editor is to get entertaining or exciting stories about normal children, the moral of which is implied rather than expressed.

1. THE CASTAWAYS OF MEADOWBANK. By Thomas Cobb.
2. THE BEECHNUT BOOK. By Jacob Abbott. Edited by E. V. Lucas.
3. THE AIR GUN. By T. Hilbert.
4. A SCHOOL YEAR. By Netta Syrett.
5. THE PEELES AT THE CAPITAL. By Roger Ashton.
6. THE TREASURE OF PRINCEGATE PRIORY. By T. Cobb.
7. Mrs. BARBERRY'S GENERAL SHOP. By Roger Ashton.
8. A BOOK OF BAD CHILDREN. By W. T. Webb.
9. THE LOST BALL. By Thomas Cobb.

Little Books on Art

With many Illustrations. Demy 16mo. 2s. 6d. net.

A series of monographs in miniature, containing the complete outline of the subject under treatment and rejecting minute details. These books are produced with the greatest care. Each volume consists of about 200 pages, and contains from 30 to 40 illustrations, including a frontispiece in photogravure.

GREEK ART. H. B. Walters. *Second Edition.*
BOOKPLATES. E. Almack.
REYNOLDS. J. Sime. *Second Edition.*
ROMNEY. George Paston.
WATTS. R. E. D. Sketchley.
LEIGHTON. Alice Corkran.
VELASQUEZ. Wilfrid Wilberforce and A. R. Gilbert.
GREUZE AND BOUCHER. Eliza F. Pollard.
VANDYCK. M. G. Smallwood.
TURNER. Frances Tyrell-Gill.
DÜRER. Jessie Allen.
HOPPNER. H. P. K. Skipton.

HOLBEIN. Mrs. G. Fortescue.
BURNE-JONES. Fortunée de Lisle. *Second Edition.*
REMBRANDT. Mrs. E. A. Sharp
COROT. Alice Pollard and Ethel Birnstingl.
RAPHAEL. A. R. Dryhurst.
MILLET. Netta Peacock.
ILLUMINATED MSS. J. W. Bradley.
CHRIST IN ART. Mrs. Henry Jenner.
JEWELLERY. Cyril Davenport.
CLAUDE. Edward Dillon.
*THE ARTS OF JAPAN. Edward Dillon.

MESSRS. METHUEN'S CATALOGUE

Little Galleries, The

Demy 16mo. 2s. 6d. net.

A series of little books containing examples of the best work of the great painters. Each volume contains 20 plates in photogravure, together with a short outline of the life and work of the master to whom the book is devoted.

A LITTLE GALLERY OF REYNOLDS.
A LITTLE GALLERY OF ROMNEY.
A LITTLE GALLERY OF HOPPNER.

A LITTLE GALLERY OF MILLAIS.
A LITTLE GALLERY OF ENGLISH POETS.

Little Guides, The

Small Pott 8vo, cloth, 2s. 6d. net.; leather, 3s. 6d. net.

OXFORD AND ITS COLLEGES. By J. Wells, M.A. Illustrated by E. H. New. *Sixth Edition.*

CAMBRIDGE AND ITS COLLEGES. By A. Hamilton Thompson. *Second Edition.* Illustrated by E. H. New.

THE MALVERN COUNTRY. By B. C. A. Windle, D.Sc., F.R.S. Illustrated by E. H. New.

SHAKESPEARE'S COUNTRY. By B. C. A. Windle, D.Sc., F.R.S. Illustrated by E. H. New. *Second Edition.*

SUSSEX. By F. G. Brabant, M.A. Illustrated by E. H. New.

WESTMINSTER ABBEY. By G. E. Troutbeck. Illustrated by F. D. Bedford.

NORFOLK. By W. A. Dutt. Illustrated by B. C. Boulter.

CORNWALL. By A. L. Salmon. Illustrated by B. C. Boulter.

BRITTANY. By S. Baring-Gould. Illustrated by J. Wylie.

HERTFORDSHIRE. By H. W. Tompkins, F.R.H.S. Illustrated by E. H. New.

THE ENGLISH LAKES. By F. G. Brabant, M.A. Illustrated by E. H. New.

KENT. By G. Clinch. Illustrated by F. D. Bedford.

ROME By C. G. Ellaby. Illustrated by B. C. Boulter.

THE ISLE OF WIGHT. By G. Clinch. Illustrated by F. D. Bedford.

SURREY. By F. A. H. Lambert. Illustrated by E. H. New.

BUCKINGHAMSHIRE. By E. S. Roscoe. Illustrated by F. D. Bedford.

SUFFOLK. By W. A. Dutt. Illustrated by J. Wylie.

DERBYSHIRE. By J. C. Cox, LL.D., F.S.A. Illustrated by J. C. Wall.

THE NORTH RIDING OF YORKSHIRE. By J. E. Morris. Illustrated by R. J. S. Bertram.

HAMPSHIRE. By J. C. Cox. Illustrated by M. E. Purser.

SICILY. By F. H. Jackson. With many Illustrations by the Author.

DORSET. By Frank R. Heath. Illustrated.

CHESHIRE. By W. M. Gallichan. Illustrated by Elizabeth Hartley.

NORTHAMPTONSHIRE. By Wakeling Dry. Illustrated.

*THE EAST RIDING OF YORKSHIRE. By J. E. Morris. Illustrated.

*OXFORDSHIRE. By F. G. Brabant. Illustrated by E. H. New.

*ST. PAUL'S CATHEDRAL. By George Clinch. Illustrated by Beatrice Alcock.

Little Library, The

With Introductions, Notes, and Photogravure Frontispieces.

Small Pott 8vo. Each Volume, cloth, 1s. 6d. net; leather, 2s. 6d. net.

A series of small books under the above title, containing some of the famous works in English and other literatures, in the domains of fiction, poetry, and belles lettres. The series also contains volumes of selections in prose and verse. The books are edited with the most scholarly care. Each one contains an introduction which gives (1) a short biography of the author; (2) a critical estimate of the book. Where they are necessary, short notes are added at the foot of the page.

Each volume has a photogravure frontispiece, and the books are produced with great care.

Anon. ENGLISH LYRICS, A LITTLE BOOK OF.

Austen (Jane). PRIDE AND PREJUDICE. Edited by E. V. LUCAS. *Two Volumes.*

NORTHANGER ABBEY. Edited by E. V. LUCAS.

Bacon (Francis). THE ESSAYS OF LORD BACON. Edited by EDWARD WRIGHT.

Barham (R. H.). THE INGOLDSBY LEGENDS. Edited by J. B. ATLAY. *Two Volumes.*

Barnett (Mrs. P. A.). A LITTLE BOOK OF ENGLISH PROSE.

Beckford (William). THE HISTORY OF THE CALIPH VATHEK. Edited by E. DENISON ROSS.

Blake (William). SELECTIONS FROM WILLIAM BLAKE. Edited by M. PERUGINI.

Borrow (George). LAVENGRO. Edited by F. HINDES GROOME. *Two Volumes.* THE ROMANY RYE. Edited by JOHN SAMPSON.

Browning (Robert). SELECTIONS FROM THE EARLY POEMS OF ROBERT BROWNING. Edited by W. HALL GRIFFIN, M.A.

Canning (George). SELECTIONS FROM THE ANTI-JACOBIN : with GEORGE CANNING's additional Poems. Edited by LLOYD SANDERS.

Cowley (Abraham). THE ESSAYS OF ABRAHAM COWLEY. Edited by H. C. MINCHIN.

Crabbe (George). SELECTIONS FROM GEORGE CRABBE. Edited by A. C. DEANE.

Craik (Mrs.). JOHN HALIFAX, GENTLEMAN. Edited by ANNE MATHESON. *Two Volumes.*

Crashaw (Richard). THE ENGLISH POEMS OF RICHARD CRASHAW. Edited by EDWARD HUTTON.

Dante (Alighieri). THE INFERNO OF DANTE. Translated by H. F. CARY. Edited by PAGET TOYNBEE, M.A., D.Litt. THE PURGATORIO OF DANTE. Translated by H. F. CARY. Edited by PAGET TOYNBEE, M.A., D.Litt. THE PARADISO OF DANTE. Translated by H. F. CARY. Edited by PAGET TOYNBEE, M.A., D.Litt.

Darley (George). SELECTIONS FROM THE POEMS OF GEORGE DARLEY. Edited by R. A. STREATFEILD.

Deane (A. C.). A LITTLE BOOK OF LIGHT VERSE.

Dickens (Charles). CHRISTMAS BOOKS. *Two Volumes.*

Ferrier (Susan). MARRIAGE. Edited by A. GOODRICH - FREER and LORD IDDESLEIGH. *Two Volumes.* THE INHERITANCE. *Two Volumes.*

Gaskell (Mrs.). CRANFORD. Edited by E. V. LUCAS. *Second Edition.*

Hawthorne (Nathaniel). THE SCARLET LETTER. Edited by PERCY DEARMER.

Henderson (T. F.). A LITTLE BOOK OF SCOTTISH VERSE.

Keats (John). POEMS. With an Introduction by L. BINYON, and Notes by J. MASEFIELD.

Kinglake (A. W.). EOTHEN. With an Introduction and Notes. *Second Edition.*

Lamb (Charles). ELIA, AND THE LAST ESSAYS OF ELIA. Edited by E. V. LUCAS.

Locker (F.). LONDON LYRICS. Edited by A. D. GODLEY, M.A. A reprint of the First Edition.

Longfellow (H. W.). SELECTIONS FROM LONGFELLOW. Edited by L. M. FAITHFULL.

Marvell (Andrew). THE POEMS OF ANDREW MARVELL. Edited by E. WRIGHT.

Milton (John). THE MINOR POEMS OF JOHN MILTON. Edited by H. C. BEECHING, M.A., Canon of Westminster.

Moir (D. M.). MANSIE WAUCH. Edited by T. F. HENDERSON.

Nichols (J. B. B.). A LITTLE BOOK OF ENGLISH SONNETS.

Rochefoucauld (La). THE MAXIMS OF LA ROCHEFOUCAULD. Translated by Dean STANHOPE. Edited by G. H. POWELL.

Smith (Horace and James). REJECTED ADDRESSES. Edited by A. D. GODLEY, M.A.

Sterne (Laurence). A SENTIMENTAL JOURNEY. Edited by H. W. PAUL.

Tennyson (Alfred, Lord). THE EARLY POEMS OF ALFRED, LORD TENNYSON. Edited by J. CHURTON COLLINS, M.A. IN MEMORIAM. Edited by H. C. BEECHING, M.A. THE PRINCESS. Edited by ELIZABETH WORDSWORTH. MAUD. Edited by ELIZABETH WORDSWORTH.

Thackeray (W. M.). VANITY FAIR. Edited by S. GWYNN. *Three Volumes.* PENDENNIS. Edited by S. GWYNN. *Three Volumes.* ESMOND. Edited by S. GWYNN. CHRISTMAS BOOKS. Edited by S. GWYNN.

Vaughan (Henry). THE POEMS OF HENRY VAUGHAN. Edited by EDWARD HUTTON.

Walton (Izaak). THE COMPLEAT ANGLER. Edited by J. BUCHAN.

Waterhouse (Mrs. Alfred). A LITTLE BOOK OF LIFE AND DEATH. Edited by. *Eighth Edition.*

Wordsworth (W.). SELECTIONS FROM WORDSWORTH. Edited by NOWELL C. SMITH.

Wordsworth (W.) and Coleridge (S. T.). LYRICAL BALLADS. Edited by GEORGE SAMPSON.

Miniature Library

Reprints in miniature of a few interesting books which have qualities of humanity, devotion, or literary genius.

EUPHRANOR: A Dialogue on Youth. By Edward FitzGerald. From the edition published by W. Pickering in 1851. *Demy 32mo. Leather, 2s. net.*

POLONIUS: or Wise Saws and Modern Instances. By Edward FitzGerald. From the edition published by W. Pickering in 1852. *Demy 32mo. Leather, 2s. net.*

THE RUBÁIYÁT OF OMAR KHAYYÁM. By Edward FitzGerald. From the 1st edition of 1859, *Third Edition. Leather, 1s. net.*

THE LIFE OF EDWARD, LORD HERBERT OF CHERBURY. Written by himself. From the edition printed at Strawberry Hill in the year 1764. *Medium 32mo. Leather, 2s. net.*

THE VISIONS OF DOM FRANCISCO QUEVEDO VILLEGAS, Knight of the Order of St. James. Made English by R. L. From the edition printed for H. Herringman, 1668. *Leather. 2s. net.*

POEMS. By Dora Greenwell. From the edition of 1848. *Leather, 2s. net.*

Oxford Biographies

Fcap. 8vo. Each volume, cloth, 2s. 6d. net; leather, 3s. 6d. net.

These books are written by scholars of repute, who combine knowledge and literary skill with the power of popular presentation. They are illustrated from authentic material.

DANTE ALIGHIERI. By Paget Toynbee, M.A., D.Litt. With 12 Illustrations. *Second Edition.*

SAVONAROLA. By E. L. S. Horsburgh, M.A. With 12 Illustrations. *Second Edition.*

JOHN HOWARD. By E. C. S. Gibson, D.D., Bishop of Gloucester. With 12 Illustrations.

TENNYSON. By A. C. BENSON, M.A. With 9 Illustrations.

WALTER RALEIGH. By I. A. Taylor. With 12 Illustrations.

ERASMUS. By E. F. H. Capey. With 12 Illustrations.

THE YOUNG PRETENDER. By C. S. Terry. With 12 Illustrations.

ROBERT BURNS. By T. F. Henderson. With 12 Illustrations.

CHATHAM. By A. S. M'Dowall. With 12 Illustrations.

ST. FRANCIS OF ASSISI. By Anna M. Stoddart. With 16 Illustrations.

CANNING. By W. Alison Phillips. With 12 Illustrations.

BEACONSFIELD. By Walter Sichel. With 12 Illustrations.

GOETHE. By H. G. Atkins. With 12 Illustrations.

*FENELON. By Viscount St. Cyres. With 12 Illustrations.

School Examination Series

Edited by A. M. M. STEDMAN, M.A. *Cr. 8vo. 2s. 6d.*

FRENCH EXAMINATION PAPERS. By A. M. M. Stedman, M.A. *Thirteenth Edition.* A KEY, issued to Tutors and Private Students only to be had on application to the Publishers. *Fifth Edition. Crown 8vo. 6s. net.*

LATIN EXAMINATION PAPERS. By A. M. M. Stedman, M.A. *Thirteenth Edition.* KEY (*Fourth Edition*) issued as above. *6s. net.*

GREEK EXAMINATION PAPERS. By A. M. M. Stedman, M.A. *Eighth Edition.* KEY (*Third Edition*) issued as above. *6s. net.*

GERMAN EXAMINATION PAPERS. By R. J. Morich. *Sixth Edition.*

KEY (*Third Edition*) issued as above. *6s. net.*

HISTORY AND GEOGRAPHY EXAMINATION PAPERS. By C. H. Spence, M.A. *Second Edition.*

PHYSICS EXAMINATION PAPERS. By R. E. Steel, M.A., F.C.S.

GENERAL KNOWLEDGE EXAMINATION PAPERS. By A. M. M. Stedman, M.A. *Fifth Edition.* KEY (*Third Edition*) issued as above. *7s. net.*

EXAMINATION PAPERS IN ENGLISH HISTORY. By J. Tait Plowden-Wardlaw, B.A.

Science, Textbooks of

Edited by G. F. GOODCHILD, B.A., B.Sc., and G. R. MILLS, M.A.

PRACTICAL MECHANICS. By Sidney H. Wells. *Third Edition. Cr. 8vo. 3s. 6d.*

PRACTICAL PHYSICS. By H. Stroud, D.Sc., M.A. *Cr. 8vo. 3s. 6d.*

PRACTICAL CHEMISTRY. Part I. By W. French, M.A. *Cr. 8vo. Fourth Edition.* 1s. 6d. Part II. By W. French, M.A., and T. H. Boardman, M.A. *Cr. 8vo. 1s. 6d.*

TECHNICAL ARITHMETIC AND GEOMETRY. By C. T. Millis, M.I.M.E. *Cr. 8vo. 3s. 6d.*

EXAMPLES IN PHYSICS. By C. E. Jackson, B.A. *Cr. 8vo. 2s. 6d.*

*ELEMENTARY ORGANIC CHEMISTRY. By A. E. Dunstan, B.Sc. Illustrated. *Cr. 8vo.*

Social Questions of To-day

Edited by H. DE B. GIBBINS, Litt.D., M.A.   *Crown 8vo. 2s. 6d.*

A series of volumes upon those topics of social, economic, and industrial interest that are foremost in the public mind.

TRADE UNIONISM—NEW AND OLD. By G. Howell. *Third Edition.*

THE COMMERCE OF NATIONS. By C. F. Bastable, M.A. *Third Edition.*

THE ALIEN INVASION. By W. H. Wilkins, B.A.

THE RURAL EXODUS. By P. Anderson Graham.

LAND NATIONALIZATION. By Harold Cox, B.A. *Second Edition.*

A SHORTER WORKING DAY. By H. de B. Gibbins and R. A. Hadfield.

BACK TO THE LAND. An Inquiry into Rural Depopulation. By H. E. Moore.

TRUSTS, POOLS, AND CORNERS. By J. Stephen Jeans.

THE FACTORY SYSTEM. By R. W. Cooke Taylor.

WOMEN'S WORK. By Lady Dilke, Miss Bulley, and Miss Whitley.

SOCIALISM AND MODERN THOUGHT. By M. Kauffmann.

THE PROBLEM OF THE UNEMPLOYED. By J. A. Hobson, M.A.

LIFE IN WEST LONDON. By Arthur Sherwell, M.A. *Third Edition.*

RAILWAY NATIONALIZATION. By Clement Edwards.

UNIVERSITY AND SOCIAL SETTLEMENTS. By W. Reason, M.A.

Technology, Textbooks of

Edited by G. F. GOODCHILD, B.A., B.Sc., and G. R. MILLS, M.A.
Fully Illustrated.

HOW TO MAKE A DRESS. By J. A. E. Wood. *Third Edition. Cr. 8vo. 1s. 6d.*

CARPENTRY AND JOINERY. By F. C. Webber. *Fourth Edition. Cr. 8vo. 3s. 6d.*

MILLINERY, THEORETICAL AND PRACTICAL. By Clare Hill. *Second Edition. Cr. 8vo. 2s.*

AN INTRODUCTION TO THE STUDY OF TEXTILE DESIGN. By Aldred F. Barker. *Demy 8vo. 7s. 6d.*

BUILDERS' QUANTITIES. By H. C. Grubb. *Cr. 8vo. 4s. 6d.*

RÉPOUSSÉ METAL WORK. By A. C. Horth. *Cr. 8vo. 2s. 6d.*

Theology, Handbooks of

Edited by R. L. OTTLEY, D.D., Professor of Pastoral Theology at Oxford,
and Canon of Christ Church, Oxford.

The series is intended, in part, to furnish the clergy and teachers or students of Theology with trustworthy Textbooks, adequately representing the present position of the questions dealt with; in part, to make accessible to the reading public an accurate and concise statement of facts and principles in all questions bearing on Theology and Religion.

THE XXXIX. ARTICLES OF THE CHURCH OF ENGLAND. Edited by E. C. S. Gibson, D.D. *Third and Cheaper Edition in one Volume. Demy 8vo. 12s. 6d.*

AN INTRODUCTION TO THE HISTORY OF RELIGION. By F. B. Jevons. M.A., Litt.D. *Third Edition. Demy 8vo. 10s. 6d.*

THE DOCTRINE OF THE INCARNATION. By R. L. Ottley, D.D. *Second and Cheaper Edition. Demy 8vo. 12s. 6d.*

AN INTRODUCTION TO THE HISTORY OF THE CREEDS. By A. E. Burn, D.D. *Demy 8vo. 10s. 6d.*

THE PHILOSOPHY OF RELIGION IN ENGLAND AND AMERICA. By Alfred Caldecott, D.D. *Demy 8vo. 10s. 6d.*

A HISTORY OF EARLY CHRISTIAN DOCTRINE. By J. F. Bethune Baker, M.A. *Demy 8vo. 10s. 6d.*

Westminster Commentaries, The

General Editor, WALTER LOCK, D.D., Warden of Keble College,
Dean Ireland's Professor of Exegesis in the University of Oxford.

The object of each commentary is primarily exegetical, to interpret the author's
meaning to the present generation. The editors will not deal, except very subor-
dinately, with questions of textual criticism or philology; but, taking the English
text in the Revised Version as their basis, they will try to combine a hearty accept-
ance of critical principles with loyalty to the Catholic Faith.

THE BOOK OF GENESIS. Edited with Intro-
duction and Notes by S. R. Driver, D.D.
Fourth Edition Demy 8vo. 10s. 6d.
THE BOOK OF JOB. Edited by E. C. S. Gibson,
D.D. *Second Edition. Demy 8vo. 6s.*
THE ACTS OF THE APOSTLES. Edited by R.
B. Rackham, M.A. *Demy 8vo. Second and
Cheaper Edition. 10s. 6d.*

THE FIRST EPISTLE OF PAUL THE APOSTLE
TO THE CORINTHIANS. Edited by H. L.
Goudge, M.A. *Demy 8vo. 6s.*

THE EPISTLE OF ST. JAMES. Edited with Introduction and Notes by R. J. Knowling,
M.A. *Demy 8vo. 6s.*

PART II.——FICTION

Albanesi (E. Maria). SUSANNAH AND
ONE OTHER. *Fourth Edition.* Cr.
8vo. 6s.
THE BLUNDER OF AN INNOCENT.
Second Edition. Cr. 8vo. 6s.
CAPRICIOUS CAROLINE. *Second Edi-
tion. Cr. 8vo. 6s.*
LOVE AND LOUISA. *Second Edition.
Cr. 8vo. 6s.*
PETER, A PARASITE. *Cr. 8vo. 6s.*
THE BROWN EYES OF MARY. *Third
Edition. Cr. 8vo. 6s.*
Anstey (F.). Author of 'Vice Versâ.' A
BAYARD FROM BENGAL. Illustrated
by BERNARD PARTRIDGE. *Third Edition.
Cr. 8vo. 3s. 6d.*
Bacheller (Irving), Author of 'Eben Holden.'
DARREL OF THE BLESSED ISLES.
Third Edition. Cr. 8vo. 6s.
Bagot (Richard). A ROMAN MYSTERY.
Third Edition. Cr. 8vo. 6s.
THE PASSPORT. *Fourth Ed. Cr. 8vo. 6s.*
Baring=Gould (S.). ARMINELL. *Fifth
Edition. Cr. 8vo. 6s.*
URITH. *Fifth Edition. Cr. 8vo. 6s.*
IN THE ROAR OF THE SEA. *Seventh
Edition. Cr. 8vo. 6s.*
CHEAP JACK ZITA. *Fourth Edition.
Cr. 8vo. 6s.*
MARGERY OF QUETHER. *Third
Edition. Cr. 8vo. 6s.*
THE QUEEN OF LOVE. *Fifth Edition.
Cr. 8vo. 6s.*
JACQUETTA. *Third Edition. Cr. 8vo. 6s.*
KITTY ALONE. *Fifth Edition. Cr. 8vo. 6s.*
NOÉMI. Illustrated. *Fourth Edition. Cr.
8vo. 6s.*
THE BROOM-SQUIRE. Illustrated.
Fifth Edition. Cr. 8vo. 6s.

DARTMOOR IDYLLS. *Cr. 8vo. 6s.*
THE PENNYCOMEQUICKS. *Third
Edition. Cr. 8vo. 6s.*
GUAVAS THE TINNER. Illustrated.
Second Edition. Cr. 8vo. 6s.
BLADYS. Illustrated. *Second Edition.
Cr. 8vo. 6s.*
PABO THE PRIEST. *Cr. 8vo. 6s.*
WINEFRED. Illustrated. *Second Edition.
Cr. 8vo. 6s.*
ROYAL GEORGIE. Illustrated. *Cr. 8vo. 6s.*
MISS QUILLET. Illustrated. *Cr. 8vo. 6s.*
CHRIS OF ALL SORTS. *Cr. 8vo. 6s.*
IN DEWISLAND. *Second Edition. Cr.
8vo. 6s.*
LITTLE TU'PENNY. *A New Edition. 6d.*
See also Strand Novels and Books for
Boys and Girls.
Barlow (Jane). THE LAND OF THE
SHAMROCK. *Cr. 8vo. 6s.* See also
Strand Novels.
Barr (Robert). IN THE MIDST OF
ALARMS. *Third Edition. Cr. 8vo. 6s.*
THE MUTABLE MANY. *Third Edition.
Cr. 8vo. 6s.*
THE COUNTESS TEKLA. *Third Edition.
Cr. 8vo. 6s.*
THE LADY ELECTRA. *Second Edition.
Cr. 8vo. 6s.*
THE TEMPESTUOUS PETTICOAT.
Illustrated. *Third Edition. Cr. 8vo. 6s.*
See also Strand Novels and S. Crane.
Begbie (Harold). THE ADVENTURES
OF SIR JOHN SPARROW. *Cr. 8vo. 6s.*
Belloc (Hilaire). EMMANUEL BURDEN,
MERCHANT. With 36 Illustrations by
G. K. CHESTERTON. *Second Edition.
Cr. 8vo. 6s.*

Benson (E. F.) DODO. *Fourth Edition. Cr. 8vo. 6s.* See also Strand Novels.

Benson (Margaret). SUBJECT TO VANITY. *Cr. 8vo. 3s. 6d.*

Bourne (Harold C.). See V. Langbridge.

Burton (J. Bloundelle). THE YEAR ONE: A Page of the French Revolution. Illustrated. *Cr. 8vo. 6s.*
THE FATE OF VALSEC. *Cr. 8vo. 6s.*
A BRANDED NAME. *Cr. 8vo. 6s.* See also Strand Novels.

Capes (Bernard), Author of 'The Lake of Wine.' THE EXTRAORDINARY CONFESSIONS OF DIANA PLEASE. *Third Edition. Cr. 8vo. 6s.*
A JAY OF ITALY. *Fourth Ed. Cr. 8vo. 6s.*
LOAVES AND FISHES. *Cr. 8vo. 6s.*

Chesney (Weatherby). THE TRAGEDY OF THE GREAT EMERALD. *Cr. 8vo. 6s.*
THE MYSTERY OF A BUNGALOW. *Second Edition. Cr. 8vo. 6s.* See also Strand Novels.

Clifford (Hugh). A FREE LANCE OF TO-DAY. *Cr. 8vo. 6s.*

Clifford (Mrs. W. K.). See Strand Novels and Books for Boys and Girls.

Cobb (Thomas). A CHANGE OF FACE. *Cr. 8vo. 6s.*

Corelli (Marie). A ROMANCE OF TWO WORLDS. *Twenty-Sixth Edition. Cr. 8vo. 6s.*
VENDETTA. *Twenty-Second Edition. Cr. 8vo. 6s.*
THELMA. *Thirty-Third Edition. Cr. 8vo. 6s.*
ARDATH: THE STORY OF A DEAD SELF. *Sixteenth Edition. Cr. 8vo. 6s.*
THE SOUL OF LILITH. *Thirteenth Edition. Cr. 8vo. 6s.*
WORMWOOD. *Fourteenth Edition. Cr. 8vo. 6s.*
BARABBAS: A DREAM OF THE WORLD'S TRAGEDY. *Fortieth Edition. Cr. 8vo. 6s.*
THE SORROWS OF SATAN. *Fiftieth Edition. Cr. 8vo. 6s.*
THE MASTER CHRISTIAN. *167th Thousand. Cr. 8vo. 6s.*
TEMPORAL POWER: A STUDY IN SUPREMACY. *130th Thousand. Cr. 8vo. 6s.*
GOD'S GOOD MAN: A SIMPLE LOVE STORY. *134th Thousand. Cr. 8vo. 6s.*
THE MIGHTY ATOM. *A New Edition. Cr. 8vo. 6s.*
BOY. *A New Edition. Cr. 8vo. 6s.*
JANE. *A New Edition. Cr. 8vo. 6s.*

Crockett (S. R.), Author of 'The Raiders,' etc. LOCHINVAR. Illustrated. *Third Edition. Cr. 8vo. 6s.*
THE STANDARD BEARER. *Cr. 8vo. 6s.*

Croker (B. M.). THE OLD CANTONMENT. *Cr. 8vo. 6s.*
JOHANNA. *Second Edition. Cr. 8vo. 6s.*

THE HAPPY VALLEY. *Third Edition. Cr. 8vo. 6s.*
A NINE DAYS' WONDER. *Third Edition. Cr. 8vo. 6s.*
PEGGY OF THE BARTONS. *Sixth Edition. Cr. 8vo. 6s.*
ANGEL. *Fourth Edition. Cr. 8vo. 6s.*
A STATE SECRET. *Third Edition. Cr. 8vo. 3s. 6d.*

Dawson (Francis W.). THE SCAR. *Cr. 8vo. 6s.*

Dawson (A. J.). DANIEL WHYTE. *Cr. 8vo. 3s. 6d.*

Doyle (A. Conan), Author of 'Sherlock Holmes,' 'The White Company,' etc. ROUND THE RED LAMP. *Ninth Edition. Cr. 8vo. 6s.*

Duncan (Sara Jeannette) (Mrs. Everard Cotes). THOSE DELIGHTFUL AMERICANS. Illustrated. *Third Edition. Cr. 8vo. 6s.* See also Strand Novels.

Findlater (J. H.). THE GREEN GRAVES OF BALGOWRIE. *Fifth Edition. Cr. 8vo. 6s.* See also Strand Novels.

Findlater (Mary). A NARROW WAY. *Third Edition. Cr. 8vo. 6s.*
THE ROSE OF JOY. *Third Edition. Cr. 8vo. 6s.* See also Strand Novels.

Fitzpatrick (K.) THE WEANS AT ROWALLAN. Illustrated. *Second Edition. Cr. 8vo. 6s.*

Fitzstephen (Gerald). MORE KIN THAN KIND. *Cr. 8vo. 6s.*

Fletcher (J. S.). LUCIAN THE DREAMER. *Cr. 8vo. 6s.*

Fraser (Mrs. Hugh), Author of 'The Stolen Emperor.' THE SLAKING OF THE SWORD. *Cr. 8vo. 6s.*
*THE SHADOW OF THE LORD. *Cr. 8vo. 6s.*

Fuller-Maitland (Mrs.), Author of 'The Day Book of Bethia Hardacre.' BLANCHE ESMEAD. *Cr. 8vo. 6s.*

Gerard (Dorothea), Author of 'Lady Baby. THE CONQUEST OF LONDON. *Second Edition. Cr. 8vo. 6s.*
HOLY MATRIMONY. *Second Edition. Cr. 8vo. 6s.*
MADE OF MONEY. *Cr. 8vo. 6s.*
THE BRIDGE OF LIFE. *Cr. 8vo. 6s.*
THE IMPROBABLE IDYL. *Third Edition. Cr. 8vo. 6s.* See also Strand Novels.

Gerard (Emily). THE HERONS' TOWER. *Cr. 8vo. 6s.*

Gissing (George), Author of 'Demos,' 'In the Year of Jubilee,' etc. THE TOWN TRAVELLER. *Second Ed. Cr. 8vo. 6s.*
THE CROWN OF LIFE. *Cr. 8vo. 6s.*

Gleig (Charles). BUNTER'S CRUISE. Illustrated. *Cr. 8vo. 3s. 6d.*

Harraden (Beatrice). IN VARYING MOODS. *Fourteenth Edition. Cr. 8vo. 6s.*

THE SCHOLAR'S DAUGHTER. *Third Edition Cr. 8vo. 6s.*
Harrod (F.) (Frances Forbes Robertson).
THE TAMING OF THE BRUTE. *Cr. 8vo. 6s.*
Herbertson (Agnes G.). PATIENCE DEAN. *Cr. 8vo. 6s.*
Hichens (Robert). THE PROPHET OF BERKELEY SQUARE. *Second Edition. Cr. 8vo. 6s.*
TONGUES OF CONSCIENCE. *Second Edition. Cr. 8vo. 6s.*
FELIX. *Fifth Edition. Cr. 8vo. 6s.*
THE WOMAN WITH THE FAN. *Sixth Edition. Cr. 8vo. 6s.*
BYEWAYS. *Cr. 8vo. 3s. 6d.*
THE GARDEN OF ALLAH. *Twelfth Edition. Cr. 8vo. 6s.*
THE BLACK SPANIEL. *Cr. 8vo. 6s.*
Hobbes (John Oliver), Author of 'Robert Orange.' THE SERIOUS WOOING. *Cr. 8vo. 6s.*
Hope (Anthony). THE GOD IN THE CAR. *Tenth Edition. Cr. 8vo. 6s.*
A CHANGE OF AIR. *Sixth Edition. Cr. 8vo. 6s.*
A MAN OF MARK. *Fifth Edition. Cr. 8vo. 6s.*
THE CHRONICLES OF COUNT ANTONIO. *Sixth Edition. Cr. 8vo. 6s.*
PHROSO. Illustrated by H. R. MILLAR. *Sixth Edition. Cr. 8vo. 6s.*
SIMON DALE. Illustrated. *SixthEdition. Cr. 8vo. 6s.*
THE KING'S MIRROR. *Fourth Edition. Cr. 8vo. 6s.*
QUISANTE. *Fourth Edition. Cr. 8vo. 6s.*
THE DOLLY DIALOGUES. *Cr. 8vo. 6s.*
A SERVANT OF THE PUBLIC. Illustrated. *Fourth Edition. Cr. 8vo. 6s.*
Hope (Graham), Author of 'A Cardinal and his Conscience,' etc., etc. THE LADY OF LYTE. *Second Ed. Cr. 8vo. 6s.*
Hough (Emerson). THE MISSISSIPPI BUBBLE. Illustrated. *Cr. 8vo. 6s.*
Housman (Clemence). THE LIFE OF SIR AGLOVALE DE GALIS. *Cr. 8vo. 6s.*
Hyne (C. J. Cutcliffe), Author of 'Captain Kettle.' MR. HORROCKS, PURSER. *Third Edition. Cr. 8vo. 6s.*
Jacobs (W. W.). MANY CARGOES. *Twenty-Eighth Edition. Cr. 8vo. 3s. 6d.*
SEA URCHINS. *Twelfth Edition. Cr. 8vo. 3s. 6d.*
A MASTER OF CRAFT. Illustrated. *Sixth Edition. Cr. 8vo. 3s. 6d.*
LIGHT FREIGHTS. Illustrated. *Fifth Edition. Cr. 8vo. 3s. 6d.*
James (Henry). THE SOFT SIDE. *Second Edition. Cr. 8vo. 6s.*
THE BETTER SORT. *Cr. 8vo. 6s.*
THE AMBASSADORS. *Second Edition. Cr. 8vo. 6s.*
THE GOLDEN BOWL. *Third Edition. Cr. 8vo. 6s.*

Janson (Gustaf). ABRAHAM'S SACRIFICE. *Cr. 8vo. 6s.*
Keays (H. A. Mitchell). HE THAT EATETH BREAD WITH ME. *Cr. 8vo. 6s.*
Langbridge (V.) and Bourne (C. Harold.). THE VALLEY OF INHERITANCE. *Cr. 8vo. 6s.*
Lawless (Hon. Emily). WITH ESSEX IN IRELAND. *Cr. 8vo. 6s.*
See also Strand Novels.
Lawson (Harry), Author of 'When the Billy Boils.' CHILDREN OF THE BUSH. *Cr. 8vo. 6s.*
Le Queux (W.). THE HUNCHBACK OF WESTMINSTER. *Third Edition. Cr. 8vo. 6s.*
THE CLOSED BOOK. *Third Edition. Cr. 8vo. 6s.*
THE VALLEY OF THE SHADOW. Illustrated. *Third Edition. Cr. 8vo. 6s.*
BEHIND THE THRONE. *Third Edition. Cr. 8vo. 6s.*
Levett-Yeats (S.). ORRAIN. *Second Edition. Cr. 8vo. 6s.*
Long (J. Luther), Co-Author of 'The Darling of the Gods.' MADAME BUTTERFLY. *Cr. 8vo. 3s. 6d.*
SIXTY JANE. *Cr. 8vo. 6s.*
Lowis (Cecil). THE MACHINATIONS OF THE MYO-OK. *Cr. 8vo. 6s.*
Lyall (Edna). DERRICK VAUGHAN, NOVELIST. *42nd Thousand. Cr. 8vo. 3s. 6d.*
M'Carthy (Justin H.), Author of 'If I were King.' THE LADY OF LOYALTY HOUSE. Illustrated. *Third Edition. Cr. 8vo. 6s.*
THE DRYAD. *Second Edition. Cr. 8vo. 6s.*
Macdonald (Ronald). THE SEA MAID. *Cr. 8vo. 6s.*
Macnaughtan (S.). THE FORTUNE OF CHRISTINA MACNAB. *Third Edition. Cr. 8vo. 6s.*
Malet (Lucas). COLONEL ENDERBY'S WIFE. *Fourth Edition. Cr. 8vo. 6s.*
A COUNSEL OF PERFECTION. *New Edition. Cr. 8vo. 6s.*
THE WAGES OF SIN. *Fourteenth Edition. Cr. 8vo. 6s.*
THE CARISSIMA. *Fourth Edition. Cr. 8vo. 6s.*
THE GATELESS BARRIER. *Fourth Edition. Cr. 8vo. 6s.*
THE HISTORY OF SIR RICHARD CALMADY. *Seventh Edition. Cr. 8vo. 6s.*
See also Books for Boys and Girls.
Mann (Mrs. M. E.). OLIVIA'S SUMMER. *Second Edition. Cr. 8vo. 6s.*
A LOST ESTATE. *A New Edition. Cr. 8vo. 6s.*
THE PARISH OF HILBY. *A New Edition. Cr. 8vo. 6s.*
THE PARISH NURSE. *Fourth Edition. Cr. 8vo. 6s.*

GRAN'MA'S JANE. *Cr. 8vo. 6s.*
MRS. PETER HOWARD. *Cr. 8vo. 6s.*
A WINTER'S TALE. *A New Edition. Cr. 8vo. 6s.*
ONE ANOTHER'S BURDENS. *A New Edition. Cr. 8vo. 6s.*
ROSE AT HONEYPOT. *Second Ed. Cr. 8vo. 6s.* See also Books for Boys and Girls.
Marriott (Charles), Author of 'The Column.' GENEVRA. *Second Edition. Cr. 8vo. 6s.*
Marsh (Richard). THE TWICKENHAM PEERAGE. *Second Edition. Cr. 8vo. 6s.*
A DUEL. *Cr. 8vo. 6s.*
THE MARQUIS OF PUTNEY. *Second Edition. Cr. 8vo. 6s.* See also Strand Novels.
Mason (A. E. W.), Author of 'The Four Feathers,' etc. CLEMENTINA. Illustrated. *Second Edition. Cr. 8vo. 6s.*
Mathers (Helen), Author of 'Comin', thro' the Rye.' HONEY. *Fourth Edition. Cr. 8vo. 6s.*
GRIFF OF GRIFFITHSCOURT. *Cr. 8vo. 6s.*
THE FERRYMAN. *Second Edition. Cr. 8vo. 6s.*
Maxwell (W. B.), Author of 'The Ragged Messenger.' VIVIEN. *Seventh Edition. Cr. 8vo. 6s.*
THE RAGGED MESSENGER. *Third Edition. Cr. 8vo. 6s.*
FABULOUS FANCIES. *Cr. 8vo. 6s.*
Meade (L. T.). DRIFT. *Second Edition. Cr. 8vo. 6s.*
RESURGAM. *Cr. 8vo. 6s.*
VICTORY. *Cr. 8vo. 6s.* See also Books for Girls and Boys.
Meredith (Ellis). HEART OF MY HEART. *Cr. 8vo. 6s.*
'Miss Molly' (The Author of). THE GREAT RECONCILER. *Cr. 8vo. 6s.*
Mitford (Bertram). THE SIGN OF THE SPIDER. Illustrated. *Sixth Edition. Cr. 8vo. 3s. 6d.*
IN THE WHIRL OF THE RISING. *Third Edition. Cr. 8vo. 6s.*
THE RED DERELICT. *Second Edition. Cr. 8vo. 6s.*
Montresor (F. F.), Author of 'Into the Highways and Hedges.' THE ALIEN. *Third Edition. Cr. 8vo. 6s.*
Morrison (Arthur). TALES OF MEAN STREETS. *Sixth Edition. Cr. 8vo. 6s.*
A CHILD OF THE JAGO. *Fourth Edition. Cr. 8vo. 6s.*
TO LONDON TOWN. *Second Edition. Cr. 8vo. 6s.*
CUNNING MURRELL. *Cr. 8vo. 6s.*
THE HOLE IN THE WALL. *Fourth Edition. Cr. 8vo. 6s.*
DIVERS VANITIES. *Cr. 8vo. 6s.*

Nesbit (E.). (Mrs. E. Bland). THE RED HOUSE. Illustrated. *Fourth Edition. Cr. 8vo. 6s.* See also Strand Novels.
Norris (W. E.). THE CREDIT OF THE COUNTY. Illustrated. *Second Edition. Cr. 8vo. 6s.*
THE EMBARRASSING ORPHAN. *Cr. 8vo. 6s.*
NIGEL'S VOCATION. *Cr. 8vo. 6s.*
BARHAM OF BELTANA. *Second Edition. Cr. 8vo. 6s.* See also Strand Novels.
Ollivant (Alfred). OWD BOB, THE GREY DOG OF KENMUIR. *Eighth Edition. Cr. 8vo. 6s.*
Oppenheim (E. Phillips). MASTER OF MEN. *Third Edition. Cr. 8vo. 6s.*
Oxenham (John), Author of 'Barbe of Grand Bayou.' A WEAVER OF WEBS. *Second Edition. Cr. 8vo. 6s.*
THE GATE OF THE DESERT. *Fourth Edition. Cr. 8vo. 6s.*
Pain (Barry). THREE FANTASIES. *Cr. 8vo. 1s.*
LINDLEY KAYS. *Third Edition. Cr. 8vo. 6s.*
Parker (Gilbert). PIERRE AND HIS PEOPLE. *Sixth Edition.*
MRS. FALCHION. *Fifth Edition. Cr. 8vo. 6s.*
THE TRANSLATION OF A SAVAGE. *Second Edition. Cr. 8vo. 6s.*
THE TRAIL OF THE SWORD. Illustrated. *Ninth Edition. Cr. 8vo. 6s.*
WHEN VALMOND CAME TO PONTIAC: The Story of a Lost Napoleon. *Fifth Edition. Cr. 8vo. 6s.*
AN ADVENTURER OF THE NORTH: The Last Adventures of 'Pretty Pierre.' *Third Edition. Cr. 8vo. 6s.*
THE SEATS OF THE MIGHTY. Illustrated. *Fourteenth Edition. Cr. 8vo. 6s.*
THE BATTLE OF THE STRONG: Romance of Two Kingdoms. Illustrated. *Fifth Edition. Cr. 8vo. 6s.*
THE POMP OF THE LAVILETTES. *Second Edition. Cr. 8vo. 3s. 6d.*
Pemberton (Max). THE FOOTSTEPS OF A THRONE. Illustrated. *Third Edition. Cr. 8vo. 6s.*
I CROWN THEE KING. With Illustrations by Frank Dadd and A. Forrestier. *Cr. 8vo. 6s.*
Phillpotts (Eden). LYING PROPHETS. *Cr. 8vo. 6s.*
CHILDREN OF THE MIST. *Fifth Edition. Cr. 8vo. 6s.*
THE HUMAN BOY. With a Frontispiece. *Fourth Edition. Cr. 8vo. 6s.*
SONS OF THE MORNING. *Second Edition. Cr. 8vo. 6s.*

THE RIVER. *Third Edition. Cr. 8vo. 6s.*

THE AMERICAN PRISONER. *Third Edition. Cr. 8vo. 6s.*

THE SECRET WOMAN. *Fourth Edition. Cr. 8vo. 6s.*

KNOCK AT A VENTURE. With a Frontispiece. *Third Edition. Cr. 8vo. 6s.*

THE PORTREEVE. *Third Edition. Cr. 8vo. 6s.*
See also Strand Novels.

Pickthall (Marmaduke). SAÏD THE FISHERMAN. *Fifth Edition. Cr. 8vo. 6s.*

BRENDLE. *Second Edition. Cr. 8vo. 6s.*

'Q,' Author of 'Dead Man's Rock.' THE WHITE WOLF. *Second Edition. Cr. 8vo. 6s.*

THE MAYOR OF TROY. *Second Edition. Cr. 8vo. 6s.*

Rhys (Grace). THE WOOING OF SHEILA. *Second Edition. Cr. 8vo. 6s.*

THE PRINCE OF LISNOVER. *Cr. 8vo. 6s.*

Rhys (Grace) and Another. THE DIVERTED VILLAGE. Illustrated by DOROTHY GWYN JEFFREYS. *Cr. 8vo. 6s.*

Ridge (W. Pett). LOST PROPERTY. *Second Edition. Cr. 8vo. 6s.*

ERB. *Second Edition. Cr. 8vo. 6s.*

A SON OF THE STATE. *A New Edition. Cr. 8vo. 3s. 6d.*

A BREAKER OF LAWS. *A New Edition. Cr. 8vo. 3s. 6d.*

MRS. GALER'S BUSINESS. Illustrated. *Second Edition. Cr. 8vo. 6s.*

SECRETARY TO BAYNE, M.P. *Cr. 8vo. 3s. 6d.*

Ritchie (Mrs. David G.). THE TRUTHFUL LIAR. *Cr. 8vo. 6s.*

Roberts (C. G. D.). THE HEART OF THE ANCIENT WOOD. *Cr. 8vo. 3s. 6d.*

Russell (W. Clark). MY DANISH SWEETHEART. Illustrated. *Fifth Edition. Cr. 8vo. 6s.*

HIS ISLAND PRINCESS. Illustrated. *Second Edition. Cr. 6vo. 6s.*

ABANDONED. *Cr. 8vo. 6s.*
See also Books for Boys and Girls.

Sergeant (Adeline). ANTHEA'S WAY. *Cr. 8vo. 6s.*

THE PROGRESS OF RACHAEL. *Cr. 8vo. 6s.*

THE MYSTERY OF THE MOAT. *Second Edition. Cr. 8vo. 6s.*

MRS. LYGON'S HUSBAND. *Cr. 8vo. 6s.*

THE COMING OF THE RANDOLPHS. *Cr. 8vo. 6s.*
See also Strand Novels.

Shannon (W. F.). THE MESS DECK. *Cr. 8vo. 3s. 6d.*
See also Strand Novels.

Sonnischsen (Albert). DEEP-SEA VAGABONDS. *Cr. 8vo. 6s.*

Thompson (Vance). SPINNERS OF LIFE. *Cr. 8vo. 6s.*

Urquhart (M.), A TRAGEDY IN COMMONPLACE. *Second Ed. Cr. 8vo. 6s.*

Waineman (Paul). BY A FINNISH LAKE. *Cr. 8vo. 6s.*

THE SONG OF THE FOREST. *Cr. 8vo. 6s.* See also Strand Novels.

Waltz (E. C.). THE ANCIENT LANDMARK ; A Kentucky Romance. *Cr. 8vo. 6s.*

Watson (H. B. Marriott). ALARUMS AND EXCURSIONS. *Cr. 8vo. 6s.*

CAPTAIN FORTUNE. *Third Edition. Cr. 8vo. 6s.*

TWISTED EGLANTINE. With 8 Illustrations by FRANK CRAIG. *Third Edition. Cr. 8vo. 6s.*

THE HIGH TOBY. With a Frontispiece. *Second Edition. Cr. 8vo. 6s.*
See also Strand Novels.

Wells (H. G.). THE SEA LADY. *Cr. 8vo. 6s.*

Weyman (Stanley), Author of 'A Gentleman of France.' UNDER THE RED ROBE. With Illustrations by R. C. WOODVILLE. *Nineteenth Edition. Cr. 8vo. 6s.*

White (Stewart E.), Author of 'The Blazed Trail.' CONJUROR'S HOUSE. A Romance of the Free Trail. *Second Edition. Cr. 8vo. 6s.*

White (Percy). THE SYSTEM. *Third Edition. Cr. 8vo. 6s.*

THE PATIENT MAN. *Second Edition. Cr. 8vo. 6s.*

Williamson (Mrs. C. N.), Author of 'The Barnstormers.' THE ADVENTURE OF PRINCESS SYLVIA. *Second Edition. Cr. 8vo. 3s. 6d.*

THE WOMAN WHO DARED. *Cr. 8vo. 6s.*

THE SEA COULD TELL. *Second Edition. Cr. 8vo. 6s.*

THE CASTLE OF THE SHADOWS. *Third Edition. Cr. 8vo. 6s.*

PAPA. *Cr. 8vo. 6s.*

*LADY PETTY ACROSS THE WATER. *Cr. 8vo. 6s.*

Williamson (C. N. and A. M.). THE LIGHTNING CONDUCTOR : Being the Romance of a Motor Car. Illustrated. *Fourteenth Edition. Cr. 8vo. 6s.*

THE PRINCESS PASSES. Illustrated. *Sixth Edition. Cr. 8vo. 6s.*

MY FRIEND THE CHAUFFEUR. With 16 Illustrations. *Sixth Edition. Cr. 8vo. 6s.*

Wyllarde (Dolf), Author of 'Uriah the Hittite.' THE PATHWAY OF THE PIONEER. *Third Edition. Cr. 8vo. 6s.*

Methuen's Strand Novels

Cr. 8vo.   Cloth, 1s. *net.*

ENCOURAGED by the great and steady sale of their Sixpenny Novels, Messrs. Methuen have determined to issue a new series of fiction at a low price under the title of 'THE STRAND NOVELS.' These books are well printed and well bound in *cloth*, and the excellence of their quality may be gauged from the names of those authors who contribute the early volumes of the series.

Messrs. Methuen would point out that the books are as good and as long as a six shilling novel, that they are bound in cloth and not in paper, and that their price is One Shilling *net*. They feel sure that the public will appreciate such good and cheap literature, and the books can be seen at all good booksellers.

The first volumes are—

Balfour (Andrew). VENGEANCE IS MINE.
TO ARMS.
Baring-Gould (S.). MRS. CURGENVEN OF CURGENVEN.
*DOMITIA.
*THE FROBISHERS.
Barlow (Jane), Author of 'Irish Idylls. FROM THE EAST UNTO THE WEST
A CREEL OF IRISH STORIES.
*THE FOUNDING OF FORTUNES.
Barr (Robert). THE VICTORS.
Bartram (George). THIRTEEN EVENINGS.
Benson (E. F.), Author of 'Dodo.' THE CAPSINA.
Bowles (G. Stewart). A STRETCH OFF THE LAND.
Brooke (Emma). THE POET'S CHILD.
Bullock (Shan F.). THE BARRYS.
THE CHARMER.
THE SQUIREEN.
THE RED LEAGUERS.
Burton (J. Bloundelle). ACROSS THE SALT SEAS.
THE CLASH OF ARMS.
DENOUNCED.
*FORTUNE'S MY FOE.
Capes (Bernard). AT A WINTER'S FIRE.
Chesney (Weatherby). THE BAPTIST RING.
THE BRANDED PRINCE.
THE FOUNDERED GALLEON.
JOHN TOPP.
Clifford (Mrs. W. K.). A FLASH OF SUMMER.
Collingwood (Harry). THE DOCTOR OF THE 'JULIET.'
Cornford (L. Cope). SONS OF ADVERSITY.
Crane (Stephen). WOUNDS IN THE RAIN.
Denny (C. E.). THE ROMANCE OF UPFOLD MANOR.
Dickson (Harris). THE BLACK WOLF'S BREED.
Dickinson (Evelyn). THE SIN OF ANGELS.

Duncan (Sara J.). *THE POOL IN THE DESERT.
*A VOYAGE OF CONSOLATION.
Embree (C. F.). A HEART OF FLAME.
Fenn (G. Manville). AN ELECTRIC SPARK.
Findlater (Jane H.). A DAUGHTER OF STRIFE.
*Findlater (Mary).** OVER THE HILLS.
Forrest (R. E.). THE SWORD OF AZRAEL.
Francis (M. E.). MISS ERIN.
Gallon (Tom). RICKERBY'S FOLLY.
Gerard (Dorothea). THINGS THAT HAVE HAPPENED.
Gilchrist (R. Murray). WILLOWBRAKE.
Glanville (Ernest). THE DESPATCH RIDER.
THE LOST REGIMENT.
THE KLOOF BRIDE.
THE INCA'S TREASURE.
Gordon (Julien). MRS. CLYDE.
WORLD'S PEOPLE.
Goss (C. F.). THE REDEMPTION OF DAVID CORSON.
*Gray (E. M'Queen).** MY STEWARDSHIP.
Hales (A. G.). JAIR THE APOSTATE.
Hamilton (Lord Ernest). MARY HAMILTON.
Harrison (Mrs. Burton). A PRINCESS OF THE HILLS. Illustrated.
Hooper (I.). THE SINGER OF MARLY.
Hough (Emerson). THE MISSISSIPPI BUBBLE.
'Iota' (Mrs. Caffyn). ANNE MAULEVERER.
*Jepson (Edgar).** KEEPERS OF THE PEOPLE.
Kelly (Florence Finch). WITH HOOPS OF STEEL.
Lawless (Hon. Emily). MAELCHO.
Linden (Annie). A WOMAN OF SENTIMENT.
*Lorimer (Norma).** JOSIAH'S WIFE.
Lush (Charles K.). THE AUTOCRATS.
Macdonell (Anne). THE STORY OF TERESA.
Macgrath (Harold). THE PUPPET CROWN.

Mackie (Pauline Bradford). THE VOICE IN THE DESERT.
Marsh (Richard). THE SEEN AND THE UNSEEN.
*GARNERED.
*A METAMORPHOSIS.
MARVELS AND MYSTERIES.
BOTH SIDES OF THE VEIL.
Mayall (J. W.). THE CYNIC AND THE SYREN.
Monkhouse (Allan). LOVE IN A LIFE.
Moore (Arthur). THE KNIGHT PUNCTILIOUS.
Nesbit (Mrs. Bland). THE LITERARY SENSE.
Norris (W. E.). AN OCTAVE.
Oliphant (Mrs.). THE LADY'S WALK.
SIR ROBERT'S FORTUNE.
THE TWO MARY'S.
Penny (Mrs. Frank). A MIXED MARAGE.
Phillpotts (Eden). THE STRIKING HOURS.
FANCY FREE.
Pryce (Richard). TIME AND THE WOMAN.
Randall (J.). AUNT BETHIA'S BUTTON.
*Raymond (Walter).** FORTUNE'S DARLING.
*Rayner (Olive Pratt).** ROSALBA.
Rhys (Grace). THE DIVERTED VILLAGE.

Rickert (Edith). OUT OF THE CYPRESS SWAMP.
Roberton (M. H.). A GALLANT QUAKER.
Saunders (Marshall). ROSE A CHARLITTE.
Sergeant (Adeline). ACCUSED AND ACCUSER.
BARBARA'S MONEY.
THE ENTHUSIAST.
A GREAT LADY.
*THE LOVE THAT OVERCAME.
THE MASTER OF BEECHWOOD
UNDER SUSPICION.
*THE YELLOW DIAMOND.
Shannon (W. F.). JIM TWELVES.
*Strain (E. H.).** ELMSLIE'S DRAG NET.
Stringer (Arthur). THE SILVER POPPY.
Stuart (Esmè). CHRISTALLA.
Sutherland (Duchess of). ONE HOUR AND THE NEXT.
Swan (Annie). LOVE GROWN COLD.
Swift (Benjamin). SORDON.
Tanqueray (Mrs. B. M.). THE ROYAL QUAKER.
Trafford-Taunton (Mrs. E. W.). SILENT DOMINION.
*Upward (Allen).** ATHELSTANE FORD.
Waineman (Paul). A HEROINE FROM FINLAND.
Watson (H. B. Marriott). THE SKIRTS OF HAPPY CHANCE.
'**Zack.**' TALES OF DUNSTABLE WEIR.

Books for Boys and Girls

Illustrated.   Crown 8vo.   3s. 6d.

THE GETTING WELL OF DOROTHY. By Mrs. W. K. Clifford. *Second Edition.*
THE ICELANDER'S SWORD. By S. Baring-Gould.
ONLY A GUARD-ROOM DOG. By Edith E. Cuthell.
THE DOCTOR OF THE JULIET. By Harry Collingwood.
LITTLE PETER. By Lucas Malet. *Second Edition.*
MASTER ROCKAFELLAR'S VOYAGE. By W. Clark Russell.

THE SECRET OF MADAME DE MONLUC. By the Author of "Mdlle. Mori."
SYD BELTON : Or, the Boy who would not go to Sea. By G. Manville Fenn.
THE RED GRANGE. By Mrs. Molesworth.
A GIRL OF THE PEOPLE. By L. T. Meade. *Second Edition.*
HEPSY GIPSY. By L. T. Meade. 2s. 6d.
THE HONOURABLE MISS. By L. T. Meade *Second Edition.*
THERE WAS ONCE A PRINCE. By Mrs. M. E. Mann.
WHEN ARNOLD COMES HOME. By Mrs. M. E. Mann.

The Novels of Alexandre Dumas

Price 6d.   Double Volumes, 1s.

THE THREE MUSKETEERS. With a long Introduction by Andrew Lang. Double volume.
THE PRINCE OF THIEVES. *Second Edition.*
ROBIN HOOD. A Sequel to the above.
THE CORSICAN BROTHERS.
GEORGES.

CROP-EARED JACQUOT; JANE; Etc.
TWENTY YEARS AFTER. Double volume.
AMAURY.
THE CASTLE OF EPPSTEIN.
THE SNOWBALL, and SULTANETTA.
CECILE ; OR, THE WEDDING GOWN.
ACTÉ.